Familienunternehmen und KMU

Edited by

A. Hack, Berne
A. Calabrò, Witten/Herdecke
H. Frank, Vienna
F. W. Kellermanns, Charlotte, Vallendar
T. Zellweger, St. Gallen

AF794010

Both Family Firms and Small and Medium Sized Enterprises (SME) feature a number of distinct behaviors and characteristics which could provide them with a competitive advantage in the market but could also lead to certain risks. The scientific series at hand presents research which provides an empirical and theoretical contribution to the investigation on these specific characteristics and their impact on business practice. The overall aim of this series is to advance the development of theory in the areas of family firm and SME management.

Edited by
Professor Dr. Andreas Hack
University of Berne

Professor Dr. Hermann Frank
Vienna University of Economics and Business

Professor Dr. Thomas Zellweger
University of St. Gallen

Professor Dr. Andrea Calabrò
University of Witten/Herdecke

Professor Franz W. Kellermanns, Ph.D.
University of North Carolina, Charlotte
WHU – Otto Beisheim School of Management, Vallendar, Germany

Thomas Wittig

Crisis and Turnaround in German Medium-Sized Enterprises

An Integrated Empirical Study

Foreword by Prof. Dr. Andreas Hack

Springer Gabler

Thomas Wittig
Witten, Germany

Dissertation Witten/Herdecke University, 2016

Familienunternehmen und KMU
ISBN 978-3-658-16385-3 ISBN 978-3-658-16386-0 (eBook)
DOI 10.1007/978-3-658-16386-0

Library of Congress Control Number: 2016956810

Springer Gabler
© Springer Fachmedien Wiesbaden GmbH 2017
This work is subject to copyright. All rights are reserved by the Publisher, whether the whole or part of the material is concerned, specifically the rights of translation, reprinting, reuse of illustrations, recitation, broadcasting, reproduction on microfilms or in any other physical way, and transmission or information storage and retrieval, electronic adaptation, computer software, or by similar or dissimilar methodology now known or hereafter developed.
The use of general descriptive names, registered names, trademarks, service marks, etc. in this publication does not imply, even in the absence of a specific statement, that such names are exempt from the relevant protective laws and regulations and therefore free for general use.
The publisher, the authors and the editors are safe to assume that the advice and information in this book are believed to be true and accurate at the date of publication. Neither the publisher nor the authors or the editors give a warranty, express or implied, with respect to the material contained herein or for any errors or omissions that may have been made.

Printed on acid-free paper

This Springer Gabler imprint is published by Springer Nature
The registered company is Springer Fachmedien Wiesbaden GmbH
The registered company address is: Abraham-Lincoln-Str. 46, 65189 Wiesbaden, Germany

Foreword

Confucius found errors to be a fruitful ground for experience, for identifying and implementing changes. We, thus, learn from our mistakes and, in extreme cases, from failure. There is a reason an important part of psychological research looks into experiential learning.

In economic practice, companies make numerous mistakes every day without being aware of them. Moreover, companies find themselves in financial trouble and are forced to file for bankruptcy on a daily basis. Accordingly, one would think that economic literature encompasses countless studies investigating companies in crises in order to derive practical recommendations from their failures. However, surprisingly, there are very few theoretical / conceptional essays and even fewer empirically substantiated works. This is mainly due to the high complexity of the issue and the special challenges encountered when collecting data in this field.

Thomas Wittig is one of the first scientists in a long time to take up the challenge of analyzing the topic of crisis management on the basis of empirical data. It is not an exaggeration to say he not only accepted the challenge, he brilliantly mastered it.

This dissertation thesis specifically focuses on the elaboration of a comprehensive and consistent conceptional crisis management model and its empirical validation. Mr. Wittig particularly explains which turnaround measures lead to success for specific causes of crises and in specific critical situations. Moreover, the special situation of family-owned companies and the influence of restructuring measures on the entrepreneurial family are described.

The theoretical relevance of the underlying research question is to be assessed as very high, since the present research is probably unique in its multifacetedness and completeness. The conceptional considerations and empirical statements have the potential to exert a fundamental influence on crisis management research in years to come. From the perspective of family company research, as a by-product, so to say, the paper also provides important clues with regard to changes of ownership and management structures in specific critical situations and crisis management. The underlying database can also be described as unique and has the potential to lay the foundation for crisis management research in the field of family-owned companies.

Groundbreaking works are expected to be based on interesting research questions, solid theoretical foundations, and strong databases, but they should also provide surprising results that shake up current beliefs and stimulate new ways of thinking. Not many papers are able to fulfil these requirements, but Thomas Wittig's thesis has.

This dissertation thesis will dominate economic discussions on crises and crisis management strategies (especially in family-owned companies) in years to come and will inspire many theoretical and empirical projects. I am confident that selected findings from this thesis will find their way into the leading journals of our community. Of equal importance is the fact that the explanations will be taken up by a broad general readership as the practical implementation of the findings are certain to increase the effectiveness of crisis management to a considerable extent. Thomas Wittig has rendered us a great service with this thesis.

Prof. Dr. Andreas Hack

Preface

The compilation of this monograph has been both a challenge and a pleasure. The topic of crisis and turnaround has been a highly relevant part of my professional life, both as manager and consultant. While the companies I worked for did experience other phases of the company lifecycle as well, the time of crisis and turnaround is, although posing a high risk for the continuation of a company, a time of dynamic changes and renewal of the corporate identity: The turnaround management includes both drastic cuts into the corporate substance as well as the opportunity to change the very character of an enterprise.

Conducting this study brought with it the opportunity to venture beyond the strategic and operational management challenges in turnaround situations, to investigate the underlying structure of the turnaround process in a depth that would be unfeasible outside a dedicated scientific research project. It allowed me to challenge and review my personal experience in the context of scientific evidence.

The accessibility of this monograph for practitioners is unfortunately obstructed by the academic setup of such a work. Nonetheless, I am convinced that this study's results, which are based on a broad base of empirical evidence and an innovative conceptual structure, can be of use in gaining additional insights into the crisis and turnaround process. These insights can offer valuable guidance for the best performance of such a process.

Obviously, this study would not have been possible without the support of many people contributing in different ways to this study.

On the scientific side, I want to thank foremost my doctoral thesis supervisor Professor Dr. Andreas Hack, who is both a brilliant scientific mind and has been a reliable and critical, but always constructive, advisor for this work. His professional guidance, both in terms of how to conduct such a research and the empirical research methodology, was invaluable for me.

I want to thank the whole team of Professor Dr. Arist von Schlippe at the WIFU (Witten Institute for Family Business), including all internal and external PHD students. I appreciated the warm welcome and especially the excellent discussions in the regular research colloquiums. Also, I want to thank Dr. Nils Kraiczy, who taught me the nuts and bolts of conducting statistical analyses. Similarly of tremendous assistance was Wilko Ufert, who invested extensive time in both literature acquisition and providing feedback and criticism on earlier drafts of this study. My thanks also go to Thomas Pichote, who shared an office with me during the whole time of this monograph's compilation, providing both support and company, but mostly firm friendship.

As this work did rely on the empirical data provided by German banks and their risk managers, I want to thank those who made it possible to contact and discuss my research objective with them. Foremost, my dear friend Dr. Holmer Glietz, who not only assisted me with his extensive contacts to the risk management departments of German banks, but who was also an important discussion partner in relating the practical side of turnaround management. Similarly, I want to thank Professor Dr. Arist von Schlippe, Michael Wiendl, Dirk Schlarmann, Felix Schwabedal and Ralph Rickassel for opening doors and establishing contacts to banks and their respective heads of restructuring.

As the foundation of this study are the empirical contributions, I want to thank Deutsche Bank, Commerzbank, DZ Bank and the German Savings Banks Association, but also all other banks that requested to remain anonymous, for the time and effort invested in the assessment of cases for this study. Specifically, I want to thank Hans-Helmut Weber, director of the credit restructuring of DZ bank, who made the success of this study his own concern and helped promote this study among his peers.

Further, I want to thank the restructuring experts that assisted in the evaluation and discussion of the conceptual model: Alban Baiker, Holmer Glietz (as mentioned above) and Felix Schwabedal, as well as the anonymous banks' risk managers. They helped to ensure that the scientifically founded conceptual model for crisis and turnaround adequately reflects the real world properties of the crisis and turnaround process.

I want to express my gratitude to my parents, especially my mother Elisabeth Wittig, for her continued support of my education and personal development. I want to conclude this preface by thanking my beloved wife Nicole, without whom and without her role in my life this work would not have been possible. To her and to my daughters Johanna und Maren I want to dedicate this book.

Thomas Wittig

Table of Contents

List of figures

List of tables

List of abbreviations

Adj.	adjusted
ANOVA	analysis of variance
BaFin	German Federal Financial Supervisory Authority
beta	regression coefficient
BGH	German Federal Supreme Court
CAPEX	capital expenditure
CCF	crisis contribution factors
CEO	chief executive officer
COX regression	proportional hazards model by Sir David Cox
CRO	chief restructuring officer
Cronbach's α	Cronbach's alpha
e.g.	for example (exempli gratia)
EOC	escalation of commitment
EPV	events per variable
et al.	et alii
etc.	et cetera
EUR	Euros (€)
F-value	cluster homogeneity measure
fin.	financial
GBP	Great Britain Pound
GNP	gross national product
HR	human resource
i.e.	that is (id est)
IDW	institute of public auditors in Germany
IDW S6	Requirements for the compilation of restructuring opinions published by the IDW
InsO	insolvency statute (federal German law)
KMO	Kaiser-Meyer-Olkin measure
KPI	key performance indicator
m	million
M&A	mergers and acquisitions

manag.	managerial
MaRisk	minimum requirements for risk management
Max.	maximum
McFadden R^2	McFadden's pseudo coefficient of determination
N	sample size
n.s.	not significant
n/a	not applicable
oper.	operational
opt.	optional
p	probability
P&L	profit and loss
p.	page
part.	partial
port.	portfolio
poss.	possibly
R&D	research and development
R^2	coefficient of determination
RBV	resource-based view
ROI	return on investment
SD	standard deviation
seg.	segment
SEW	socioemotional wealth
Sign.	significance
simpl.	simplified
stand.	standardized
TMT	top management team
t-stat.	t-statistic
UK	United Kingdom
US	United States of America
USD	US Dollars
VIF	variance inflation factor
vs.	versus

1 Introduction

1.1 Motivation

A company crisis threatens the future existence of a firm (Arogyaswamy et al., 1995; Hauschildt et al., 2006; Pandit, 2000; Slatter, 1984; Trahms et al., 2013; Witte, 1981). Yet unfortunately, company crises occur frequently (Arogyaswamy et al., 1995; Bibeault, 1982; Hambrick & Schecter, 1983; Schendel et al., 1976; Slatter, 1984; Sudarsanam & Lai, 2001). Trahms et al. (2013) found 50% of the S&P 500 firms experience a decline in a five-year period. Buschmann (2006) found one out of four firms in crisis within a ten-year period. Eichner (2010) found 30% of the companies in his UK, US and German sample in distress within 6 years. Company crises are not solely dependent on macroeconomic conditions, indicated by the fact that these also occur in growing industries. A recent study found over 15% of all researched software firms in decline in the boom period from 1990 to 1996 (Ndofor et al., 2013). While the occurrence of crisis is common, the recovery from crisis is far from certain. The empirically observed recovery rates range from 57% to 72% (Buschmann, 2006; Eichner, 2010; Jostarndt, 2007; Sudarsanam & Lai, 2001).

In a nutshell:

- Company crises endanger the existence of a firm.
- Company crises are common.
- Company crises have poor survival rates.

Consequently, the research on how to reverse a crisis and enhance the possibility of recovery, turnaround research (similarly defined e.g., by Cater & Schwab, 2008; Chowdhury & Lang, 1993; Eichner, 2010; Harrigan & Porter, 1983; Pearce & Robbins, 1993; Pearson & Clair, 1998), is in my opinion one of the most relevant and interesting subjects in economics.

While the first publications in this research stream mainly addressed the topic of bankruptcy prediction (e.g., Altman, 1968), the focus has shifted to the reversal of crisis, the turnaround, i.e., finding the correct strategies and activities to manage the crisis and allow the recovery of the company.

Despite the fact that the understanding of crisis and turnaround has significantly improved since the early days of research in the 1960s, the results up until today have not been satisfying. I want to highlight three specific concerns as the cornerstones of my motivation and the starting point for the research questions of this study:

- Missing relevancy and consistency
- Missing integration
- Focus on large publicly-traded companies

Missing relevancy

The practitioners' perception of the research stream can be illustrated by quoting Winn (1993; p. 48), who stated: "While companies facing near-bankruptcy, market losses, or substandard performance are increasing in frequency, strategy researchers have provided little help for the managers charged with turning around deteriorating performance." Unfortunately, this statement, made over 20 years ago, was essentially reconfirmed, albeit with more considerate words by Trahms et al. (2013; p. 1297), stating that: "Indeed, what we do not know or what is currently understudied far outweighs what is known about decline and turnaround." In reviewing the empirical and conceptual contributions concerning crisis and turnaround management characteristics, the amount of contradicting empirical and conceptual findings for many variables, especially concerning the correct measures in turnaround, is irritating (for an overview, cf. chapter 4). To sum up, it can be established that evidence in turnaround research is highly inconsistent (Cater & Schwab, 2008; Eichner, 2010; Faghfouri, 2013; Pandit, 2000; Trahms et al., 2013) and much of the variance is unexplained (Eichner, 2010; Sudarsanam & Lai, 2001).

Missing integration

The turnaround situation is complex. Common approaches struggle to adequately reflect these complexities (Arogyaswamy et al., 1995). A specific weakness is the inadequate integration of all the relevant aspects of the crisis and turnaround process (Liou & Smith, 2006; Pandit, 2000; Pearce & Robbins, 1993). There is both a lack of integration between the research of company crisis and turnaround research (Trahms et al., 2013), and a general neglect of the context of turnaround, as it remains "largely ignored" (Pandit, 2000; p.42). While research has shown, for many variables individually, that they do have an impact on the turnaround result, there has been up until now no integrated turnaround model with a reasonable level of complexity, which integrates all relevant elements from crisis, turnaround actions and context.

This neglect is surprising, insofar as most turnaround publications draw heavily upon the contingency theory (see section 2.1.4). One of the essential assumptions of the contingency theory is the insight that any strategy is contingent on the situation it is applied to (see section 2.3.1).

The focus on large publicly-traded companies

The focus on large publicly-traded companies (Cater & Schwab, 2008; Faghfouri, 2013) might have its reasons (e.g., the availability of company data), but implicitly, this research approach ignores the largest part of the economy. According to Günterberg (2012), companies with a turnover below EUR 50m accounted for 99.7% of all companies, 60.8% of the employees and 39.1% of the total turnover in Germany in 2009. Depending on the respective definition, 55% – 70% of these companies are family firms (Klein, 2000). But the turnaround research specifically focused on family firms is very limited (see section 2.4.2). The few studies published have shown that there are significant differences between publicly-traded companies and family firms, but their findings have been largely disregarded by mainstream turnaround research.

Because medical analogies have a long tradition in turnaround research (Eichner, 2010; Faghfouri, 2013; Pearce & Robbins, 1993; Schendel et al., 1976; Sudarsanam & Lai, 2001), I want to illustrate my perception of the research situation in many studies by using a medical analogy.

Imagine a medical study conducted for a group of patients without assessing their symptoms (crisis characteristics), age, gender and background (context) and characterizing all possible treatments with a single digit number of general options (turnaround actions). Now imagine this study being done only for female patients living in the Berlin area (large publicly-traded companies), but the results being generalized for the whole population. It is not hard to imagine that the results of this study would be neither meaningful nor consistent with similar studies using different settings, and that a treatment based on this research would probably not be helpful or might even be dangerous to most of the population.

While this metaphor might be exaggerated, it illustrates the central issues in the field of turnaround research. These constitute the foundation and main motivation for this study. I want to contribute to the research field by aiming at an integrated model, which includes all relevant variables, to describe and explain crisis and turnaround for the far largest share of the company population. This study, in my assessment, successfully widens the research approach, being conducted as an overview study, integrating all relevant factors for the turnaround in a holistic approach. I am hopeful that this paves the way to a better assessment of the turnaround situation and its influencing factors, thus ultimately increasing survival rates in turnarounds.

1.2 Research questions and contributions

To address the issues of an integrated, relevant approach for medium-sized enterprises, this study focuses on four key questions, whose answers should contribute substantially to the research:

1. What are the conceptually relevant factors influencing the turnaround success?
2. Which conditions enhance turnaround success?
3. Are there common patterns in and out of crisis?
   What is their respective performance?
4. How is the relation between family and family firm affected by crisis and turnaround?

What are the conceptually relevant factors influencing the turnaround success?

The identification of the relevant factors is the foundation for conducting this study. To answer research questions two to four, a well-founded conceptual model is required to perform empirical research with an operationalized model of the crisis and turnaround process. The model design and elements need to be well-founded in conceptual and empirical research contributions, in order to build upon the achievements of the research field (Figure 1).

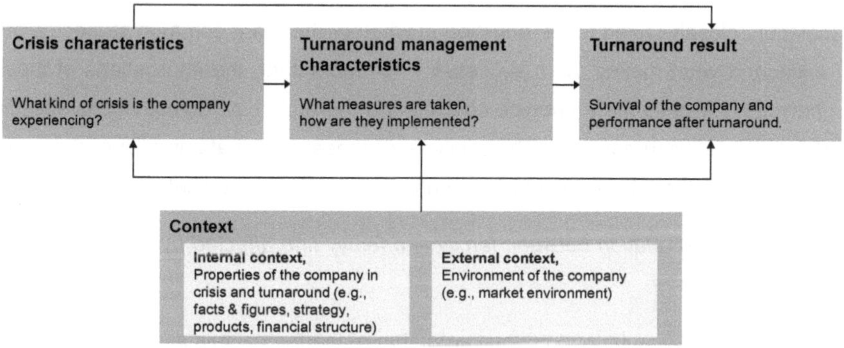

Figure 1: Elements and relations in the crisis and turnaround situation.
Source: Own illustration.

Which conditions enhance turnaround success?

The second question is the gist of the matter of turnaround research. I pose this question in a broader sense than is done in most other studies by aiming not at a single aspect, but rather employing an integrated view of the crisis and turnaround process. Explicitly, the study is not limited to turnaround actions and their impact on turnaround success, but investigates the complete setting of the crisis and turnaround process as fully as possible, i.e., how the crisis characteristics, turnaround management characteristics and the context change the probability of turning around a company in crisis, as well as their effect on the performance of the company after turnaround.

Are there common patterns in and out of crisis?

What is their respective performance?

The investigation of specific patterns and their respective impact on performance is common for both crisis and turnaround research (Asquith & Gertner, 1994; Eichner, 2010; Hauschildt et al., 2006). As both dimensions are reflected in the model developed, I want to address this issue for crisis and turnaround management separately. To understand, if there are common ways into crisis and what they might be, is, in my estimation, closely linked to the question of whether there are common strategies out of crisis and what makes them successful. To understand the implications of these archetypes, I assess the archetype specific and the archetype combinations specific performance after turnaround. The analysis of these combinations allows a conclusive analysis of the interaction between crisis and turnaround archetypes.

How is the relation between family and family firm affected by crisis and turnaround?

A family firm is characterized by the ownership of the family. It is assumed that crisis and turnaround are a challenging time, not only for the company, but also for the relation between family and family firm (Rüsen, 2008). I explore how the family role, specifically family control and family ownership, is altered by crisis and turnaround. Based on empirical data, I investigate if there are specific effects between the crisis characteristics, the turnaround management characteristics and the context on the changes on the one hand, and the family role in the firm on the other hand.

The empirical analysis relies on data specifically collected for this study from restructuring experts working in German banks. In a sampling process with 22 different banks, I was able to sample 209 valid cases of mid-sized companies in distress entering a turnaround. The contributing banks range from large companies like Deutsche Bank, Commerzbank, DZ Bank and Postbank to smaller institutes, and from all three pillars of the German banking system (see section 5.1.3). They represent an aggregated balance sheet value above 50% of the balance sheet sum of all German banks.

In answering the research questions, this study contributes to the research field in three areas:

Basis for future research

The integration of all relevant variables in one analysis allows future researchers to select relevant variables in their studies, contributing to more consistency in the results.

Guidance for practitioners and firms

The results offer guidance in terms of crisis assessment and applicability of turnaround actions. They highlight focal points influencing the turnaround result, allowing for improving the recovery chances of companies.

Basis for a turnaround rating system

Based on the integrated model and the key factors identified in the empirical analyses, it should be possible for banks to set up an ongoing turnaround risk rating system for the distressed debtors in their portfolio. This could provide an improved basis for credit decisions, collateral evaluation and covenant management.

I want to emphasize that this study does not aim to understand the details of specific turnaround mechanics, and it might be questioned if such insight is possible at all outside of specific case studies. Instead, this study's purpose is to open up new vistas, by reflecting the complexity of the turnaround situation with an appropriate modeling approach, allowing a broader overview of the crisis and turnaround process.

1.3 Outline of study

To achieve the aforementioned results, this study is structured in nine consecutive chapters (Figure 2).

While this introduction gives insights into the motivation and research gaps and provides a glimpse of the general research approach, it is chapter 2 in which the current state of the research in the field of crisis and turnaround is presented. This is achieved by introducing selected meta-studies, empirical works and family-firm-specific publications. Through this summary approach, a concise overview of the field of crisis and turnaround research is given, at the same time locating this work within the research field.

In chapter 3, the theoretical groundwork for this study is laid. Key terms and definitions are selected and refined with regard to their appropriateness for the chosen research approach. The framework, compiled and developed in chapter 3, provides the basis and context for the conceptual model, developed in chapter 4. The model is designed with the specific aim of implementing all important aspects of the turnaround situation found in conceptual and empirical literature. Chapter 4 portrays the model variables in detail. For each model dimension, propositions are derived concerning the specific relation to the post-turnaround performance of the company. To ensure practical relevancy, all elements of the model are intensively discussed with restructuring practitioners.

In chapter 5, the sampling process is presented, including a brief overview of the study participants. Further, the chapter contains the descriptive data analysis concerning basic statistical properties of the sample. Concluding this chapter, data simplifications and modifications are introduced and performed.

The regression-based analysis of the data is the topic of chapter 6. This chapter is targeted at analyzing the relation between each model component and the post-turnaround performance. The focus of this chapter is the identification of significant factors for turnaround success and their interaction. After a univariate regression between each model variable and the turnaround result, more complex statistical models are analyzed in three steps:

- *Complete models* implement all variables of the conceptual model into a complex statistical regression calculation.
- *Partial models* reflect the relations between specific aspects of crisis and specific aspects of turnaround to allow simpler, but meaningful models for each aspect.
- *Simplified models* use a reduced number of statistically determined model variables to explain post-turnaround performance.

In chapter 7, cluster analysis, as an exploratory method, is used to identify specific archetypes in the sample. The analysis is performed sequentially for the crisis characteristics and the turnaround management characteristics. For both, the clustering analysis is followed by an analysis of the cluster properties and the cluster-specific result, i.e., the mean post-turnaround performance of each cluster. Concluding this chapter, both cluster analyses are combined to picture the inter-cluster relation and their impact of the post-turnaround performance, i.e., for which configurations of crisis archetypes and turnaround archetypes success can be expected.

In chapter 8 the focus moves to the special perspective of family firm shareholders. The impact of crisis and turnaround on the role of the family in a family firm is the topic of this chapter. Focusing on successful restructuring cases, the relations between any of the conceptual model variables and changes of family ownership and control are analyzed. This analysis is completed by investigating the clusters found in chapter 7 for their respective impact on the family role change.

This study concludes in chapter 9 with a comprehensive discussion of the analyses and results and provides an outlook for possible future research.

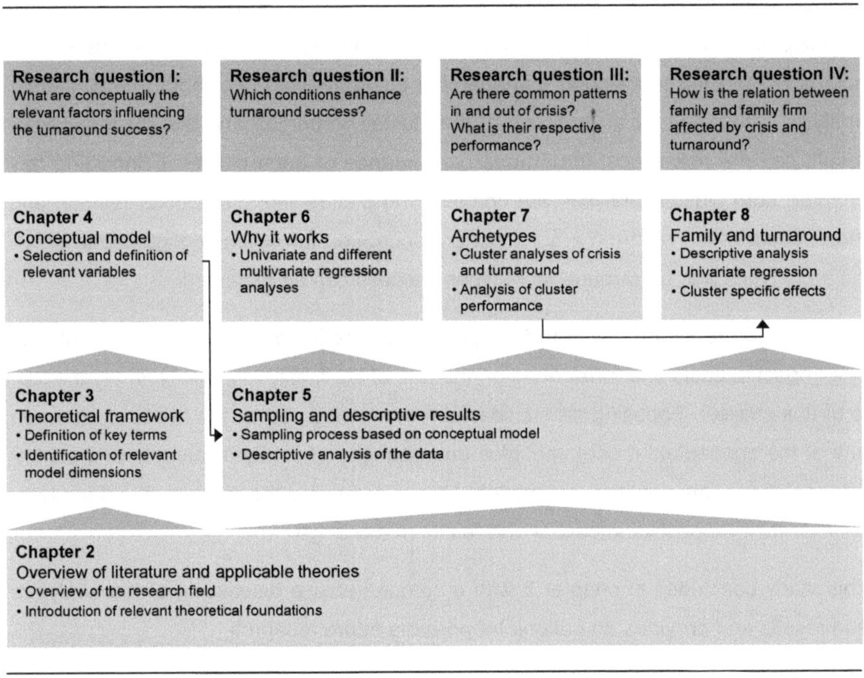

Figure 2: Chapter structure.

Source: Own illustration.

2 Overview of literature and applicable theories

An exhaustive review of existing literature on crisis and turnaround would by far exceed the scope of this work, both due to the diversity and number of publications in the research field. To offer some guidance, I introduce selected works, which have carried out such extensive research. This is covered in the first part of this chapter (section 2.1). Simultaneously, these works provide the basis for my analyses, highlighting the key publications and contributions that served as a starting point for my literature research.

The second part of this chapter is dedicated to the presentation of pivotal empirical works in the crisis and turnaround research. The approaches used to gain empirical insight into the workings of crisis development and turnaround management have been as diverse as the different theoretical lenses employed (see Eichner, 2010 and section 2.1.4 for further information). I focus on three studies, two of which are methodologically similar to my study (Eichner, 2010; Sudarsanam & Lai, 2001), and one that is unique in their contribution to the field of crisis characterization (Hauschildt et al., 2006).

The third section consists of a short summary of key theories, which are referred to throughout the study. For reasons of brevity and clarity, I forgo a thorough introduction, instead focusing on the highlights of these theories (section 2.3).

The last section of this chapter is dedicated to family firms and their characteristics which play an important role among the German medium-sized companies and thus in my research sample. These are briefly discussed, highlighting properties that distinguish them from non-family firms. This is extended by introducing two family-firm-specific works on crisis and turnaround, followed by a similarly brief introduction on the foremost family-firm-specific extensions of the presented theories, as well as one family-firm-specific theory.

2.1 Selected literature reviews

There are five works among the various meta-studies and literature reviews, which are briefly presented in this section, all of them covering different aspects of and approaches to the crisis and turnaround publications.

The two earliest works are Pearce and Robbins (1993) and John (1993). Pearce and Robbins (1993) is a seminal work, firmly introducing the notion of a turnaround consisting of two steps – retrenchment and recovery. Nearly all publications in turnaround research today reference this work as a theoretical basis for conducting research. It can be attributed to the contingency theory, which is a subcategory of strategic management research (see section 2.3.1).

The second, John (1993), was published roughly at the same time, but from the perspective of financial management research. While researching the same subject, the contrast between the two works shows the very different perceptions of financial management and strategic management research concerning crisis and turnaround.

Pandit (2000) is, in contrast, explicitly a meta-study. Without aiming to contribute new theoretical concepts, it highlights very clearly the shortcomings of the turnaround research up until the time of its publication. A major strength of his work is the detailed comparison of the different approaches used in empirical studies. Unfortunately, many of the concerns raised in this work remain valid today.

By contrast, the study of Eichner (2010) is not a conceptual work or a meta-study, but an empirical publication. Nonetheless, it contains an extensive literature overview, from which Eichner developed a very structured presentation of the turnaround research up until the date of publication. He highlights the most important works in both of the two different approaches, financial management and strategic management research. Additionally, he further subdivides the research streams, bundling the different publications into theoretical lenses, thus giving a brief and structured overview of the state of research.

The latest work presented here, Trahms et al. (2013), is an updated study in the tradition of Pearce and Robbins (1993). It reviews the major research contributions of the last 20 years as a basis for an update of the two-stage turnaround model as well as an agenda for future research.

2.1.1 The conceptual work of Pearce and Robbins (1993)

As stated by the authors, the main objective of their study is to promote retrenchment as a key element of the restructuring process. At the time of publication it had not yet been generally accepted that retrenchment activities, i.e., cost and asset reduction measures, are necessary components of turnaround management for most crisis cases. The study changed this profoundly.

The foundations for their conceptual two-stage turnaround structure are nine studies, starting from 1976, researching turnaround. Derived from them, the study proposed a unified model including the following elements (Figure 3):

- The crisis with *internal and external factors* causing it.
- *Crisis severity* as a key element of the crisis properties.
- Clear definitions and terms to unify the different *stage models* found in earlier publications, thus inventing and consolidating the notion of two-stage turnaround consisting of *retrenchment and recovery.*
- *Interaction* between the different elements.

The key assumption of their structural model is that the character of retrenchment and recovery are determined by different variables. The severity of the crisis mainly affects the intensity of the retrenchment activities: For high severity (e.g., imminent bankruptcy), asset retrenchment is required; for lower severity (e.g., sales decline), cost retrenchment is sufficient. The crisis factors, on the other hand, affect the nature of the recovery response. Internal factors demand efficiency related responses (i.e., process and structure), while external factors demand entrepreneurial responses (i.e., product and marketing).

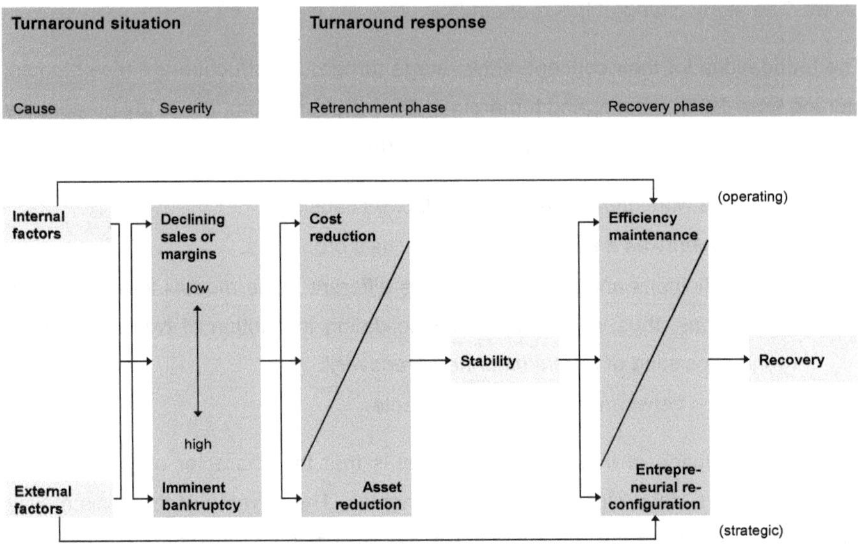

Figure 3: Pearce and Robbins' turnaround process model.
Source: Pearce and Robbins (1993).

Today, this basic model is widely accepted. But from the work's perspective, it aimed to achieve two targets:

- Firstly, the *unification of terminologies.*
- Secondly, arguing for the general *necessity of retrenchment.*

As of today, a majority of studies makes use of the two-stage process framework, which indicates that the authors achieved their aim. Weaknesses and limitations of this framework, for example that it only includes long-term declines and not shock-induced declines, are commonly ignored by others using this framework (e.g., Arogyaswamy et al., 1995).

The necessity to retrench and to focus on retrenchment activities when declining stood in stark contrast to an obsession with growth that was assumed common for managers at that time by this study. While in some publications it is sometimes questioned if retrenchment is required under all circumstances (Arogyaswamy et al., 1995; Faghfouri, 2013), the notion of retrenchment as a common crisis necessity is accepted.

For this study, the work of Pearce and Robbins (1993) is one of the early cornerstones in terms of the general understanding of the crisis and turnaround process. As such, many of the structural elements it introduced are integrated in this study's model.

2.1.2 The survey of John (1993)

The difference between John's financial management and Pearce and Robbins's strategic management perspective is already obvious due to their divergent perception of the crisis phenomenon. While Pearce and Robbins's work focuses on the internal and external factors causing the crisis and retrenchment and recovery actions to counter them, John's financial management study addresses financial distress (i.e., the shortfall of cash to fulfill the firm's obligations) and contracts, which need to be altered to allow the company to fulfill its obligations again. As contractual alterations are, much more than management actions, dependent on the respective legal framework, it is important to note that John (1993) was written with the US legal situation in mind.

In developing a model for managing financial distress, the work assessed the characters of the financial obligations. This resulted in the following structure:

- A company is *in distress* if it cannot fulfill all its hard (i.e., legally binding) obligations with its liquid (i.e., short term convertible in cash) assets.
- Measures to counter distress can be:
  - The liquidation of hard assets (e.g., machinery).
  - The alteration of hard contracts (i.e., renegotiation of debt contracts).
  - The issue of claims against future cash flows to finance the current (hard) obligations (e.g., new debt).

From a financial management perspective, the company is mainly a structure of cash flows. The key to averting financial distress is aligning these cash flows. This might be simplified by the formula of 'reducing the outflowing and increasing the inflowing cash.'

At the same time, the focus of financial management research is not on the operational cash flow, but on changing the financially-induced cash flow. This can either be renegotiation of debt – by changing terms of obligations or even converting debt to equity – or raising new sources of liquidity – through selling assets or new debt. The operational activities of the company itself are a black box, generating or consuming cash. The distress itself is seen as a situation and not as a process, the process view being the common perspective of strategic management research.

While the perspective is very different from the strategic management approach, both are valid perceptions and simplifications of the actual situation of a company in financial distress/ crisis. But both research perspectives are – in many cases up until today – disjunctive.

As a consequence, for this study, the financial management perspective as presented, e.g., by John (1993), highlights the need to set up a complete model, integrating the financial management research perspective.

2.1.3 The meta-study by Pandit (2000)

Pandit's meta-study performed an extensive review of 47 contributions to the field of research and turnaround. The judgment about the general performance of the research field and the quality of the contributions is very negative. The main criticism of turnaround research is related to its inconclusiveness, main reasons for this are, according to Pandit:

- Poor research design due to *poor definitions*, for example, the lack of consistency in the definitions used in turnaround studies for turnaround situations.
- Poor research design due to *simplistic explanations*, for example, the complexity of the turnaround situations is not reflected by the research design.
- Lack of a firm theoretical grounding of the studies, showing a weakness he deems as '*theoretical neglect.*'

These items lead the author to suggest measures to improve the general quality of the research in the field of crisis and turnaround:

- Better *definitions*: There should be clear conceptually founded definitions of the constructs used in the research design, especially for the definition of the turnaround situation. He suggests characterizing a turnaround situation as a threat to the company's continued existence if radical action is not taken.
- Better *research questions*: He suggests using the framework of Pettigrew (1988) as a conceptual basis to embrace all relevant aspects of turnaround: content, process and context. The latter two, in particular, are largely ignored, oversimplifying the studies' design.
- Better *methodology*: He assesses two general trends: small sample studies with depth and large sample studies with a very limited scope. He suggests using a methodological pluralism and established systematic research protocols, to better grasp and understand the turnaround situation.

Unfortunately, as of today, for many contributions in the crisis and turnaround research, according to my personnel assessment, the criticism of Pandit (2000) is still valid.

For my study, the topics and concerns raised by Pandit (2000) constitute an important element of the motivation to overcome the limitations perceived for large sample studies. I aim to achieve this by setting up a conceptual model integrating all relevant aspects of content, process and context: At the same time, by not doing a small sample study, but rather assessing a larger sample of firms, contributing to a broader understanding in terms of an integrated overview of the crisis and turnaround situation.

2.1.4 The literature overview by Eichner (2010)

The work of Eichner (2010) is an empirical study and definitely not intended as a dedicated literature review. Nonetheless, as an introductory part of his monograph, Eichner drafted a structure of the turnaround research stream, attributing key contributions on a first level to the respective theoretical perspectives and on a second level to specific theoretical lenses (the notion of theoretical lenses draws on Bowman & Singh, 1993).

The first of the two top-level categories is the *financial management research*. It consists of five theoretical lenses:

- *Bankruptcy prediction* is one of the earliest theoretical lenses of the financial management research. One of the most important contributions is the bankruptcy prediction model by Altman (1968). Other works are Routledge and Gadenne (2004); Smith and Graves (2005).
- *Market for corporate control* is a perspective viewing the economy as a competition of management teams for corporate resources. The turnaround situation can be seen as a struggle for control between different stakeholders. Contributions to this theoretical lens include Denis and Kruse (2000); Gilson (1990); John et al. (1992); Khanna and Poulsen (1995).
- *Capital structure* theory employs a perspective on a company consisting of different classes of financing, with the focus on the relation between debt financing, equity financing and the market value of the firm. With respect to turnaround, this research lens focuses on the alteration and conversion of debt and equity. Works attributed to this lens include Franks and Sanzhar (2006); Gilson (1989); Gilson et al. (1990); M. C. Jensen and Meckling (1976); Kraus and Litzenberger (1973); Lai and Sudarsanam (1997); Lang et al. (1995); Myers (1977); Ofek (1993); Whitaker (1999).
- *Theory of workouts* addresses the problems introduced into the workout process (restructuring of debt) by public debt holders. In contrast to bank debt holders, public debt holders introduce inefficiencies into the process. Works attributed to this lens include Asquith and Gertner (1994); Brown et al. (1994); Gertner and Scharfstein (1991); C. James (1995); Jostarndt (2007).
- The *stakeholder theory* is described as a hybrid between financial management and strategic management research. It structures the turnaround process by introducing the different stakeholders and their specific interest into the turnaround process. The amount of research is limited (Buschmann, 2006; Nothardt, 2001).

In contrast to the financial management research, the *strategic management research* consists of a larger number of publications and a broader variety of six theoretical lenses:

- *Industrial organization* focuses on the positioning of firms within their industry. The most popular work within this lens is the publication by Porter (1985). This theoretical lens is used relatively seldom in turnaround research, one of a few works attributed to it is Francis and Desai (2005).
- *Contingency theory* is the most popular of the theoretical lenses (for a more detailed introduction, please refer to section 2.3.1). Contingency theory states that there is no single optimal strategy, but a strategy is contingent on the specific setting of each firm. A sample of the broad variety of works are: Arogyaswamy et al. (1995); Barker and Mone (1994); Barker et al. (2001); Castrogiovanni and Bruton (2000); Chowdhury and Lang (1993); Hofer (1980); Pearce and Robbins (1993, 1994); Robbins and Pearce (1992); Schendel and Patton (1976); Schendel et al. (1976); Thietart (1988).
- *Theory of gestalts* assumes that there are a limited number of strategic configurations to which a specific performance can be attributed (for more information, please refer to section 2.3.4). This lens consists of a smaller number of works, among them Hambrick and Schecter (1983); Miller (1981).
- The theoretical lens *strategy process* refers to assessing the turnaround as a process consisting of content, process and contextual variables. Works attributed to this include Pettigrew (1988) and Pandit (2000).
- The *crisis management* perspective focuses on how crisis emerges and structurally analyzes the crisis variables. It is mainly driven by German authors. These include Bergauer (2001); Grape (2006); Hauschildt et al. (2006); Krystek (1980).
- The *organizational decline* literature is similarly focused on the process of crisis development and patterns in this process. It is the parallel, largely disjunctive, US research stream similar to *crisis management* in Germany. It consists, for example, of Kim S. Cameron et al. (1987); Clapham et al. (2005); S. J. Freeman and Cameron (1993); Love and Nohria (2005).

For my study, the contingency framework contributes most to the theoretical foundations (section 2.3.1). Second to this is the theory of gestalts (section 2.3.4), which is the foundation for the archetype analysis conducted in chapters 7 and 8. Despite using these as main lenses, for the development of the conceptual model I draw on all of the presented works and perspectives to derive the relevant variables with the aim of integrating them into a consistent conceptual framework (see Figure 4 and Chapter 4).

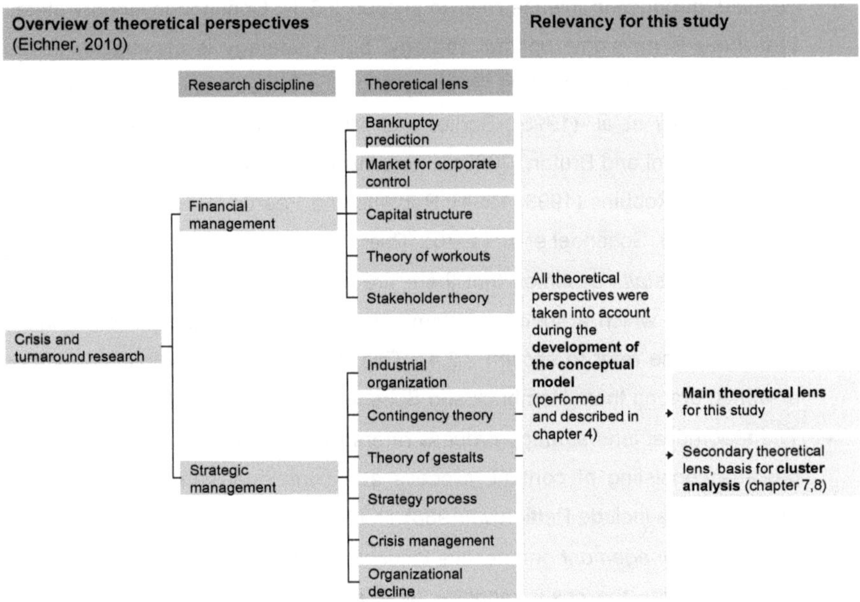

Figure 4: Alternative theoretical perspectives and their relevancy for this study.
Source: Eichner (2010), complemented by the respective relevance for this study.

2.1.5 The review by Trahms et al. (2013)

The review performed by Trahms et al. (2013) is conducted in the tradition of Pearce and Robbins (1993). Analyzing 40 empirical articles from a time span between 1993 and 2012, they found the model of Pearce and Robbins (1993) lacking in the ability to reflect the complexity of the phenomena found in the empirical studies. To cope with this gap, the authors introduced response factors into the classical two-stage model (Figure 5). In this respect, the work is similar to other authors (e.g., Arogyaswamy et al., 1995; Faghfouri, 2013), who also extended the original model of Pearce and Robbins (1993) with additional elements.

The response factors influence the company's reaction to a crisis. These factors are grouped in three categories: 'Managerial cognition,' 'strategic leadership' and 'stakeholder management.'

Apart from introducing these factors, the work extends the definitions of the original model, redefining the categories 'retrenchment' and 'recovery' to more broadly defined 'operational measures' and 'strategic measures.' The review also extends the result dimension to a continuum of possible turnaround outcomes ranging from failure via moderate recovery to the best case of sharp-bend recovery.

Besides these model extensions, the study points out unanswered research questions related to three main areas:

- *Resource orchestration*: Open questions related to this area refer to how the management and mismanagement of resources change crisis and turnaround. This ranges from the question of how timing affects the outcome to the quality of the management in this regard and its cognition impacting the resource orchestration.
- *Strategic leadership*: Open questions concerning strategic leadership refer to the actions, quality of and interactions within the company's management, including CEO and top management team (TMT).
- *Stakeholder management:* These open questions refer to the handling and interactions with the stakeholder, ranging from their motivation structures to power struggles and interpersonal relationships between management and stakeholders.

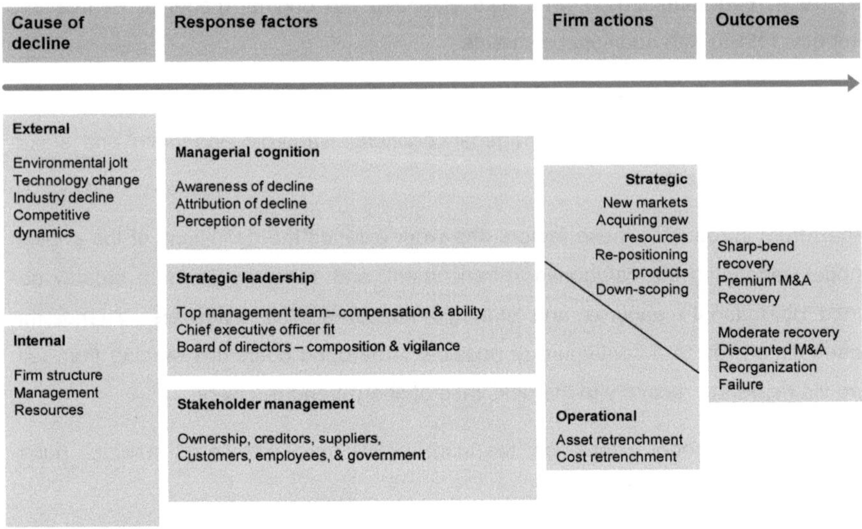

Figure 5: Trahms' model of organizational decline and turnaround.
Source: Trahms et al. (2013).

The impact of this work on my study is twofold. On the one hand, it raises important questions that are partially reflected in the composition and structure of the conceptual model. On the other hand, it specifically highlights the need to add more complexity to the turnaround modeling approaches, if researchers want to understand the observed phenomena in the crisis and turnaround process. This is consistent with one of the key aims of this study.

2.2 Selected empirical evidence

Many empirical works have been published researching the process and relevant factors in crisis and turnaround. I have selected three studies that use a partially integrated approach (Eichner, 2010; Sudarsanam & Lai, 2001) or contribute to the characterization of the crisis (Hauschildt et al., 2006).

The discussions of these studies follow five steps for each work: model design, empirical data, statistical methodology, results and conclusive assessment.

2.2.1 The study by Sudarsanam and Lai (2001)

Model design (Figure 6)

The study by Sudarsanam and Lai (2001) was the first study integrating financial and strategic management perspectives (Eichner, 2010) in turnaround research. In their model, the turnaround management content is reflected by four categories of restructuring measures: Operational restructuring, asset restructuring, managerial restructuring and financial restructuring. While operational restructuring and managerial restructuring are directly operationalized as variables, the other two are subdivided. Asset restructuring is subdivided into asset sales, acquisition and internal CAPEX. Financial restructuring is differentiated into dividend cut/ omission, equity issue and debt restructuring. This results in eight variables describing the content of the turnaround management.

The model is supplemented by five additional variables. The characterization of the crisis is based on the variables 'internal problems' and 'severity of the crisis.' The internal context is limited to the variable 'size' (of the company) while the external context is described by two variables: 'Industry condition' and 'economic condition.'

The result dimension is a binary variable for turnaround success, based on the z-score (Altman, 1968), which is a combined indicator for the proximity to bankruptcy. Using the z-score, the distress measurement of the company is done, defining both the beginning and end of distress.

The model analyzes three time periods – the first year of distress and the two years after that.

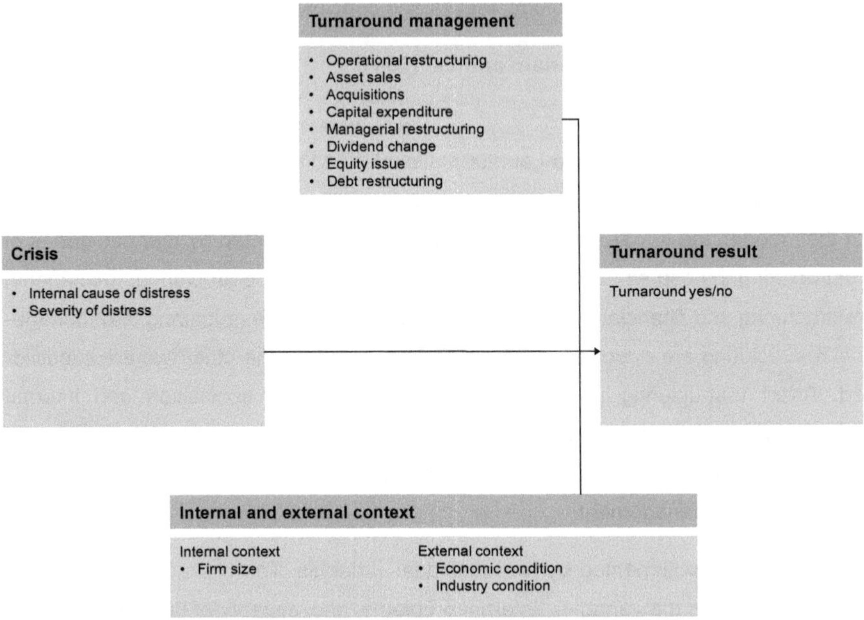

Figure 6: Model design used in the study of Sudarsanam and Lai (2001).

Source: Variables used by Sudarsanam and Lai (2001), structured according to this study's theoretical framework (chapter 3).

Empirical data

The study is based on 166 UK firms that experienced financial distress between 1985 and 1993. All companies were listed on the London Stock Exchange. The model is operationalized using specific financial figures for each variable. The figures originate from different financial databases. This limits the study to firms both publicly listed and present in these databases, and consequently above a certain size (market capitalization above GBP 10m).

Statistical methodology

The study employs parallel logit and linear regression analyses. The main models are a logit and a linear multivariate regression with the turnaround success as dependent variable and all other variables (without interaction effects) as predictor variables.

Results

The adjusted R^2 of the linear regression – comparable to the results in chapter 6 of this study – is 0.257. Thus the regression explains 25.7% of the variance of the result variable. Significant variables are 'operational restructuring,' which is negatively associated with recovery; 'dividend change,' which is positively related, 'debt restructuring,' which again has a negative effect, and the last significant variable is 'crisis severity,' which is negatively related to recovery.

Conclusive assessment

While originating from a mainly financial management perspective, the study includes many elements from strategic management research, specifically from the contingency approach (section 2.3.1). The integration of both financial and strategic management perspectives is, in my opinion, an indication that it is both possible and necessary to consider both perspectives in one model. The structure of the model is plain, limited to a small number of variables. The crisis variables in particular are not on a similar level of complexity with the turnaround management variables (two for crisis vs. eight for turnaround management). Determining cause and effect relations is thus very difficult at best. At the same time, the internal context variables are limited to one – the firm size – which is an even lower level of detail.

The data source – financial databases, which refer to annual statements – raises the possible problem of 'window dressing' in crisis proximity (Pandit, 2000) and thus manipulated financial numbers may impact the analysis.

Besides these concerns, this study's approach is the first of a kind in respect to the integration of different research perspectives, and thus the foundation upon which both Eichner (2010) and this study build.

2.2.2 The study by Eichner (2010)

Model design (Figure 7)

This study's model consists of a large number of variables, grouped into independent variables, control variables and a dependent variable.

The binary independent variables define the turnaround management. These 23 variables are structured in five categories: Operational restructuring, managerial restructuring, portfolio restructuring, financial restructuring, and process characteristics. Additionally, all these variables are assessed twice for different time periods during turnaround. This essentially doubles the number of independent variables to 46 by discerning early distress (i.e., the first year and second year), from the late restructuring phase (i.e., the third and fourth year of distress).

As control variables, 10 context factors are included in the analysis, covering the topics of internal context (firm size, leverage, growth opportunities, profitability and severity of distress), distress causation (industry crisis and type of crisis) and external context (geography, industry sub segment and distress year).

The binary dependent variable is based on the term free cash flow minus interest expenses. If this is negative after four years of turnaround, it indicates failed, if positive, successful turnaround.

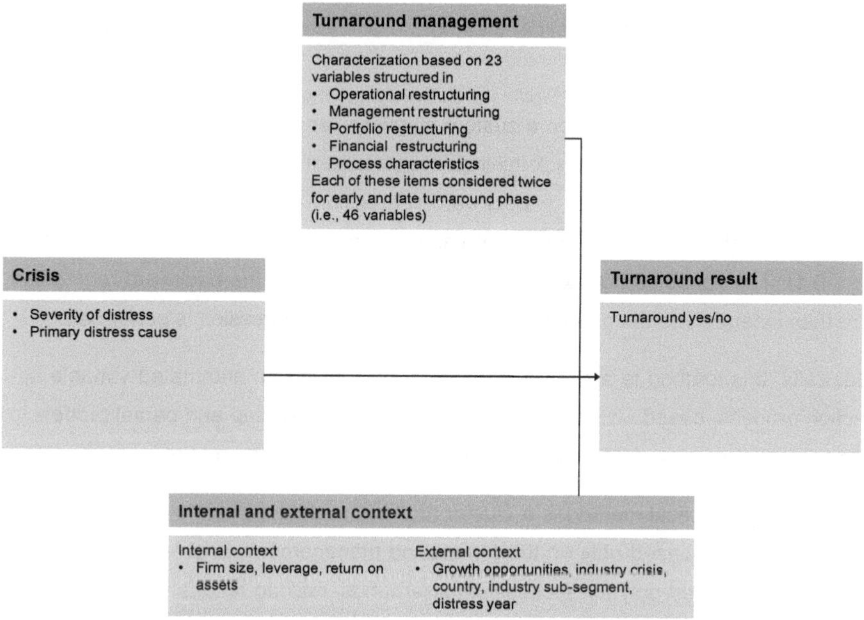

Figure 7: Model design used in the study of Eichner (2010).
Source: Variables used by Eichner (2010), structured according to this study's theoretical framework (chapter 3).

Empirical data

The analyzed cases are companies located in the US, UK and Germany. The analysis is based on publicly-traded industrial manufacturing firms with annual sales above USD 50m. As selection criteria, the firms had to have experienced distress (i.e., the shortfall of free cash flow compared with interest) in the time frame from 1996 to 2005.

To collect the relevant empirical data, financial data bases (for firm and market data), press releases/ad-hoc releases of the firms (using e.g., the database Factiva) were evaluated.

This concluded in a data set of 151 firms, for which all required information was available.

Statistical methodology

Eichner (2010) used two statistical methods to analyze his data: logistic regression and cluster analysis.

His statistical model is based on a custom stepwise variable selection approach: In a first step, variables not fulfilling a minimum requirement ($p < 0.25$) in a univariate regression are excluded. Then, a backward regression is performed for four partial models, selecting for each a subset of variables, but based on a different threshold ($p < 0.1$). The variables not excluded by the univariate and the backward regression are then inserted into the main model for which the final regression is performed.

Basically, this method is a simplification procedure using an automated variable selection process, based on univariate regression in the first step and partial models in the second step, all with the same dependent variable (turnaround yes/no).

The second statistical method is a cluster analysis to detect clusters of similar turnaround strategies, based only on the turnaround management variables of the model. This was performed only for successful turnarounds, making an analysis of the comparative performance of these strategies impossible. The result is limited to a content description of successful turnaround clusters.

Results

The complete logistic regression model yields a McFadden R^2 of 0.48 with 10 significant variables. Thus, it explains 48% of the result variable's variance with 10 significant predictor variables. A second measure common for logistic regression is the number of cases, which would be correctly sorted; in this respect, it could attribute 85.4% to the correct outcome (turnaround yes/no).

In the cluster analysis, six archetypes emerge, which are interpreted as a straight extension and detailing of the four operating turnaround strategies found by Hofer (1980).

Conclusive assessment

The study is a big step forward compared to the work of Sudarsanam and Lai (2001) that it drew upon. The resulting R^2 value is impressive and shows that the model is able to explain a significant part of the turnaround result distribution. In addition, the performance of the conceptual model development is excellent and thus the foundation for the structure used in this study.

While the execution of the regression itself is flawless, I have conceptual concerns related to the significant late variables with negative effects on the turnaround success, for example, 'late CEO change' or 'late plant closure.' These late variables are an important part of the final model (late variables are 6 of the 10 significant variables identified). My concerns relate to the fact that these late measures might be symptoms of an already doomed turnaround instead of the reason for its failure. It is very possible that these late measures were implemented as a last resort because earlier measures did not work and the turnaround was already failing, indicating a reverse cause-effect relation.

From the perspective of model design, the work is focused on the content of turnaround management. The number of context factors is limited and the operationalization of the crisis with only two variables (compared to 46 turnaround management variables) is a severe limitation of its scope.

As the cluster analysis only considered successful turnarounds, it is regrettably not possible to investigate performance differences between the clusters.

Overall, this study is a seminal work in the structural modeling of the turnaround process. It is the foundation and reference for the modeling and analyses done in this study.

2.2.3 The study by Hauschildt et al. (2006)

Model design (Figure 8)

The research field of crisis characterization shows only a very limited number of empirical contributions. The study of Hauschildt et al. (2006), which includes the findings of Hauschildt (2000), is one of the few works developing a systematic (and detailed) approach to categorizing crisis phenomena. The model consists of 67 'crisis causes,' which are grouped into four main segments: 'Person-influenced causes,' 'organization causes,' 'operative causes' and 'financial causes.'

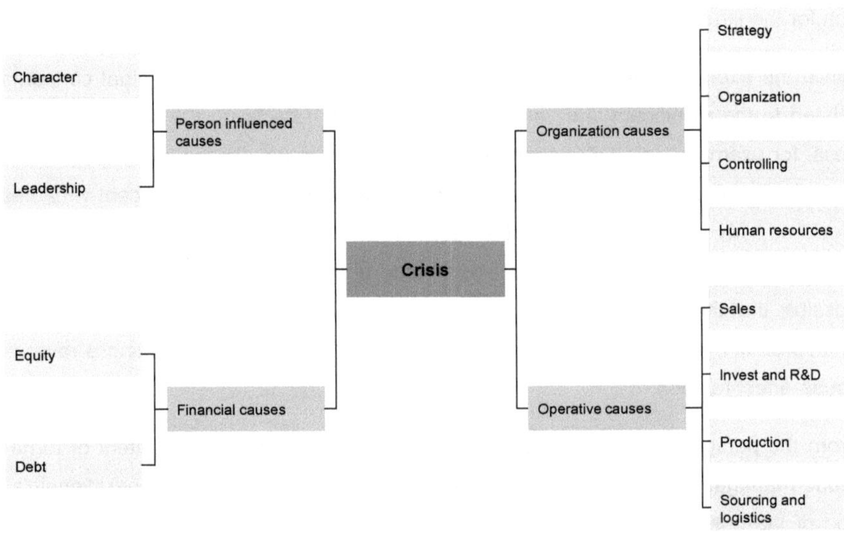

Figure 8: Model design used in the study of Hauschildt et al. (2006).
Source: 'Crisis spider' by Hauschildt et al. (2006).

Empirical data

The study contains three different analyses – two of which were previously published (Hauschildt, 2000).

The analyses draw on two different data sources. The first and the third analyses are based on publications in a popular weekly German business magazine (*Manager Magazin*). For the first analysis, 72 articles of a series about failing firms due to bad management (German series title: *Missmanagement*) from 1971 to 1982 were gathered. The third step is based on 53 articles from 1992 to 2001 in the same magazine.

This data base is – as admitted by the authors – heavily influenced by the journalists' biases. Also, as a consequence of the data sources being a magazine series focusing on the managers responsible for crisis, the model mostly addresses management performance.

The second analysis is based on data of 142 failed firms in the year 1988. These data originate from the files of a large German bank.

Statistical methodology

Based on these data sets, three cluster analyses (using Ward's algorithm) were performed, grouping the data sets into clusters according to their crisis characteristics. The study discloses only very limited information about the specific statistical methodology.

Results

The first analysis yields four clusters: 'Technologically endangered companies,' 'companies with uncontrolled growth,' 'companies with patriarchal leadership' and 'companies on crumbling pillars.'

The second analysis adds two clusters to the result of the first analysis: 'Dependent companies' and 'companies with unsuitable employees.'

The third analysis yields different, but similar, results: 'CEO with character weaknesses,' 'companies with inter-personal interaction defects,' 'companies with operating defects,' 'companies with institutional defects' and 'companies with unexpected sales problems.'

Conclusive assessment

While the process quality of the study shows some weaknesses, it used a rather broad basis to identify many different aspects of a crisis. The data sources are heavily biased with regard to the results, personalizing the company in crisis and attributing all issues to the management. This point of view thus significantly limits the perspective on other aspects of the company.

Nonetheless, this data collection is a significant contribution to the development of the conceptual model regarding crisis characterization, especially due to the limited data availability in this area.

2.3 Introduction of selected applicable theories

In the course of this publication, there are some theories that I will refer to frequently. This section presents a very brief introduction into the general ideas behind these theories with specific reference to their application to the crisis and turnaround research and thus to this study. As this is not an in-depth introduction to the theory itself, it is recommended that interested readers take the referenced publications into account.

2.3.1 Contingency theory

Contingency theory is a behavioral theory attributed to the work of Woodward (1965). Her work was based on research about US industry in the 1950s and 1960s. Woodwork noted that the firms' organizational structures correlated with the production technologies employed. Specifically, the 'fitting' organizational structures differ, for example, in terms of control span, depending on the batch sizes (small volume vs. mass production). Later she generalized these findings – still focused on production and technology – to a contingency theory of production processes, stating that the factors' technology, market situation, product diversity and size affect the appropriate organizational setup.

This leads to the perception of an organization as contingent on its specific situation, not as a static entity, but continuously adapting to changes of internal and external factors.

This production-process focused approach has since been generalized (see e.g., Morgan, 1997). Its fundamental principle states that there is no universally applicable best strategy, but that the optimal strategy for a given company depends on its specific situation. The best way to manage an organization is *contingent* on the internal and external factors influencing a situation. Commonly, these are the factors market and competitor situation and the available resources of the company.

This results in the key elements of the contingency theory (Morgan, 1997):

1. There is no 'optimal' strategy or organization per se.
2. A company has to achieve a match between itself and the environment.
3. Internally, a company has to achieve a fit between its internal functions.
4. The main task of management is to ensure this alignment and to adapt to internal and external changes.

Due to its flexible application, contingency theory is one of the most popular management theories, not only for turnaround, but also generally in management research (Eichner, 2010). Its intuitive structure allows the reflection of all kinds of management decisions in a factor-based model. Due to the contingent-result relationship, these models can also be straightforwardly evaluated in empirical studies.

The same is the case for the crisis and turnaround research. Here it is not only applicable for the turnaround measures themselves, but also for the assessment of the crisis. Hereby it leads to the perception of a crisis as the consequence of a misalignment between a firm, its resources, and the environment (Porter, 1985; Trahms et al., 2013). This perspective allows the crisis to be assessed not as induced by external causes driving a company into distress, but as a result of the company's failing to adapt to the changing environment and thus causing the crisis itself through maladaptation.

An exemplary utilization of the contingency theory for turnaround research can be found in the model of Pearce and Robbins (1993) presented in section 2.1.1. It defines the content of turnaround management as contingent on the crisis causes and the crisis severity, while similarly defining the beginning of the recovery phase as contingent on having achieved financial stability. This intuitive applicability and flexibility make contingency theory the most popular theoretical lens for crisis and turnaround research (see section 2.1.4). For this study as well, contingency theory is the main theoretical foundation applied.

2.3.2 Principal-agent theory

The principal-agent theory is founded in the publication of M. C. Jensen and Meckling (1976). At its core, it scrutinizes the abstract situation of the 'principal' delegating a task to an 'agent.' For the specific research context of this study, this usually refers to the situation of a company's operational management, where the owner (principal) of a company is delegating the task of managing it to a manager (agent).

The key idea behind the principal agency theory is that the owner (principal) has different interests and other information available than the agent (manager) (Eisenhardt, 1989). These asymmetries in both information and interest lead to inefficiencies, which are referred to as agency costs, as the principal has to implement instruments (with concurring costs) to avert the agent from acting against his interest.

These asymmetries are:

- *Hidden actions*, i.e., activities of the agent that cannot be monitored or ex post attributed to the agent by the principal.
- *Hidden information*, i.e., the principal has less available information than the agent.
- *Hidden characteristics*, i.e., the principal is not aware of certain characteristics of the agent.

It is assumed that the agent uses his privileged situation to act in his own favor or perform acts that are not in line with the interest of the principal. To reduce the impact of these effects, the principal implements instruments to reduce and govern these effects (e.g., monitoring systems or variable compensations). These instruments incur costs and are the first element of the so-called agency costs. The second part of the agency costs is incurred by activities or missing activities of the agent itself that are not in line with the interest of the principal. This research stream relies heavily on building mathematical models, which usually aim at analyzing (and minimizing) the total agency costs.

The theory is empirically testable and it is both supported by and contributes to organization theory, although it has also been criticized as too narrow and even dangerous (Eisenhardt, 1989).

The principal-agent theory is not one of the primary theoretical lenses used in turnaround research (Eichner, 2010). For this study, it is important for two reasons: its application in the family firm research (see section 2.4.3) and its application to the interactions between management and shareholder in the specific situation of crisis and turnaround.

2.3.3 Resource-based view (RBV)

The resource-based view essentially perceives a firm – as the name of the theory suggests – as a bundle of resources. While its origins go back to the 1950s, the theory has been consolidated and established in the publication of Wernerfelt (1984) and found wider acceptance after the publication of Barney (1991). It has been assessed to be one of the most influential theories in the history of management research (Kraaijenbrink et al., 2010). The theory aims to explain, based on their available resources, why firms within the same industry show different performance.

The key concepts of the theory are the following (Barney, 1991):

- Firm resources are broken down into *physical capital* (e.g., assets), *human capital* (e.g., knowledge) and *organizational capital* (e.g., processes), which are controlled by a firm and can be used to implement strategies that increase efficiency and effectiveness of the firm
- Resource characteristics:
    - *Valuable*: Allowing implementing value-creating strategies.
    - *Rare*: Not available for any or at least most competitors.
    - *Imperfectly imitable*: Cannot be imitated by competitors.
    - *Non-substitutable*: Cannot be substituted by other resources.
- *Competitive advantage* is a value-creating strategy implemented by using resources that are currently not implemented by any competitor. To achieve competitive advantage, a company needs resources that are valuable and rare.
- *Sustainable competitive advantage* is a competitive advantage that cannot be duplicated by any competitor. To achieve sustainable competitive advantage, a company needs resources that are valuable, rare, inimitable and non-substitutable.

While the theory is criticized (Kraaijenbrink et al., 2010), there is a significant amount of empirical and conceptual findings supporting it as a valid construct to explain phenomena found in strategic management research.

The resource-based view is also used in turnaround research (see e.g., Thornhill & Amit, 2003) and is referred to during the development of the conceptual model. It also is one of the key theories in family firm research (see section 2.4.3).

2.3.4 Theory of gestalts

The theory of gestalts is a specific application of the contingency theory, developed by Miller (1981). He criticizes five properties of the contingency theory based research:

- Simplistic statistical methods, like correlation coefficients or bivariate analyses.
- An ignorance of context leading to very different results in different studies.
- Analyses searching for a single path to success, ignoring the fact that there might be multiple and different successful strategies.
- Cross-sectional studies ignoring cause-effect relations and the process perspective (especially the issue of timing aspects).
- Simplistic cause-effect relations of a company adapting to the environment, ignoring the fact that the managerial set-up of a company influences this relation.

The theory of gestalts is based on the fundamental assumption that there are a limited number of common patterns – the 'gestalts,' in environmental, organizational, and strategy-making variables – that account for a large percentage of cases. These can be identified, for example, by using cluster analysis.

This method allows the consideration of many variables in a contingency setting where traditional regression methods would fail to detect significant relations (as the statistical power decreases with an increasing number of variables – see section 6.1.2). Based on the theory of gestalts, these complex data sets are subdivided into archetypes. These subsets can then be analyzed more meaningfully than the complete data set, as they share a gestalt-specific homogeneity.

The theory of gestalts is relevant for this study as it provides the fundament for the second statistical analysis performed. The first statistical analysis (chapter 6) is focused on linear regression models identifying relevant (single) variables and their relation to the turnaround result. In chapter 7, on the other hand, the second statistical analysis investigates for common archetypes (clusters), relying on the theory of gestalts. These archetypes are then characterized and analyzed. Chapter 8 utilizes both approaches – regression and clustering – for the analysis of the family role change in crisis and turnaround.

This twofold approach allows considering two very different perspectives, the first focused on the details, the second on the big picture. The combination of the two perspectives is expected to yield a much more differentiated insight than both methods alone.

2.4 Introduction to selected family firm research

Among the medium-sized companies in Germany, family firms play an important role. It was found that, depending on definition, sample and country, between 35% and 99% of all firms are family firms (Gómez-Mejía et al., 2007). This is consistent with this study, in which 85% of all firms in the sample are fully or partly owned by founding families (see section 5.2.1).

The high relevance of family firms within the sample does require introducing some key facts about family firms and their theoretical foundations.

This section introduces family firm definitions, elaborating on the diverse possibilities to grasp this phenomenon (see section 2.4.1). Afterwards, it covers two selected studies of family firms in crisis and turnaround (see section 2.4.2) and concludes with the introduction of relevant family firms theories (see section 2.4.3).

2.4.1 Definition of family firms

Unfortunately, there is no generally accepted standard in family firm research to determine whether a firm is a family firm (Ahlers, 2014; Astrachan et al., 2002; Cater & Schwab, 2008; Faghfouri, 2013).

The definition of the family firm is based mainly upon two different approaches, the 'components of involvement' and the 'essence' approach (Chrisman et al., 2005). The 'components of involvement' is based on actual measurable metrics which define the level of interaction between family and company. These are commonly 'management role,' 'ownership share' or 'governance structure' (Chrisman et al., 2005).

The 'essence' approach is based upon the assumption that mere involvement of the family is not sufficient. The family must influence the firm with a certain family business-specific behavior before it is an 'actual' family firm (Chrisman et al., 2005).

As the 'components of involvement' approach allows a definition along empirically measurable features, I draw upon them in mapping the role of the family in respect to the company as part of the contextual dimension of the conceptual model (see section 4.6.). I focus on the aspects of ownership and management, thus roughly following the approach of Block (2010) in his study about family firms and downsizing.

Similar to many other authors, I restrict the family aspect of the family firm definition exclusively to founding families and their descendants (Anderson & Reeb, 2003; Faghfouri, 2013; Gómez-Mejía et al., 2007). Thereby I do not set a strict ownership limit, above which a firm is defined as family firm. Instead, all firms with any family ownership are considered in my respective analyses and the ownership percentage is incorporated as a context variable.

As the relation between family and family firm changes with each generation of the family (Gómez-Mejía et al., 2007), the family firm generation is included as a context factor in the conceptual model.

2.4.2 Selected studies on family firms in crisis and turnaround

Similar to the introduction for crisis and turnaround research, this section briefly presents only two, but central, publications in the research field of family firms in distress.

In contrast to the diverse field of general crisis and turnaround research, the details of how the cause-effect relations differ in the crisis specifically for family firms has not been sufficiently researched. Most studies about crisis and turnaround refer exclusively to publicly listed companies (Cater & Schwab, 2008; Faghfouri, 2013; Rüsen, 2008); examples for such studies are e.g., Barker and Duhaime (1997); Eichner (2010); Hambrick and Schecter (1983); Sudarsanam and Lai (2001).

Both of the works presented in this section are indeed the only two family firm oriented publications discussed in the extensive review of Trahms et al. (2013). Although addressing a similar research subject, the two publications are very different. While the first is a case study, using two cases to develop hypotheses for specifics and commonalities between family and non-family firms in distress and turnaround (Cater & Schwab, 2008), the second is an empirical work using publicly available information about Spanish oil mills to develop – based on very specific settings – a theory stating that family firms have complementing non-financial goals as part of their decision process (Gómez-Mejía et al., 2007).

While the differences between family firms and non-family firms in regard to crisis and turnaround management have been researched, if not sufficiently, there is virtually no research on how the crisis affects the relation between family and company in regard to ownership and control, a topic I analyze in chapter 8.

2.4.2.1 The case study of Cater and Schwab (2008)

This case study analyzes the crisis and turnaround process of two cases. Out of 20 companies contacted, the respective companies agreed to participate in the study. The data collection occurred over a two-month interview period with the top management teams of both companies.

The findings cover the following eight propositions for the retrenchment phase:

- Top management changes:
    - Strong ties between family management and family business reduce the ability to change top management.
    - Replacement candidates in the family for the top management are limited and may also block a management change.
    - Consensus orientation of the decision processes reduces the ability to execute the decision to change the top management.
    - Informal management systems make the transition to a new manager more difficult.
- External advice and expertise
    - Internal orientation reduces the willingness of the company to invite external specialists support during turnaround.
    - Good integration of non-family employees into the company supports hiring external specialists.

- Altruistic motives and long-term goal orientation
    - Altruistic motives help to implement retrenchment moves that are necessary in turnaround.
    - Long-term goal orientation supports retrenchment actions, even if these only help the company long term.

These propositions influence, but do not fundamentally change the crisis and turnaround process. According to the authors, this influence modifies the applicability of turnaround moves. Implicitly, it also changes the probability of turnaround success, although the authors do not elaborate on that relation.

This case study is relevant for this work, as it illustrates that there are specific differences between family and non-family firms in a fundamentally similar process. As I integrate the family-ownership as a context variable into the conceptual model, its effect on the turnaround result is part of the analysis, and the study of Cater and Schwab (2008) offers some guidance in their interpretation.

2.4.2.2 The study of Gómez-Mejía et al. (2007)

This study is not dedicated to crisis and turnaround, but it shows very transparently that family firms are willing to run higher risks than non-family firms under specific circumstances. Probably due to similar reasoning, the study was, despite not being explicitly about turnaround, also included in the turnaround research review by Trahms et al. (2013).

Due to this indirect connection, a brief introduction of the setting is required. The study is based on a very specific property of the Spanish oil mill market. These oil mills have the option of joining a co-op, a decision that – as it is described by the authors – brings only advantages in terms of financial incentive and risks. But as a consequence of joining a co-op, owner families would lose their family influence on the business.

Model design

Of the several models in the study, I want to focus on the model describing the factors influencing the decision to join a co-op.

While the decision of the company to join a co-op is the dependent variable, there are 21 independent variables in the model. Of these, I want to highlight four variables related to family ownership.

The first is the family ownership (yes/no); the other three specify a combination of ownership and control of the family by using a three-stage operationalization:

- Stage 1: Founding family as owners and managers.
- Stage 2: Descendants and managed by the family.
- Stage 3: Descendants and managed by external managers.

The other 17 variables reflect different internal and external context factors for the transaction, e.g., size, technology, and gross national product.

Empirical data

The empirical data covers 1,237 firms during a 54-year period. The required information was obtained from the annual data of the government mandate registries (for the oil mills themselves) and other public data sources (for other variables, e.g., for the gross national product).

Statistical methodology

The regression is performed as COX regression, a hazard rate prediction model the authors use to predict the release of control (i.e., joining a co-op) with the described data set.

Results

The authors were able to show that family-run oil mills are less willing to join a co-op, thus accepting higher risks and less profit in exchange for family control. At the same time, the authors also show that with increasing family stages (explained in 'model design') this family-specific effect is reduced.

Conclusive assessment

While the study is only indirectly linked to the crisis and turnaround research, it shows clearly that family firms act differently – and will do so in the context of crisis and failure risks as well. Explicitly, the authors show (in an initial assessment), that for family firm-owned oil mills the risk of failure is higher than for non-family-owned oil mills.

While there is no direct application of these findings in my study, it reconfirms that the characteristics of family firms have to be included in the conceptual model. This research was also the foundation for the development of the SEW theory (see section 2.4.3.3).

2.4.3 Introduction of selected applicable theories for family firms

For family firms, there are three basic theories that have received most of the attention in research: Principal-agent theory, the resource-based view and, since 2007, the socioemotional wealth theory (SEW) (Berrone et al., 2012; Chrisman et al., 2010; Pijanowski, 2014; Siebels & zu Knyphausen-Aufseß, 2012).

While the first two are straightforward applications of existing theories to family firms, socioemotional wealth (Gómez-Mejía et al., 2007) is a family-specific theoretical construct (see section 2.4.2.2). These three theories are briefly introduced in the following sections.

2.4.3.1 Principal-agent theory for family firms

Many family firms are also family managed (descriptive details for the sample of this study are presented in section 8.4). In this, the typical family firm deviates from the otherwise typical constellation of shareholder and managers: For family firms, ownership and management are often in the same hand.

Drawing on the principal-agent theory, it could easily be concluded that, due to the alignment of interest, both elements of the agency costs disappear. There is no need for monitoring and controlling instruments, nor is there an agent not acting in the best interest of the principal.

While this seems like a logical conclusion, it was shown that there are agency costs present in family firms (Schulze et al., 2001). Family firms with family managers also use typical principal-agent mitigating instruments, e.g., variable compensation. At the same time, the authors showed evidence for family-specific principal-agent issues, for example, related to conflicts among family owners.

It seems that from a principal-agent perspective there are differences between a family and a non-family firm, but that these are not one-directional, i.e. not only agency cost reducing.

Specifically for the purpose of this study, it is assumed that there are effects that can be explained by the principle agency theory. In the context of bankruptcy proximity there are obviously different interests of principal and agent. While the agent, i.e., the employed manager, is much more willing to file for insolvency (to follow the legal regulations and avoid retributions), the principal, i.e., the shareholder, will usually lose his stake in the company (share value is usually zero after insolvency) and is thus interested in resolving the crisis and will probably file for insolvency as late as possible. It could be concluded that a family manager, as manager and owner, will thus balance both interests and file for insolvency at a later time than the employed non-family manager.

2.4.3.2 Familiness – RBV

In the context of the resource-based view (RBV) Habbershon and Williams (1999; p. 11) characterize "the unique bundle of resources a particular firm has because of the systems interaction between the family, its individual members and the business" as 'familiness.' The definition of familiness encompasses positive resources – referred to as 'distinctive familiness' – as well negative resources – referred to as 'constrictive familiness.'

Sirmon and Hitt (2003) further differentiate these resources by categorizing them:

- *Human capital*, for example, the family members' skills and capability, commitment and loyalty of employees to the company.
- *Social capital*, for example, goodwill with stakeholders.

- *Survivability capital*, for example, the willingness of the family to contribute resources beyond the point where a 'normal' shareholder would do this.
- *Patient capital*, i.e., the fact that families are willing to invest with longer ROI perspectives.
- *Governance capital*, i.e., the identity of agent and principal simplifying the governance structures.

The core ideas of family-firm-specific resources are tightly linked to the turnaround capability of a company. The main aspects of the theoretical construct have a direct impact on the ability to turn around a company (most obviously survivability capital).

2.4.3.3 Socioemotional wealth (SEW)

The theory of socioemotional wealth (SEW) is based upon the empirical study conducted by Gómez-Mejía et al. (2007), which was presented in section 2.4.2.2. The study found that family firms are willing to accept a higher risk in order to retain control of the family firm. To explain this behavior, which seems irrational from the perspective of financially-based reasoning, the SEW construct was developed.

SEW states that the commercial targets of a family firm are complemented by non-commercial targets, which add a different kind of wealth to the owning family, the socioemotional wealth.

The SEW was operationalized by Berrone et al. (2012), deriving a five dimensional construct to define the relevant aspects of SEW:

- *Family control and influence* refer to the family's need to influence decisions and the course of the company.
- *Identification of family members with the firm* refers to the family members' perception of the company as part of their identity.
- *Binding social ties* refer to the wish that the company be perceived positively by society, stakeholders and community beyond what could be explained by expected financial returns.
- *Emotional attachment of family members* refers to the fact that a family firm is perceived not as a financial vehicle, but as an entity to which there is an emotional connection.

- *Renewal of family bonds through dynastic succession* refers to the wish to hand over the family business to future generations.

For the context of crisis and turnaround, the SEW-driven behavior of a family firm also changes the turnaround probability. It could be assumed that a family shareholder is willing to invest funds in the company beyond what a rational investor would be willing to do. At the same time, other options, like bringing in new shareholders with additional funds, might be less desirable for the shareholders of a family business.

3 Theoretical framework

Crisis and turnaround research lacks a commonly accepted conceptual framework for the relevant aspects of the crisis and turnaround situation. Most terms employed are ambiguous in their meaning, depending on their research perspective and lens (section 2.1.4) and the definition chosen in the respective study. This fact was discussed by Pearce and Robbins (1993) in their seminal work in the early 1990s, and it is still the case today, as pointed out in more recent works (e.g., Faghfouri, 2013; Liou & Smith, 2006; Pandit, 2000; Trahms et al., 2013).

This chapter introduces and defines the key terms used in this study to describe the elements of the crisis and turnaround process. It establishes the theoretical framework as well as the structural context for the conceptual model developed in chapter 4.

A foundation for these definitions is provided by the conceptual presentation of the basic research context, based upon the introduction of the general phase model of crisis and turnaround (section 3.1). This general model is extended by a short excursus elaborating the specifics of the German restructuring process of bank-financed companies and its implications for this study.

Afterwards, the aspects of crisis are introduced with a focus on the two key aspects: crisis diagnostics and crisis typology (section 3.2). Crisis diagnostics focuses on the answer to the question of how to determine whether there is a crisis. Crisis typology seeks an answer to how to characterize the properties of a crisis.

Subsequently, the key aspects of the actual turnaround are introduced (section 3.3): process and content of the turnaround management.

The last two sections (section 3.4 and 3.5) discuss the possible results and the internal and external context of the crisis and turnaround process.

3.1 Basic research context

Using the most fundamental and broadest perspective, the crisis and turnaround process for any company can be characterized by a sequence of three phases (Figure 9):

- *Crisis emerging*: Crisis develops and crisis is perceived.
- *Turnaround management*: Actions against crisis are taken.
- *Turnaround result*: Crisis is averted or company fails.

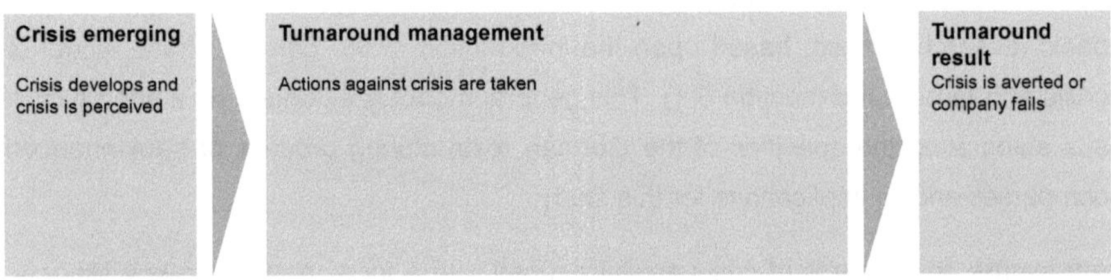

Figure 9: Basic three stage turnaround model.

Source: Underlying concept of all crisis and turnaround phase models (e.g., Arogyaswamy et al., 1995; Faghfouri, 2013; Pearce & Robbins, 1993; Pearson & Clair, 1998; Smith & Graves, 2005; Trahms et al., 2013).

Some phase models deviate from the basic sequence of phases and supplement them with additional elements that not only describe the sequence of phases in a crisis and turnaround process, but either add additional context variables to the phase models (e.g., Trahms et al., 2013), differentiating the turnaround activities by characterizing the reactions types (e.g., Pearson & Clair, 1998), or by compiling decision trees in the phase models itself (e.g., Arogyaswamy et al., 1995). In the case of Trahms et al. (2013), these are so-called 'response factors,' which determine how the unique resources and properties of a company change and define the responses to a distress situation. In the case of Arogyaswamy et al. (1995), a flow is added to the model by allowing phases to repeat themselves under certain conditions in an if/else-like decision tree.

In this study, I want to clearly separate the phases (i.e., the sequence of events) from the various variables, ranging from the crisis properties and the turnaround activities to the contextual variables, as they influence these phases and each other. This distinction is required as this study aims to develop a better and more detailed understanding of the relations between the elements of the conceptual model. Using one of these more complex phase models would imply (by the assumptions inherent in each model) too many restrictions on the research subject, thus limiting the possible findings.

For this reason, I rely on a – compared to some of models mentioned above – a simpler but well-established phase model, which is detailed in the following sections.

3.1.1 Five-stage crisis and restructuring model

The five-stage model (Figure 10) is an extension of the very rudimentary three-phase model introduced previously (Figure 9). It extends this model detailing the 'turnaround management' into three sub-stages: 'Turnaround plan,' 'retrenchment' and 'recovery.'

This five-stage model is conceptually widely accepted and is directly adapted from Eichner (2010), but ultimately relies on the works of earlier publications (Bibeault, 1982; Böckenförde, 1996; Pearce & Robbins, 1993; Robbins & Pearce, 1992), and it is used in a similar form in other studies as well (Buschmann, 2006; Grape, 2006). It assumes a certain sequence of phases and events, which have been found to be common to most, if not all crisis and restructuring cases.

- Stage 1: *Crisis emerging* – a distress situation develops through different stages (see section 3.2 for further details). This process can either be a situation of longer decline or instigated by a sudden event. The end of this stage is marked by the perception of the crisis and the company being acknowledged as 'in distress.'

- Stage 2: *Turnaround plan* – based on the perception of the crisis in Stage 1, a plan for how to overcome this crisis is developed. It prescribes the activities later implemented in Stages 3 and 4. The turnaround plan is synonymously also referred to as restructuring opinion or turnaround concept.
- Stage 3: *Retrenchment*: 'Stop the bleeding' – the first phase of turnaround management is focused on activities to cut costs and losses, with financial stabilization being the key retrenchment target.
- Stage 4: *Recovery*: 'Return to growth' – the second phase of turnaround management is focused on long-term restructuring. The focus is to return to a stable business model and – if possible – growth.
- Stage 5: Turnaround success or failure – the results become visible. After this phase, there is either a successful or a failed turnaround.

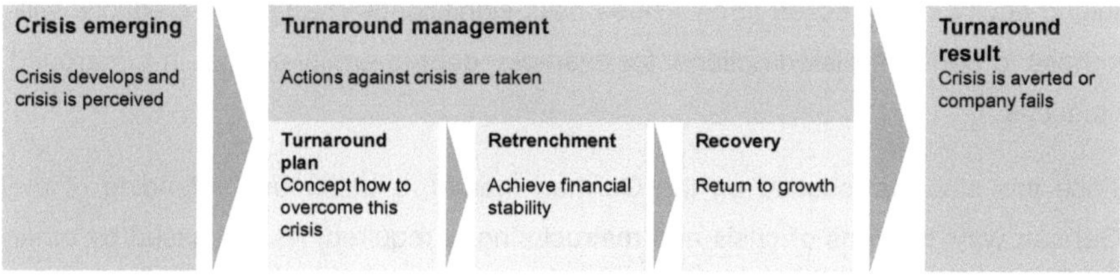

Figure 10: Five stage turnaround model.
Source: Adapted from Eichner (2010).

Per definition, the crisis is present during the complete process with the exception of the very last stage, when it is either averted or has led to a failure of the company, thus the term 'crisis' is used to describe stages 1 to 4 of this phase model. Similarly, turnaround management starts with the *turnaround plan* and lasts until the results of the respective activities are visible. Thus the term 'turnaround management' covers stages 2 to 4.

3.1.2 Specifics within the crisis and turnaround process in Germany

Most studies focus their analysis on only one country, but some authors compare the crisis and turnaround process in different countries. While these are very similar in many aspects, the studies have found some country specific characteristics. Suzuki (1985) found that differences between the process in Japan and the US were mostly due to different corporate financial structures in the two countries, with the US-firms relying more on equity financing and the Japanese firms more on bank financing. Eichner (2010) shed light on differences in the turnaround of publicly-traded companies in the US, UK and Germany and found, for example, that German companies had a tendency to rely more on CAPEX increase and product innovation as well as CEO removal compared to the other two countries. Jostarndt (2007) revealed that there are additional risks for creditors in Germany compared to other markets, if acquiring equity in distressed firms. These risks significantly change the creditors' willingness to perform related actions, for example, debt-to-equity-swaps, in turnaround situations.

Since this study is focused on the German market, a better understanding of the 'German way' in terms of crisis and restructuring is required. As discussed by other authors (Buchalik, 2004; Jostarndt, 2007; Langer et al., 2012), the properties of the crisis and turnaround process in Germany are heavily influenced by the banking system regulations. They determine how banks have to handle their 'bad loans,' i.e., any credits for which the repayment is doubtful; this includes – per definition (see section 3.2.2) – loans to companies in crisis.

The regulation framework forces banks to comply with a specific process. I want to highlight three key elements of the regulatory framework, which are significant for this study:

- Minimum requirements for risk management ("Mindestanforderungen an das Risikomanagement"; BaFin, 2012), *MaRisk*
- German Bankruptcy Act ("Insolvenzordnung"), *InsO*
- Decisions of the German Federal Supreme Court ("Bundesgerichtshof"), *BGH*

The *MaRisk* is a key document released by the German Federal Financial Supervisory Authority ("Bundesanstalt für Finanzdienstleistungsaufsicht") abbreviated BaFin. It regulates the organizational structure and processes to manage risks in financial institutions. Specifically, it defines the mandatory requirements for the management of 'bad loans' ("Problemkredite"), i.e., loans for which the repayment is doubtful:

- *Organizational structure within the bank*

  Risk assessment and risk management on the one hand and sales organization on the other hand, are to be separate up to the level of the board of directors.
- *Risk assessment of banks*

  Credit risks have to be assessed regularly by using an evolving credit rating system, which is suitable to identify bad loans.
- *Loan management*

  The risks of these bad loans have to be managed according to an explicitly defined process.
- *Regulations for continued lending*

  If a bank considers maintaining the business relationship with a company, which is the borrower and customer of a 'bad loan,' the following restrictions apply:
  - The responsibility for this company (as customer) has to be transferred from the sales department to a separate restructuring department in the bank's organization (including different staff and a separate reporting line up to the board of directors).
  - The bank has to require the company to present a turnaround plan to assess the feasibility of successfully turning around the company and thus allow the repayment of the loans. That assessment has to be positive.
  - The bank (i.e., the restructuring department of the bank) has to supervise the progress of the turnaround process.

The German Bankruptcy Act (*InsO*) forces the bank to restrict itself from directly influencing the company's decisions. If it directly influences the company's policies, it would act similarly to a shareholder. As a consequence, the bank would risk its loans being treated as (unsecured) equity in case of insolvency.

Through its decisions in related court cases, the German Federal Supreme Court (*BGH*) has defined and regulated many aspects of the turnaround process. The requirements of the turnaround plan were one of the key subjects of its decisions.

These specific requirements and other regulations with respect to the turnaround plan have been compiled by the *Institute Of Public Auditors In Germany* ("Institute der Wirtschaftsprüfer"), the IDW, into an industry standard for turnaround plan requirements, the *IDW S6* (IDW, 2012). The key elements of this standard are:

- The turnaround plan has to be set up by an independent third party.
- The turnaround plan has to analyze in detail the causes of the crisis and the current state of decline.
- A detailed assessment of the company and the company's market has to be part of the turnaround plan.
- Specific measures have to be included to address the causes of decline and the current crisis.
- A long-term vision of the company as well as an integrated P&L and cash flow plan have to be incorporated.

These requirements force the restructuring process in Germany in a specific structure (see also Buchalik, 2004; Rüsen, 2008). To understand the implications for the process of turnaround management enforced by this regulatory framework, these are specified for each stage of the five-stage turnaround model introduced previously (Figure 11):

- Stage 1: Crisis emerging
  As soon as the risk management systems of the bank assess the credit risk of the company as problematic, i.e., the outstanding debt is judged a 'bad loan,' the bank will shift the responsibility internally from a sales representative to a risk manager (and thus to a different department). The responsible risk manager then requires the company to draft a turnaround plan, as otherwise the bank has to cease the business relationship. This would imply that all current credit lines be cancelled and all due and undue loans would have to be repaid. As this would, in most cases, require companies to file for insolvency, the company usually complies with this requirement.
- Stage 2: Turnaround plan
  The company assigns a third party – for example, a specialized consultant or an auditor – to draw up a turnaround plan. This plan has to implement all re-

quirements defined by the regulatory framework and past court decisions (see above) to be accepted by the bank.

- Stage 3 & 4: Retrenchment and recovery
  If the turnaround plan is assessed as feasible and accepted by the bank, the implementation of the defined restructuring measures is carried out. During this process, the bank is required to oversee the turnaround process with ongoing monitoring.
- Stage 5: Failed or successful turnaround
  If the turnaround is successful, the risk manager transfers the responsibility for the formerly distressed company back to the sales department. In the case of a failed turnaround and insolvency, the bank is one of the parties involved in the insolvency proceeding (according to *InsO*), which is usually handled by a different department of the bank.

The risk managers and the respective risk management departments are – compliant with *MaRisk* – organized very similarly in most banks. The names employed for both experts and departments vary. These departments are called special credit management, credit risk management, risk office, restructuring, credit restructuring, intensive care, workout or central customer service. In this study, I refer to these departments and the experts working there uniformly as the banks' risk management departments and the banks' risk managers.

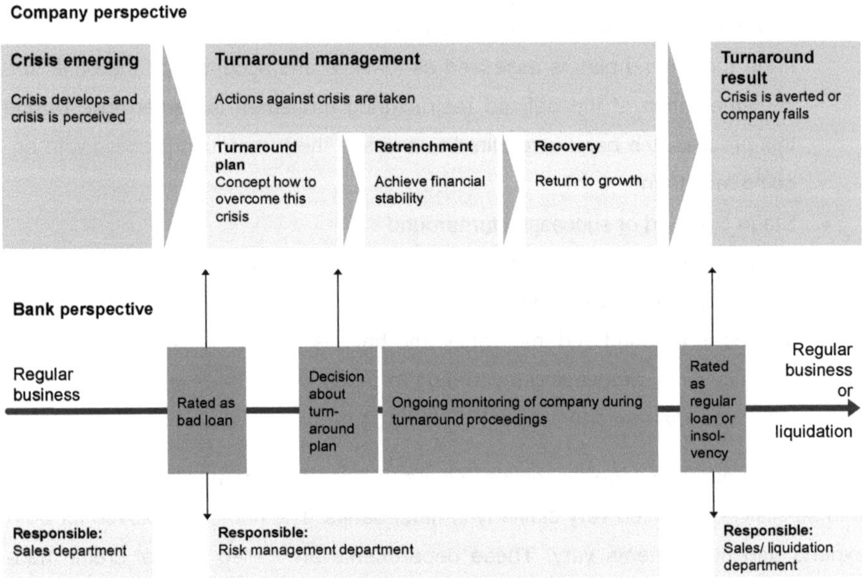

Figure 11: Company and bank perspectives on crisis and turnaround process.
Source: Own illustration.

3.1.3 Implications for the data collection process

This study's empirical data is collected by questionnaire from German banks' risk managers. The rationale for this – in terms of crisis and turnaround research – new approach is based on five key reasons: Availability of information, overcoming survival bias, independent witness function, regulatory required information and crisis and turnaround experience.

- *Availability of information* about crisis and turnaround is generally difficult. Especially if the research does not examine publicly listed companies, which most published works deal with (e.g., Buschmann, 2006; Eichner, 2010; Hauschildt et al., 2006; Jostarndt, 2007; Robbins & Pearce, 1992; Sudarsanam & Lai, 2001), the research is often limited to case studies (e.g., Cater & Schwab, 2008).

Banks, on the other hand, employ risk managers working solely on crisis and turnaround cases that are not limited to listed companies and are thus a rich source of information.

- Any analysis not relying solely on publicly available data, but also on company-provided information (e.g., by interviewing company executives or using other data provided by the company), is usually limited to surviving companies. Thus, many turnaround studies face the issue of *survival bias*. The challenge of survival bias has been addressed by several authors – not limited to the context of turnaround research (Eichner, 2010; Grinblatt & Titman, 1989; Healy & Palepu, 1988; Lie, 2005; Ndofor et al., 2013; Trahms et al., 2013).
  The specialists working in the banks' risk management departments are not biased in this respect, as they experience both surviving and non-surviving companies and are able to report on both kinds of cases.
- Using the company itself – and thus the company's management or data produced by the management – as data sources of empirical turnaround research has been found biased. Pandit (2000) reported that the company's management has a tendency to use 'window dressing.' Trahms et al. (2013) use managerial response factors in their stage model, implying a very different perception of the crisis depending on the management's peculiarities. Other authors have found that managers tend to attribute crisis to external instead of internal factors (Barker & Patterson, 1996; Cater & Schwab, 2008).
  The German banks' risk managers, on the other hand, come into play only after the crisis is present, avoiding the necessity of defending past decisions (as discussed in the context of 'escalation of commitment' by Faghfouri, 2013 for managers) and play no active role in the crisis management (legal implication of the *InsO*). This makes them an *independent witness* for a less biased view of the crisis and turnaround of a company.
- Due to the regulatory requirements concerning content and quality of the restructuring plan as well as the *regulatory obligation to monitor the progress of the turnaround*, the bank specialists have access to a vast pool of information concerning context, crisis and turnaround management (see section 3.1.2). This information is prepared and compiled prior to the time the turnaround

management begins and updated, up until the responsibility is transferred back to the sales department or the company files for insolvency.

- Due to the mandatory organizational separation of the risk management department in the bank's organization, the risk managers work solely on crisis and turnaround cases. Based on their *experience,* they are able to judge a company based on a significant number of supervised cases. In this, they differ from the management of a company, which usually bases its judgments on one or a small number of cases with which they are familiar. This should support the notion of a more realistic assessment by the banks' risk managers.

As with most research approaches, certain limitations result from using the banks' risk managers as information sources; these limitations impose specific restrictions on the conceptual model and the data collection structure. They originate in two key factors: The protected customer-bank relationship and the effort to answer the questionnaire.

- The *protected customer bank relationship* in Germany imposes limitations on what banks can share about their customers (see section 5.1.1). Especially in the case of sensitive topics, like financial distress and turnaround, it is extremely important that the identity of the companies involved remain undisclosed. This requirement is of specific relevance for the sample collection process.
- The complexity of the information that can be collected from risk managers is further limited by the willingness of the participants to *invest time*, leading to the simple equation: More information requested in the questionnaire equals fewer cases contributed. This inherently limits the number of variables that can be implemented in the conceptual model.

Balancing these issues is an important challenge for this study. Consequently, the choice of banks' risk managers as sample sources has an impact on both the fundamental definitions chosen and implicitly on the structure of the conceptual model.

3.2 Crisis

While the definition of the term 'company crisis' massively influences the scope and content of research, especially of an empirical analysis, there is currently no consistent definition (Faghfouri, 2013; Liou & Smith, 2006; Trahms et al., 2013). An interesting pair of articles, one by Robbins and Pearce (1992) and the response of Barker and Mone (1994), illustrates this. The response is critical in that it maintains that an inadequate definition of crisis leads to misleading conclusions and erroneous recommendations to practitioners. Robbins and Pearce (1992) used 'relative performance decline' as the criterion for inclusion of a firm in their sample and 'relative performance improvement' as a dependent variable, showing that retrenchment is positively related to this improvement. Barker and Mone (1994) showed that this diluted the sample because firms with very different severity of crisis are compared. They showed that the severity of the decline positively influences the retrenchment probability. While for the retrenching firms the relative improvement (from their very bad performance) is higher, the absolute performance after retrenchment is lower than that of the non-retrenching firms, concluding in a much more skeptical assessment of retrenchment. This example reconfirms the need for meaningful definitions and the requirement to include all relevant contextual variables in order to reflect possible ambiguities in the analysis.

To avoid similar issues, the definition and characterization of *company crisis* for this study are discussed in three steps. In a first step, the fundamental crisis definition and the relevant crisis stages – based on two different stage models – are introduced.

In the subsequent sections, the two crisis dimensions relevant for the conceptual model are discussed. These are the crisis *diagnosis*, i.e., the decision on the criteria for the presence of a crisis, and the crisis *typology*, i.e., how to describe the nature of a crisis.

3.2.1 Definition of crisis and crisis stages

To define the term, I follow a plain definition of company crisis commonly used and recommended in literature (Arogyaswamy et al., 1995; Hauschildt et al., 2006; Pandit, 2000; Slatter, 1984; Trahms et al., 2013; Witte, 1981):

A company crisis is present when the future existence of the company is threatened unless radical action is taken to improve the company's performance.

To allow a further characterization and specification there are two dimensions (Hauschildt et al., 2006) that can be used to assess the state of crisis. These are:

- Differentiation by *severity* of crisis
- Differentiation by *perception* of crisis

The differentiation of sequential phases of crisis by severity is commonly used in the literature (Eichner, 2010 ; Hauschildt et al., 2006; Pandit, 2000). In relation to the five-stage crisis and restructuring model, all these crisis stages usually occur during the *crisis emerging* phase. These severity-based crisis models include a minimum of three phases (definitions adapted from Eichner, 2010), sometimes extended to more phases, e.g., five phases for IDW (2012):

- *Strategic crisis* – slowing of sales growth, loss of market share.
- *Performance crisis* – earnings below cost of capital, earnings below industry mean, up to negative earnings.
- *Liquidity crisis* – interest coverage shortfall, negative free cash flow, cash shortage.

It is assumed that a company in a crisis situation sequentially passes through all steps of the crisis development, if adequate measures to avert the respective crisis phase are not implemented. The associated effort required to avert the crisis increases with each crisis stage (Hauschildt et al., 2006; IDW, 2012).

The differentiation by perception of the crisis is based on how the company's stakeholders perceive the ongoing distress situation (Hauschildt, 2000; Hauschildt et al., 2006). The model is differentiated into two phases: latent and manifest crisis. In the latent crisis phase, the crisis is present but not perceived by the stakeholders (especially banks), while in the latter phase, the crisis is acknowledged by the company's stakeholders.

Both phase models reflect a different aspect of crisis and can be employed simultaneously. For the purpose of this study, to homogenize the case structure and maximize the availability of information from the banks' risk managers, the relevant crisis cases stage is defined as follows (Figure 12):

All cases relevant for this study experience a manifest liquidity crisis prior to the turnaround management activities.

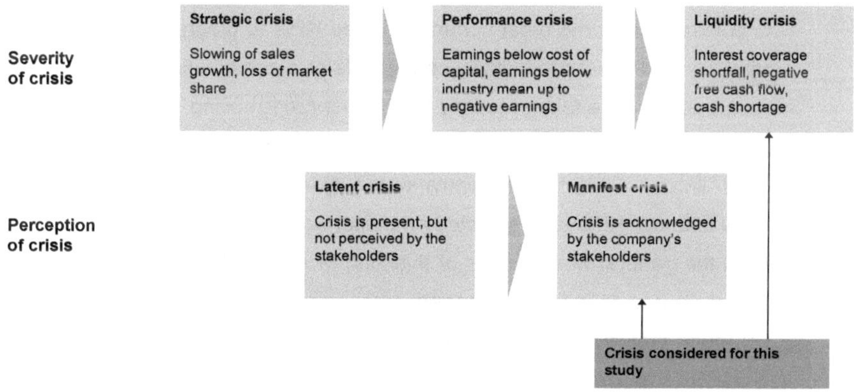

Figure 12: Stage models of crisis severity and perception.
Source: Adapted from Hauschildt et al. (2006).

3.2.2 Crisis diagnosis

The seemingly simple question, "When is there a crisis?" becomes difficult when operationalizing the term for empirical research and inherently determines the scope of the analysis. Unfortunately, as Trahms et al. (2013; p.1302) found in their extensive literature review examining 40 empirical works, "there are currently no set standards for measuring decline and turnaround."

The wide diversity of different measures can be differentiated in three main approaches based on the respective criteria. Following the logic of Pandit (2000) (see also similar classification approaches by Cater & Schwab, 2008; Eichner, 2010; Faghfouri, 2013; Trahms et al., 2013) these are: Firm-KPI-based, benchmark-based and expert-opinion-based.

- *Firm-KPI-based approaches* use company KPIs to define a threshold that, when reached, implies per definition a company crisis. In most cases these KPIs belong to the financial metrics. Pearce and Robbins (1993) had already stated that the most common approach to diagnosing a crisis is that of judging a company to be in distress if it has experienced several years of financial profit decline. Similarly and more recently, in the review of Pandit (2000), it was confirmed that the most commonly used KPIs to diagnose crisis are still profitability and asset productivity coefficients or a combination of these. Similar approaches were taken recently by Eichner (2010) using interest coverage, i.e., cash-flow-based diagnosis, and Sudarsanam and Lai (2001) using the z-score (Altman, 1968), which calculates the proximity to bankruptcy based on several financial KPIs (see selected empirical works in section 2.2).
  One of the general weaknesses of this kind of approach is the unreliability of financial figures found in distressed companies. Cater and Schwab (2008; p.34) found that "approaches based only on financial measures are often limited due to 'creative' accounting practices, orientation on the past, and inaccurate accounting information." Similar criticism is brought forward by Pandit (2000) with a focus on the tendency to do 'window dressing' in distress situations.
- *Benchmark-based approaches* use the comparison between benchmark data and the firm's performance to assess the presence of a company crisis. Pandit (2000) finds it less common than the firm-KPI-based approaches. He finds two main ways to conduct the comparison, which differ in respect to the relevant benchmark: The first is based on the comparison with GNP data, the second on industry specific benchmarking.

While the industry benchmarks are seen as superior to the GNP benchmarking, both approaches are seen as highly controversial due to the limited diagnosis quality of these methods (Pandit, 2000).

- *Expert-opinion-based approaches* are least commonly used. Pandit (2000) found only two studies (Robbins & Pearce, 1992; Zimmerman, 1989) relying on them. More recently, Cater and Schwab (2008), in their work about family firms, use a similar approach.

  Pandit (2000) sees advantages in the expert-opinion-based diagnosis due to its being able to consider contextual information as well, which takes the heterogeneity of the cases into consideration; but on the other hand, he addresses concerns that expert-opinion-based decisions might be highly subjective.

In the context of this study's data source – the banks' risk managers – I use an expert-opinion-based approach. Restricting them explicitly to cases of a manifest liquidity crisis (see section 3.2) I rely on the banks' judgment to decide whether there is a crisis. As this assessment is indirectly founded on the banks' regulated risk management and rating systems, the risk of subjectivity should be sufficiently compensated. This leads to the definition as follows:

A company is experiencing a company crisis if the bank treats the loans of the company as 'bad loans' and transfers the responsibility for the client to the bank's risk management department.

3.2.3 Crisis typology

When analyzing the crisis, most works use the 'cause' of the crisis as key characteristic. According to Pandit (2000), this is the most commonly researched context factor for turnaround. The characterization of the crisis is commonly seen as an important precondition for the decision about the correct turnaround management activities (Arogyaswamy et al., 1995; Faghfouri, 2013; Liou & Smith, 2006; Pearce & Robbins, 1993; Trahms et al., 2013). Variables referred to as causes for crisis are also used in the selected empirical studies as presented in section 2.2 (Eichner, 2010; Sudarsanam & Lai, 2001).

3.2.3.1 Review of existing frameworks

There are two relevant aspects in the existing crisis specification frameworks discussed here: The crisis characterization, i.e., what kind of variable is used to describe the crisis; and the crisis model, i.e., the structure in which these variables are modelled.

3.2.3.1.1 Crisis characterization

When categorizing these causes, most publications with a conceptual focus use the dichotomy of internal and external causes for crisis without further definition or differentiation. The terms stem from the popular model by Pearce and Robbins (1993; section 2.1.1).

Internal causes for crisis are defined as all causes originating within the company, while *external causes* originate outside the company itself.

My criticism of this intuitive approach is twofold:

- The usage of the term 'cause' implies that there is a single reason at the root of the decline that triggers the crisis.
  In my interpretation, this is in violation of the contingency theory's perception of a company. Its fundamental principle is that a crisis originates in errors in the "alignment between a firm, its resources and the environment" (Trahms et al., 2013; p.1289).
  In my view there is an obvious discrepancy between this definition and the usage of the term 'crisis cause' on the one hand, but also between this definition and the dichotomy in internal and external causes.
  The contingency theory-based conception of a crisis as misalignment implies that the three elements (firm, resources and environment) are no longer in sync. For this definition, it is irrelevant whether the external environment or the internal properties have changed.
  Thus in my view, the term 'cause' is, although very intuitive, extremely misleading, when applied to a company's crisis as it suggests a simple cause-effect relationship instead of a complex balance that was distorted by possibly multiple factors.

Using the example of a company in decline in a changing market environment, the difficulty in answering the question of causes can be illustrated by two exemplary questions, which are difficult to answer at the time of the turnaround plan compilation:
"Are the conflicts in the management caused by the pressure of reduced margins or did the conflicts in the management hinder its adaptation to changing markets?"
"Did the market development cause the market share loss due to changing competition or were the investments in key products insufficient or incorrect?"

- On the other hand, the categories of internal and external causes, without further differentiation (also in current crisis models e.g., by Trahms et al., 2013), contain very limited information about the properties of the crisis. Thus for the purpose of this study, while accepting that the differentiation by internal and external is fundamentally meaningful, I employ a more detailed and differentiated approach to analyze the character of crisis.

3.2.3.1.2 Crisis models

When reviewing crisis models, there are two possible ways to differentiate the crisis properties: The first, based on the theory of workouts; and the second, based mainly on German crisis management research (see subsection for a classification of the different research streams 2.1.4).

The framework by Asquith and Gertner (1994) is an example of the first. This framework was also used and extended by Eichner (2010).

It classifies crises into four categories:

- *Overleverage,* i.e., debt is too high for the company to service.
- *Overexpansion*, i.e., the firm is investing too much money in growth.
- *Operating profitability,* i.e., the company's profit is low compared to industry average.
- *Industry level operating profitability,* i.e., while the company is in line profit-wise with the industry average, the industry itself has a profit issue.

This classification is based on a financial analysis. The authors first run simulations for each of these traits – presupposing those are absent – and supplant the company's financial figures with those of an average company, thus determining the trait whose elimination would most improve the company's situation and is therefore the primary cause of the crisis.

Still, using the term 'cause' (as Eichner, 2010 does) in this context is in my opinion misleading, as it implies that this analysis is able to identify a cause-effect relationship leading to the crisis. Instead, it analyzes the current crisis symptoms to establish a classification. Also, the categorization in only four types of crises is limited with respect to the level of detail and thus in the information content.

On the other hand, the crisis management strain of research uses a different segmentation. It is mostly based on German publications, of which I have selected the rather current work of Hauschildt et al. (2006), because it is a reliable summary, update and confirmation of earlier publications (see details in subsection 2.2.3). This study disregards the common separation between internal and external causes for crisis and classifies them as follows:

- Person-influenced causes ("Personengeprägte Ursachen").
- Organizational causes ("Institutionelle Ursachen").
- Operative causes ("Erfolgswirtschaftliche Ursachen").
- Financial causes ("Finanzwirtschaftliche Ursachen").

In this structure, the authors assign a total of 67 different phenomena to these topics. While this differentiation is richer in terms of information content and detail, it does not provide any approach for a structured operationalization in an empirical work. But at the same time, it illustrates the complexity of possible crisis scenarios that need to be reflected in the crisis typology.

3.2.3.2 Typology approach for this study

The requirements for a typology of the crisis for this study differ from the frameworks presented above. The requirements for a meaningful typology in respect to this study are twofold: A *symptom-based typology* with a certain amount of *similarity between the crisis model and the turnaround management model*.

- *Symptom-based typology* reflects the decision to abandon the common approach of using 'causes' to characterize the crises. By the time, the turnaround plan is drafted the crisis has already progressed through several stages (see subsection 3.2). At this point, the causal effects leading to the crisis are extremely difficult to assess. The focus should instead be on the situation at hand at the time the turnaround plan is drafted, i.e., an assessment of the symptoms not the causes. This approach is implicitly similar to the approach of Asquith and Gertner (1994) and Eichner (2010), which depends on financial KPIs, without analyzing the underlying causes.

  The analysis of symptoms instead of causes results in both more meaningful questions to the interview partners, as well as a more objective analysis.
- The requirement for *similarity between crisis model and the turnaround management model* is based on the assumption that crisis properties demand specific turnaround management responses and a specific turnaround strategy (as stated explicitly or implicitly e.g., by Arogyaswamy et al., 1995; Eichner, 2010; Hofer, 1980; O'Neill, 1986; Pearce & Robbins, 1993; Schendel et al., 1976; Starbuck et al., 1985; Stopford & Baden-Fuller, 1990; Trahms et al., 2013). To analyze these as cause-effect relations, a similarity between the model of turnaround activities and crisis properties is needed, in structure as well as in the level of detail of the models.

These requirements lead to two central decisions in the research framework: To describe the crisis properties with crisis contribution factors (CCFs) and to characterize the crisis with a model structure similar to the turnaround management model.

3.2.3.2.1 Crisis characterization using crisis contribution factors

To assess the properties of the crisis, I want to concentrate on the information available at the time the turnaround plan is drafted. The assessment of the crisis should be based on factors that contributed to it, as perceived at the time the turnaround plan is drawn without regard to the question, "What came first?" i.e., the question about the cause or the blame. To implement this approach, I employ a construct labeled as *crisis contribution factor* (CCF).

The crisis contribution factors include all aspects allowing or promoting the crisis. It moves the focus away from the much more complex question of causality in the crisis to reflect all crisis elements, as these can be assessed at the time of the turnaround plan compilation:

A crisis contribution factor is an internal or external factor that contributes to the development, progression or worsening of the company's crisis.

3.2.3.2.2 Crisis model structure

The model structure of the crisis characterization is based on two levels. On the first level, it relies on the very common separation of internal and external factors contributing to the crisis (as already introduced). Specifically, I treat all aspects related to the company – including the shareholders – as internal characteristics, whereas, all factors contributing to the crisis from outside the company are treated as external factors.

Internal crisis contribution factors are differentiated similarly to the turnaround management characterization structure defined by Eichner (2010) (based on the work of Sudarsanam & Lai, 2001). These are differentiated into four categories: Operational, managerial, portfolio, and financial crisis contribution factors.

- *Operational crisis contribution factors* consist of all aspects of the operation, processes, organization and structure of a company. These range from investments, added-value depth, financial processes as well as organizational aspects.

- *Managerial crisis contribution* factors consist of all factors originating from top management personnel as well as – in the case of family firms – influence of the family on the management.
- *Portfolio crisis contribution factors* range from product to market decisions and assessments as well as product properties and M&A decisions.
- *Financial crisis contribution* factors originate in the financing structure and the dividend policy of the company.

While this chapter defines the fundamental design concepts for the conceptual model (Figure 13), the details and the content of the model are discussed and introduced in chapter 4.

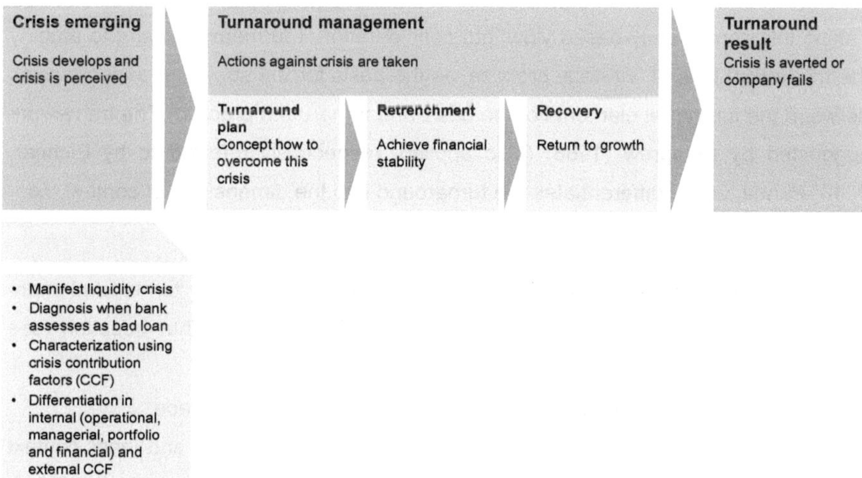

Figure 13: Framework development – crisis.
Source: Own illustration.

3.3 Turnaround management

The reversibility of a company crisis is the fundamental assumption of all turnaround research (explicitly stated, e.g., by Cater & Schwab, 2008; with reference to the seminal work of Porter, 1985). The underlying premise of most studies is, further, that overcoming the consequences of a crisis depends on choosing the correct actions (Harrigan & Porter, 1983; Pearce & Robbins, 1993), which depend mainly on the crisis characteristics (Arogyaswamy et al., 1995; Hofer, 1980; Schendel et al., 1976). Different actions can lead to failure or successful turnaround for very similar companies (Schendel & Patton, 1976).

This explains the application of the contingency theory (see section 2.3.1) as the main theoretical lens in turnaround research (see section 2.1.4) and thus the conviction that there is no optimal strategy for all cases, but that the best strategy for a company depends on its specific situation.

Taking this contingency-based view into consideration, I furthermore want to employ the theoretical lens of 'strategy process' as the basis for the structural dependencies between the individual elements of the crisis and turnaround process. The framework suggested by Pettigrew (1988) (also applied, respectively referred to by Eichner, 2010; Pandit, 2000) differentiates the turnaround into the dimensions of content, context and process:

- *Content* comprises the actual measures taken during the turnaround management. The content can be obtained by asking the 'What'-question (see sections 3.3.3 and 4.5).
- *Context* refers to the setting in which the turnaround takes place.
  It is further differentiated into the outer (company external) and inner context (company internal). The context can be identified as the answer to the 'Why'-question.
  In this study, the context of turnaround management refers extensively to the crisis characteristics (see sections 3.2 and 4.4), but also to the internal and external context factors (see sections 3.5 and 4.6).
- *Process* reflects the answer to the 'How?'- question. It refers to the nature of execution of the content of turnaround activities (see sections 3.3.2 and 4.5.5).

3.3.1 Turnaround plan

The first step of turnaround management is the turnaround plan. It is both an assessment of the crisis up until time of the plan's compilation and the prerequisite of the implementation of the turnaround activities.

Due to the structure of the data collection process described in section 3.1.3, the turnaround plan is in most cases the primary repository for information about the company for the banks' risk managers. The turnaround plan content and structure, as elaborated in section 3.1.2, is for German companies with bank financing determined by German laws and regulations. The turnaround plan has to contain both information about the crisis of the company as well as information about the turnaround management and the scenarios and business plans for the post-turnaround future of the company (IDW, 2012). The regulatory requirements specifically demand that such a plan plausibly present the transition from the company's state today to a future successful turnaround by detailing and describing that process.

Hence, the definition for the turnaround plan is:

The turnaround plan describes a turnaround strategy that consists of restructuring moves aimed at overcoming the diagnosed crisis and crisis contribution factors.

3.3.2 Process of turnaround management

The two-stage turnaround management implementation model as proposed (or rather consolidated from other authors) by Pearce and Robbins (1993) is widely accepted and valid today. It was reconfirmed more recently, as it could be shown that a company can be correctly assigned into the different stages by using a classification based on a discriminant analysis of financial ratios (Pearce, 2007).

- *Retrenchment*, the first stage of turnaround management comprises restructuring activities targeted at stabilizing the company and stopping the ongoing decline. This is commonly described as "belt tightening" (Hambrick & Schecter, 1983; p.239) or "stopping the bleeding" (Arogyaswamy et al., 1995; p. 497) and aims at short-term stabilization by cutting the costs and reducing the negative cash flow. These activities range – depending on the severity of the crisis from asset sales (severe crisis) to cost reduction (less severe) activities (Pearce & Robbins, 1993). The outcome of this first implementation stage is the short-term stabilization of the company.

- In the second stage, *recovery*, the restructuring moves are targeted on returning the company to normal growth and recovering from the crisis state to a 'normal' business setting. These moves range, depending on the severity, from efficiency maintenance (less severe) to entrepreneurial reconfiguration (severe) (Pearce & Robbins, 1993).

While this logic is widely accepted and supported, it is challenging to operationalize in an empirical study. Eichner (2010) modeled it in his study by defining fixed time frames, i.e., the retrenchment phase as the first two years and the recovery phase as the second two years of turnaround. I am skeptical of this approach, as a purely time-based classification has severe limitations. It does not consider the fact that for (quickly) failing turnaround cases there might be no recovery phase at all. Instead these companies might face an ongoing recurrence of retrenchment moves, as stabilization efforts fail. On the other hand, some recovery-oriented activities are commonly already started early in the turnaround. In fact, it is one of the main results of Eichner's study that new product development in the first two years contributes significantly to turnaround success, thus challenging his underlying time-based definition.

A second way to approach the operationalization in an empirical study is by sorting all restructuring moves depending on their content. Arogyaswamy et al. (1995) define per restructuring move, whether it is a retrenchment move or a recovery move in nature. In my opinion, this approach is also limited, as the same restructuring move can have a different character – in terms of retrenchment vs. recovery – depending on the specific setup of the turnaround. A relevant example can be made of the restructuring move employee '*layoff*.' It can be either a typical retrenchment-oriented, cost-saving measure, or part of a long-term strategic decision to outsource specific production steps and to focus investments on other production steps and thus recovery oriented.

As a consequence, this study uses and adapts the model of the restructuring moves by Eichner (2010) (discussed in detailed in the following section), but without the segregation into early and late – retrenchment and recovery – moves. While there is no explicit segregation of the restructuring moves into retrenchment and recovery for the research purpose of this study, this perspective is an implicit part of the modeling approach as discussed in chapter 4 and it is revisited in chapter 7 in discussing the results of the clustering analysis.

3.3.3 Content of turnaround management

Similarly to the crisis typology (see section 3.2.3), the content of turnaround management, i.e., the individual restructuring moves, have to be operationalized for this empirical study. For the crisis typology, this study departed with the existing frameworks and defined a new structure. In contrast, the structure of turnaround management and its defining elements, the restructuring moves, are adapted from a framework established and employed by two research studies (already presented in section 2.2). Sudarsanam and Lai (2001) integrated the financial perspective and the strategic management perspective in their framework (for the theoretical lenses and research streams see section 2.1.4). This framework consisted of eight very broadly defined, 'restructuring strategies,' to reflect activities during turnaround management. Eichner (2010) extended these to a model with a total of 23 different turnaround variables. In terms of completeness and complexity, this model is best suited as a foundation for this study.

While the individual restructuring moves, which are defined for each category, are adapted, completed and changed for this study (see chapter 4), the general structure of the turnaround model is directly adopted. The restructuring moves in the turnaround management are classified into four main categories: Operational, managerial, portfolio and financial restructuring moves.

- *Operational* restructuring moves cover all measures changing investments and value-add. These include the 'typical' cost saving measures like layoffs and other cost management activities, but also organizational and process changes to support turnaround.
- *Managerial* restructuring moves include all activities changing management team and management structure of a company.
- *Portfolio* restructuring reflects changes in the company portfolio ranging from product and market decisions to M&A activities.

- *Financial* restructuring ranges from internal to external financing moves, addressing working capital reductions, dividend changes, shareholder contributions and debt modifications.

For details concerning the individual restructuring moves please refer to chapter 4.

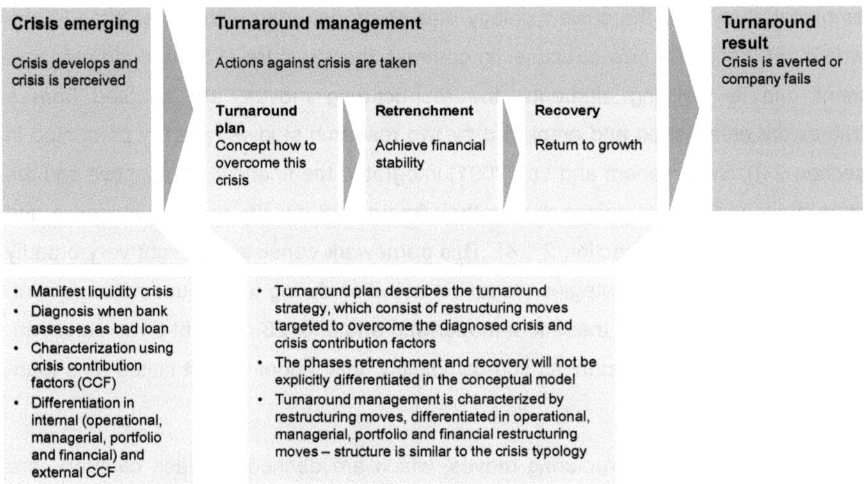

Figure 14: Framework development – turnaround management.
Source: Own illustration.

3.4 Result of turnaround management

The counterpart of the criteria for diagnosing the crisis, discussed in section 3.2.2, is the assessment of the turnaround result and the company's post-turnaround situation. Similar to the diagnosis of the crisis, this question is also more complex than the seemingly intuitive categorization in successful and failed turnaround.

In the discussion of the result of turnaround management, the specific issue of the owner family perspective is addressed in addition to the company perspective. In chapter 5 it is shown that 85% of the companies in this study's research sample have family shareholders, making their specific properties a relevant part of the theoretical framework.

Consequently, I focus in this study on two topics when analyzing the turnaround result:

- The *company perspective,* focusing on the outcome for the company itself, its post-turnaround situation and the success or failure of turnaround.
- The *owner family perspective,* investigating the relation between shareholding family and company and how it is changed by crisis and turnaround.

3.4.1 Company perspective

Trahms et al. (2013; p. 1302) conclude in their meta-study, reviewing 20 years of empirical turnaround research, that the usage of a binary variable for failed or successful turnaround, while very common "fails to capture the richness and nuances of organizational performance." This limitation is already reflected in the model by Pearce and Robbins (1993), as it allows for more than the two possible outcomes of turnaround (liquidation, moderate recovery and recovery). Following this line of reasoning, Pearson and Clair (1998; p.67) suggested using a continuum perspective for the turnaround result, as "no organization will respond in a manner that is completely effective or completely ineffective." This leads to the following model design decision:

The quality of the turnaround result for the company, i.e., its situation after turnaround, is measured with an interval variable, allowing for more than the binary results of failed and successful turnaround.

Besides the decision about the type of variable, the second question is when it is measured, i.e., when the turnaround management phase is over. Some studies consequently use the same parameter employed for diagnosing the crisis with the very same threshold to diagnose the successful end of the crisis. When the parameter crosses the crisis-threshold in the other direction, the crisis, and thus the turnaround management, is successfully completed; if this is not the case after a maximum time period, the turnaround has failed (e.g., among others Eichner, 2010; Schmuck, 2013). Others use similar approaches, but with different thresholds for entering the crisis and leaving the turnaround management state (e.g., Buschmann, 2006; Nothardt, 2001); some use different parameters altogether for entering and leaving the crisis stage (e.g., Sudarsanam & Lai, 2001).

These approaches have little relevance for this study, as I use a similar expert-opinion-based approach for the end of the turnaround and for the crisis diagnosis (see section 3.2.2). While for the diagnosis of crisis the transfer from the banks' regular customer service department to its risk management department was the relevant trigger, the return of the customer responsibility from the risk management to the regular customer service shall also be the trigger for the successful end of the turnaround management phase (This successful end is the precondition for the turnaround quality measurement as discussed before.).

Similarly, the turnaround is considered failed if a company files for insolvency while in the hands of the bank's risk management department. In the cases of insolvency, the responsibility for the company is usually handed over from the bank's risk management department to a specialized liquidation department; hence, there is no further information available about these cases from the interview partners. Thus, there is no quality measurement for the cases of companies filing for insolvency. These are treated per definition as a failed turnaround and those companies as non-surviving companies. Whether the companies partly or fully recover from insolvency proceedings is not a consideration in this study.

A successful turnaround is achieved when the responsibility for a company as a bank's customer is returned from the risk management department to the regular customer service department. The quality of the successful turnaround is measured (as defined) with an interval variable.

A failed turnaround has to be concluded when the company files for insolvency.

3.4.2 Owner family perspective

The family firm is a system of two major components: the family and the company (see section 2.4.1). Block (2010) analyzed how family ownership and management change the probability of a company implementing downsizing measures. While investigating the influence of the family firm properties on the turnaround success by considering these as context factors (see section 3.5.1), I also want to consider a different perspective by analyzing how crisis and turnaround change the relation between family and firm. Specifically, how the two defining elements – family ownership and family control (Block, 2010) – are affected by a crisis and the subsequent turnaround process.

As Rüsen (2008) states in his study about turnaround in family firms, based on interviews with over 100 experts, even a successful turnaround can end the relationship between family and company, i.e., the family is no longer a shareholder, or it can change the control of the family, i.e., the family plays a different role in the company's top management. Because the banks' risk managers only possess information about successful turnarounds, this family-firm-specific turnaround result, i.e., family management role and family ownership after crisis, is only available for successful turnarounds, as defined in section 3.4.1.

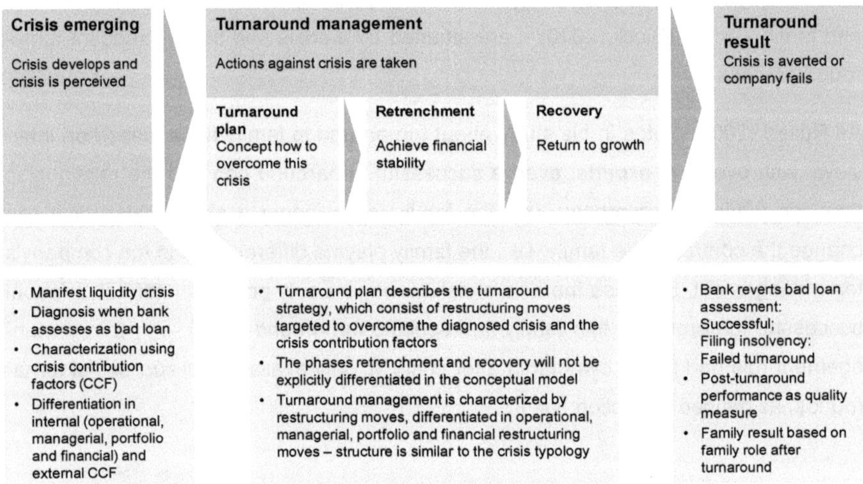

Figure 15: Framework development – turnaround result.
Source: Own illustration.

3.5 Internal and external context

The most important context for the turnaround process is the crisis, as the characteristic traits of crisis determine the responses (see section 3.2). While the integration of this dependency in research is already limited (Trahms et al., 2013), it is even more so with regard to other contextual dimensions, like company properties and market environment. Pandit (2000; p.42) stated that the "severity of the crisis, attitude of stakeholders, firms outer context, firms historical strategy" have been "largely ignored" in the literature. He assessed a general tendency to limit studies to a few variables, thus severely limiting the insight given. Similar conclusions have been reached by Arogyaswamy et al. (1995) and Trahms et al. (2013).

To gain a better understanding of the complexity and richness of the crisis and the turnaround process, as well as its most defining properties, this study aims to implement all relevant dimensions of the turnaround situation into an integrated conceptual model.

Using the approach of congruence between the different model dimensions, this work adapts the basic differentiation introduced with regard to crisis typology (see section 3.2.3) and distinguishes on the top level between internal and external contextual elements. Internal context variables are all variables relating to the setup of the company including shareholding, while external variables include elements referring to market setup and development.

3.5.1 Internal context

Currently, to the best of my knowledge, there is no model that reflects all contextual variables within a structure framework. Thus, for this study, I have implemented such a structured model, based on an extended review of all relevant works in this field and the topics and variables proposed in conceptual and considered in empirical works. The detailed references per variable are discussed in the context part of the conceptual model in section 4.6.

The relevant main categories of this structured model are: Company facts, management, company strategy and products, company financing and role and function of family in family firms:

- *Company facts* combine the basic figures that describe a company in terms of size and setting.
- *Management* addresses the situation of the CEO and the management team of the company
- *Company strategy and products* refer to the historical strategy and its effect on the company situation.
- *Company finance* further details the financial situation of the company itself as well as its relation with lenders.
- *Role and function of the family* is based on the relevant dimensions defining family firms (see section 2.4.1).

3.5.2 External context

The external context of a company is based on the industry's situation and market perspectives, as these reflect the growth opportunities of a company and thus the going concern value (Eichner, 2010; Varaiya et al., 1987). This affects the options of the company on the one hand, but also significantly affects the behavior of stakeholders in the company (Morrow et al., 2007; Moulton et al., 1996; Ndofor et al., 2013; Trahms et al., 2013).

While other elements – like new regulations and legislative changes – might have an impact on the turnaround process, this study chooses to focus solely on the widely mentioned and recommended dimension of market context, i.e., the growth perspective of the market segment.

3.6 Summary

In the course of this chapter, the definitions and the relevant dimensions of the research framework are introduced (Figure 16).

The understanding of the overall crisis and turnaround process is defined and further specified for the different stages of the turnaround. This included a specific focus on the crisis and turnaround situation in Germany, as this frames and explains key definitions chosen for this study.

Concerning the framework for the conceptual model, four dimensions are introduced: Crisis, turnaround management, turnaround result and the internal and external context.

In the following chapter, this framework is populated with "operationalizable" variables for each of these dimensions.

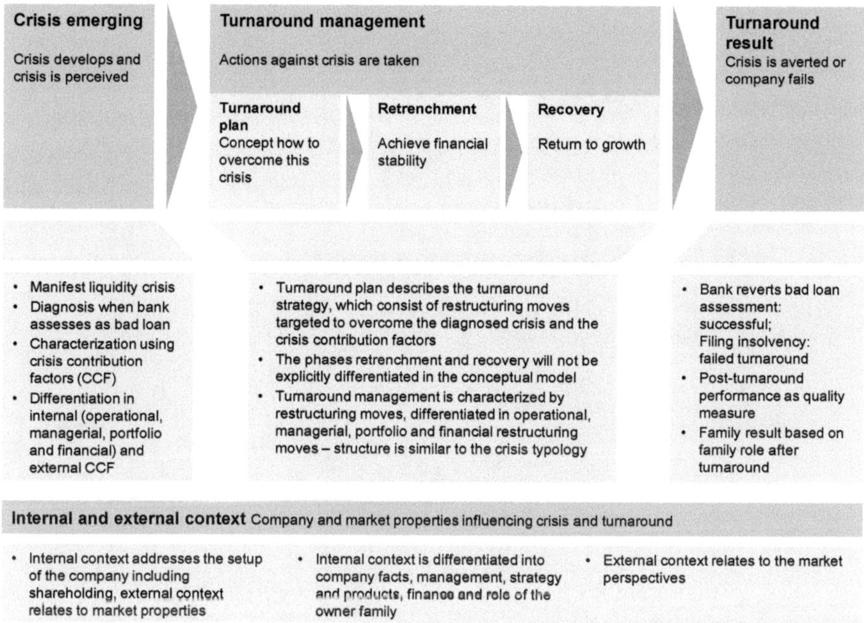

Figure 16: Framework development – complete framework.

Source: Own illustration.

4 Conceptual model

While the theoretical foundation is addressed in chapter 3 by discussing the theoretical framework and the major model design decisions and determining the relevant dimensions of this study's research model, this chapter is dedicated to substantiating these dimensions with conceptual content. For each of the dimensions, this has to be carried out in a way that the research goal is supported.

The decision about the model's complexity as well as the criteria for the number of and the choice of variables is a relevant precondition for the model development process. In this respect, the model's complexity raises a challenge already laid out very briefly in chapter 3. As the empirical data sampling process relies on the input of the banks' risk managers, it is expected that the number of relevant cases submitted decreases with every increase in requested details. At the same time, the statistical power of any analysis also decreases with the number of variables (see section 6.1.2).

This conflict is inherent to turnaround research, as analyzed by Pandit (2000) in his meta-study. He stated that it is 'usual' that in large number studies an increasing number of cases come at the expense of reduced depth of the analytical research. On the other hand, it has been found that the turnaround situation is characterized by a high number of influencing variables. In their extensive literature review, Liou and Smith (2006) found a gap between published research and the general research desideratum as already issued 13 years earlier by Pearce and Robbins (1993; p.12) "that further research would need to investigate the interrelationships between the four components of the turnaround process already identified: The turnaround situation, the 'retrenchment' response, the 'recovery' response and the level of turnaround success achieved." It seems intuitively compelling that a more complete model, considering variables of all these dimensions, also yields more meaningful results.

To develop a model to be meaningful in this regard, as a first step, a robust set of criteria is established, which is applied during the model design. These criteria for the model setup are discussed in section 4.1.

Following the recommendation of Sudarsanam and Lai (2001), this study focuses on a homogenous research sample. In section 4.2, homogeneity criteria are presented and discussed. The fact that this study's sample is limited to specific companies is mentioned in section 3.1.2 with regard to nationality. This criterion is supplemented by additional restrictions concerning the industry sector and company size.

The first section discussing the actual conceptual model elements addresses the dependent variable: turnaround result (section 4.3). In the next sections, all aspects of the model (Figure 17) are covered sequentially – starting with crisis (section 4.4) and turnaround management (section 4.5) concluding with the internal and external context (section 4.6). The chapter concludes with the owner family perspective of the turnaround result (section 4.7) and the character of the model variables (section 4.8).

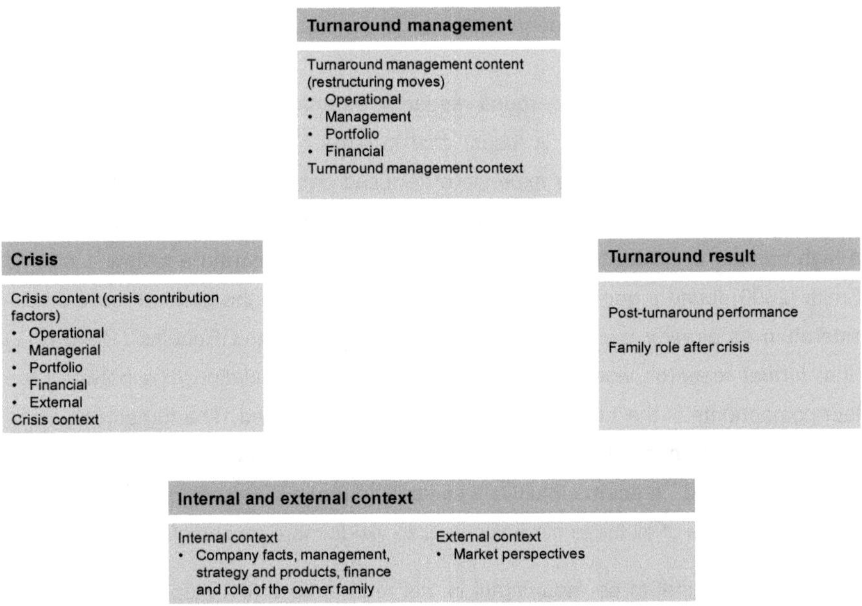

Figure 17: Conceptual model structure derived from theoretical framework.

Source: Own illustration.

4.1 Research criticism and modeling approach

The starting point for my modeling approach is the review of the current status and limitations of empirical turnaround research. In reviewing the models and approaches used by other authors, some shortcomings and thus areas for improvement have already been touched on in chapters 1 to 3.

The main symptoms of the weaknesses in many empirical studies can be summarized by the following three issues:

- Inconclusiveness; missing relevancy of results.
- Missing integration of the crisis characteristics, especially their effects on turnaround management and on the turnaround result.
- Missing integration of context variables.

The inconclusiveness and missing relevancy of results is the harshest possible assessment of any research. For many factors, different empirical studies have yielded different, even contradicting results. The analytical findings are highly inconsistent (in addition to the examples discussed in the course of this chapter, cf. by Cater & Schwab, 2008; Eichner, 2010; Faghfouri, 2013; Pandit, 2000; Trahms et al., 2013) and much of the variance is unexplained (Eichner, 2010; Sudarsanam & Lai, 2001).

Pandit (2000) characterized the situation of the research stream by referring to a statement by Winn (1993; p. 48): "While companies facing near-bankruptcy, market losses, or substandard performance are increasing in frequency, strategy researchers have provided little help for the managers charged with turning around deteriorating performance." This has not changed, as recently confirmed by Trahms et al. (2013; p. 1297), who stated: "Indeed, what we do not know or what is currently understudied far outweighs what is known about decline and turnaround." In my opinion, these fundamental weaknesses can be attributed largely to the other two issues raised: The lack of integration regarding both crisis and context.

The lack of consideration of the crisis characteristics in turnaround research was criticized by Pandit (2000). In his meta-study aimed at the improvement of turnaround research, he found that only 21% of the 47 studies reviewed considered the crisis properties as determining factors of the turnaround. Similarly, Trahms et al. (2013) in a more recent literature review found little integration of the research about decline and turnaround. This is surprising, insofar as the connection between the causes of decline and the correct turnaround strategy are conceptually agreed upon by many authors, starting with Pearce and Robbins (1993), and throughout many publications since then (e.g., Arogyaswamy et al., 1995; Faghfouri, 2013; Liou & Smith, 2006; Pearce & Robbins, 1993; Trahms et al., 2013).

Even more obvious is the missing integration of internal and external context in most empirical studies. According to Pandit (2000), the context of the firm and its impact on the turnaround result remains 'largely ignored' in empirical research; according to my assessment, this is largely unchanged up until today. It has been addressed more recently in conceptual works: Trahms et al. (2013) introduced the concept of response factors into their turnaround model, which are essentially contextual variables shaping the response of a company to crisis; Faghfouri (2013) identified 14 variables in his literature review. The empirical studies presented in chapter 2 of this work emphasize the importance of context variables and include a limited number of four (Sudarsanam & Lai, 2001) and ten (Eichner, 2010).

Medical analogies have a long tradition in turnaround research. Starting with Schendel et al. (1976; p.11), who referred to a company in crisis as the "weakened corporate body," many other authors have since then employed similar metaphors (e.g., Faghfouri, 2013; Pearce & Robbins, 1993; Sudarsanam & Lai, 2001). For illustrations sake, I want to extend this analogy by framing the empirical turnaround research as a medical study: the company as patient, the crisis as illness and the turnaround management as cure. This makes the absurdity of common approaches obvious:

A medical study ignoring the patient properties (age, gender, and medical history) and his or her illness (symptoms diagnosis) while concentrating solely on the impact of a single digit number of treatments would make no sense. It would be like medical researchers researching the question, "Does it generally make sense to cut off a patient's leg?" without having any data on the correspondent diagnosis or the patient (i.e., without having any anamneses). Not only would it be very difficult to obtain any statistically significant results for this question, but also the question itself is not highly relevant.

As a result of this fundamental criticism, I want to define four main setup criteria for the development of the conceptual model in this study:

- *Limitation to a homogenous research sample* – thus reducing the number of influencing factors and variables that need to be considered.
- *Consideration of all relevant dimensions of the turnaround situation* – including the properties of the crisis, the turnaround strategy chosen, the result of the turnaround management and the context variables influencing the aforementioned dimensions.
- *Congruence in complexity in these dimensions* – the variables of each dimension of the model should have a similar level of complexity and a comparable structure as far as applicable, to allow a meaningful analysis of cause-effect relations.
- *The principle of visibility and relevancy* – the variables considered by the research model have to be both relevant for the analysis and visible with the data sources used. They have to have real life relevancy and applicability for practitioners as well.

Based on these criteria, the conceptual model as detailed and presented in the remaining part of this chapter was developed in an iterative approach. It used a bottom-up research review combined with an evaluation phase.

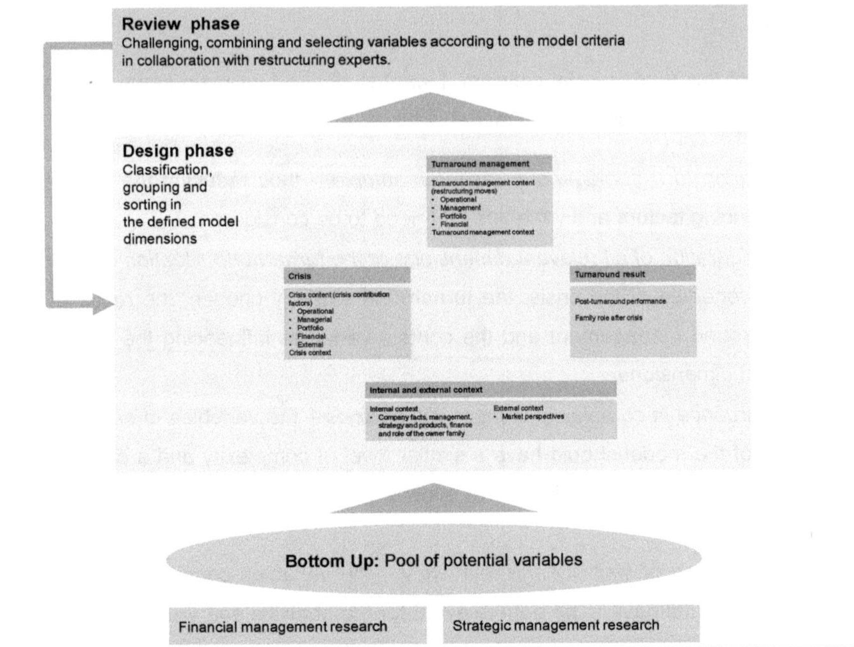

Figure 18: Iterative conceptual model design process – bottom-up research review and evaluation.
Source: Own illustration.

In the bottom-up research review, all relevant variables discussed in selected conceptual and empirical works were initially considered. The starting points for the selection of the literature were the studies discussed in section 2.1, complemented by database research. Based on the model structure, the variables candidates were classified, grouped, and structured into the different categories of the model dimensions as presented in chapter 3.

In an iterative review of all these variables together with restructuring experts (see Appendix 1 – list of restructuring specialists), these variables were challenged, combined and selected according to the four setup criteria discussed, resulting in the final conceptual model presented in this chapter.

4.2 Homogeneity of the research sample

Following the recommendation of Sudarsanam and Lai (2001) for further research and the practice of other studies (Eichner, 2010; Robbins & Pearce, 1992), the homogeneity of the sample is important to allow a "robust testing" (Eichner, 2010; p. 125) in empirical analysis. A higher diversity in the research sample would require more context variables to reflect this diversity in the model and to avoid interference. Consequently, this would have a negative impact on the statistical power of the model (see section 6.1.2) and the expected amount of contributed cases (see section 3.1.3). Thus the statistical detection of effects would decrease due to both less comparable and thus inherently different cases in the samples as well as more variables and fewer cases per variable.

For this study I decided to limit the selection of relevant cases in the following dimensions:

- Industrial sector
- Nationality
- Company size
- Date of distress situation

The limitation to manufacturing firms follows the recommendation of Eichner (2010), although it was proposed even earlier, for example, by Liou and Smith (2006); Pearce and Robbins (1993); Sudarsanam and Lai (2001). Sudarsanam and Lai (2001) justified this by the impact of the industry characteristics on turnaround strategies in general and the limitations which non-industry specific research would thus have.

Depicting the differences between common business models in the different sectors of economy, i.e., farming, service industry, real estate, financial industry and industrial manufacturing serve to illustrate the rationale for this statement. These have different business processes, competitive advantages and risk patterns and thus presumably are also different in the crisis and turnaround process. This concludes in the following definition:

The cases analyzed in this study are companies in the manufacturing sector.

The limitation to German companies is based on the sampling strategy, as discussed in section 3.1.2. The specifics of the German crisis and turnaround process are the starting point for the data collection approach chosen. This study is thus to be limited to companies that are subject to the regulatory framework in Germany. Besides this study specific item, there are other nation-specific influences on the crisis and turnaround process (Eichner, 2010; Suzuki, 1985), as already addressed in section 3.1.2. This restriction thus supports the homogeneity of the sample as well as the sampling strategy:

The cases analyzed in this study are companies with headquarters in Germany.

A significant part of the research in the field of crisis and turnaround has focused on large, publicly-listed companies. This limitation of the research stream has been addressed explicitly in some works (Cater & Schwab, 2008; Faghfouri, 2013; Rüsen, 2008). All the empirical studies reviewed in section 2.2 belong to this category of works (Eichner, 2010; Hauschildt et al., 2006; Sudarsanam & Lai, 2001). If a reason for this decision is explicitly discussed in the respective studies, it is the availability of published information. For publicly-traded companies, there are many standardized and non-standardized sources of information available, from public ad-hoc information to balance statements and databases. Most importantly, this information is usually available for failed turnaround cases as well, thus avoiding the issue of survival bias (see section 3.1.3).

This is in conflict with the relevance of the small and medium-sized companies, called the “Mittelstand” in the Germany economy. There is no strict and common definition of “Mittelstand”. The definitions are usually based on company turnover, with an upper limit between EUR 50m to EUR 500m (different "Mittelstand" definitions are reviewed in Langer et al., 2012). According to Günterberg (2012), “Mittelstand” accounted for 99.7% of all companies, 60.8% of the employees and 39.1% of the total turnover in Germany in 2009, even though Günterberg employed a rather restrictive definition of “Mittelstand” limiting it to companies with a turnover below EUR 50m.

Besides its overall importance, the focus on the “Mittelstand” market segment is supported from another perspective: As it is – per definition – comprised of companies smaller than those publicly listed, there are overall more potential cases of crisis and turnaround, which implies a significantly larger parent population for the sample collection. This should support the sampling process, as the banks' risk managers are assumed to have more companies in their respective portfolios fitting in this segment than larger companies.

For the purpose of this study, and also due to the data collection strategy chosen, I also need to implement a lower turnover limit, excluding very small companies from the sample. This has at its root two reasons: the differences in business processes and the availability of information:

- Small businesses below a certain turnover threshold usually have a very *simple organizational structure*, focused on the person of the founder, owner or managing director of the company. Many business processes that exist in larger companies are missing, thus crisis and turnaround are radically different. In relation to the crisis development, the limited size, for example, few employees, means that the illness or resignation of a single employee can cause a crisis situation. Other factors cannot contribute to crisis as the necessary complexity, for example organizational issues, is generally not present. Recovery is similarly different, as a wage waiver by the owning manager can constitute a turnaround strategy. Allowing small companies into the sample would thus add to the heterogeneity I want to avoid.
- Below a certain loan exposure, banks do not invest significant effort in their 'bad loan' cases. In addition, these companies would not be able to afford a third party turnaround plan compilation. Thus the information available from risk managers for very small companies is sparse.

Concerning the upper limit for companies relevant for this study, I chose to follow the definition used by the *Association of German Banks* (Bankenverband, 2000), defining 'Mittelstand' with an upper limit of EUR 500m turnover. Concerning the lower limit, I follow the definition of the European Commission, defining EUR 10m as the lower limit of medium-sized companies (European Commission, 2003). This concludes in the definition of the relevant company range:

The cases analyzed in this study are companies with a turnaround above EUR 10m and below EUR 500m.

As discussed before (see section 3.2), further limitations apply in respect to the character of the crisis, as it has to be both a manifest and a liquidity crisis. To permit a meaningful analysis, it is restricted to cases for which at the time of the data collection the turnaround management phase has ended, either with a successful or failed turnaround.
Concerning the date of the distress situation, I consider only crises that occurred after the year 2000. This ensures that the risk managers select cases for which information is sufficiently available.

Elaborating on the definition in section 3.2, the basic population of this study can be captured by adding this last restriction:

The cases analyzed in this study are companies that experienced a manifest liquidity crisis after the year 2000 and for which the crisis has ended either with a successful turnaround or insolvency.

4.3 Model of the turnaround result – company perspective

Employing the company perspective, the outcome of the crisis and turnaround process can be measured with a single variable, sharing its name with the respective model dimension, the '*turnaround result.*'

The complexity and the challenges in measuring the turnaround result are discussed in section 3.4.1. Both the definitions of failed and successful turnaround are derived there. As mentioned, the approach of using only binary variables has been criticized heavily in the conceptual research, but despite these conceptual concerns, empirical research has struggled to use more multi-valued variables.

For this study, I want to face these concerns by measuring the '*turnaround result*' for the company using an interval variable measuring the 'post-turnaround performance.' The variable incorporates the failed turnaround as the lower end of the scale, while increasing values reflect a higher post-turnaround performance. This implements some of the conceptually discussed elements of the result dimension, while still allowing a rather straightforward operationalization.

The dependent variable 'turnaround result' reflects the performance of the company in distress after the turnaround has either been successful or failed.

It ranges from

- *the lowest value, reflecting a failed turnaround (insolvency), to*
- *the highest value, which reflects a performance above pre-crisis level.*

The full extent of possibilities in terms of turnaround result scenarios as introduced by Trahms et al. (2013), include more cases, such as discounted merger and acquisition (M&A), premium M&A and sharp-bend recovery. However, they are not included in the model for two reasons:

- The option of M&A during the turnaround process brings an additional dimension into the variable, as it does not reflect the company itself, but the decision of the shareholders about the ownership of their asset, i.e., whether to keep or sell their shares. The turnaround of the company would then be carried out by the new owner of the company. In this respect, it is not an essential part of the company-oriented view of turnaround.
- The aspect of duration and timing, i.e., the length of the turnaround as reflected in 'sharp-bend recovery' by Trahms et al. (2013), was explicitly excluded from this research (as it has been also discussed for different reasons in respect to the turnaround phases, see 3.3.2), since it does not reflect the core research questions. If this aspect were included in the turnaround result dimension, the criteria of congruency (section 4.1) would require it to be reflected in all other relevant dimensions (i.e., crisis, turnaround management and context).

These additions would not add enough analytic value to justify the inflation of variables in the model and the resulting increase in complexity. Instead, a key target of this conceptual model is to adequately integrate all relevant dimensions of the crisis and turnaround situation as the basis for the empirical analyses in the chapters 5 to 8.

4.4 Model of the crisis

As concluded in section 3.2.3, the model of the crisis is structured in distinct categories for each different crisis characteristic. These characteristics are described mainly by resorting to crisis contribution factors. The categories are introduced in section 3.2.3.2 and are sequentially discussed and fleshed out with variables for each model dimension in this section (section 4.4.1 to section 4.4.5).

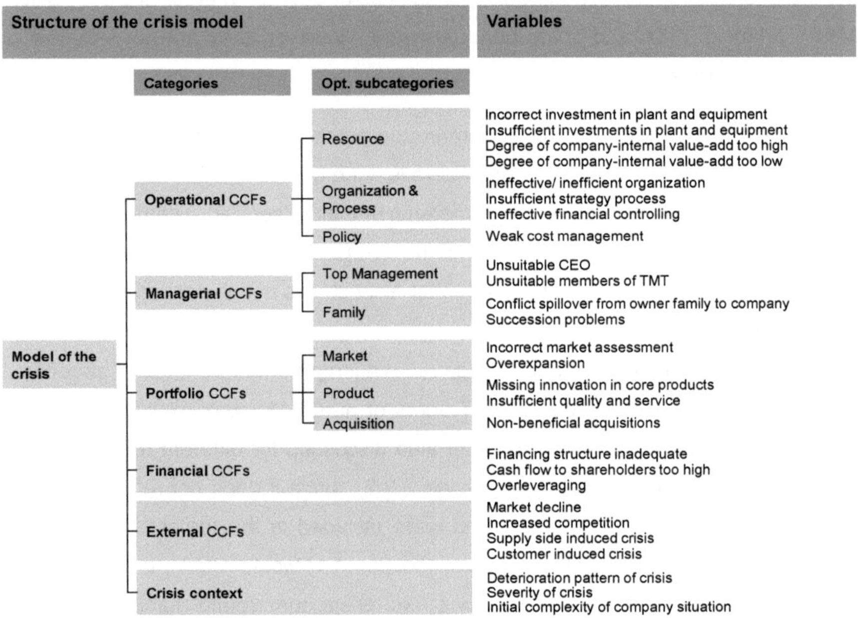

Figure 19: Model of the crisis.
Source: Own illustration.

The differentiation of context, content and process used by Pettigrew (1988) to describe turnaround strategies can also be applied to the subject of crisis. To the best of my knowledge, this has not been done before in the literature, but the application is rather straightforward.

The crisis content is sufficiently addressed by the typology using crisis contribution factors (CCFs) as explained above. While many aspects of the crisis context are part of the internal and external context and are thus addressed in section 4.6 – the model of the internal and external context – some crisis-exclusive context items are part of the model of the crisis. These items, the decline pattern, the severity of the crisis and the complexity of the company situation are in summary defined as 'crisis context' and are discussed as the last part of the conceptual model of the crisis (see section 4.4.6).

This section concludes with the discussion of propositions for the crisis model, (section 4.4.7).

4.4.1 Operational crisis contribution factors (operational CCFs)

As introduced in section 3.2.3, the crisis typology is an extension of the framework used by Eichner (2010) to classify restructuring moves. This is also applied to group the operational CCFs, following the criteria of congruency, introduced in section 4.1, i.e., striving for similar structures for the different model dimensions.

This approach results in three subcategories for the operational CCFs: resource-related CCFs, organizational and process-related crisis CCFs and policy related CCFs.

- *Resource-related CCFs* refer to factors contributing to the crisis originating in the resources of the company. These range on the monetary side from investment problems to physical resources issues.
- *Organizational and process-related CCFs* address all issues arising from the structure and the business processes of the company. Starting from the overall organizational structure to specific important processes like strategy development and financial management.
- *Policy-related CCFs* describe issues in the operating strategies of the company. These do not address single processes, but have a general application throughout the company as policy (e.g., insufficient cost management).

4.4.1.1 Resource-related CCFs

The resource-related CCFs considered for this research address two aspects: investment activities and vertical integration.

When analyzing the investment behavior, there are two seemingly opposite, but not necessarily contradictory CCFs: incorrect and insufficient investments. For all their apparent similarity, they are – especially in conceptual literature – often mentioned only summarily, even though both factors have very different impacts on the company and are not mutually exclusive. This is why, for the operationalization in this study with the target to identify cause-effect-relations, the two factors need to be addressed separately.

CCF 'incorrect investment in plant and equipment' comprises all investment activities that are either unnecessary, unrelated to the company business strategy, too complex or not technically mature, and thus contribute to the crisis.

Incorrect investment activities as summarized in this factor contribute to a company's crisis through CAPEX's not contributing to company success. This CAPEX reduces the company's assets and options by draining cash reserves for unnecessary investments. This topic is discussed in conceptual and empirical literature within the generalized context of incorrect investment (Hauschildt et al., 2006; IDW, 2012), but also framed in different subcategories, for instance, incorrect investment in real estate and excess capacity (Grape, 2006; Hauschildt et al., 2006); investment in new and untried technology (Hauschildt et al., 2006); leading to high start-up costs (Slatter, 1984); overcapacity (Grape, 2006; Hauschildt et al., 2006); and managerial misuse of resources (Trahms et al., 2013).

CCF 'insufficient investments in plant and equipment' comprises missing investment activities that contribute to outdated production equipment and/or to a non-state of the art production procedure, thus contributing to the crisis through higher maintenance, higher scrap rate, higher frequency of breakdowns and quality issues.

This CCF addresses the issue of investment backlog: The strategy and the core business of the company are not supported adequately by investments in the company's assets, thus weakening the company's performance. Hauschildt et al. (2006) used the terms 'too-late investments,' 'investment-fatigue' and 'outdated technology.' Similar items were addressed by other authors (Cater & Schwab, 2008; Grape, 2006; B. L. Hedberg et al., 1976; Starbuck et al., 1985), who found a lack of investments in the company's core competencies as a frequent source of crisis. The topic is addressed with similar content, but framed as 'inertia,' blocking the change of capital equipment (Grinyer & Spender, 1979), as side-effect of over diversification (Johnson, 1996) or as failure to update traditional capabilities and resources (Liou & Smith, 2006; Trahms et al., 2013). Other authors addressed the consequences of missing investments, for example, a high scrap rate (Böckenförde, 1996) and inefficient production (Schendel & Patton, 1976).

The second group of CCFs addresses the topic of vertical integration and the depth of added value. Similar to the investment activities, these two CCFs seem contradictory, but are in fact not incompatible. They refer fundamentally to decisions about the value-add of the company, which can contribute to a crisis by being either too deep or too low. Both factors can, per se, be relevant in a company at the same time, but in different processes or different production steps. They are addressed conjointly as inappropriate value depth (IDW, 2012).

Most publications do not address production-specific items like value-add in crisis companies in their research. But as I am looking at manufacturing firms, the production process is, per se, a core of the company's business processes; decisions concerning its fundamental design have significant impact on the overall company situation. This is also supported by the model discussions with the restructuring specialists conducted to develop this model (see Appendix 1 – list of restructuring specialists).

While vertical integration is typically seen in strategic research as a portfolio topic, it is restricted here to production-specific issues. While it could still be argued to address these items as portfolio CCFs, the structure of the CCFs did convince me to address the value depth issues as operational instead of portfolio CCFs. This prevents a fragmented presentation of the production and process related factors.

CCF 'degree of company-internal value-add too high' comprises all cases in which a crisis is promoted by a company doing too much 'by itself.' Services are provided within the company instead of procured on the market; this leads to investments outside of core competencies missing out on specialization, higher costs and lower performance.

This CCF addresses an item often found in German "Mittelstand" companies – the refusal to rely on external partners, performing most value-add themselves. While Hauschildt et al. (2006) addressed the item specifically in terms of 'missing specialization' and 'uneconomical production instead of procurement,' Trahms et al. (2013) summarized this as 'misuse of resources.'

CCF 'degree of company-internal value-add too low' comprises all cases in which a company performs key processes or process steps by purchasing external services, and crisis promotion originates from, for example, higher prices, worse quality or services.

This CCF refers to a situation where crucial elements of the business processes of the company are purchased and not part of the company's portfolio, limiting the company's influence on these processes with negative impact. Hauschildt et al. (2006) referred to these items as the phenomena 'dependencies on suppliers' and 'fragmented production process.'

There are additional topics related to human resources, which are not included in the final version of this model. Hauschildt et al. (2006), for example, referred to them in terms of 'too high or too low payment of personnel,' 'high headcount' or 'low performance employees.' These items are also mentioned in other crisis-oriented publications (Grape, 2006; IDW, 2012; Slatter, 1984).

These crises-related human resource topics can be generalized as two general issues promoting crisis in a company: The quantity and the substandard quality of personnel:

- The wrong quantity, i.e., having either too many or too few employees, is an obvious performance problem for a company. Having too many employees impacts the financial performance due to higher costs, while too few employees cause performance problems due to inadequate execution capacity. This topic is addressed in a broader fashion by the context factor 'slack resources,' which is discussed in section 4.6.1.
- The quality of personnel refers to substandard qualification or motivation of the company's employees. Concerning the management level, the topic of quality

is addressed by the factors introduced in 4.4.2. From the perspective of the banks' risk managers, the general quality of employees is not visible and assessable and was thus not considered in the model (application of the criterion of visibility, introduced in section 4.1).

4.4.1.2 Organization and process-related CCFs|

The three organizational and process-related CCFs are closely related. The first one, CCF *'ineffective/ inefficient organization,'* covers all general aspects of weaknesses of the company's processes and organization, while the two others, CCF *'ineffective financial controlling'* and CCF *'insufficient strategy process,'* address two specific and important processes enabling crisis development.

CCF 'ineffective/ inefficient organization' comprises any weaknesses in the organization and processes leading to crisis promotion due to a lack of performance of business processes, for example, too many hierarchical layers, bad preparation or execution of decisions, unclear competencies and responsibilities.

The literature has prominently discussed management systems and their role in crisis. The issues concerning the decision-making process in a company have been addressed in the literature as promoting crisis development (Liou & Smith, 2006); at the same time the quality of decision making is prone to change in a crisis (D'Aunno & Sutton, 1992), thereby intensifying the crisis (Bozeman & Slusher, 1979; Staw et al., 1981).

Related, but with a different focus, other authors (Arogyaswamy et al., 1995; Liou & Smith, 2006) have addressed the issues of clear responsibilities and competencies in the management team as crisis promoting. These can lead to conflicts and blame games between departments and managers.

Both these topics illustrate that the crisis development process is promoted by weaknesses in the management system, and thus can be self-enforcing. Firstly, the crisis and the pressure it causes on the organization worsen the efficiency and efficacy of collaboration and thus compromise process quality; and, secondly, a weak organization and processes may delay or even block the correct handling of crisis.

In their study, Hauschildt et al. (2006) found items like 'overly/insufficiently organized,' 'centralism and missing delegation,' 'coordination issues' and 'weak (production-) steering processes.' In relation to the last item, other authors (Bibeault, 1982; Slatter, 1984) highlighted the relevance of a lack of operating controls for crisis development. Böckenförde (1996) and Slatter (1984) emphasized the relevancy of generally inefficient processes and communication for the crisis development. Specific business processes are addressed as important factors with respect to production, sales (Böckenförde, 1996; Slatter & Lovett, 1999) and distribution (Schendel et al., 1976).

CCF 'insufficient strategy process' comprises process weaknesses in terms of development or communication of the company's strategy that promote crisis.

The topic of strategy development and its effect on crises was a key motivational factor in the study by Pearce and Robbins (1993; p. 613). As they pointed out, management is often "transfixed in their desire for expansion" in the evaluation of options for the company's strategy and thus does not consider other valid options. Hauschildt et al. (2006) also addressed the topic of strategy development in the items 'fanatic growth orientation' (similar to Pearce & Robbins, 1993), 'bad timing of strategic decisions' and 'missing planning process.'

A number of authors explicitly see poor strategy formulation (Grinyer & Spender, 1979; IDW, 2012; Johnson, 1996; Liou & Smith, 2006) or even an absence of company strategy (Bergauer, 2001; IDW, 2012) at the root of many or most restructuring necessities.

CCF 'ineffective financial controlling' comprises all weaknesses related to the financial processes in a company that lead to a weak or deficient financial steering of the company and thus promote crisis, including insufficient reporting or reporting quality, missing or unreliable operating figures.

The topic of financial processes and their quality is a relevant item for turnaround research. Hauschildt et al. (2006) fanned out the spectrum of possible items: 'Defects in bookkeeping and calculation,' 'incorrect attribution of costs to company segments and products,' 'missing consolidated statements,' 'missing resource planning' and 'strict budget orientation.' Financial mismanagement has been found in other studies to be a major cause of crisis in companies (Arogyaswamy et al., 1995; Grinyer et al., 1988; Liou & Smith, 2006; Sudarsanam & Lai, 2001), specifically in respect to calculating costs (Böckenförde, 1996), lack of planning and forecasting (Schendel et al., 1976), insufficient or sabotaged controlling (IDW, 2012; Slatter, 1984) or missing human resource quality in the financial function (Bibeault, 1982).

4.4.1.3 Policy related CCFs

Relying on the policy definition from Eichner (2010; p. 80) as "operating strategies, concerning a firms relationship to its suppliers and customers, (...) for the improvements of (...) costs," I adopt this approach for CCFs.

While this definition is based on the application of policies for turnaround management (these are discussed in section 4.5.1), operating strategies of companies can also be – although with limited applicability – seen as contribution factors for crises. In this respect, this category is limited to only one main factor with a broad definition.

CCF 'weak cost management' comprises all aspects of insufficient cost control and cost steering impairing the company's performance and thus promoting crisis.

With respect to this CCF, publications emphasize the issue of cost adjustment with changing external and internal circumstances, for example, sales decline, as important for crisis development (Bibeault, 1982; Böckenförde, 1996; Grape, 2006). The issue of high purchasing prices compared to competitors (Hauschildt et al., 2006) and faulty cost control processes (Cater & Schwab, 2008; B. L. Hedberg et al., 1976; Schendel et al., 1976; Slatter & Lovett, 1999) are the other two items commonly found.

Insufficient cost management is also seen as an aspect of the more generalized issues of poor resource management (Trahms et al., 2013).

4.4.2 Managerial crisis contribution factors (managerial CCFs)

"Top managers are often the villains of crisis." This statement by Starbuck et al. (1985; p.183) emphasizes both the importance, but also the responsibility, of management for the crisis development.

Consequently, the management and governance system has received significant attention in turnaround studies as found by Trahms et al. (2013) in their overview of 20 years of turnaround research. Based on their literature review, they proposed an adaption of the basic turnaround model of Pearce and Robbins (1993) (see section 2.1.1) by including 'response factors,' which determine the reaction of a company to a crisis. These 'response factors' consist solely of elements characterizing the management reaction to a crisis. The subcategories they suggested were 'managerial cognition,' 'strategic leadership' and 'stakeholder management.' Although these categories perfectly illustrate the importance of management for crisis and turnaround research, the research framework decisions laid out in section 3.3.2 make them inapplicable to this empirical study in a direct fashion. The elements of the 'response factors' are included implicitly in both the managerial CCF and the model of internal context in section 4.6.1.

The managerial CCFs are structured in two subcategories: Top management and family.

- The top management CCF's include all issues arising from the actions and behavior of the company's top management including the CEO and the top management team and their (unintentional) promotion of the crisis.
- The family CCFs focus on the crisis aspects arising specifically for firms with family owners. Specifically, these variables reflect the (unwilling) promotion of the crisis that can arise from the interconnection between the owning family and the firm.

As mentioned above, the properties of the managerial setup of a company are not only reflected by the CCFs introduced here, but also by model elements belonging to the internal context variables, which are discussed in section 4.6.1. These are – among others – the length of time the CEO has been with the company before the crisis and details about the family-company relation.

4.4.2.1 Top management CCFs

The heterogeneity of research on management impact on crisis and turnaround requires some initial clarification about the way this subject is addressed, before discussing the individual CCFs.

The term 'management mistakes,' as used by many works, has an ambiguity that makes it inapt for empirical research. As ultimately the management is responsible for steering a company, any crisis can be attributed to actions or inactions of the management (see e.g., Bibeault, 1982; Faghfouri, 2013; John et al., 1992; Nothardt, 2001; Schendel et al., 1976; Slatter & Lovett, 1999; Starbuck et al., 1985; Whitaker, 1999 and many others).

If defining organizational performance and thus crisis as "results from the alignment between a firm, its resources, and the environment" (Trahms et al., 2013; p.1289) and if ensuring this alignment and anticipating required changes are the main task of the top management, then any crisis can be attributed to the management's not taking the correct actions to reestablish or maintain this alignment.

In conclusion, 'management mistakes' as the cause of crisis is not a meaningful category for crisis typology. The informational content would only be minimal and insufficient to differentiate one crisis from another.

Using crisis contribution factors instead of causes partially reduces this dilemma (see section 3.2.3.2 for details). Labeling 'management mistakes' as causes would entail management always or never being the ultimate cause for crisis: Always the ultimate cause, as the reactions of the management enable or avert the crisis. Never the ultimate cause, as external factors are usually part of the picture if the management misaligns the company in respect to environment and resources.

Instead of using 'management mistakes' to describe the managerial CCF's, I want to focus on management as a group of persons and their suitableness for the company specific situation, thus focusing on their performance and their (presumably unwilling) contribution to the crisis.

To allow a more detailed analysis of top management, two functions are distinguished: the CEO, who leads the company and the top management team (TMT), consisting of all managers directly reporting to the CEO. This results in two different CCFs to describe the role of the management in the crisis.

A CCF 'unsuitable CEO' is identified as a CEO with lack of abilities or an unsuited personality, which leads to promoting the crisis through insufficient crisis perception/ acknowledgement as well as individual or professional errors.

In relation to the role of the CEO and his or her impact on the company's performance in a crisis and declining situation there are three items discussed in literature:

- *Missing awareness* of decline, i.e., the CEO does not acknowledge and act upon the crisis.
- *Inability to change* the strategy and thus the company, i.e., the CEO is not able to recognize that the strategies applied before are no longer valid in the current situation.
- Various *issues with internal or external stakeholders*, i.e., the CEO does not carry out meaningful stakeholder management.

The topic of *missing awareness* is commonly addressed insofar as a crisis progressing in a downward spiral is attributed mainly to managerial inaction (Barker & Mone, 1994; Hoffman, 1989; Lovallo & Kahneman, 2003; Schendel et al., 1976; Starbuck et al., 1985; Sudarsanam & Lai, 2001; Weitzel & Jonsson, 1989). The timing of management's acknowledgement of the existence of a crisis (the earlier the better) has a significant impact on the options available for the company to avert the crisis (Furrer et al., 2007; Pajunen, 2006; Trahms et al., 2013).

The *inability to change* was described by Hauschildt et al. (2006) very vividly as managers 'clinging to concepts successful in the past;' similar notions have been expressed in different terms by other authors (Arogyaswamy et al., 1995; Barr et al., 1992; Bergauer, 2001; B. Hedberg & Jönsson, 1977; Liou & Smith, 2006; Nystrom & Starbuck, 1984).

A specific aspect of this inertia to implement necessary changes is the issue of escalation of commitment (EOC). Faghfouri (2013; p.60) summed up the basic idea of EOC in relation to crisis and turnaround, stating that it "is that managers who have invested time, effort, money, passion and enthusiasm in projects will ignore warning signals and continue investing in spite of setbacks." The personal investment in 'old' strategies blinds the managers to the necessity of giving up or adapting these strategies and thus in some cases write off investments into these 'old' strategies.

Issues with internal or external stakeholders reflects the role of the CEO as the main representative of the company towards stakeholders (Jostarndt, 2007). His key role in stakeholder management allows the CEO to dominantly influence the relations toward important stakeholders. This is a central point of the empirical study of Hauschildt et al. (2006) using the terms 'one man regime,' 'nepotism,' 'patriarchal leadership,' 'avoidance of conflict' and 'conflict with stakeholders' to illustrate many aspects of this weakness. Similar issues, specifically with patriarchal leadership, have been addressed by other authors (Bibeault, 1982; Grape, 2006; Slatter, 1984).

CCF 'unsuitable members of TMT,' is defined by lacking abilities or unsuited personality of TMT members, promoting the crisis through individual or professional errors, including conflicts within the management team and with employees.

Similar to the CEO, the TMT plays an important role in steering the company. Many of the items mentioned for the CEO are also applicable for the individuals in the TMT, although moderated by the fact that they do report to the CEO and follow his directions. The team performance aspect and the interaction within the team are distinctive items for the top management *team.* Crisis-inducing issues with the team's performance have been attributed to ineffective communication and increased conflict (Arogyaswamy et al., 1995; Grape, 2006; IDW, 2012), the TMT's behavioral integration (Carmeli & Schaubroeck, 2006) and ineffective TMT compensation (Trahms et al., 2013) and missing TMT ability (Bergauer, 2001; Slatter, 1984; Trahms et al., 2013).

There is also a negative effect between the progressing financial distress and the TMT's performance, as distress promotes conflict and competition between the team members (D'Aunno & Sutton, 1992).

4.4.2.2 Family CCFs

Family firms are characterized by the interconnection of family and firm (see section 2.4.1). For the purpose of this study, the focus is on how the family can (unwillingly) promote crisis development.

Two CCFs are considered for this model, addressing the key elements of family and firm connection: Ownership and control (see 2.4.1).

While the ownership aspect is reflected by the CCF *'conflict spillover from owner family to company,'* the control aspect is reflected by the CCF *'succession problems.'*

CCF 'conflict spillover from owner family to company' comprises all conflicts within the family that promote the crisis of the company.

Conflict in families and crisis of family firms seem to be closely connected, as found by Rüsen (2008): He concluded in his interview study with more than 100 interview partners that conflicts between family members and conflict of interest within families are two of the four family-firm-specific causes for crisis he identified. The other two are related to succession and incompetent family managers and are mapped in the CCF '*succession problems*' and '*unsuitable CEO*' (see section 4.4.2.1).

Rosenbauer (1994) researched the interaction between family and company in respect to crisis development. The study found two key issues allowing the transfer of conflict from the system family to the system company: trans-system transfer and diverging system interests. Issues arising from trans-system transfer of conflicts can occur based on current or historic conflict, which are common in each family, but affect decisions and behavior in the professional environment of a firm. Issues arising from diverging interest might involve family shareholders' private priorities influencing the company strategy. As example Rosenbauer found charitable activities of a shareholder influencing the dividend policy. Ward (1997) also identified the issue of conflicts originating from disparate family goals.

While these studies investigate why these conflicts occur, other authors have simplified the matter by plainly referring to 'family shareholder disputes' as a factor for crisis (Hauschildt et al., 2006; IDW, 2012).

CCF 'succession problems' is defined by the promotion of crisis by all possible negative effects of trans-generational handover of a firm within the family, including a lack of suitable successor, conflict in the succession, loss of contacts and network of the predecessor, too much change by a successor and company tailored to fit the predecessor.

The family succession is a time of specific vulnerability for family firms (e.g., Ahlers, 2014; Cater & Schwab, 2008; Davis & Harveston, 2001; Faghfouri, 2013; Hauschildt et al., 2006; Longenecker & Schoen, 1978; Miller et al., 2003; Rüsen, 2008; Sharma et al., 2003). This might be related to the fact that for many family firms the trans-generational handover is more than a simple transfer of control (see SEW theory – section 2.4.3.3) and thus is loaded with specific expectations and emotions.

The main reasons for a problematic succession are the inability of the predecessor to hand over (let go) the business and the availability of a willing and able successor:

- The lack of ability to hand over can show itself in two regards. The first aspect is a lack of a proper planning and preparation for the succession (Lansberg, 1988; Sharma et al., 2001); the second concerns issues the predecessor might have in ceding the actual control (Bibeault, 1982; Bjuggren & Sund, 2001; Cater & Schwab, 2008; de Vries, 1994; Dyer, 1986; Handler, 1994; Sharma et al., 2001; Ward, 1997).
- Availability of a suitable successor is the second important factor. In most cases, it is simply driven by the limited pool of management resources from which to choose a family member as manager, as well as their willingness to work in a management role in the family business (Dyer, 1989; Sharma & Irving, 2005).

4.4.3 Portfolio crisis contribution factors (portfolio CCFs)

If the operational aspect describes 'how' a company is managed and the managerial aspects 'who' does it, then the portfolio aspects are about 'what' a company is producing and reflect the strategic setup of a company.

The portfolio-related CCFs are structured in three subcategories: Market-related CCFs, product-related CCFs and acquisition-related CCFs.

- *Market-related CCFs* concern the decision of the company on the markets in which it is active, both new and existing markets.
- *Product-related CCFs* address issues with respect to product features, both product innovations and product quality and service.
- *Acquisition-related CCFs* relate to M&A as crisis facilitator.

4.4.3.1 Market-related CCFs

There are two market-related CCFs, the first addressing the perception of the market, i.e., how a wrong market assessment contributes to crisis; the second relates to the possible consequences of extensive growth strategies, i.e., overexpansion and over-diversification.

CCF 'incorrect market assessment' comprises all crisis-inducing factors stemming from misestimating the market development or (future) market requirements. These range from quantitative errors concerning market growth to qualitative mistakes concerning product properties.

Referring back to the definition of crisis as the consequence of a misalignment "between a firm, its resources, and the environment" (Trahms et al., 2013; p. 1289), misjudgments of the future market requirements and market developments are often a prerequisite for the misalignment (IDW, 2012). This can happen simultaneously for many companies within a market segment due to environmental changes (Donaldson, 1994; Faghfouri, 2013; Grinyer et al., 1988), for example, in cases of a technological innovation redefining a market segment. It can also happen when an individual firm misjudges its specific market and competitive landscape (IDW, 2012).

The resulting issues, as a consequence of this misjudgment, range from wrongly following a general market euphoria, for example, as occurred during the reunification of Germany (Grape, 2006), to incorrect timing estimations of market developments (Hauschildt et al., 2006) and growth overestimation (Hauschildt et al., 2006; Schendel et al., 1976; Slatter, 1984). Similar misjudgments were found by Hauschildt et al. (2006) regarding the product requirements with the items 'out-of-time product properties' and 'too narrow or too wide product portfolio.'

CCF 'overexpansion' comprises all aspects of growing and diversifying too much or too fast. This promotes the crisis on account of growth-related financing issues, unmanaged complexity through growth, operating losses in new markets and with new products.

One of the key motivations for the seminal work by Pearce and Robbins (1993; p. 613) was the notion that American executives are focused on growth: Their "preoccupation with growth is widely reported as the number one internal cause of corporate financial decline." A similar statement was made by Hauschildt et al. (2006) using the term 'fanatic desire to grow market share.' The importance of growth and the resulting problems in terms of overexpansion and over-diversification is common in literature (Bibeault, 1982; Finkin, 1985; IDW, 2012; Robbins & Pearce, 1992; Slatter, 1984; Slatter & Lovett, 1999). Besides the direct effect of growth, it seems that the intention to grow also reduces the willingness to consider crisis symptoms and warning signals (Heany, 1985).

The direct risks of growth are reconfirmed by the surprising fact that more companies fail in growing industries than in declining industries (Moulton et al., 1996).

An indication of the relative importance of overexpansion as a crisis factor can be given based on the work of Eichner (2010): He found 20% of the companies in his sample could be assigned to this category in his four-category crisis diagnostic framework. This illustrates the importance of this aspect of crisis, although the more differentiated approach of my model might significantly change that number.

Over-diversification as a crisis promoting factor has also been discussed in literature (Faghfouri, 2013; Hoskisson et al., 1994; Markides, 1995) with specific respect to the competitive cost disadvantages through diversification and market entry costs (Slatter, 1984).

4.4.3.2 Product-related CCFs

Product properties can be a factor for a crisis in two ways, either through missing product properties, i.e., product innovation, or underperforming properties, i.e., product quality.

CCF 'missing innovation in core products' specifies a situation promoting the crisis, in which missing innovation is the reason why the products of a company are not technically state of the art, with properties below market and competition standards.

The failure to develop new and update current products is a common aspect of crisis research (Cater & Schwab, 2008; Grape, 2006; Hauschildt et al., 2006; B. L. Hedberg et al., 1976; Liou & Smith, 2006; Slatter, 1984; Starbuck et al., 1985) caused, for example, by organizational inertia (Grinyer & Spender, 1979). Other studies employ the complementary market perspective. But by attributing decline to technological market changes (Bibeault, 1982; Dowell & Swaminathan, 2006; Grape, 2006; Grinyer & McKiernan, 1990), these authors have described only the other side of the same coin, as this similarly expresses the failure to follow the relevant technological trends in a company's market.

Other authors find innovation issues arising out of insufficient (Böckenförde, 1996; Hauschildt et al., 2006) or unfocussed R&D activity (Hauschildt et al., 2006) or due to neglect of the core business in the context of diversification (Slatter, 1984). Trahms et al. (2013) employed the resource perspective, framing reduced R&D activities as ineffective resource usage, which leads to crisis.

CCF 'insufficient quality and service' comprises all aspects of insufficient performance of a company, in terms of both product and service quality, which promote crisis. This includes, for example, a high number of customer claims, bad customer service, bad logistics or other weaknesses concerning product-supporting services.

The topic of product and service quality has not received much attention in research on crisis and turnaround. Related items do surface, however, as 'issues with on-time delivery' (Böckenförde, 1996; Grinyer et al., 1988; IDW, 2012) or as 'quality issues with products and services' (Grinyer et al., 1988; IDW, 2012). The last item was generalized by Hauschildt et al. (2006), who identified in his sample the category 'too high, too low quality' of products.

4.4.3.3 Acquisition-related CCFs

Acquisitions that negatively impact the company's performance are a factor that has been discussed more frequently in research.

CCF 'non-beneficial acquisitions' comprise acquisition of companies or assets, promoting crisis. The specific reasons for this might be, for example, that an acquisition is too large, too complex or an acquisition target itself is in a crisis situation.

It seems there are two ways an acquisition can contribute to a crisis. The first is a badly-executed, acquisition-caused integration problem, for example, insufficient managerial and financial control (Slatter, 1984; Slatter & Lovett, 1999), or missing complementarity (Trahms et al., 2013). Secondly, the acquisition of a company already in distress can lead to distress for the acquiring company (Grape, 2006; Slatter, 1984; Slatter & Lovett, 1999). Hauschildt et al. (2006) elaborated that in many cases companies cannot resist a non-beneficial acquisition if it is perceived as a bargain.

Both ways were generalized by Sudarsanam and Lai (2001) in attributing decline to 'bad M&A decisions.'

4.4.4 Financial crisis contribution factors (financial CCFs)

The financing of a company can significantly contribute to a company's crisis. In contrast to strategic management research, financial management research has mostly regarded turnaround as a financial issue, perceiving the crisis as an imbalance between cash flows. An overview of the comparison of both research streams by Eichner (2010) can be found in section 2.1.4.

He found that Sudarsanam and Lai (2001) conducted the first empirical study to integrate the financial management and strategic management research perspective. Their model was extended and adapted by Eichner (2010) in his research model.

Following the criteria of congruency the companies' financing is also integrated as part of the crisis contribution factors into the conceptual model. There are three different financial CCFs considered, which promote the crisis in different ways: *'Structure of financing,' 'dividend to shareholders'* and *'overleveraging.'*

CCF 'financing structure inadequate' comprises all situations, in which the financial structure is unsuitable, too complex or too expensive and thus promoting crisis. This might be, for example, due to non-matching maturities, usage of unsuitable or uncontrolled financial instruments.

The inadequacy of financial structure has been found as crisis contributor in several ways, ranging from choosing financial instrument and structures, which cannot be sufficiently controlled by the company (IDW, 2012; Slatter, 1984), to mismatching maturities between the companies obligation and its financing (Hauschildt et al., 2006; IDW, 2012; Slatter & Lovett, 1999) and generally too high interest payments due to debt and financing conditions (Grape, 2006; Hauschildt et al., 2006).

Rising interest rates as a consequence of macroeconomic changes cause financial distress (Altman & Hotchkiss, 2006). While it might be an issue of overleveraging (see below) becoming visible by rising interest rates, it can also be a matter of mismatching maturities: If a company has flexible interest rates for its debt but at the same time has long-term fixed price agreements with customers, this would constitute an inadequate debt structure for the business model, i.e., the customer contract situation.

While an inadequate financing structure might exist at the beginning of a crisis, it can also be a crisis accelerator, if, for example, the loan agreements with the bank allow adjusting interest rates based on the bank's risk assessment of the company, thus being an indirect consequence of losing stakeholder support (see Arogyaswamy et al., 1995).

The CCFs *'financing structure inadequate'* and *'overleveraging'* are closely related. The symptom for both factors is identical: high interest payments. But the underlying problems are distinctively different – wrong structure vs. wrong amount – and thus are presumably the corrective actions. Following the criterion of congruence (see section 4.1), it is necessary to integrate both as separate CCFs in the conceptual model.

CCF 'cash flow to shareholders too high' refers to cases when dividend or other cash out to shareholders is too high and thus promotes crisis. This includes cash out to other shareholder-affiliated companies or entities.

Hauschildt et al. (2006) depict the extreme cases of this under the picturesque term 'extravagance in the private area,' referring to the case of shareholders draining the cash reserves of a company due to private cash requirements. Similar issues of conflict between shareholder and company requirements have also been found for corporate holding shareholders draining their subsidiaries (Grape, 2006).

Specifically, family shareholders are found to expropriate wealth from family firms by related party transaction and special dividends (Anderson & Reeb, 2003).

The limited coverage of dividends as crisis factors is in contrast to the intensive discussion of dividend cuts as restructuring instrument (see section 4.5.4). Through application of the criterion of congruency, the inclusion of one item requires the integration of the other. Specifically, it enables one to analyze the questions of whether there is a relation between excessive dividend before crisis and dividend cuts and what their combined effect on the post-turnaround performance is.

CCF 'overleveraging' describes a situation of crisis promotion in which the amount of debt becomes unaffordable for the company, as the monetary requirements of interest and amortization payments cannot be generated from operational cash flow, thus prohibiting the company from meeting principal payments.

The issue of overleveraging has been a prominent item for crisis research (Bibeault, 1982; Grape, 2006; IDW, 2012; John et al., 1992; Robbins & Pearce, 1992; Slatter, 1984).

'Overleveraging' is one of the three crisis categories used by Asquith and Gertner (1994) and later one of four categories in the adaption by Eichner (2010). Both of them found around 10% of their respective sample to be in that category.

Even before, Kraus and Litzenberger (1973) proved arithmetically that the increased leverage does also increase the probability of bankruptcy. This was reconfirmed in practice by Altman and Hotchkiss (2006) finding that the increased leveraging of US companies was a reason for liquidity crisis situations.

4.4.5 External crisis contribution factors (external CCFs)

The external CCFs reflect the issues originating outside the company itself insofar as these contribute to the crisis.

These factors are not to be seen as mutually exclusive from the internal CCFs, as these commonly occur together with internal issues of the company. For example, '*increased competition*' and '*insufficient investments in plant and equipment*' can together be two key factors fueling a crisis scenario, i.e. a company neglecting necessary investments in a market with increasing competitive pressure.

The external CCFs originate in two areas: The market setup, with market development and the competitive situation as its main aspects, and the stakeholder situation with the two important stakeholder groups: Customers and suppliers.

Market development is addressed by the CCF '*market decline.*' The decline is not differentiated by the scope of the contraction. In other words, it is irrelevant whether the industry, the national economy or the worldwide economy is contracting. From the company perspective, only the effect on the company is of relevance, and in this, the scenarios of decline are similar.

The competitive situation is addressed by the CCF '*increased competition.*' Again, I do not differentiate the reason for this competitive increase, whether there are new competitors or more aggressive competition in shrinking markets. The pressure on the company is the same.

The customer side is reflected by the CCF '*customer induced crisis.*' This addresses issues regarding the relation with customers.

The supplier side is reflected by the CCF '*supplier-side induced crisis.*' It addresses issues of the relation with the suppliers. It also includes general issues with the (raw) material market.

CCF 'market decline' comprises all factors, induced by shrinking markets that contribute to a crisis. This includes, for example, customer purchasing in low-cost countries, cyclical or permanent market decline, and substitution of products by new technology.

To avoid concerns about this item, I want to briefly clarify the model structure in relation to market development as a factor for crisis and turnaround. The market development as a whole is addressed with three distinct model variables:

- The CCF *'market decline'* refers to the market influence only insofar as it contributes to the development of the crisis
- The turnaround management context variable *'development of market segment during turnaround'* refers to the market dynamics during the turnaround process (section 4.5.5)
- The external context variable *'long-term growth perspectives of market segment'* addresses the long-term development of the relevant market segment (see section 4.6.2)

Together, the three variables allow one to clearly distinguish between 'sick industries,' for example, due to technological substitution, and regular cyclical decline, for example, due to a macroeconomic recession (Altman & Hotchkiss, 2006).

Industry contractions and market decline have been discerned as factors responsible for company crisis (Altman & Hotchkiss, 2006; Bibeault, 1982; Kim S Cameron et al., 1988; Grape, 2006; Whetten, 1987) although the effects of these factors are lower than the firm specific effects on the company's performance (Short et al., 2007). The underlying reasons have been further differentiated into environmental jolts (Park & Mezias, 2005), technological changes (Dowell & Swaminathan, 2006) or demographic effects (Grinyer & McKiernan, 1990).

The notion of a declining market's negatively influencing companies is unanimously agreed upon and immediately clear. In this context, the important research question is: "Why do different companies experience a very different impact on their survival?" This has been researched with diverse results using a population ecology perspective (Whetten, 1987; Zammuto & Cameron, 1982) and relative competitive market positions (O'Neill, 1986; Thietart, 1988). In many cases, the retention of a certain minimum turnover for a company is seen as a precondition to continuing operation in declining markets (Hofer, 1980; Schendel et al., 1976).

In his sample of 151 US, UK and German firms, Eichner (2010) found around 20% to which he attributed the category of industry decline. A similar number was identified by Asquith and Gertner (1994). Grinyer et al. (1988) found the topic of falling revenue for 60% of their sample, most commonly (50% of the sample) due to cyclical effects.

CCF 'increased competition' comprises the effects of a changing and more challenging competitive landscape in a company, thereby promoting a crisis. This includes, for example, the market entry and the formation of new competitors, changing behavior of competitors or higher efficiency of other market players.

Increased competitive pressure has been a commonly discussed factor for crisis development in research publications (Bergauer, 2001; Bibeault, 1982; Böckenförde, 1996; Grinyer & McKiernan, 1990; Robbins & Pearce, 1992; Schendel et al., 1976; Slatter, 1984; van Witteloostuijn, 1998). Slatter (1984) differentiated price and product competition. The first is based on product features, the second on product prices. The CCF *'increased competition'* can be linked to the CCF *'market decline.'* The competition in declining markets usually increases, as the market cannot support the pre-decline capacity (Kim S Cameron et al., 1988). Whetten (1987) conceptualized this by differentiating deaths of organizations based on markets as their ecological niches. Based on this perspective, he distinguished between deaths due to inability to perform in a stable ecological niche and deaths due to the shrinking of the ecological niche. Specifically for shrinking ecological niches, companies must achieve a top competitive position to survive. Its position has to be high enough in the ranking that it is among the share of companies able to survive in this niche. This fuels competitive pressure in the respective market.

Independent of *'market decline'* the competitive situation can also change in stagnating or growing markets, either due to competitive behavior based on strategy changes or new competitors entering the market. Altman and Hotchkiss (2006) further analyzed the underlying causes of increased competition and identified the topics of deregulation, international competition, overcapacity in the industry, and high new business formation rates as causing a lack of liquidity for companies. Barney (1991) added new products or services by competitors to this list.

O'Neill (1986) found that increasing competition was a factor for more intensive turnaround activities. Johnson (1996) analyzed that downscoping, i.e., the opposite of diversification, is related to the competition in the business field, as the management of diversified assets becomes problematic under challenging conditions.

Conceptual research often does not differentiate between customers and suppliers in their work. Instead in many cases these are summarily referred to as stakeholders (see e.g., Liou & Smith, 2006; Pandit, 2000; Trahms et al., 2013). But to serve my research objective, the separation is necessary in the conceptual model, due to the fact that supplier-induced crisis contribution affects the company differently, i.e., mostly with operational and cost effects, than customer-induced crisis factors, i.e., mostly with revenue and price effects.

CCF 'supply-side-induced crisis' addresses crisis-promoting effects coming from the supplier relations. This includes, for example, price increases for raw materials and purchased services and products, availability problems of purchased articles and services, bankruptcy of key suppliers or change of payments terms.

CCF 'customer induced crisis' comprises all negative effects from the customer relation(s), which contribute to a crisis. These are, for example, forced price decreases (especially in the case of dependency on few customers), reduction of the company's share in the total customer demand, loss of key customers or loss of receivables, e.g., due to insolvent customers.

Supplier-induced factors might involve quality issues, both in terms of product and logistics (Böckenförde, 1996), reliance on few suppliers or single sources (Hauschildt et al., 2006; Slatter, 1984) and raw material price increase (Hauschildt et al., 2006; Schendel et al., 1976; Slatter, 1984).

Customer-induced factors can range from straight volume reductions (Böckenförde, 1996), to dependency on key customers (Hauschildt et al., 2006; Slatter, 1984), to customers in distress, specifically in the case of built-to-order products, (Grape, 2006) to disadvantageous pricing agreements, such as with long-term fixed sales prices (Hauschildt et al., 2006).

4.4.6 Crisis context

The crisis contribution factors are elaborated in sections 4.4.1 to 4.4.5, while the crisis-specific context factors are discussed in this section.

The crisis specific context factors comprise three items: The pattern of the crisis, the severity of the crisis and the initial complexity of the turnaround situation.

The crisis context variable 'deterioration pattern of crisis' refers to the dynamic of the crisis progress. These dynamics range from

- *slow decline over several years to*
- *sudden crisis caused by an event.*

There is a consensus in the research that there are different velocities of crisis development (Cater & Schwab, 2008; Faghfouri, 2013; Park & Mezias, 2005). The underlying factors are explained from both the external perspective, with the antipodes of gradual change in the competitive environment and environmental jolts (Hambrick

& D'Aveni, 1988; Park & Mezias, 2005; Trahms et al., 2013), and the internal perspective, with the polar opposite's gradual slowdown vs. precipitous financial decline (Pearce & Robbins, 1993).

When it comes to the effect of the different decline patterns on the turnaround probability, the literature is sparse. Arogyaswamy et al. (1995) concluded that in the case of a slower decline process, a CEO change may reduce the effectiveness of recovery strategies.

The crisis context variable 'severity of crisis' refers to the state of the crisis at the time the turnaround plan is drafted. The severity ranges are:

- *less serious crisis state*
- *very serious crisis*

The notion of severity of the crisis has received more attention in the research. While this study only considers companies that are experiencing a liquidity crisis, i.e., a specific and rather advanced crisis stage (see section 3.2.1), the severity within this crisis stage can still differ for different companies' crises.

There is a conceptual consensus that severity has a negative influence on turnaround probability (Nothardt, 2001; Slatter & Lovett, 1999; Smith & Graves, 2005; Sudarsanam & Lai, 2001; Whitaker, 1999). The crisis severity as influencing factor for the turnaround was introduced in the model of Pearce and Robbins (1993). They postulated that more severe crises require more intensive measures in the retrenchment phase (see section 2.1.1), suggesting asset reduction for more severe and cost reduction for less severe crises. Despite its acknowledged relevancy, Pandit (2000) found and criticized that there is no consistent application of the severity of the crisis as a context factor in empirical research.

In empirical works, severity is often measured using the z-score (Altman, 1968). The z-score is based on several financial company data and is designed to measure the proximity to bankruptcy. It has been applied in multiple empirical works (Eichner, 2010; Francis & Desai, 2005; Robbins & Pearce, 1992; Sudarsanam & Lai, 2001).

Eichner's (2010) analysis of the severity's impact on turnaround shows no conclusive result for his sample. Others found negative impact on the turnaround probability (Francis & Desai, 2005). Lai and Sudarsanam (1997) found effects of the crisis severity on the content and the pace of restructuring, but not on the turnaround result.

The crisis context variable 'initial complexity of company situation to implement turnaround' refers to the situation of the company at the time the turnaround is drafted. The number, character, security situation and strategies of the financing partners, complexity of financing, role and behavior of unions, key suppliers and key customers can influence this. The complexity can thus range from

- *simple to*
- *very complex.*

In the critical phase after the turnaround plan has been drafted and before the turnaround actions begin, there are preconditions to be met to allow the implementation of the turnaround plan. Most importantly, this is whether the bank assesses the turnaround plan to be feasible; otherwise the bank is not permitted to retain the business relationship with the company (see section 3.1.2 for the restructuring process in Germany and its regulatory components). Stakeholder support, which is usually required to implement the turnaround plan, is usually one of these preconditions. This can contribute to a high level of complexity depending on the specific situation. A high number of financing partners with different interests and different initial situations poses a more complex framework than a one-bank-only situation. Similarly, unions, suppliers and customers and their relation with the company can change the complexity depending on their willingness to support the turnaround process.

These issues have been, for example, addressed by Arogyaswamy et al. (1995) who noted that factors beyond the crisis itself, time constraints, resource limitation and missing stakeholder support, add to the challenges of the situation. At the same time, stakeholders might add complexity to the process by trying to influence the turnaround implantation to serve their interests (Buschmann, 2006).

These contradicting challenges of a turnaround situation have been adequately described by Trahms et al. (2013; p.1278):

"Concerns and challenges managers face when executing an organizational turnaround (. . .).

1. first, managers must improve performance (. . .)

2. (. . .) context of increasing stakeholder conflict as different constituents jostle to protect their interests.

3. Despite the imperative for decisive action to turn around performance, managers of declining firms make decisions with diminished managerial discretion as greater supervision by boards and increased restrictions by creditors, bondholders, banks, and suppliers all limit their power."

4.4.7 Propositions for the model of crisis

As has been discussed in the model development section of the crisis characteristics, the availability of conceptual and empirical information on the crisis characteristics impact on the *'turnaround result'* is extremely limited. In fact, in many cases – as discussed – if there is information available, it is also inconclusive and contradicting.

Nonetheless, there is – as discussed before – the conceptual consensus that the character of the crisis does have an impact on the result of the turnaround process:

Proposition 1: The characteristics of the crisis do have an effect on the 'turnaround result,' as some or all of the specific characteristics of the crisis impact the distribution of the performance of the company after the turnaround.

This proposition is evaluated in chapter 6 by using different linear regression models to analyze this relation using empirical data.

Furthermore, it is assumed that there is a relation between the crisis characteristics and the appropriate turnaround strategy chosen, reflected in the following proposition:

Proposition 2: The characteristics of the crisis influence the turnaround strategy of a company, specifically impacting the probability of certain restructuring moves during the turnaround (content), but also the restructuring process.

The analysis of Proposition 2 is beyond the scope of this study, but is an important relation in respect to the conceptual model. Besides the fact that it is an interesting field for further research, this proposition also results in a statistical relation between crisis characteristics and turnaround management characteristics. These relations affect limitations for the statistical analyses (i.e., correlation between different factors in the regression analysis as well as possible multi-collinearity in linear regression), which are addressed in section 5.2.2 (Correlations) and 6.4.2 (Multi-collinearity).

The third proposition is based on the theory of gestalts (Miller, 1981), which postulates that there are specific configurations of strategic moves or strategy-defining variables, leading to a limited number of archetypes (section 2.3.4).

I assume that while the crisis itself is different for each company – especially, when analyzing it with the broad number of variables – there are specific underlying common crisis patterns, which can be identified in the sample data:

Proposition 3: There are common sets of crisis characteristics that allow for grouping the collected empirical data into a limited set of crisis archetypes, which can be meaningfully specified. These archetypes share certain key characteristics allowing for a distinctive segregation between them.

The related analysis is conducted in chapter 7.

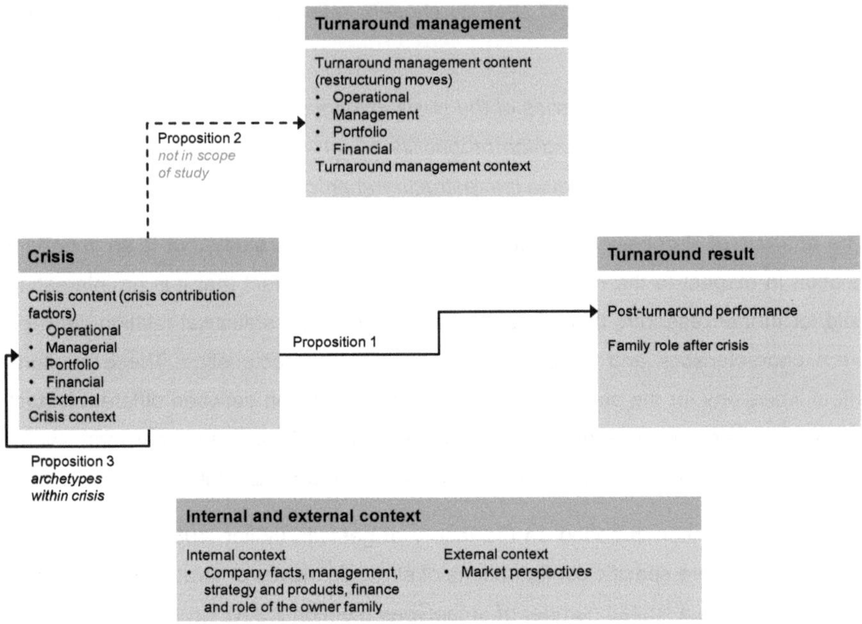

Figure 20: Conceptual model structure – crisis propositions.
Source: Own illustration.

4.5 Model of the turnaround management

Turnaround management is characterized as the set of actions a company performs to battle the crisis. Applying the contingency theory (see section 2.3.1) it can be assumed that there is no universally correct turnaround management. The correct set of actions is determined by the specifics of the company and the crisis.

This relation directly relates to the modeling criterion of congruency (see section 4.1): The different dimensions of this study's model should have a similar level of complexity and a similar structure as far as applicable.

Consequently, the turnaround management model is structurally similar to the model of the crisis as far as this is possible (Figure 21), the exception being CCFs that have no corresponding turnaround management action, for example, the external crisis contribution factors, which have no correspondent in the turnaround management model.

While the structure of the crisis typology as detailed in section 4.4 is a transference of the turnaround management framework developed by Eichner (2010), the structure of the turnaround management model is an adaptation and extension of Eichner's model. The common top-level structure is defined by the following elements (see section 3.3.3):

- Operational restructuring
- Managerial restructuring
- Portfolio restructuring
- Financial restructuring

While similar in structure, there are three important aspects in which the model of the turnaround management differs from Eichner's approach:

- Interpretation of the categories – portfolio vs. operational restructuring.
- Content of the model – bottom-up model development approach.
- Research object – medium-sized companies vs. publicly-traded companies.

Eichner's definition for the category of portfolio restructuring is rather narrow. Only transactional moves (M&A activities, i.e., sales and purchase of companies) are assigned to this category. This narrow interpretation is expanded by this model (see section 4.5.3) by adding strategic portfolio changes without M&A aspects, resulting in the categories 'portfolio restructuring by strategy change' (without M&A aspects) and 'portfolio restructuring by transaction.' In this, I follow the broader definition used by Sudarsanam and Lai (2001).

While adapting the structure by Eichner (2010), the content of the model is determined by a bottom-up variable selection process (see section 4.1) for each of the categories. The pool of variables forming the starting point of this selection process originates from many different research contributions, referenced in the respective sections. The selection was performed according to the criteria and procedure defined in section 4.1.

A contingency to this selection process is the research sample (see section 4.2) and the sample collection process (see section 3.1.3). Eichner (2010) analyzed publicly listed companies from Germany, US and UK in distress. This study, in contrast, is focusing on medium-sized companies, restricted by specific criteria to ensure the sample homogeneity. This implies necessary adaptations of the structure to reflect the different setup.

The final part of this section presents the modeling of the turnaround management context (section 4.5.5). Its variables define the specific relevant context of turnaround management: Market development during turnaround and quality of the stakeholder management. The general company context is addressed in section 4.6 instead.

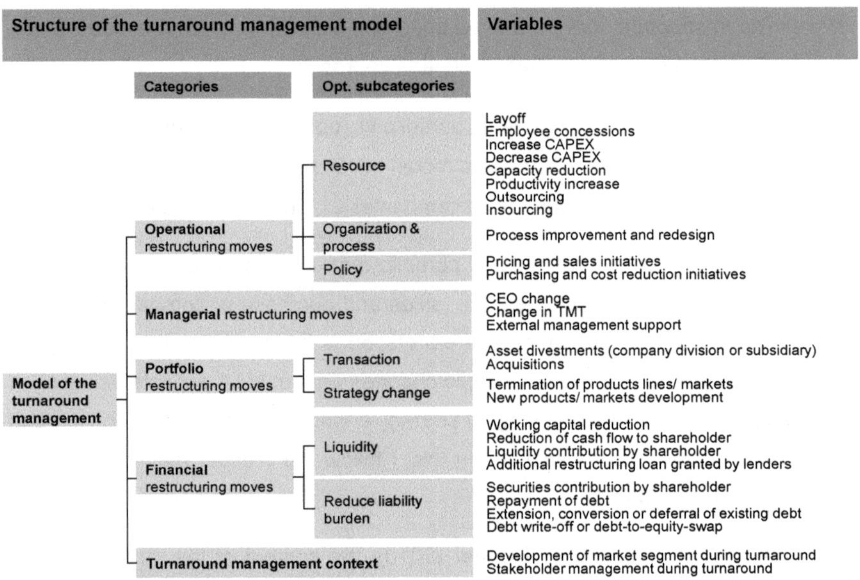

Figure 21: Model of the turnaround management.

Source: Own illustration.

4.5.1 Operational restructuring moves

Operational restructuring has been seen as an important part of turnaround management in multiple studies. The term was first employed by Hofer (1980), who set operational restructuring as the first activities to be executed by any company in turnaround. In his view, it is an integral part of the retrenchment phase. The actual term 'retrenchment' was introduced later by Pearce and Robbins (1993). The goal of operational restructuring is the reduction of costs and the increase of efficiency (Hofer, 1980; Slatter, 1984).

In their empirical study, Sudarsanam and Lai (2001) used 'operational restructuring' as a general variable, summarizing all operational activities. They found over 50% of the UK firms in their sample using operational restructuring moves.

Eichner (2010; p.52) defined 'operational restructuring' as "substantial changes to operational resources, organization and process as well as policies." This definition inherently already specifies the subcategories to structure this topic: 'Resource restructuring,' 'restructuring of organization and processes' and 'policy restructuring.'

- *'Resource restructuring'* comprises all restructuring moves used to alter the resources of or the usage of resources by a company.
- *'Restructuring of organization and processes'* comprises all moves targeted on changing the structure or processes of a company.
- *'Policy restructuring'* aims to change overall operational strategies.

Each of these categories is further defined and discussed in the respective following sections.

4.5.1.1 Resource restructuring moves

Resource restructuring moves affect the resources of a company and apply changes to their utilization. These resources include human capital, investments and the manufacturing capabilities of a firm.

The restructuring moves addressing the human resources of a firm concern changes in the headcount and changes of the costs per capita. The first of the restructuring moves is '*layoff*,' i.e., the reduction of the number of personnel employed by a firm and the second is '*employee concessions,*' i.e., the reduction of the employee compensation.

The restructuring move 'layoff' consists of all activities aimed at reducing the number of employees working for a firm. These are formal layoffs as well as dissolution contracts with or without settlements.

'*Layoff*' as a restructuring move is a common measure, the discussion of which engenders controversy in discussions.

John et al. (1992) found layoffs to be the most frequent operational restructuring measure taken. In empirical analyses layoffs have been found to have positive performance effects (Kang & Shivdasani, 1997; Khanna & Poulsen, 1995). However, in one study, the positive performance was only found for companies with organizational slack (Love & Nohria, 2005).

Much has also been said conceptually about the downsides of layoffs, as they cause a decline in morale (Arogyaswamy et al., 1995; Slatter, 1984; Suzuki, 1985) and cause more valuable employees to leave (Filatotchev & Toms, 2006).

Nixon et al. (2004) has even reported an empirically-supported negative influence on the turnaround success. Bowman et al. (1999) reported a mixed effect on shareholder returns, depending on the studies they reviewed.

Eichner (2010) was unable to find any significant effect of this restructuring move on the turnaround success when carried out in the first two years of turnaround, a phase he defined as the retrenchment phase. He did, however, find a significant negative impact if layoffs were executed in the second two years of a turnaround, which he defined as the recovery phase. For the findings of Eichner's study it is unclear if the restructuring move directly affects the turnaround result or if the cause-effect relationship is reversed, as in the case of poorly performing turnaround layoffs could resulting from the need for additional cost-saving measures. So, it is possible that the restructuring cases with late layoffs are more likely to fail because the performance was already impaired.

It can be concluded that there is no clear consensus in the literature whether layoffs influence turnaround success positively or negatively, although clearly they do play an important role in many restructuring cases as found in turnaround research.

Also, there is no consensus whether the move *'layoff'* belongs to the retrenchment or to the recovery phase of turnaround. Although clearly a cost-reduction activity and thus intuitively attributed to retrenchment, some publications argue that it belongs to recovery activities because of its long-term effects. Some even have argued 'downsizing' should be a third category in addition to retrenchment and recovery (DeWitt, 1993; Faghfouri, 2013; S. J. Freeman & Cameron, 1993) and downsizing has sometimes been directly operationalized as employee reduction (Love & Nohria, 2005).

The restructuring move 'employee concessions' includes all activities targeted at the reduction of costs per employee in a company. These might be, for example, the reduction or waiver of special payments, salary reductions, waiving or postponing of contractually agreed salary increases.

Employee concessions receive considerably less attention than layoffs. With respect to the cost perspective, many of the reasons and arguments for layoffs can be directly applied to employee concessions. Similarly, employee concessions are targeted at reducing personnel costs, with the main difference of focusing on the cost per employee instead of on the headcount. At the same time, the applicability is generally limited: According to Slatter (1984; p.180), common employee concession topics like "cutting wages, salaries and bonuses" and "postponement or freezing of pay increases" are "more difficult to implement." Employee concessions are conceptually supported for the German market with two possible effects: Deferral of payments and reduction of costs (Böckenförde, 1996).

On the empirical side, data is sparse. John et al. (1992) found 20% of the companies in his sample using wage cuts as a measure. Arogyaswamy et al. (1995) reported the example of Chrysler, which was able to agree to concessions with the union to support the company in a struggling automotive industry.

Rüsen (2008) found in over 100 interviews with family firms and restructuring specialists in Germany that family firm employees more willingly agreed to employee concessions than those of other firms. He attributes this to the privileged relation between family owners, firm and employees.

The second couple of restructuring moves address the topic of investments during turnaround management. '*Increase CAPEX*' and '*decrease CAPEX*' are diametrically opposed restructuring moves along the same metric and are thus discussed jointly.

The restructuring move 'increase CAPEX' describes an increase of the investment activities compared to the situation before turnaround management; this can range from new machinery to infrastructure. This restructuring move might also be a prerequisite for the implementation of other restructuring moves such as 'new product/ market development' and 'insourcing.'

The restructuring move 'decrease CAPEX' describes a decrease of the investment activities compared to the situation before the turnaround management. This restructuring move might be complementary to other restructuring moves such as 'outsourcing' and 'capacity reduction.'

In situations of financial distress and limited liquidity, the question of how to proceed with investment activities is obviously challenging for any company. The topic has been discussed in literature with diverse results.

Pearce and Robbins (1993) focused on investment reduction as one of the possible options to retrench a company. In many cases, the topic of CAPEX reduction has been included in general terms like downsizing or asset sale, implying accordingly reduced investment activities (Liou & Smith, 2006; Sudarsanam & Lai, 2001; Trahms et al., 2013). Harrigan (1980) suggested that firms with a good market position in contracting markets should strengthen their capabilities with investments to freeze out competitors.

Sudarsanam and Lai (2001) employed the perspective of cost reduction through added CAPEX by investing in equipment, reducing production costs and speeding up market reaction time and thus strengthening the competitive advantage, complementing operational restructuring (e.g., layoffs). They could not find any significant relation between CAPEX increase and turnaround result, but concluded that both recovery and non-recovery firms intensively use CAPEX increase as a restructuring move. In their study Schendel and Patton (1976) found that specifically during the retrenchment phase, there were significantly higher investments for successful turnarounds in comparison to their failed counterparts. Eichner (2010) analyzed both restructuring moves in his empirical analysis and finds no significance in turnaround success for either of them. However, he detected a more frequent use of the '*increase CAPEX*' restructuring move for the German firms in his sample compared to the ones from US and UK. Similarly, he found that highly-leveraged companies act more defensively on CAPEX decisions during turnaround management.

The last four restructuring moves in the category of resource restructuring address the actual production setup of the manufacturing firms analyzed. The restructuring moves '*capacity reduction,*' '*productivity increase*' and the oppositional couple '*outsourcing*' and '*insourcing*' all concern changes in the core process production.

The restructuring move 'capacity reduction' comprises all activities to reduce the output capacity. These include closing or partly closing plants or reducing the runtime of the machines in production, for example, through cancelation of work shifts.

As discussed previously, most research studies contributing to the field deal with publicly-traded companies, while this work focuses on medium-sized companies (see section 4.2). The general category 'asset reduction' for large companies commonly includes two aspects, which are assessed separately in my model. These are capacity reduction (discussed here), on the one side, and, on the other side, asset divestment (discussed in section 4.5.3.1).

For the first aspect, research focused on larger companies has often used plant closures as proxy to operationalize capacity reduction (Buschmann, 2006; Eichner, 2010). In smaller companies, or even one-plant companies, a broader definition is needed. The term *'capacity reduction'* has to include plant closures as well as similar measures on a smaller scale. The topic of the sale of plants is addressed separately within the restructuring move *'asset divestment'* (see 4.5.3). A plant sale would count as an instance of both restructuring moves at the same time, as capacity reduction and asset sales are both achieved by the same transaction.

Capacity reduction is one element of 'downsizing' as a general turnaround strategy (briefly mentioned in the discussion of the restructuring move '*layoff*'). 'Downsizing' can be further itemized by differentiating between different scopes of downsizing (DeWitt, 1998; Love & Nohria, 2005). While shrinking the company with a similar portfolio is defined as downscaling, a reduction of the portfolio is described by the term downscoping. This differentiation is also implicit in this study. *'Capacity reduction'* is an aspect of downscaling, with its focus on the reduction of the existing production capacity, while downscoping is addressed by the portfolio-changing restructuring moves discussed in section 4.5.3. The restructuring move '*outsourcing*' (see below) is a specific facet of downscoping focused on the production process, not on the product portfolio.

Kang and Shivdasani (1997) found that 5% of the Japanese and 16% of the US firms conduct plant closures. Buschmann (2006) found no significant effects of plant closures on turnaround success. Eichner (2010) found no significant effect of plant closures in turnaround if conducted in the first two years of turnaround, but that plant closures in the subsequent two years significantly impede turnaround success. Concerns about this approach similar to the ones mentioned in the discussion of the restructuring move '*layoff*' can be directly applied here.

The restructuring move 'productivity increase' includes all activities to increase productivity of a production. This can be human or equipment productivity, extending also to yield increase and automation. Sometimes these restructuring moves are also implemented as production strategies, for example, lean production.

Pearce and Robbins (1993) included measures to increase the company's efficiency in the cost reduction efforts (as part of the retrenchment activities). In their conclusion, these cost-reduction measures are relevant for less severe crises, while for more severe crises asset-reduction strategies should be applied. Arogyaswamy et al. (1995; p.502) emphasized the importance of efficiency-increasing measures, as these can "stabilize the competitive position of the firm by lowering costs, and the risk of insolvency in the short term is lessened by improving cash flow."

Eichner (2010) addressed the topic of productivity by using the variable 'asset productivity increase.' He finds no significance for this variable on turnaround probability. Other studies have found efficiency measures are frequently used (John et al., 1992) and have shown a relation to successful turnarounds (Finkin, 1985; Hambrick & Schecter, 1983).

The structure of the production process and the value-add done by a firm are important for any manufacturing firm. Thus the value-add depth changes during turnaround are important resource restructuring moves. Similarly to other crisis and turnaround aspects concerning details of production properties of manufacturing firms, the existing turnaround research contributes little to this topic.

The pair of restructuring moves 'outsourcing' and 'insourcing' both reflect changes to the added-value depth of a company. They are consequently discussed jointly.

The restructuring move 'outsourcing' labels measures to reduce the company's value-add by purchasing production steps, services and products externally.

The restructuring move 'insourcing' consists of measures to increase the company's value-add by introducing new production steps and production technology formerly purchased externally, for example, for quality or cost reasons.

The restructuring move 'outsourcing' is a specific facet of downscoping, with a cost reduction element to it. It allows the company to focus on key production steps (downscoping aspect) and improve the cost situation (cost aspect). Its scope ranges from single production steps to services like, e.g., logistics, and might even extend to the decision to purchase and trade products instead of producing them. In the research stream about turnaround, the level of detail to bring up such production improvement actions is usually not attained, although it can be assumed that outsourcing is implicitly part of the items in the discussion of retrenchment measures.

Hofer (1980) suggested that, in cases of competitive disadvantages in terms of production costs, subcontracting of major parts of the production to suppliers is a way to take advantage of their better position regarding the economies of scale, and adds that flexibility might be another reason for subcontracting.

The topic of 'insourcing' is often only implied in more general terms like resource recombination. Morrow et al. (2007) suggested combining measures like new products,

M&A and new processes (new processes are a consequence of insourcing), and finding a positive relation with value creation in distressed firms. *'Insourcing'* is also sometimes subsumed in the topic of R&D investments, as new production processes often imply R&D efforts for a company (IDW, 2012).

4.5.1.2 Organizational and process-restructuring moves

The aim of organizational and process restructuring is to change the structure of a company to cope with inefficiencies and improve the company's performance. These activities address the processes organization and the organizational structure:

- The *process organization* is the structure of the business and support processes, i.e., the way the workflow within an organization is organized, including process interfaces and responsibilities.
- The *organizational structure* is the hierarchical structure of an organization including management and decision-making structure and reporting lines.

As the possibilities to adjust organization and processes vary, I decided upon a single, broadly-defined restructuring move to address these topics summarily.

The restructuring move 'process improvement and redesign' comprises all changes in an organization including, for example, changes in the organizational structure, hierarchical structure, responsibilities, and process optimization with respect to workflow and interfaces.

A variety of restructuring moves and different terms that can be related to 'process improvement and redesign' as defined by this study, have been discussed in literature. Besides the fact that all of them are targeted at an improvement of the organization and processes, they often reflect the different management trends at the respective time of publication. The terms and content range from implementation of strategic business units (Sudarsanam & Lai, 2001), changes in the organizational structure (O'Neill, 1986), organization design (Schendel, 1993), change of the management system (Robbins & Pearce, 1992), decentralization of power and elimination of hierarchy levels (Bergauer, 2001; Slatter & Lovett, 1999) to improving decision making processes (Arogyaswamy et al., 1995).

Hannan and Freeman (1984) emphasized a downside of process improvement and organizational changes. They point out that in the short term reorganization impedes the company's performance, an effect that increases with company complexity and reorganization duration, thus increasing the risk of failure.

The analysis of this restructuring move in empirical works is less common, as it is extremely difficult to grasp. Most empirical studies use financial numbers to identify restructuring moves, which is difficult for organizational changes. Eichner (2010) used employee productivity (turnover per employee) as an indirect proxy for organizational improvements. While this is a valid approach, it can be diluted by the effects of other activities, such as '*layoff*' or '*outsourcing.*'

Organizational changes are commonly assigned to the recovery phase of turnaround due to the long-term orientation of this measure.

4.5.1.3 Policy-restructuring moves

Policy restructuring moves do not just address the improvement of existing business processes. These moves are characterized by an effort beyond the routine business processes to achieve cost saving and growth targets not reachable in day-to-day operations. They usually constitute a discontinuation of the common business policy before turnaround management.

The moves integrated in the conceptual model address two specific areas of interest and are often executed in a crisis situation to support and improve the financial situation of a company. These are *'pricing and sales initiatives'* and *'purchasing and cost reduction initiatives.'*

The restructuring move 'pricing and sales initiatives' comprises all initiatives to raise product prices and/or to increase sales volume.

The topic of sales growth in turnaround has been addressed frequently in literature (Arogyaswamy et al., 1995; Eichner, 2010; Hambrick & Schecter, 1983; Schendel & Patton, 1976; Sudarsanam & Lai, 2001), but the topic of price adjustments has seldom been addressed. Hofer (1980) suggested increasing prices if price sensitivity and demand elasticity allow implementing this step with positive cash flow effects.

Eichner (2010) employed the restructuring move 'organic sales growth' – opposing growth through acquisition – in his study, but finds no significant effect on the turnaround success. Yet he determines that companies with overexpansion issues are more likely to implement this restructuring move to utilize idle capacities. Similarly, Buschmann (2006) used it in his research with significant effect if revenue generation was long-term oriented. Nothardt (2001) found sales-increasing turnaround actions to be one of the most important positive factors in his German sample. Hambrick and Schecter (1983) found price increases more frequent in successful than in failing turnarounds.

The restructuring move 'purchasing and cost reduction initiatives' comprise all initiatives to reduce purchasing costs and lower other non-personnel expenses.

Cost reduction measures are turnaround supporting activities according to many turnaround publications (among others Hambrick & Schecter, 1983; Hofer, 1980; O'Neill, 1986; Pearce & Robbins, 1993). The details on how to achieve these cost reductions are often not further differentiated. The topics of renegotiation of prices with suppliers (Bergauer, 2001; Finkin, 1985; Slatter & Lovett, 1999) and the reduction of other operating expenses, for example, by using expense control mechanisms (O'Neill, 1986) have been explicitly mentioned.

General cost-reduction strategies are commonly seen as part of the retrenchment phase in turnaround management (see e.g., Pearce & Robbins, 1993).

4.5.2 Managerial restructuring moves

Managerial restructuring comprises all alterations made to the company's management during turnaround management. It has been a highly controversial topic throughout management research (Trahms et al., 2013).

The role of management in turnaround is two-fold: In the internal perspective, the management is responsible for steering the company safely through the crisis, while at the same time it is the face of the company in relation to stakeholders (external perspective) (Slatter & Lovett, 1999). In order to regain or maintain the trust of stakeholders and to change the course of the company, management restructuring has been seen as a prerequisite for changes in turnaround by many authors (Barker et al., 2001; Bibeault, 1982; Clapham et al., 2005; Grinyer & Spender, 1979; Hofer, 1980; Nystrom & Starbuck, 1984; Slatter, 1984; Slatter & Lovett, 1999) and the new management as the facilitator of organizational renewal (Clapham et al., 2005).

To operationalize managerial restructuring, I want to use the differentiation already introduced in the model of the crisis (see section 4.4.2) following the criteria of congruency (see section 4.1), which I also deem the best structure to analyze the impact of key managerial restructuring decisions. In doing so, I separate the restructuring moves: *'CEO change,' 'change in TMT,'* adding the restructuring move *'external management support.'*

The restructuring move 'CEO change' is defined by the replacement of the CEO of the company by a new manager to steer the company through the crisis.

In many publications, the replacement of the CEO has been seen as a precondition or in nearly all cases necessary element of any crisis management strategy (Bibeault, 1982; Hofer, 1980; Schendel et al., 1976; Slatter, 1984; Starbuck et al., 1985). In most cases, this is justified by the assumption that the management of a formerly successful company will have difficulties parting with their formerly successful strategies (see section 4.4.2) and leaving old habits behind. This impedes the application of the required, sometimes radical, changes if the same person remains in charge. Beyond the internal role of the CEO, the change of a CEO is additionally an important signal to stakeholders, indicating that there are changes being implemented to avert or to resolve the crisis (Slatter, 1984; Slatter & Lovett, 1999). In some cases, the company will even be pressured by external stakeholders, especially its creditors, e.g., the loan-giving banks, to remove a CEO (Bruton et al., 2003). This is supplemented by the fact that the CEO characteristics best suited for the turnaround implementation differ from those characteristics of a CEO who has managed the company before in times of growth (Hofer, 1980; Slatter & Lovett, 1999).

Other authors have addressed the downside of a CEO change. Arogyaswamy et al. (1995) emphasized that the removal process will lead to a loss of knowledge and cause friction in the handover. But they conclude that a CEO change is necessary if the cause of crisis is internal. Jenter and Kanaan (2015) partly confirmed that notion, as they found CEO removals to be less likely in an industry crisis if the company is performing better than its competitors.

Empirically, studies have found evidence that a CEO change had a positive effect on turnaround results (Grinyer et al., 1988), on the share price development (Bonnier & Bruner, 1989; Coughlan & Schmidt, 1985; Warner et al., 1988); others, however, report no significant effect (Weisbach, 1988) or negative effects (Khanna & Poulsen, 1995). Ndofor et al. (2013) found the positive effect to be contingent on growing markets. Sudarsanam and Lai (2001) could find no significant relation between CEO change and turnaround success.
Eichner (2010) analyzed the effect of early (first two years) and late (second two years) change of the CEO on the turnaround success and found significant effects for both, but positive only in case of early changes; in the case of late changes the effect was negative. Again, it can be argued that in the case of late changes these effects are found due to a reverse cause-effect relation, i.e., an already failing turnaround is causes a late CEO change and the change is a symptom not a cause of failure. He also found a higher occurrence of CEO changes in Germany than in UK or US companies.

The restructuring move 'change in TMT' is defined by changes to the top management team (TMT), i.e., changes to the managers directly reporting to the CEO.

The discussion of management changes is often focused on the CEO. The TMT, as the group of managers steering a company, receives significantly less attention. Management changes and CEO changes are not always distinguished from one another and a significant part of the key arguments concerning CEO change can be directly applied to the topic of TMT change.

When the role of the TMT is addressed, the team aspect is often addressed specifically. Filatotchev and Toms (2003) showed that the diversity of boards is related to the company's survival. Barker et al. (2001) found TMT changes to be related to enable strategy and organizational adjustment – thus supporting turnaround. Withers et al. (2012) suggested relations between the character of the crisis and the identification of the TMT member as part of the team, and the relation of the team members to the CEO, which influenced his decision to leave the company voluntarily during a crisis. In summary, as found in the meta-analysis by Liou and Smith (2006), the evidence of senior management changes is inconclusive.

The restructuring move 'external management support' comprises the support of the company's management by external management consultants, including the employment consultants as directors (e.g., as CRO) and interim managers.

Turnaround situations are not routine business and cause additional challenges for management like eroding stakeholder support, internal inefficiencies, or deteriorating internal firm climate (Arogyaswamy et al., 1995). The set of strengths, which managers need to possess in other phases of the company development, for example, identifying market opportunities and exploiting growth potential, are not suitable for helping to manage these additional challenges (Pearce & Robbins, 1993). Thus, external management expertise might be required, supplementing the internal managers' know-how about products and markets with specialized turnaround know-how. This role is often filled by specialized management consultants (Böckenförde, 1996; Cater & Schwab, 2008), who bring in restructuring experience and support the organization to learn to handle the crisis.

A second task for these external consultants is helping the company to regain creditor support and credibility by functioning as an unencumbered contact person for these creditors (Rüsen, 2008). In Germany, the regulations recommend banks use external restructuring specialists to perform an ongoing review of the turnaround development (BaFin, 2012). Unfortunately, to the best of my knowledge, there are no empirical studies analyzing the effect of this external management support on the turnaround probability.

4.5.3 Portfolio restructuring moves

Portfolio restructuring is defined as changes to the company's product and/or market segments. Following Sudarsanam and Lai (2001), this includes both portfolio changes due to internal strategic decisions and portfolio changes that are achieved through M&A transactions. In contrast to this broader definition, Eichner (2010) suggested a more restricted approach, only attributing M&A decisions to this topic, while moving the strategic portfolio restructuring move 'products innovations' to operational restructuring.

As these two possibilities, M&A based portfolio changes and internal decision based portfolio changes, are equally valid but fundamentally different, they are discussed sequentially in two subcategories. While both obviously involve a strategic decision, the first is prominently defined by its M&A transaction aspect. The portfolio-restructuring moves are thus subdivided into the two categories: 'Portfolio restructuring by transaction' and 'portfolio restructuring by strategy change,' only the first involving M&A transactions.

Concerning the topic of the general contribution of portfolio restructuring, Grinyer et al. (1988) found that implementation of long-term focused activities (besides cost-saving issues) is found more often in companies achieving a successful turnaround than for their unsuccessful counterparts. Their understanding of these long-term measures is similar to the portfolio restructuring moves as defined here. They deduced that addressing operational issues is necessary, but not sufficient to achieve turnaround.

Downsizing, a notion already discussed in the context of operational restructuring moves (see section 4.5.1), has the two aspects downscoping and downscaling (DeWitt, 1998). Downscoping describes the strategy to reduce a company to the profitable activities by shrinking its portfolio. This means to give up on non-core and non-profitable activities. This might involve both discontinuing and selling these activities. All retrenching portfolio actions can be attributed to downscaling.

4.5.3.1 Portfolio-restructuring moves by transaction

M&A activities can be clearly differentiated into two main options: Buying and selling assets. The two types of transactions have very different motivations and produce very different effects. The objects of these transactions might be assets or subsidiaries, depending on the specific structure of the transaction and the company performing it. But this has little influence on intention and effects of the restructuring move, and despite their difference in content, these actions are not mutually exclusive.

The restructuring move 'asset divestments (company division or subsidiary)' is defined by the distressed company's sale of plants, plant locations, and/or subsidiaries as well as of parts of plants or company divisions.

Asset divestments are the second aspect of the general notion of asset reductions in turnaround (Pearce & Robbins, 1993). The first aspect, capacity reductions, is discussed in section 4.5.1.1. Asset reductions are discussed as a general retrenchment strategy to battle a very severe crisis (as opposed to cost cutting, for a less severe crisis) and play a significant role in turnarounds. As Pearce and Robbins (1993; p.186) pointed out, "divestment of subsidiaries is perhaps the most common turnaround strategy." The importance and relevancy of asset sales has been supported by many other authors (Bergauer, 2001; Hofer, 1980; John, 1993; Lasfer et al., 1996; Slatter & Lovett, 1999). There are two general motivations for divestment in a crisis situation: generating cash flow through asset sale and divestment of activities not fitting the core business, i.e., downscaling (Eichner, 2010). The decision to part with assets is supported by low utilization of capacity (Sudarsanam & Lai, 2001). Achieving all targets at the same time can be challenging. It has been shown that the weakest unit is usually not the one to be sold (Trahms et al., 2013).

Other authors have addressed the risk of 'fire sales,' stating the concern that distressed asset sales are discounted due to the inherent urgency of the situation and possibly the overall industry situation (Shleifer & Vishny, 1992). This discount can be seen either as inherent costs of crisis management (John, 1993) or even as the implicit costs of leveraging (Shleifer & Vishny, 1992).

The decision to carry out asset divestments depends on the structure of the distressed firm. It was shown that of the firms using that option most have more than one division, while the firms not using it mostly have only one (John, 1993). This suggests that such a restructuring move might be more likely to be found within larger firms.

Many studies found evidence of positive effects of asset sales on turnaround performance (Asquith & Gertner, 1994; Denis & Kruse, 2000; Francis & Desai, 2005; Robbins & Pearce, 1992), while only one study found negative effects (Chowdhury & Lang, 1996). Morrow et al. (2007) found that asset divestment supports value creation in declining firms. Others (Bowman et al., 1999; Buschmann, 2006; Sudarsanam & Lai, 2001) reported divestments with refocusing having no effect on average. Eichner (2010) found that assets sales in the early stage of turnaround have a positive effect on turnaround success, while sales in the later turnaround stage have a negative effect. He also found this move more frequently for firms in shrinking markets.

The restructuring move 'acquisitions' comprises purchasing subsidiaries, shares in other companies, founding joint ventures or acquiring assets, such as plants, divisions, or other business activities from other companies.

The notion of investing in other companies and assets in a situation of financial distress might seem counterintuitive. But there are valid reasons to make an acquisition if the necessary resources are available (e.g., through cash flow generating measures) during turnaround, motivations discussed in the research are discounted capacity increase and new brands (Schendel & Patton, 1976) as well as diversification and new products (Schendel et al., 1976; Slatter & Lovett, 1999). The notion of acquisition in turnaround has been supported by several authors (Arogyaswamy et al., 1995; Robbins & Pearce, 1992; Slatter, 1984) up to the present.

Morrow et al. (2007) found evidence that adding resources through mergers or acquisitions supports value creation in declining firms, but only if these mergers add non-imitable competitive advantages (see RBV in section 2.3.3); otherwise they found a negative effect. No significant effects of this turnaround move have been found by Khanna and Poulsen (1995), and Sudarsanam and Lai (2001) found negative effects. According to Bowman et al. (1999), acquisitions with refocusing generate no improvements on average (based on 169 companies).

Analyzing the relation between the buyer and the acquisition object, it has been found for the case of declining markets that related acquisitions perform better than unrelated acquisitions (Anand & Singh, 1997).

4.5.3.2 Portfolio-restructuring moves by strategy change

While the topic of portfolio changes by M&A activities have received significant attention in turnaround research, the publications are much sparser on strategy-related portfolio changes. I assume two key reasons for this: Firstly, the outside visibility and thus the ability to analyze transactional changes is much better than that of strategy changes, and secondly, while strategy changes are purely internal adjustments in a company, the complexity of distressed asset sales are much more interesting – both from a scientific point of view, but also for investors.

The differentiation in regard to the strategy-related portfolio restructuring moves is similar to transaction-related restructuring moves. There is the possibility to reduce the portfolio by using the restructuring move '*termination of products lines /markets*' or to extend the portfolio by using the restructuring move '*new products/ markets development*.' Again, these actions are not mutually exclusive.

The restructuring move 'termination of products lines/markets' comprises the cessation of products, product lines or business segments as well as the withdrawal from markets or market segments.

When comparing the restructuring move '*asset divestment*' with this restructuring move, there are similar motives and effects: While strategic portfolio reductions cannot achieve an inflow of cash, as found for divestments, they follow the same logic of withdrawing from non-core activities, i.e., downscaling and thus share the same motivation. To that extent, a significant part of the conceptual arguments concerning divestments are also applicable for this restructuring move: An important motivation for downscaling measures is to reallocate the remaining sparse resources to the core product/ market combinations (see e.g., Pearce & Robbins, 1993). This product/ market refocusing may range from deletion of customers and markets, closure of losing business units to complete withdrawal from certain markets (Bergauer, 2001; Grinyer et al., 1988; Slatter, 1984; Slatter & Lovett, 1999).

It has been found that in times of poor performance, companies tend to refocus on their core product/ market segment by discontinuation of high technologies (Ketchen & Palmer, 1999).

The restructuring move 'new product/ market development' comprises new product development and new market entry. New product development includes product innovation as well as new market segment and product lines.

Entering new markets or producing new products in a distressed situation is challenging as resources are limited. But in some cases, a change of the company's product and market segments is necessary for survival. Thus this restructuring move is in line with the notion of refocusing the business on promising product and market segments (Bergauer, 2001; Eichner, 2010; Faghfouri, 2013; Hambrick & Schecter, 1983; Pearce & Robbins, 1993).

To illustrate the necessity of such a turnaround move, I want to use the example of a company serving its market with a product that will be substituted in the near future. No combination of operational, managerial and financial restructuring activities can suffice to achieve turnaround. For this specific company, the only valid turnaround option is to enter the market with new products.

In the empirical turnaround studies, restructuring moves involving innovation and expansion to new markets have often been neglected (e.g., missing in Bowman et al., 1999; Ofek, 1993; Sudarsanam & Lai, 2001).

Eichner (2010) found significant positive effects from product innovation on turnaround success. Morrow et al. (2007) found that declining firms are able to create value by adding new products (and implicitly, also new processes and technologies), but only if these add new, non-imitable competitive advantages to the company. Ndofor et al. (2013) found that new product introductions are specifically important for turnaround in growing markets. Grinyer et al. (1988) found diversification into new product and markets to be less frequent in failed than in successful turnarounds. Latham and Braun (2009), on the other hand, have shown that continued spending on innovation reduces the probability of survival.

In his study, Eichner (2010) found new product development to be more frequently employed by German companies than by US and UK companies. Bolton (1993) found that firms depend on the availability of slack resources (see 4.6.1.3) to implement innovation.

4.5.4 Financial restructuring moves

Financial restructuring differs from the other three categories of restructuring moves in the way it affects the company. Financial restructuring directly and solely influences the company's liquidity and debt situation, and it therefore directly touches a defining element of this study's definition of the crisis (see section 3.2.2). In contrast, the other restructuring moves affect the company's liquidity indirectly by changing the company's performance. While, for example, asset divestments also directly influence liquidity, they – unlike financial restructuring moves – at the same time drastically change the business of the company.

Financial restructuring moves, especially direct liquidity inflow from shareholders and banks, immediately relieve the crisis situation of a company by directly 'curing' the symptom of the manifest liquidity crisis. But on the other hand, it targets *only* illiquidity as a symptom of the crisis, without resolving the root of the crisis, the substandard performance draining the company's resources.

This relation between financial restructuring moves on one side and operational, managerial and portfolio restructuring moves on the other side is reflected in a division in the literature, where financial management research and strategic management research often appear as separate, detached fields (see comparison in section 2.1.4). For financial management research, financial restructuring is a research focus and the crisis is commonly treated only as an adjustment problem between capital structure and the company. From the perspective of strategic management publications, the financial aspects of turnaround are neglected. Crisis is treated as an adjustment problem between market and the company.

The first attempt to integrate both perspectives is the study of Sudarsanam and Lai (2001), which in turn is the starting point for the structure introduced by Eichner (2010). For the purpose of this integrated model, I follow and extend the definitions of these two authors and include alterations to the financing and the capital structure of a company in the turnaround management model, insofar as they "relieve the strain of interest and debt payments" (Sudarsanam & Lai, 2001; p.187) or are "either capable of improving the liquidity position (. . .) or alleviating the burden of financial liabilities" (Eichner, 2010; p.55). Concerning the categorization, I differentiate into 'liquidity improvement' restructuring moves and restructuring moves to 'reduce the financial liability burden,' thereby following John (1993).

4.5.4.1 Liquidity improvement restructuring moves

Liquidity improvement restructuring moves comprise all restructuring moves with the purpose of directly and positively affecting the liquidity of a company.

There are two restructuring moves considered: the internal restructuring move *'working capital reduction'* and the external restructuring move *'reduction of cash flow to shareholder.'*

The restructuring move 'working capital reduction' comprises activities that increase the payment periods to suppliers, reduce the payment periods to customers and/or minimize inventory.

General cash flow improvement measures have been discussed and supported as important for turnaround success (see e.g., Arogyaswamy et al., 1995; Sudarsanam & Lai, 2001). Working capital reduction is an intuitively correct operating measure to increase the company's cash reserves. It has been discussed in the relevant turnaround literature (with financial perspective) and conceptually supported by several authors (Eichner, 2010; Finkin, 1985; Slatter & Lovett, 1999; Whitney, 1999). It does include the introduction of factoring (Böckenförde, 1996), which – from the financial perspective – is a reduction of the payment period to customers.

Empirically, *'working capital reduction'* has been found to be used frequently (Bergauer, 2001), with positive significance (Hambrick & Schecter, 1983) but also with insignificant results by others (Buschmann, 2006; Chowdhury & Lang, 1996; Eichner, 2010).

The restructuring move 'reduction of cash flow to shareholder' comprises the reduction/ cut of dividends or other profit distributions, reduction or suspension of repayment of shareholder loans, reduction or suspension of payment to shareholder associated companies (e.g., rent payments to property-owning holding companies).

This restructuring move refers to the reduction of all possible cash flow setups intended to transfer liquidity to shareholders. As most publications address publicly-traded companies, the diversity of cash flow setups is limited and these are simplify reflected by the term dividends respectively dividend reductions/ omissions.

Dividends have two effects: They reduce liquidity and equity. Dividend cuts prohibit these effects and thus support turnaround (e.g., Bergauer, 2001; John, 1993). The downside of dividend cuts is that these might send an alarm signal to shareholders about the state of their investment, as dividends are perceived as an indication of the management's expectations of future earnings (Healy & Palepu, 1988).

Dividend cuts are a common measure, for the typical distressed firm, "the initial dividend reduction represents a cut of more than 70%," as found by DeAngelo and DeAngelo (1990; p.1416) for a sample of distressed US firms, and are specifically relevant for large firms (John et al., 1992).

Concerning the impact of dividend cuts on turnaround success, positive (Healy & Palepu, 1988; G. R. Jensen & Johnson, 1995), insignificant (Buschmann, 2006; Lie, 2005), and negative (Sudarsanam & Lai, 2001) effects have been found.

External financing sources contributing liquidity to a company can be differentiated by the source of capital – shareholders vs. other lenders.

The restructuring move 'liquidity contribution by shareholder' is defined by a positive cash flow from shareholders or associated companies as equity or shareholder loan.

The contribution of liquidity by new or existing shareholders appears to be a favorable restructuring move (Eichner, 2010). As the external financing equivalent of dividend cuts, there is no doubt conceptually that the strengthening of liquidity and equity is a stabilizing move for any company in distress (Böckenförde, 1996; Buchalik, 2004; Buth & Hermanns, 2004; Slatter, 1984). Besides the financial aspects, it is an important signal to all stakeholders that the shareholders have confidence about the future of the company (Buchalik, 2004; Rüsen, 2008). In some cases the debt structure and the debt contracts even enforce equity increasing measures by the company to avoid breaching these (DeAngelo & DeAngelo, 1990).

This relation between shareholder and creditors does raise an important issue that makes a unilateral equity increase during the turnaround management unattractive for shareholders. Due to the fact that the security situation of the creditors increases with the new equity, this step can be seen as a wealth transfer from the equity increasing party to the creditors and is thus not favorable to the contributing party (Jostarndt, 2007) unless the value of the going concern exceeds the wealth transfer.

The empirical results have ranged from positive (Buschmann, 2006; Jostarndt, 2007) to insignificant (Eichner, 2010; Sudarsanam & Lai, 2001) and negative (Castrogiovanni & Bruton, 2000) findings.

The restructuring move 'additional restructuring loan granted by lenders' comprises all additional liquidity contributed as loans, credit lines, mezzanine capital, bonds or other forms of financing.

In many restructuring cases, additional financing for the restructuring effort is required (see e.g., Eichner, 2010). If the shareholders are unable or unwilling to contribute additional funds, liquidity has to be raised from debtors (Böckenförde, 1996). New loans are a common form of financial restructuring (see e.g., Slatter, 1984).

Similar to the case of wealth transfer from equity contribution to creditors, new loans constitute a wealth transfer from creditors to shareholders (and to the existing creditors not participating in the new loan). This is why in such cases the creditors often insist on security compensations, for example, the shareholder contributing either liquidity or additional securities (i.e., personal wealth or illiquid personal assets) to the company (Buchalik, 2004; Rüsen, 2008). This step is reflected in the following section (as a capital structure move) by the restructuring move 'securities contribution by shareholder.'

From a bank's perspective, the contribution of new loans can be argued for as follows: Rather than forcing a premature liquidation of the company's assets (which are the securities of the loans) and risk the loans being repaid below nominal value, it can make sense to issue new loans against future cash flows generated by the assets and avoid the liquidation losses (John, 1993). Obviously, this only makes sense if the bank assesses the turnaround as feasible and the going concern value is significantly above the liquidation value plus the value of the new loans. In their analysis of 76 firms, Asquith and Gertner (1994) found that banks rarely (< 10% of the cases) contribute new financing in a crisis.

4.5.4.2 Restructuring moves to reduce the financial liability burden

The adjustment of the financial structure can contribute to reducing the liability burden on the company. To achieve this, there are four different restructuring moves considered: *'Securities contribution by shareholder,' 'repayment of debt,' 'extension, conversion or deferral of existing debt'* and *'debt write-off or debt-to-equity-swap.'* These measures can be characterized by their impact on the current loan contracts, the cash flow involved and actual balance sheet effects.

- *'Securities contribution by shareholder'* is a change of the loan agreements that improves the security situation of the lending banks. It does not involve any cash flow or balance sheet effects. Contractually, a third party acts as guarantor for debt, reducing the debt-associated risk by adding new collateral. This step has the purpose of ensuring the ongoing support of the bank, possibly including additional restructuring loans.
- *'Repayment of debt'* does not necessarily involve any loan contract changes. It improves the balance sheet situation by reducing the debt and thus the debt/equity ratio. It also has a direct cash flow effect (the repayment of the debt itself) and future cash flow effects (reduction of future interest payments and debt repayments).
- *'Extension, conversion or deferral of existing debt'* is a straightforward change of the loans contracts. It does not involve any balance sheet changes or immediate cash flow effects. Depending on the specific changes, it has an impact on future cash flows, P&L statements and balance sheets.
- *'Debt write-off or debt-to-equity-swap'* is a balance sheet focused measure and changes the loan contracts significantly. It does not involve cash flow effects. Future cash flows and P&L statements are altered.

The restructuring move 'securities contribution by shareholder' comprises all kinds of additional security contributions by shareholder and shareholder associated companies. These securities might be a personal guarantee by shareholders, pledging of other assets and subordination of shareholder loans.

This restructuring move is unimaginable for most publicly-traded companies. It is hard to imagine common stockholders pledging personal assets to secure the company's security situation. For this reason, this restructuring move has received no attention by scholars and studies focused on publicly-traded companies. For the special case of family firms in the group of private firms, Cater and Schwab (2008; p.43) found that during turnaround "family members were willing to personally sacrifice for the firm temporarily to an astonishing degree (e.g., pay cuts, investment of private funds)." As discussed regarding the contribution of funds in section 4.5.4.1, it is often the case that the shareholders have either no funds available to contribute or the assets of the shareholders cannot be easily liquidated. In this case, guarantees by the shareholder replace liquidity contributions and improve the security situation of lenders (Buth & Hermanns, 2004; Rüsen, 2008), thus allowing additional restructuring loans or the retention of existing credit lines. Similarly to the contribution of liquidity, this restructuring move is also a strong signal to all stakeholders that the shareholders believe in the future of the company.

This step has been attributed specifically to family firms in crisis (Rüsen, 2008).

The restructuring move 'repayment of debt' is defined by the repayment of outstanding debt to lenders. This debt repayment can be in the form of loans, credit lines and bonds, among others. The repayment might be combined, for example, with asset divestments.

As the company experiencing a crisis – as defined for this study – is, per se, having liquidity issues, it will usually not have the funds to repay debt by itself. This move does commonly require other restructuring moves to facilitate internal or external sources of cash flow. For this restructuring move, the source of liquidity is irrelevant and can originate from operational measures, assets sales or shareholder liquidity (similar definitions, e.g., Eichner, 2010; John, 1993). This measure is also conceptually supported by other authors (Slatter, 1984; Sudarsanam & Lai, 2001).

Empirically, debt repayment with positive effect on stock prices (Lang et al., 1995) and debt repayment without effect on turnaround (Eichner, 2010) have been both found, as well as the correlation that successful turnarounds utilize debt repayment less frequently than their control group (Grinyer et al., 1988).

The last two financial restructuring moves are generally referred to as 'debt restructuring.' The target of debt restructuring is reducing or deferring the payments arising out of the current debt of the company. John (1993; p. 61) has specified debt restructuring as "replacing an existing debt contract by a new contract with (i) a reduction in the required interest or principal payments, (ii) extension of maturity, or (iii) placement of equity securities (common stock or securities convertible into common stock) with creditors."

A common perspective is to perceive debt restructuring as a substitute for the bankruptcy filings, as it would be necessary if firm and lender were unable to agree on a change in contract. It is thus seen as a privatized bankruptcy (M. C. Jensen, 1991, 2010) but conducted more informally and with a more efficient cost structure for both sides than common insolvency proceedings. This informality limits the application of debt restructuring in complex environments driven, for example, by a large number of debtors, high information asymmetries and conflicts between creditors (John, 1993).

The relevance of privatized bankruptcy proceedings has been empirically shown. Gilson et al. (1990) found in their study that 47% of the firms in their sample could avoid Chapter 11 by debt restructuring. Sudarsanam and Lai (2001) found that more (10%) of the companies failing in turnaround use debt restructuring than the successful cases (3%).

For this study, I distinguish these steps by the extent of the debt changes in the two restructuring moves *'extension, conversion or deferral of existing debt'* and *'debt write-off or debt-to-equity-swap.'*

The restructuring move 'extension, conversion or deferral of existing debt' comprises changes in the costs (interest rates), deadline and terms of an existing loan.

Extension, conversion or deferral of existing debt is to mitigate the debt contract. The nominal value remains unchanged, but there might be interest rate reductions and repayment deferral. These changes can also extend to changed, removed or newly implemented covenants. On the other hand, debt write-off or debt-to-equity-swaps change the debt's nominal value, either by writing it off, or by trading it for volatile equity shares.

This 'softer version' of debt restructuring is supported by a significant number of authors (Gertner & Scharfstein, 1991; Gilson, 1989, 1990; John, 1993; Ofek, 1993; Sudarsanam & Lai, 2001).

Empirically, there have been varying results ranging from positive (Bowman et al., 1999) to insignificant (Asquith & Gertner, 1994; Eichner, 2010), to negative (Sudarsanam & Lai, 2001).

The restructuring move 'debt write-off or debt-to-equity-swap' comprises a waiver of quota of the company's debt or the conversion of debt to equity shares.

From the banks' perspective, this is the most extreme possible restructuring move and thus the 'harder' version of debt restructuring. In viewing waiver and debt-to-equity-swap within the same restructuring move, I follow the definition of Eichner (2010), arguing for similar characteristics, regardless of whether the debt is waived or converted (similarly defined by Jostarndt, 2007).

Obviously, this restructuring move is limited to cases in which the creditors see an upside through this transaction. The necessary conditions are straightforward to draft: The turnaround plan and thus future cash flow expectations (especially for conversion to equity) have to be higher than the liquidation value. The bank will not make any concessions if the value of the securities is near the loan value (Asquith & Gertner, 1994). Thus the turnaround move is more viable in the presence of growth opportunities (Gertner & Scharfstein, 1991; C. James, 1995) and if there are no legal limitations (Jostarndt, 2007).

The empirical data concerning the impact on the turnaround result is limited. There have been positive findings (C. James, 1995) as well as negative (Buschmann, 2006). Eichner (2010) did find a negative impact on turnaround success for this restructuring move in his late turnaround phase (second two years), but this analytic structure is not without issues (see section 2.2.2 for my concerns).

4.5.5 Turnaround management context

The turnaround management context concludes the model of turnaround management. While the general context of the crisis and turnaround process is covered in section 4.6, the specific contextual properties are addressed in this section. Two variables are selected for this part of the model, the first one relating to the situation of the relevant market segment during the turnaround management, the second to the stakeholders in the turnaround process.

The crisis context variable 'development of market segment during turnaround' refers to the relevant market segment of the company during the turnaround management. These developments range from

- *Contraction to*
- *Stagnation, to*
- *Growth.*

The '*development of market segment during turnaround*' refers to specific developments during the turnaround. This is different from the CCF '*market decline*' as discussed in section 4.4.5., as this factor is related to the time before the turnaround management. 'Development of market segment during turnaround' is also different from the long-term growth perspective of the market segment, which refers to the general lifecycle situation of the industry and is discussed in section 4.6.2. IDW (2012) emphasizes that it is crucial to differentiate between the long-term development and short-term cyclical effects of the industry or the economy to determine the correct restructuring measures.

The development of the market during the turnaround implementation impacts turnaround results twofold (see also Pandit, 2000; Whetten, 1987 for an assessment of the general relevance of market development on turnaround). Contracting markets impede sales prices and sales volumes; consequently, the operating cash flow in turn affects liquidity, assets and thus turnaround probability. Market contractions also have a signaling function for stakeholders, indicating difficulties for the company and thus eroding stakeholder support. A successful turnaround – which is often linked to growing turnaround (Schendel & Patton, 1976) – is much more difficult to achieve.

Downturn in markets changes the applicability of some restructuring moves (Barker & Mone, 1994; Hambrick & D'Aveni, 1988; Krueger & Willard, 1991), the most obvious example being the sales of assets, which will be discounted even further in a downturn situation (John, 1993).

Empirical considerations of the market context are not common, but Bibeault (1982) found market change contributed to recovery in 16% of the successful recoveries. At the same time, Sudarsanam and Lai (2001) found no significance in the GDP development (i.e., the general market situation, not the specific industry of the company) on the turnaround success.

The crisis context variable 'stakeholder management during turnaround' refers to the quality of the information provided to and involvement of key stakeholders (e.g., banks, customers, suppliers and employees) during turnaround. The quality of stakeholder management can range from

- *bad to*
- *very good*

'Stakeholder management during turnaround' addresses the challenge of managing the relevant stakeholders during turnaround. This does not reflect the *content* of turnaround management, but the *process* aspect of turnaround management (i.e., It is not about what is done, but about how it is done.). Specifically, it is not to be confused with the stakeholder-related (content-oriented) issues reflected in several of the crisis contribution factors (e.g., *'unsuitable CEO'* or *'supplier/customer-induced crisis'* in section 4.4.2 and 4.4.5, respectively) nor with the content of what is agreed on with the stakeholders (e.g., *'employee concessions'* or *'debt-to-equity-swap'* discussed in section 4.4.1.1 and 4.4.4, respectively). This context factor refers to the process quality of the interaction with the stakeholders.

Securing stakeholder support is a key task in the turnaround situation (see e.g., Liou & Smith, 2006; Trahms et al., 2013). As the stakeholders become aware of the crisis situation, their focus and interests change compared to the situation pre-crisis (Pajunen, 2006): Employees are concerned about job security, suppliers and banks about their credit risk and customers about their supply security. Identifying the key stakeholders and their management is essential for turnaround success (Arogyaswamy et al., 1995; Liou & Smith, 2006; Slatter, 1984; Slatter & Lovett, 1999) as supporting stakeholders can provide resources usually not available to declining firms (Arogyaswamy et al., 1995). Liou and Smith (2006; p.17-18) defined a very broad spectrum of possibilities to conduct these stakeholder management activities; these may involve "manipulative, substantive or even purely symbolic actions to increase stakeholders' perception of their power and participation in the company's activities, to highlight or clarify the benefits rather than the potential costs of continued commitment and improve their general perception/concept of the company and its credibility."

In case of insufficient stakeholder management, there is the risk that each of these stakeholders follows only his particular interest, thus damaging the turnaround efforts as a whole (Buschmann, 2006; Rosenblatt & Mannheim, 1996; Rosenblatt et al., 1993). For example, unions can attempt to block restructuring moves they perceive as threatening to their resources or influence (Meyer & Zucker, 1989).

The empirical research on the role of stakeholders in turnaround is fragmented (Trahms et al., 2013). It has been shown that distressed firms with a high level of stakeholder support are more likely to survive (Smith & Graves, 2005). Aside from the work of Buschmann (2006), finding negative effects of high bank influence, positive effects of high shareholder influence and positive effects if there are high dependencies of stakeholders on the company, there has been no detailed research except for case studies. This was reflected by Trahms et al. (2013; p.1294) admonishing that "this area of research could benefit from the application of stakeholder theory to present a more robust understanding of how the divergent interests and claims of stakeholders are manifested and sorted during decline and how this process affects turnaround outcome."

4.5.6 Propositions for the model of turnaround management

Following the approach of an exploratory study to evaluate the relevance and relative importance of different elements of the crisis and turnaround process, I also want to define broadly structured propositions for the model of turnaround management.

Therefore, the first proposition for the model of turnaround management is an echo of Proposition 1:

Proposition 4: The characteristics of the turnaround management have an effect on the 'turnaround result,' as some or all of the specific characteristics of the turnaround management will impact the distribution of the performance of the company after the turnaround.

Proposition 4 is addressed in the linear regression models analyzed in chapter 6.

As turnaround management aims to alleviate the effects of the crisis of the company, it has to be assumed that the characteristics of the turnaround management change the effects of the crisis characteristics on the *'turnaround result.'*

Proposition 5: The characteristics of the turnaround management change the effect of the crisis characteristics on the 'turnaround result,' thereby affecting the relation between the crisis characteristics and its impact on the performance of the company after turnaround.

Proposition 5 allows for a very large number of interactions between crisis characteristics and turnaround management characteristics. As the statistical analysis is constrained by the availability of empirical data (see section 6.1.2), this study limits the research to specific interaction effects. A classification scheme for these effects and the choice of effects analyzed is discussed and conducted in section 6.2.

Similar to the archetypes of crisis, I also analyze the turnaround strategies for common archetypes, accordingly leading to the next proposition:

Proposition 6: There are common sets of turnaround management characteristics, allowing for grouping the collected empirical data into a limited set of turnaround archetypes, which can be meaningfully specified. These archetypes share certain key characteristics, allowing a distinctive segregation between them.

The related analysis for Proposition 6 is performed in chapter 7.

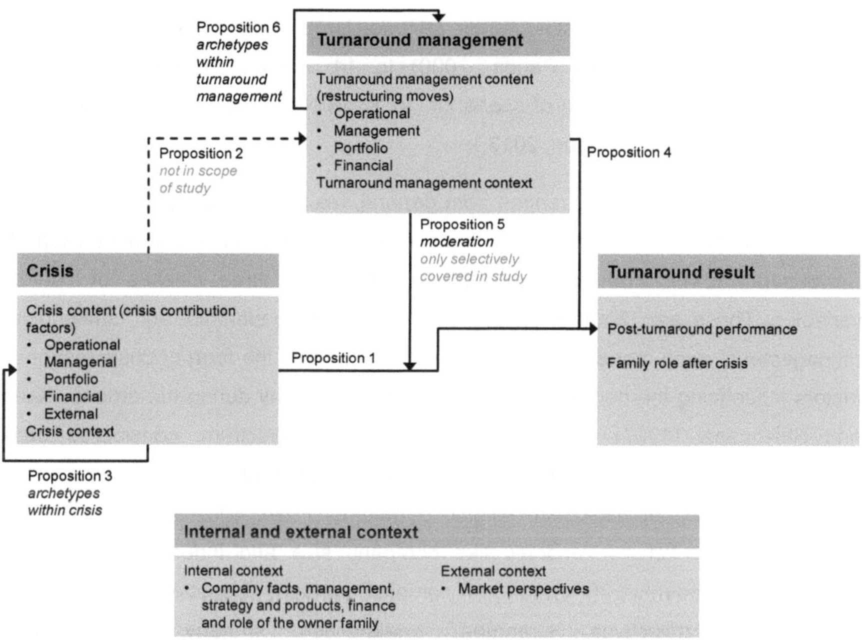

Figure 22: Conceptual model structure – turnaround management propositions.
Source: Own illustration.

4.6 Model of internal and external context

The model of internal and external context describes the general contextual elements of the crisis and turnaround process. The context variables that are part of and specific to the crisis itself (section 4.4.6) as well as those specific to the turnaround management (section 4.5.5) are included in the respective model dimensions. In contrast, this section addresses the factors that influence both crisis and turnaround.

The literature on context variables is rich in suggestions about which variables might play a crucial role in the crisis and turnaround process. But there is no coherent modeling approach attempting to integrate them into a model that could be directly operationalized. The suggestions vary greatly in the complexity and in the selection of variables considered as crisis and turnaround context, both in number and content.

The complexity in terms of the number of variables ranges from only four relevant context variables (severity; stakeholder attitude; firm's outer context and historical strategy, as suggested by Pandit, 2000) to 14 variables (These range from 'computer-assisted simulation of scenarios' to 'knowledge and understanding of the specific company' by Faghfouri, 2013.).

The content of the variables ranges from general, mainly managerial contextual factors (Trahms et al., 2013), to specific stakeholder settings of Japanese firms (Kang & Shivdasani, 1997). Trahms et al. (2013) introduced three classes of context variables; These are: 'Managerial cognition,' 'strategic leadership' and 'stakeholder management,' each modeled as a process component in the form of crisis response factors influencing the decisions and options of a company during turnaround. Kang and Shivdasani (1997), on the other end of the spectrum, considered bank relationship, block shareholders, managerial shareholding and keiretsu-membership – belonging to either Mitsubishi, Mitsui, Sumitomo, Fuyo, DKB or Sanwa. Others have suggested control variables like company size and industry classification (Routledge & Gadenne, 2004), to more complex company characteristics, for example, 'company objectives,' 'strengths,' 'weaknesses,' 'strategy,' 'structure' and 'control/information' systems (Ashta & Tolle, 2005).

While most of these conceptual and empirical works contributed additional insights to the research field, there is no approach to integrate all relevant variables into a shared model to evaluate their relative importance as well as the strength and significance of their impact on the crisis and turnaround process and its performance.

As it is the aim of this study to develop a model reflecting all important aspects of crisis and turnaround, based on the modeling guidelines introduced in section 4.1, this section is dedicated to doing both: introducing a structure and discussing the relevant variables for the internal and external context.

Similar to the model of the crisis (see section 4.4), the top-level separation of the company context into internal and external context variables is intuitively given. This similarity between the model of the crisis and the model of internal and external context is also a direct consequence of applying the criterion of congruency (see section 4.1).

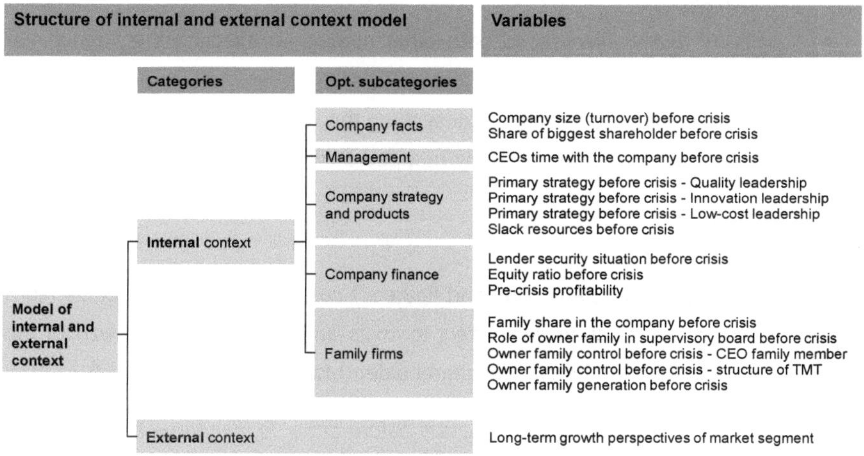

Figure 23: Model of the internal and external context.
Source: Own illustration.

4.6.1 Internal context

Due to the variety of different internal context variables, these are classified in groups with similar content. My literature review unfortunately did not result in an applicable and compatible model structure, as was the case with the model of turnaround management (see section 4.5). A direct extension of an existing model, comparable to the crisis model (see section 4.4) is also not feasible.

The following structure is both a loose reference to the model of the crisis and the model of turnaround management and a meaningful aggregation of the identified variables from literature. The resulting subcategories are:

- *Company facts* (new category without correspondence to the other two model dimensions).
- *Management* (as in both other models – reflecting the management aspect).

- *Company strategy and products* (similar to both other models – reflecting the portfolio aspect).
- *Company finance* (similar to both other models – reflecting the finance aspect).
- *Role and function* of the family (describing the role and influence of the family on and in the company, similarly mapped in the result model – see section 4.7).

4.6.1.1 Company facts

When addressing the company facts and figures, I concentrate on two aspects highlighted by several researchers in respect to crisis and turnaround: The size of the company and the share of the biggest shareholder (blockholder).

The context factor 'company size (turnover) before crisis' is measured by the annual turnover. It ranges from

- *the lower limit of EUR 10m to*
- *the upper limit of EUR 500m*

While the company size as a context factor is present in many studies, it is measured using different metrics. Some studies have used the turnover level (see e.g., Eichner, 2010) others have referred to balance sheet numbers like the total assets of a company (Sudarsanam & Lai, 2001) or the number of employees. The decision to use turnover as a defining number with the upper and lower limits is based on the definition of German "Mittelstand" and its application for this study (see section 4.2).

The notion that a company's size has an influence on turnaround success is common (as found by Francis & Desai, 2005), but authors tend to differ concerning the direction of this influence, i.e., if greater size is increasing or decreasing turnaround probability. The assumption of a negative relation is based on an assumed slower reaction (inertia) of bigger firms to apply changes in response to crisis (Hannan & Freeman, 1984) and higher complexity (Indro et al., 1999). On the other hand, organizational ecologists have theorized about a 'liability of newness,' decreasing the probability to fail with the age and thus the size of a company (J. Freeman & Hannan,

1989), similarly reflected by the notion that large firms have lower growth rates but better survival chances (Sutton, 1997).

Empirically, there have been studies finding better recovery chances (Jostarndt, 2007; Smith & Graves, 2005) or no effects (Eichner, 2010; Sudarsanam & Lai, 2001).

At the same time, firm size seems to also affect the content of turnaround management, i.e., the restructuring moves chosen. As discussed in section 4.5.3.1, divestments are not applicable for smaller firms without enough assets to divest. This was reconfirmed by Ofek (1993), showing empirically that the firm's size is positively related to the probability of operational and asset restructuring measures. At the same time, it could be shown that smaller firms are more risk averse in turnaround situations than the larger comparison group (Audia & Greve, 2006).

The context factor 'share of biggest shareholder before crisis' is determined by the equity share of the single largest shareholder in the company. It ranges from

- *0% to*
- *100%*

The notion of ownership concentration as a factor influencing the turnaround is not as common as the consideration of company size, but it has been a topic of debate.

It has been found by some researchers that there is a positive relationship between higher ownership concentration and turnaround success (Bethel & Liebeskind, 1993; Kang & Shivdasani, 1997). Daily and Dalton (1994) found firms with institutional investors less likely to go bankrupt; Trahms et al. (2013) attributed this to the fact that these investors, as blockholders, are more active in turnarounds to save their assets, as they cannot easily sell their shares. Others found lower turnaround performance in the special case of subsidiaries, despite the of the parent company's access to resources (Bradley et al., 2011).

Blockholders, like company size, seem to influence the decisions made by the company in turnaround. That is, blockholders increase the probability of equity increase (i.e., shareholder liquidity contribution) (Shleifer & Vishny, 1986).

4.6.1.2 Management

The role of the management in crisis and turnaround is a widely discussed topic, as noted in section 4.4.2 for the crisis and 4.5.2 for turnaround management. The duration of time the CEO has been with the company before the crisis is one of the key context aspects and completes the CEO specific information reflected in the CCFs and restructuring moves.

The context factor 'CEOs time with the company before crisis' relates to the CEO's time in his or her current position before the crisis.

It is conceptually assumed that long-term CEOs tend to judge a situation based on perceptions and strategies of the past, especially if these have been successful before. This attitude might be incorrect and unfitting at the time of the crisis (Barr et al., 1992; Hauschildt et al., 2006; Nystrom & Starbuck, 1984). Especially if drastic changes are required, it is difficult for the existing management to radically change their routines (Sudarsanam & Lai, 2001).

Although their finding is based on experiments with MBA students only, not actual turnaround data, Musteen et al. (2011) reached different results, as they found that increasing maturity and experience of managers increased both the perception of crisis severity and extent of retrenchment actions.

With slightly different results, Barker and Patterson (1996) found that managers who have been with the company a shorter time, tend to attribute the decline to internal, longer-employed managers rather than to external causes. This is reflected in the actual behavior of companies, as the extent to which companies exchange managers to overcome inertia in turnaround increases the longer managers have been with the company (Barker et al., 2001).

Pointing in a different direction are the empirical findings of Daily and Dalton (1995). They found a significantly higher turnover of directors (and thus a shorter time for the managers with the company) for bankrupt firms than for the control group.

4.6.1.3 Company strategy and products

The business strategy of a company has a significant impact on both the character of possible crisis scenarios, as well as on the options for restructuring that company. To grasp the business strategy, two aspects are included, which are discussed in the literature and fulfill the modeling criteria (see section 4.1): *'Primary strategy of the company before crisis'* and *'slack resources before crisis.'*

The context factor 'primary strategy of the company before crisis' refers to the main business strategy a company follows to conduct its business. These refer to the following distinct categories:

- *No clear strategy*
- *Cost leadership*
- *Quality leadership*
- *Innovation leadership*

Options two to four reflect the three distinct strategies that organizations use to gain competitive advantage (Schuler & Jackson, 1987), while the first option reflects the absence of such a distinct strategy.

The historic strategy of a company is an important context factor for crisis and turnaround (Pandit, 2000; Slatter & Lovett, 1999). But Pandit (2000) found Slatter (1984) to be the only study that considered the historical strategy as a variable: Slatter found that the historical strategy especially influenced the recovery phase. Depending on the company's historic strategies, the options for a company differ. For example, a company with a low-cost leadership strategy will have more difficulties introducing new products than a company with an innovative leadership strategy.

Conceptually, this was supported in one later contribution (Faghfouri, 2013). As a context factor in drafting turnaround plans, the respective standard in Germany (IDW, 2012) also requires the analysis of the business model and specifically refers to 'basis strategies' as an analysis element.

The context factor 'slack resources before crisis' refers to the level of organizational slack in a company. This level can range from:

- *lean organization – no slack, to*
- *normal organization – medium slack, to*
- *inflated organization – high slack*

The level of organizational slack is discussed throughout literature as a common contextual factor. It plays the most significant role in the model of Arogyaswamy et al. (1995), who define organizational slack along with the severity of the crisis, as the only two contextual factors in the crisis development.

For an organization with structural slack resources, retrenchment and downsizing (in the sense of downscaling as discussed in section 4.5.1 based on DeWitt, 1998) can be implemented without gravely impeding the organizational performance. Organizational slack is thus seen as a precondition for extensive downsizing (Faghfouri, 2013; Love & Nohria, 2005). It could also be shown that organizational slack works as an enabling factor for turnaround moves like acquisitions (Wan & Yiu, 2009), as organizational slack allows an organization to shoulder the additional organization stress.

4.6.1.4 Company finance

While the financial crisis contribution factors (section 4.4.4) and the financial restructuring moves (section 4.5.4) cover all aspects of financial factors and measures contributing to or averting a crisis, there are contextual elements to the company's financials that influence crisis and turnaround. These range from the debt situation from the lenders side, '*lender security situation before crisis,*' to the debt leverage and equity situation, '*equity ratio before crisis,*' but also cover the historic P&L performance '*pre-crisis profitability.*'

The context factor 'lender security situation before crisis' refers to the average securities of the loans to the company. It is significant for the liquidation risks of the lenders of the company. These can range from:

- *very bad to*
- *very good.*

The risk situation and thus the behavior of the debtors as key stakeholders of the turnaround management are assumed to be influenced by the impact a failed turnaround would have on the value of their (pre-crisis) loans, as well as influencing their willingness to contribute additional liquidity to the company (Rüsen, 2008). Insolvency does not financially impact a fully-secured lender, whereas lenders with insufficient securities might lose the complete debt under similar circumstances. It is conceptually assumed that if the going concern value (for the lenders) is significantly above the liquidation value, the support by the lenders will improve (M. C. Jensen, 2010) to avoid a liquidation scenario. This is supported by the findings that in the case of a high share of intangible (and thus hard to liquidate) assets the lenders are more willing to compromise (Gilson et al., 1990).

On the other hand, a low security situation of lenders might reduce the willingness of shareholders to contribute liquidity, as this would constitute a significant wealth transfer from shareholder to lenders (Gertner & Scharfstein, 1991; Myers, 1977).

If the security situation between the different debtors is very divergent, it might correspondingly determine their behaviors (This specific factor is intentionally not part of the model, as it would have required a significant number of additional variables to be properly reflected.). In this situation, the interests of the discernible debt classes might differ, reducing the probability of turnaround (John, 1993). Specifically, well-secured lenders might be willing to compromise on non-value changing restructuring activities like covenant changes, but will usually not agree to any measures reducing their loan value (Asquith & Gertner, 1994).

The context factor 'equity ratio before crisis' refers to the equity share of the balance sheet and thus to the leverage situation of the company. This equity ratio is assessed in relation to the business model and ranges from

- *too low to*
- *very high.*

The leverage situation is already part of the crisis contribution factors (see section 4.4.4). For the context aspect, I want to consider this information independently from its contribution to a crisis; high leverage does not necessarily contribute to a crisis, but might still change the options in turnaround. For this context factor, much of the information discussed for the respective financial crisis contribution factors (section 4.4.4) is also relevant.

Financial leverage as context factor can be perceived in two contradictory ways:

- From one perspective, a more highly leveraged company is more likely to experience a crisis. The fixed payment of interest and repayments of debt decrease the cash flow. Thus, the vulnerability to operational cash flow effect increases (Eichner, 2010).
- The probability for a successful turnaround of a more highly leveraged company is higher for two reasons:
  A high debt level increases the incentive to establish a monitoring system and counteract an upcoming crisis immediately (M. C. Jensen, 2010). Higher bank debt also increases the likelihood of successful out-of-court solutions (debt restructuring) for a company (Gilson et al., 1990; Ofek, 1993).

Empirically, Eichner (2010) found no effect for the variable leverage on turnaround success in his sample, but found that for highly leveraged companies the frequency of cash-draining turnaround moves like acquisitions or investments is reduced.

The context factor 'pre-crisis profitability' refers to the profitability of the company before the crisis. This ranges from

- *low (5%; return on sales) to*
- *medium (5%-10%), to*
- *high (>10%).*

The specific intervals chosen are based on the discussions with the restructuring experts (Appendix 1 – list of restructuring specialists), specifically the banks' risk managers involved in these discussions.

Pre-crisis profitability affects the crisis and turnaround process in a two-pronged way: On the one hand, it is assumed that firms with higher pre-crisis profitability have a more robust business model, and due to their historical performance, more substance (i.e., assets) than lower profit firms. On the other hand, a higher pre-crisis profitability is perceived by the stakeholders as proof of concept, showcasing the potential earning level of the company. It is assumed that a higher pre-crisis profit encourages all stakeholders to support turnaround. This has been researched conceptually and is uncontested in the literature (Eichner, 2010; Faghfouri, 2013; Routledge & Gadenne, 2004).

In empirical studies, pre-crisis profitability has also been found to have a positive effect on turnaround (Campbell, 1996), but insignificant in others (Eichner, 2010; Sudarsanam & Lai, 2001).

4.6.1.5 Family firms

Cater and Schwab (2008) concluded in their case study that family firms are in many ways very similar to other companies in turnaround; but they identify certain factors which separate them from the firms: 'Strong ties to the family firm,' 'small pool of replacement candidates,' 'consensus orientation,' 'informal management systems,' 'internal orientation,' 'integration of non-family employees,' 'altruistic motives,' 'and long-term goal orientation.' Being a family firm seems to have a significant impact on the process of a company crisis and turnaround (as discussed already in section 2.4). Consequently, the context variables describing the family firm and the role of the family in the company are included in this model of crisis and turnaround.

The term 'family firm' is not applied to just any privately owned firm (For the different definitions of the family firm refer to section 2.4.1.). In this study, the term is explicitly only applied to firms owned by founding families of the respective company and their descendants. This definition is in line with other authors (Anderson & Reeb, 2003; Gómez-Mejía et al., 2007).

To operationalize the role and function of the family in the distressed company, I use variables defining the family firm in three key aspects:

- *Ownership*
- *Involvement* of the family members in the management
- *Generation* of the family

These context variables have a different quality for the empirical analysis performed in this study. While the variable 'ownership' is a valid context variable for the empirical analysis of the data in all statistical analyses (see chapters 6, 7 and 8), the other two dimensions can only be analyzed meaningfully within the group of firms with family ownership (see chapter 8). Thus, in the empirical analysis in chapters 6 and 7 only the aspect of ownership is statistically analyzed, while in chapter 8 the details concerning control and generations are part of the analysis.

The context factor 'family share in the company before crisis' refers to the ownership share held in the company by the founding family and their descendants. It ranges from

- *0% to*
- *100%.*

Family ownership changes the situation of a company in crisis and turnaround. As elaborated below, family firms experience both a different crisis development and also differ in terms of the selected turnaround moves.

On the negative side, there is the issue of reduced professionalism (e.g., among many others Chua et al., 2009; Martínez et al., 2007; Schulze et al., 2001) and reduced monitoring systems in the case of shareholding managers (Johnson et al., 1993). The SEW theory (see section 2.4.3.3) adds additional complexity, as the question remains as to how family firms balance the SEW requirements with the need for survival (Trahms et al., 2013).

With both positive and negative effects on the crisis development, the internal orientation of family firms (Cater & Schwab, 2008) is an additional factor. It might improve performance, but reduce the recognition of external threats. Similar ambiguity is there for the risk adversity of family firms, again with both positive (H. S. James, 1999; Le Breton-Miller & Miller, 2006; Zellweger, 2007) and negative effects such as reduced R&D effort (Gómez-Mejía et al., 2007).

The long-term focus of business policy allows less short-term oriented management (Chua et al., 1999; H. S. James, 1999; Le Breton-Miller & Miller, 2006; Sirmon & Hitt, 2003; Zellweger, 2007), which is similarly reflected by less focus on growth rates or high ROI decisions (Górriz & Fumás, 1996; Harris et al., 1994; Tagiuri & Davis, 1992).

For turnaround management, the restructuring moves are also affected by family ownership, both in application frequency and applicability, (Cater & Schwab, 2008).

These range from a tendency to hesitate in implementing harsh retrenchment-oriented turnaround moves (Block, 2010; Cater & Schwab, 2008; Faghfouri, 2013; MacKenzie, 2002; Rüsen, 2008) to similar hesitation in radical departure from formerly successful strategies (Cater & Schwab, 2008; Ward, 1997). A very sensitive area is the topic of top management changes; these are especially difficult if managers are family members and shareholders (Cater & Schwab, 2008; MacKenzie, 2002). This move is further limited by the restricted pool of replacement candidates if a family-internal solution is pursued (Cater & Schwab, 2008). Family firms have also been found to be both reluctant to employ and challenging to work with for external specialists (consultants), providing support in a crisis situation (Cater & Schwab, 2008; MacKenzie, 2002).

Rüsen (2008) found indications for advantages of family firms in terms of stakeholder support during crisis: The unique relationship structures of family firms provide an additional resource in gathering turnaround support from stakeholders (employees, customers and suppliers).

Exclusive to family firms is the applicability of the crisis contribution factors *'conflict spillover from owner family to company'* and *'succession problems,'* both of which are part of the crisis model (see section 4.4.2.2).

Empirically, it has been demonstrated that family firms fail more often (Gómez-Mejía et al., 2007; Lansberg, 1988). Gómez-Mejía et al. (2007) found evidence that family firms are willing to run additional risk to secure the family ownership and control in a company, explaining this with the concept of SEW.

To allow a finer-grained analysis of the influence of the family on the company, there are three distinct variables that are considered for the model. As they all address one aspect of family firms, these are discussed conjointly.

The context factor 'owner family control before crisis – CEO is family member' refers to the CEO position in the company. There are two options:

- *yes*
- *no*

The context factor 'owner family control before crisis – structure of TMT' refers to the top management team (TMT) and its members. There are three options:

- *only family members,*
- *family and non-family members,*
- *only non-family members.*

The context factor 'role of owner family in supervisory board before crisis' refers to the role of the family in the supervisory board. There are four options:

- *no supervisory board,*
- *only family members in supervisory board,*
- *family and non-family in supervisory board,*
- *only non-family in supervisory board.*

While these variables reflect different dimensions of family influence on the company, they all refer to the level of influence (control) a family has on the company.

The supervisory board is a direct link between shareholder and management. Family in the supervisory board constitutes no direct involvement in the operational business, but an institutionalized controlling instance. A detailed analysis of function and role of supervisory boards in family firms was compiled by Faghfouri et al. (2015), concluding that specifically for family firms, supervisory boards play an important role in monitoring the management of the company (see below). The families' role as CEO and in the TMT constitutes direct operational involvement. It is a fact that "there are usually family members in the TMT of a family business" (Faghfouri, 2013; p. 69), which affects how the company conducts business.

Family managers show other and different characteristics than external managers, with both positive and negative consequences.

Related to the characteristics of the managers themselves, it has been found that management changes are less frequent (Tsai et al., 2006), bringing longer tenure with the company and thus high standards of performance, but also inertia to adapt to market changes and exploit new opportunities (R. Jensen, 2003) and reduced entrepreneurial behavior (Zahra, 2005). The selection method of new CEOs, specifically the focus on family members as managers, increases the risk of having an unsuitable CEO or unsuitable TMT members (Astrachan & Kolenko, 1994; Dyer, 1989; Tagiuri & Davis, 1992).

In the development of the crisis, shareholding managers have been found to reduce R&D spending more strongly than their non-shareholding counterparts (Latham & Braun, 2009). Similarly, shareholding managers are less likely to apply retrenchment activities without immediate cash effect (Ofek, 1993), like closing plants or laying off employees, which was more recently reconfirmed for family firms by Block (2010), a second example of neglect of long-term targets, but with different focus.

Concerning the role of the supervisory board, Rüsen (2008) found that external (non-family) members can provide important immediate support to the management and the family in the development of the crisis. Similarly, Faghfouri et al. (2015) in their empirical analysis found increased crisis readiness of family firms with supervisory boards compared to firms without. A similar effect was not found for non-family firms.

The context factor 'owner family generation before crisis (majority of shares)' refers to the generation holding the majority of the shares before the crisis. The options are:

- *Founder generation,*
- *2nd generation,*
- *3rd and later generation.*

The generation of family firms influences the relation of the family to the company.

The progression through time is often described by stage model. Gómez-Mejía et al. (2007; p.109) referred to these by "founding-family-controlled and managed firms (first stage), ownership and management by extended family (second stage), and ownership by extended family, professionally managed firms (third stage)." Their study showed that, with the ongoing stages and thus the progressing generations, the relations between family and company weaken. The author assumes that this might also be relevant in the crisis and turnaround process.

4.6.2 External context

Concerning the external context of the crisis and turnaround situation, many elements of the external influence are covered in the external crisis contribution factors (see section 4.4.5) and the turnaround management context (see section 4.5.5). The remaining external context factor is the long-term perspectives of the market segment in which the company is active.

The context factor 'long-term growth perspectives of market segment' refers to the long-term perspectives of the relevant market segment of the company. This does not refer to the short-term development of the market segment, but the longer-term perspectives of the market. These developments range from

- *contraction, to*
- *stagnation, to*
- *growth.*

Growth perspectives allow a higher valuation of the company's equity. These growth opportunities can only be realized if a company has a going-concern forecast (i.e., achieves a successful turnaround), and should thus support turnaround success (Eichner, 2010; Slatter & Lovett, 1999). These growth opportunities enable the company to use a wider set of financing instruments, as found by C. James (1995) and later confirmed by Kahl (2002), and make it more likely to gain additional funding from banks up to debt-to-equity-swaps (Liou & Smith, 2006).

Growth opportunities reduce the applicability of asset- and cost-reduction moves and increase the applicability of investment and growth-oriented restructuring moves (O'Neill, 1986; Slatter, 1984). Ndofor et al. (2013) found that cost and asset retrenchment negatively influence the turnaround performance in growing environments.

Empirically, the relation between growth opportunities and turnaround probability could not be confirmed by the empirical analysis of Eichner (2010). Moulton et al. (1996) even found that more firms fail in growing than in declining industries. The failing firms in growing industries showed a phenomenon described as 'forced debt-funded growth.' Empirically, they found these firms to be characterized by a higher financial leverage risk and a higher strategic growth risk.

4.6.3 Proposition for the model of internal and external context

Similar to the other two model dimensions, I define propositions for the model of internal and external context.

Based upon the discussion of the individual model elements, the first proposition follows Propositions 1 and 4:

Proposition 7: The internal and external context will have an effect on the 'turnaround result,' as some or all of the specific characteristics of the internal and external context management will impact the distribution of the performance of the company after the turnaround.

Proposition 7 is addressed in the linear regression models analyzed in chapter 6. The analysis of Proposition 7 does not cover the context variables related to the role and function of the family in the firm before the crisis; these are analyzed in chapter 8 instead, as part of the family-specific analysis.

The internal and external context further enriches the possibilities for interaction effect between variables. This results in three additional propositions:

Proposition 8: The internal and the external context of the company will influence the crisis characteristics of a company, specifically impacting the probability of certain crisis contribution factors leading to the crisis.

Proposition 9: The internal and the external context of the company will influence the turnaround strategy of the company, specifically impacting the probability of certain restructuring moves.

Proposition 10: The internal and external context change the effect of the crisis characteristics or the turnaround management characteristics on the 'turnaround result,' thereby affecting the relation between the crisis characteristic as well as the turnaround management characteristics and their impact on the performance of the company after the turnaround.

The analysis of propositions 8, 9 and 10 are not part of the analysis in this study; as discussed before, it is important to consider these dependencies and relations in order to address these by analyzing possible statistical limitations, i.e., correlation between different factors in the regression analysis as well as possible multicollinearity issues in the linear regression – see section 5.2.2 (Correlations) and 6.4.2 (Multicollinearity). As it is a common issue for all statistical analysis of complex real word topics, the addition of too many variables would not allow any meaningful analysis.

The propositions addressing the specific topic of family firms are laid out and discussed in chapter 8.

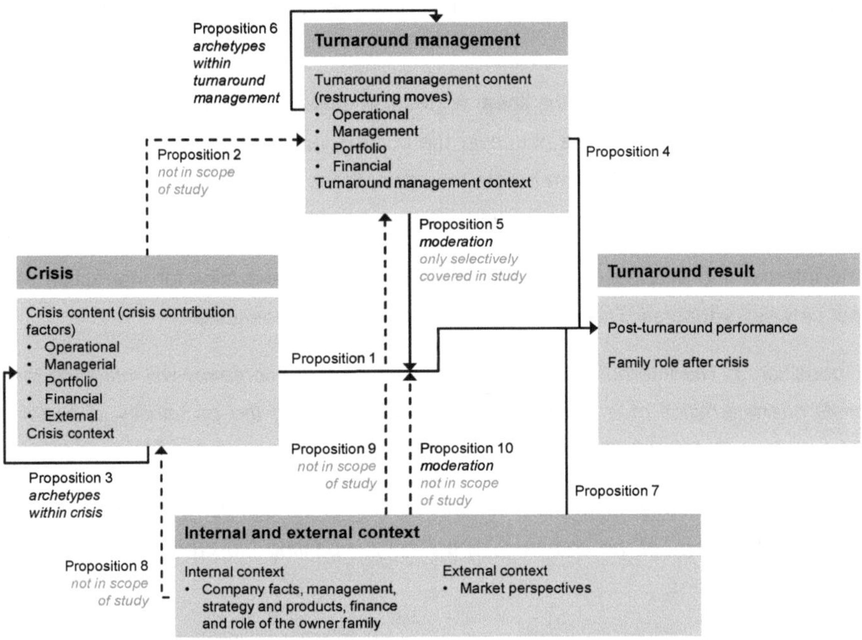

Figure 24: Conceptual model structure – context propositions.
Source: Own illustration.

4.7 Model of the turnaround result – owner family perspective

From the company's perspective, the result of turnaround management is discussed in section 4.3. As family firms are defined by the relation between family and company, the turnaround can – apart from its impact on the company – have an effect on the role and function of the family for the company after the crisis (see chapter 8).

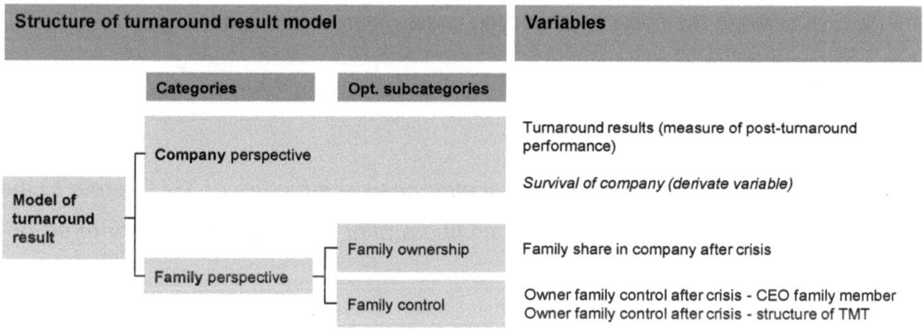

Figure 25: Model of the turnaround result.
Source: Own illustration.

To reflect these changes three of the internal context variables defining the family role in the company (see section 4.6.1.5) are also evaluated after turnaround. These are:

- *Ownership* in the company (one variable), i.e., how many shares does the company still hold in the company after the crisis.
- *Control* of the company (two variables), i.e., what is the operational influence of the family in the company after the crisis.

The result variable 'family share in the company after crisis' refers to the ownership share the founding family and their descendants hold in the company after the crisis. It ranges from

- *0% to*
- *100%.*

The result variable 'owner family control after crisis – CEO is family member' refers to the CEO position in the company after the crisis. There are two options:

- *Yes*
- *No*

The result variable 'owner family control after crisis – structure of TMT' refers to the top management team (TMT) and its members after the crisis. There are three options:

- *only family members*
- *family and non-family members*
- *only non-family members*

The changes of these variables during the turnaround are part of the analysis conducted in chapter 8. That analysis is focused on the condition and circumstances leading to a loss in control and ownership of the family in the family firm. These variables are only part of the sampling process, if the company's turnaround does not fail. For failed turnarounds, this information would not be available to my data source – the banks' risk managers (see section 3.1.3).

4.8 Variable operationalization

As discussed in section 3.4, there is a significant difference between the variables employed by both Eichner (2010) and Sudarsanam and Lai (2001), the two empirical studies that provide an important foundation for this work, on the one hand and the variables employed by this work on the other hand. While both these studies relied on a binary approach to measure their variables (yes/no) for restructuring moves and context factors, my model uses scale variables.

For Eichner (2010), the decision for binary variables is consistent throughout the model as a whole. His modeling started with the definition of turnaround success as a binary variable, i.e., successful, if cash flow after four years is above the given crisis threshold, otherwise not. He then applied a similar logic using binary variables throughout all variables including restructuring moves and context variables.

Based on the literature research, for this study I decided to reflect the *'turnaround result'* using a scale variable (see section 3.4.1 and section 4.3) reflecting both failed turnaround and post-turnaround performance of the company. In my assessment, this allows a more meaningful measurement of the situation after turnaround. A similar approach has been chosen for all other model elements, thus integrating more information, not only by the number of variables in the conceptual model, but increasing the information content also for each variable:

- The crisis contribution factors address the relative importance of a crisis characteristic for the crisis as a whole. Thus, not only the presence of a factor is evaluated, but the individual contribution to the crisis.
- The restructuring moves are measured similarly. Each variable does not simply reflect whether a specific turnaround move is part of the turnaround strategy, but instead what its relevance for this strategy is. This allows a more differentiated analysis, based not only on their presence but also on their relative importance.
  To illustrate the advantage of this approach, I want to refer to the fact that nearly all turnaround strategies – as shown in the descriptive analysis of the empirical data in section 5.2 – include some level of layoff. But for the character of the turnaround management, it makes a difference if layoffs are the most relevant restructuring move as part of an asset-cutting strategy or a move with minor importance for the overall strategy to outsource a single production step.
- The context variables are similarly assessed on a scale level. For these variables, the respective scales differ based on the variable content (see section 4.4.6, 4.5.5 and 4.6 for the variable details and 5.2.1.1, 5.2.1.2 and 5.2.1.3 for the variable coding).

4.9 Summary

The conceptual model, as it is laid out in this chapter, aspires to implement all relevant variables of the crisis and turnaround process. These are selected following a bottom-up approach, integrating variables discussed by different research streams and authors in many different contexts. The discussions of these variables show diverse and often contradictory results of different studies for the same variables. The ongoing verification of this model with restructuring experts (see Appendix 1 – list of restructuring specialists) ensures that this model additionally reflects the actual real world situation adequately.

The analysis of this model with real world data in chapters 5 to 8 allows a better understanding of the relative importance of the different elements for the turnaround situation and their concurrence in specific archetypes (see Figure 26 for the graphical illustration of the model with all relevant propositions for this study).

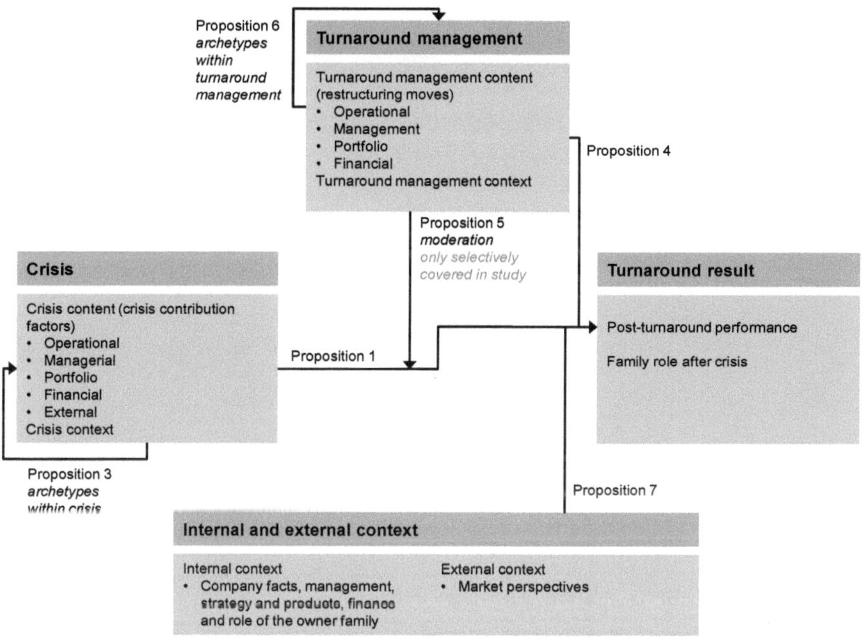

Figure 26: Conceptual model with relevant propositions for this study.
Source: Own illustration.

5 Sampling and descriptive results

The conceptual model developed in chapter 4 provided the basis for the sampling process conducted between October 2014 and February 2015. In this chapter, the details, including inherent limitations and restrictions of the sampling process, are discussed (section 5.1), preceding the descriptive data analysis (section 5.2.1 and 5.2.2), which is in turn followed by a limited model simplification, a result of the descriptive analysis (section 5.2.3).

5.1 Sample collection

As discussed in section 3.1, this study relies on banks' risk managers as a source of empirical information about failed and successful turnaround cases. It specifically relies on their professional experience with distressed companies from the turnaround plan to the turnaround result in order to analyze the crisis and turnaround process. To reiterate, the key reasons for choosing them as witnesses of the turnaround process (see section 3.1.3 for more details) are that bank risk managers:

- Only become involved after the crisis has manifested.
- Have access to the turnaround plan (detailing the crisis characteristics and the planned turnaround).
- Are continuously informed during the ongoing turnaround.
- Have no direct responsibility or influence on the company.

These characteristics, required by German regulations, allow reliance on their consistent applicability.

The following section describes the conduct of data collection during the sample stage of the study.

5.1.1 Key parameters of the sample collection process

A company's crisis – even if it has been successfully resolved – is not a topic that most companies want discussed in a scientific publication linked to their name. Additionally, bank secrecy and data protection laws in Germany forbid banks from publishing any information – including, but not limited to sensitive details about crisis and turnaround – to the public or any other non-bank employees. This influences the design of the conceptual model, and it also has implications for the sampling procedures.

To permit any bank and its employees (i.e., the risk managers) to participate in this study, anonymity is guaranteed on two levels:

- The anonymity of the bank's customers in distress (company assignability).
- The anonymity in respect to the link between cases and individual banks (bank assignability).

The anonymity of the companies themselves (company assignability) has to be guaranteed to ensure that the relevant regulations protecting the client-customer-relation would not be violated. Company assignability affects the study in two ways: in the design and content of the questionnaire, as well as in the process of the data collection.
At the same time, the anonymity of the banks (bank assignability) in respect to their cases is similarly important, not because of legal requirements, but as those responsible in the bank would object to the possibility of bank-to-bank benchmarking. Involuntarily releasing this information could lead to a possible backlash from three different sides: the bank's top management; regulation authorities, who could question the adequacy of the bank's risk management; and even from their customers.

The second challenge in the sampling procedure addresses how to motivate a bank and its employees to participate in this study. The knowledge gain for the participating banks was the key narrative in convincing them to spend the time and effort to support this study. Due to the inherent complexity of the turnaround situation and the characteristics of the conceptual model, the assessment of each case required approximately 30 minutes, excluding additional research in the bank's files. The German regulation authority BaFin (2012; p.11) specifies as an additional task that the risk management department responsible for the distressed cases "support the management in the implementation and advancement of the risk supervision and controlling processes" ("Unterstützung der Geschäftsleitung bei der Einrichtung und Weiterentwicklung der Risikosteuerungs- und -controllingprozesse"). Building upon this requirement, I was able to argue that insights gained into key parameters of the crisis and turnaround process as a result of this study are valuable to the banks in advancing their risk management procedures.

As this line of argument makes participation in the study a strategic decision, the contact to the banks had to be the heads of the bank's risk management department. The executive's involvement was also required to obtain a centralized approval for participation in the study. Formal and informal internal approval was required before the banks' risk managers were willing and able to submit any questionnaires – even anonymously – to the study. As a supporting factor, the active support of the head of risk management and his (in all cases, the department heads were male) internal promotion of the study to his employees was crucial to generate a significant number of contributions.

5.1.2 Operational conduct of the sampling process

To ensure the highest level of transparency possible, I provide a more detailed description of the operational conduct of the sampling process than is usually done in other empirical studies, especially since usual metrics, such as the response rate, cannot be provided due to the rigorous demand for anonymity.

The operational implementation of the sampling process was based on an online questionnaire (see Appendix 2 – questionnaire) hosted on the online survey platform Qualtrics (for detailed information please refer to www.qualtrics.com).

With each bank, a kick-off meeting with the relevant head of risk management served as the starting point of the sample collection process. Its key elements were a presentation of how the bank might benefit from the study, a detailed presentation of the questionnaire and the specifics of the sampling process.

The online questionnaire was accessed using a bank specific login code allowing multiple usages. According to the heads of risk management, a risk-manager-specific login would have decreased the response rate and the quality of responses due to concerns about anonymity on that level. The bank's anonymity was guaranteed; the cases were saved anonymously, allowing only for tracking the number of submitted cases per bank, so bank executives could review participation of their respective teams.

Supported and promoted by the head of risk management, all of the bank's risk managers were asked to submit actual crisis and turnaround cases from their professional experience, limited by the restrictions as defined in the conceptual model (see section 4.2.) The sampling period for each bank was limited to four to six weeks with continuous progress monitoring.

During the sampling period, the validity of the questionnaire was reconfirmed twofold. During the initial detailed discussions of the content of the questionnaire and all subsequent meetings with the heads of risk management, no concerns about misunderstandings or misleading questions could be identified. At the same time, the number of risk managers who contacted me during the sampling period for support with the questionnaire was limited to two cases.

To support the participation of the risk managers, additional incentives were used to promote the contribution of cases. For each case, there was a donation of EUR 10 to a good cause. Additionally, each risk manager was able sign up for his own copy of a consolidated result report.

5.1.3 Result of the sampling process

The sampling process was finished by February 2015. A total of 213 cases was submitted by the participating banks. Four cases are excluded, due to data inconsistencies and missing information, which results in a total number of 209 valid responses (Figure 27).

These responses are based on contributions from 22 banks and the German Savings Banks Association (the association directly distributed the questionnaire to their member banks). Based on the 2012 version of the list of the 100 largest German banks (Hirschmann, 2015), 9 of the 10 largest banks contributed to this study. Of these, Deutsche Bank, Commerzbank, DZ Bank and Postbank agreed to be mentioned by name – all of the other banks requested to remain anonymous. According to the Association of German Banks, the total balance sheet value of all German banks is EUR 8.3 trillion (Bethge, 2014; 2013 figures). The cumulative balance sheet of the participating banks is above 50% of this value.

The German banking system – unlike the banking systems of other countries – is built on three so-called pillars (Koetter, 2013):

- Commercial – privately-owned banks.
- Savings – owned by regional governments.
- Cooperative – owned by member-depositors.

In this study, all relevant pillars are represented: 5 (most of them very large) commercial banks, 14 savings banks and 3 cooperative banks (number is limited as these mostly small banks have centralized their management of distressed assets in dedicated institutions).

It is thus assumed that the study is representative of the German banking system and – indirectly – of the companies financed by banks experiencing crisis and turnaround.

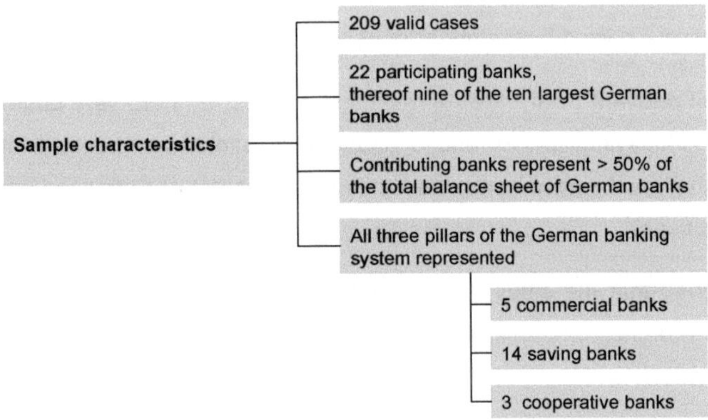

Figure 27: Sample characteristics.
Source: Own illustration.

5.2 Results

This section is dedicated to an initial assessment of the collected empirical data. The analysis of the data's descriptive characteristics provides the basis for the statistical data analysis using regression models (chapter 6 and 8) and clustering algorithms (chapter 7 and 8).

The assessment follows three sequential steps. The first step is the per-variable analysis and interpretation of the key descriptive statistics. The second step is the analysis of the relations between variables, i.e., the correlation matrix. The first two steps form the groundwork for the model simplification as the last step.

5.2.1 Descriptive statistics

The descriptive statistics are addressed separately, one subsection per model dimension, following the logic of the conceptual model.

Each subsection covers the following elements:

- Introduction of the coding scheme used to operationalize the variables.
- Presentation of the empirical descriptive results.
- Discussion of the descriptive results.

In a minority of empirical studies (one of the few doing this is Eichner, 2010), the descriptive statistics are discussed in the context of prior studies to assess and analyze commonalities and differences. In the case of this study, a comparison would not be meaningful for two key reasons: the deviating level of differentiation and the decision to use interval instead of binary variables.

- This study's conceptual model is designed to reflect the full complexity of the turnaround situation, and the approach thus differs from the partial and simplified models used by most other studies. This is especially apparent when comparing the level of differentiation used to describe the model dimensions, starting with the model of the crisis. This study uses 27 variables to characterize the crisis. It might be possible to compare it with the three-variable based characterization by Asquith and Gertner (1994) or the four-variable based characterization of Eichner (2010), but that would hardly be meaningful. The characterization scheme of Hauschildt et al. (2006) with 67 variables, aggregated to ten categories, which is used in his empirical evaluation, is structurally incompatible with the characterization applied by this study.
  For the model dimension of turnaround management, this study employs 28 variables compared to eight (Sudarsanam & Lai, 2001). Eichner (2010) on the other hand uses a slightly smaller number (23) of partly comparable variables. For the model of the internal and external context, there is to the best of my knowledge, no study using a similar number of variables.
- The second reason a comparison would not be meaningful is the decision to use interval instead of binary variables (see section 4.8) throughout the model. This allows a more nuanced analysis, especially for the '*turnaround result.*' Most other studies use binary variables for failed or successful turnaround and reflect this throughout their model, both to describe the crisis and the applica-

tion of restructuring moves (e.g., Asquith & Gertner, 1994; Eichner, 2010; Schmuck, 2013; Sudarsanam & Lai, 2001).

To illustrate, the comparison between the relative importance of a crisis contribution factor (e.g., with a mean of 3.46) with a binary variable stating a percentage value for a similar factor (e.g., with an occurrence rate of 67%) is not meaningful. In my assessment, using data transformation, e.g., mean split, to compare the two different kinds of variable would also not yield meaningful information due to the structural differences.

5.2.1.1 Crisis

As shown in Table 1, the coding of the individual crisis contribution factors is based on five-level Likert scales to characterize the impact on the development of the crisis. The three additional crisis context variables' coding is also based on a five-level Likert scale using a variable specific scale.

Variable	Remarks and coding
Each of the crisis contribution factors	Reflecting the relevance of each factor to the crisis of the company. Likert scale: From 1 = not relevant to 5 = highly relevant
Deterioration pattern of crisis	Likert scale: From 1 = sudden event to 5 = long-term decline
Severity of crisis	Likert scale: From 1 = less critical stage to 5 = highly critical stage
Initial complexity of company situation to implement turnaround	Likert scale: From 1 = simple to 5 = very complex

Table 1: Variable coding of the crisis variables.

The assessment of the crisis contribution factors and the crisis context variables are based on the descriptive statistics shown in Table 2.

Regarding the investment-related CCFs, *'incorrect investment in plant and equipment'* is more common (mean = 2.9; SD = 1.54) – although with a comparably high standard deviation – than *'insufficient investments in plant and equipment'* (mean = 1.96; SD = 1.23). Similarly for the internal value-add, here a too-high value-add (mean = 2.32; SD = 1.36) is also more common than a too-low value-add (mean = 1.6; SD = 0.88).

It seems that among the crisis companies in the sample, the companies that are too 'heavy,' i.e., have been investing too much in the wrong items and have an overly high internal value-add, are more common than companies that are too 'slim,' not investing enough with an overly-low internal value-add.

Regarding the organizational and process-related CCFs, the item of *'ineffective financial controlling'* is the most relevant of all CCFs in the model (mean = 4.24; SD = 1.05) and has a standard deviation on the low end of the spectrum. Nearly as highly relevant as, but slightly less frequent, are the other three process- and policy-related characteristics: *'weak cost management'* (mean = 3.9; SD = 1.04), *'ineffective/ inefficient organization'* (mean = 3.84; SD = 1.10) and *'insufficient strategy process'* (mean = 3.53; SD = 1.26).

It can be concluded that the average company crisis is consistently and strongly promoted by organizational and process weaknesses, with particular focus on the financial process capabilities.

The managerial contributions from the CCF *'unsuitable CEO'* (mean = 3.70; SD = 1.26) and the CCF *'unsuitable members of the TMT'* (mean = 3.38; SD = 1.21) both show a high relevance with emphasis on the CEO role. By comparison, the family-related crisis contribution factors show a lower relevance, both for *'conflict spillover from owner family to company'* (mean = 2.06; SD = 1.41) and *'succession problems'* (mean = 2.22; SD = 1.48).

When considering only companies with any family ownership (N = 178), the respective means increase only slightly, for *'conflict spillover from owner family'* to company' to 2.24 and for *'succession problems'* to 2.43 (information is not included in Table 2). For family firms, the succession, which commonly involves operational management, seems to play a more important role in the crisis development than the indirect effects of conflicts originating in the owning family.

Regarding the portfolio-related CCFs, the *'incorrect market assessment'* plays a dominant role (mean = 3.46; SD = 1.30), followed by *'overexpansion'* (mean = 2.76;

SD = 1.45) and *'insufficient quality and service'* (mean = 2.41; SD = 1.29). The lowest frequencies in this category are found for *'non-beneficial acquisitions'* (mean = 2.17; SD = 1.56) and *'missing innovation in core products'* (mean = 2.14; SD = 1.25). *'Non-beneficial acquisitions,'* displaying one of the highest standard deviations of all variables, indicates that this variable, while showing little relevance on average, is a high crisis contributor for some cases.

Among the portfolio-related CCFs, the incorrect perception of the market is on average more relevant than the CCFs describing actual portfolio issues.

Regarding the three financial CCFs, the factor *'overleveraging'* seems to be the predominant item (mean = 3.63; SD = 1.32), followed by *'financing structure inadequate'* (mean = 2.95; SD = 1.45). The last factor in this group, *'cash flow to shareholders too high,'* has a much lower average relevance (mean = 2.24; SD = 1.31).

It can be concluded that too much debt is much more critical for crisis development than the structure of financing or the cash flow to shareholders.

Concerning the external CCFs, the *'customer induced crisis' plays* the most important role (mean = 3.47; SD = 1.26) in crisis development, followed by *'increased competition'* (mean = 3.16; SD = 1.31) and *'market decline'* (mean = 2.85; SD = 1.50), while the role of the suppliers, reflected by the CCF *'supply-side induced crisis'* (mean = 2.35; SD = 1.21) is by comparison less important.

The average *'deterioration pattern of crisis'* (mean = 2.94; SD = 1.43) is very close to the middle of the respective five-level Likert scale (middle of scale = 3.00). At the same time, it shows a comparably high standard deviation indicating the existence of different deterioration patterns in the sample; it seems both theoretical scenarios ('sudden crisis' and 'long-term decline') occur.

At the same time, the variable *'severity of crisis'* (mean = 4.08; SD = 0.96) indicates that most cases are in a very severe crisis state when the turnaround begins. This is supported by the comparably low standard deviation of this variable, a finding that matches the content of the crisis stage models (see section 3.2.1), as the study is, per se, limited to crises that have already progressed to the severe stage of liquidity crisis (see section 4.2). The mean of the variable *'initial complexity of company situa-*

tion to implement turnaround' is an indication of an on-average fairly complex situation (mean = 3.58; SD = 1.12).

In summary, the assessment of the properties of the crisis variables shows that the three most frequent CCFs all stem from the process- and policy-related operational CCFs; these are *'ineffective financial controlling,' 'weak cost management'* and *'ineffective/ inefficient organization.'*

The three variables with the highest standard deviation and thus the highest differentiating properties are much more diverse: *'Non-beneficial acquisitions,' 'incorrect investment in plant and equipment'* and *'market decline.'* This finding is consistent with the content of these variables. As they have all a yes/no characteristic, it seems that these factors are either present and thus play an important role in the crisis or they are not present at all.

Variable	Mean	Median	SD
Operational crisis contribution factors			
Incorrect investment in plant and equipment	2.90	3	1.54
Insufficient investments in plant and equipment	1.96	1	1.23
Degree of company-internal value-add too high	2.32	2	1.36
Degree of company-internal value-add too low	1.60	1	0.88
Ineffective/ inefficient organization	3.84	4	1.10
Insufficient strategy process	3.53	4	1.26
Ineffective financial controlling	4.24	5	1.05
Weak cost management	3.90	4	1.04
Managerial crisis contribution factors			
Unsuitable CEO	3.70	4	1.26
Unsuitable members of TMT	3.38	4	1.21
Conflict spillover from owner family to company	2.06	1	1.41
Succession problems	2.22	1	1.48
Portfolio crisis contribution factors			
Incorrect market assessment	3.46	4	1.30
Overexpansion	2.76	3	1.45
Missing innovation in core products	2.14	2	1.25
Insufficient quality and service	2.41	2	1.29
Non-beneficial acquisitions	2.17	1	1.56
Financial crisis contribution factors			
Financing structure inadequate	2.95	3	1.45
Cash flow to shareholders too high	2.24	2	1.31
Overleveraging	3.63	4	1.32
External crisis contribution factors			
Market decline	2.85	3	1.50
Increased competition	3.16	3	1.31
Supply side induced crisis	2.35	2	1.21
Customer induced crisis	3.47	4	1.26
Crisis context			
Deterioration pattern of crisis	2.94	3	1.43
Severity of crisis	4.08	4	0.96
Initial complexity of company situation to implement turnaround	3.58	4	1.12

Table 2: Descriptive statistics of the crisis variables.

N = 209.

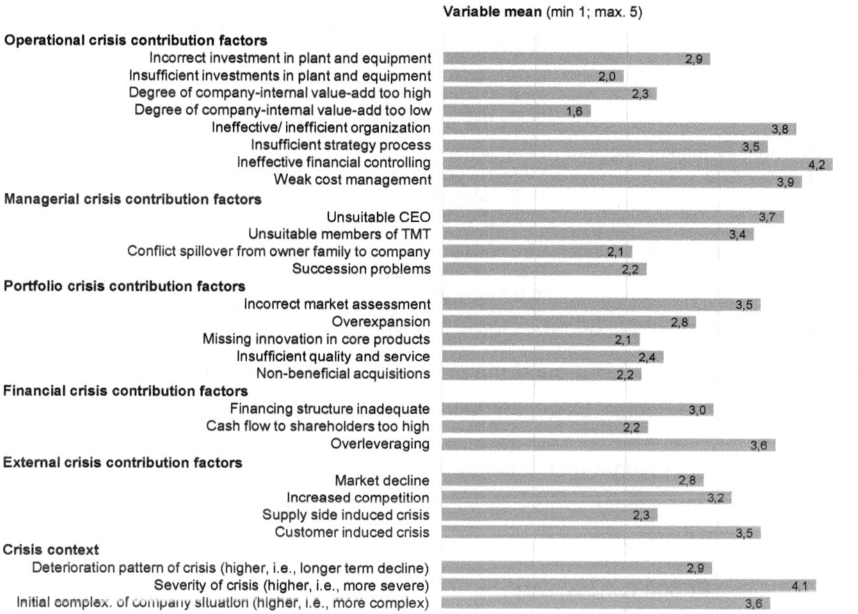

Figure 28: Mean comparison for crisis characteristics.

Source: Own illustration.

5.2.1.2 Turnaround management

The coding for the turnaround management variables (Table 3) is very similar to the crisis variables (Table 1). The relevance of the restructuring moves for the turnaround strategy of the company are reflected in a five-level Likert scale, from '1' reflecting the absence of any relevance to '5' reflecting a high relevance of that specific restructuring move for the strategy.

The two variables describing the turnaround management context are also coded based on a five-level Likert scale. In both cases, the scale reflects the 'quality' of the variable from the lowest/ worst value to the highest/best value.

Variable	Remarks and coding
Each of the restructuring moves	Reflecting the relevance of each restructuring move for the turnaround of the company. Likert scale: From 1 = not relevant to 5 = highly relevant
Development of market segment during turnaround	Likert scale: From 1 = contraction by 3 = stagnation to 5 = growth
Stakeholder management during turnaround	Likert scale: From 1 = very poor to 5 = very good

Table 3: Variable coding of the turnaround management variables.

The discussion of the turnaround management variables is conducted in a similar way to the crisis variables, based on their respective mean and standard deviation.

Among the 11 operational restructuring moves, four show a comparably high mean with low standard deviation: *'Process improvement and redesign'* (mean = 4.07; SD = 1.01), *'purchasing and cost reduction initiatives'* (mean = 3.93; SD = 1.01); *'productivity increase'* (mean = 3.76; SD = 1.19), and *'pricing and sales initiatives'* (mean = 3.72; SD = 1.07).

This indicates that policy measures and process changes are often and consistently implemented as part of a turnaround strategy.

Sorted by their means, these are followed by a second class of two measures with lower means and higher standard deviations: *'Layoff'* (mean = 3.43; SD = 1.28) and *'employee concessions* '(mean = 3.23; SD = 1.32). Following this logic, the next set of operational moves is on average less relevant, but with even higher standard deviation: *'Capacity reduction'* (mean = 2.78; SD = 1.49), *'decrease CAPEX'* (mean = 2.78; SD = 1.49) and *'outsourcing'* (mean = 2.11; SD = 1.32). The remaining two operational restructuring moves seem to be consistently seldom applied: *'Increase CAPEX'* (mean = 1.92; SD = 1.18) and *'insourcing'* (mean = 1.72; SD = 1.04).

The conclusion is a diverse picture of operational restructuring: Process and policy measures are almost always addressed, usually supplemented by human resource cost reductions and selectively enhanced by defensive retrenchment actions like reduced capacity and outsourcing.

Among the managerial restructuring moves the *'CEO change'* (mean = 3.11; SD = 1.71) has a lower average relevance than *'change in TMT'* (mean = 3.70; SD = 1.37), but *'CEO change'* is at the same time the restructuring move with the highest standard deviation in the model.

This finding is in line with the expectations, as the change of a CEO is a differentiating factor. Either it is not done at all and thus of no relevance for the turnaround, or, if there is a change, it has a high significance for the turnaround.

The restructuring move *'external management support'* (mean = 4.44; SD = 0.91) has the highest mean of all variables combined with one of the lowest standard deviations. It appears that external management support is nearly always involved in turnaround. This leads to the decision to exclude this variable from further analyses in my statistical models, due to its limited information content (see section 5.2.3).

In the portfolio restructuring, three of the four restructuring moves share similar descriptive parameters. These are *'asset divestments (company division or subsidiary)'* (mean = 2.34; SD = 1.60), *'termination of products lines/ markets'* (mean = 2.80; SD = 1.49) and *'new products/ markets development'* (mean = 2.93; SD = 1.39). All these variables show a mid-range mean (compared with all other restructuring moves), but a comparably high standard deviation. This suggests that these moves are selectively employed, depending on the companies' situation.

The restructuring move *'acquisitions'* (mean = 1.31; SD = 0.85) is very different. It has the lowest mean of all restructuring moves and also a low standard deviation. Thus it does not appear to be a relevant move in virtually any turnaround strategies. Consequently, this variable is also omitted in the statistical analyses (details see section 5.2.3).

The financial restructuring moves show a more diverse picture. On the one hand *'working capital reduction'* (mean = 3.64; SD = 1.10) seems to be employed in consistently in most restructuring cases. In this respect the financial restructuring is similar to the – also in the operational implementation similar – process- and policy-related operational restructuring moves.

The next group of measures combines a high-range mean with a high standard deviation. *'Liquidity contribution by shareholder'* (mean = 3.27; SD = 1.61), *'additional restructuring loan granted by lenders'* (mean = 3.25; SD = 1.58), *'securities contribution by shareholder'* (mean = 3.04; SD = 1.55) seem to be frequently, but selectively, employed in turnaround situations. This makes sense, as they all address the main issue of crisis companies – liquidity shortage. It seems that the fitting instrument to address the liquidity issues is selectively chosen depending on the cases' properties.

'Reduction of cash flow to shareholder' (mean = 2.78; SD = 1.47), *'extension, conversion or deferral of existing debt'* (mean = 2.66; SD = 1.35) and *'repayment of debt'* (mean = 2.43; SD = 1.46) have a medium mean, again with a high standard deviation, which does fit the content of the measures, as these require certain preconditions to be implemented.

The last item, which is the restructuring move of last resort from the banks' perspective, '*debt write-off or debt-to-equity-swap*' (mean = 1.86; SD = 1.48) has fittingly one of the lowest means of all restructuring moves.

The turnaround context sheds more information on the setting of the turnaround situation. The *'development of market segment during turnaround'* (mean = 2.95; SD = 1.09) is on average only slightly below the stagnation case (stagnation = 3.00), while the *'stakeholder management during turnaround'* (mean = 3.29; SD = 1.14) is assessed rather positively.

I want to close the discussion of the descriptive statistics of the turnaround management variables similarly to that of the CCF in the section before, by highlighting the three most relevant restructuring moves. These are *'external management support,' 'process improvement and redesign'* and *'purchasing and cost-reduction initiatives.'* The first one appears to be a requirement in bank-driven turnaround (see 5.2.3). The second and the third are consistent with the most relevant CCFs. It seems logical that as process issues commonly contribute to crisis (see section 5.2.1.1) that the countering restructuring moves are similarly relevant.

The most differentiating restructuring moves in terms of the respective standard deviations are '*CEO change*,' '*liquidity contribution by shareholder*' and '*asset divest-*

ments (company division or subsidiary).' The first one is quite intuitive, as it reflects the important decision of whether or not to change the head of the company. The second depends on a very specific precondition of the shareholder setting. A shareholder, who is willing and able to support the company during a crisis, will be of high relevancy for the turnaround. Asset divestment – as retrenchment moves for the most serious crises (compare e.g., Pearce & Robbins, 1993) – seems to be an infrequent but highly differentiating decision for a company in distress.

Variable	Mean	Median	SD
Operational restructuring moves			
Layoff	3.43	4	1.28
Employee concessions	3.23	4	1.32
Increase CAPEX	1.92	1	1.18
Decrease CAPEX	2.26	2	1.34
Capacity reduction	2.78	3	1.49
Productivity increase	3.76	4	1.19
Outsourcing	2.11	2	1.32
Insourcing	1.72	1	1.04
Process improvement and redesign	4.07	4	1.01
Pricing and sales initiatives	3.72	4	1.07
Purchasing and cost reduction initiatives	3.93	4	1.01
Managerial restructuring moves			
CEO change	3.11	4	1.71
Change in TMT	3.70	4	1.37
External management support	4.44	5	0.91
Portfolio restructuring moves			
Asset divestments (company division or subsidiary)	2.34	1	1.60
Acquisitions	1.31	1	0.85
Termination of products lines/ markets	2.80	3	1.49
New products/ markets development	2.93	3	1.39
Financial restructuring moves			
Working capital reduction	3.64	4	1.10
Reduction of cash flow to shareholder	2.78	3	1.47
Liquidity contribution by shareholder	3.27	4	1.61
Additional restructuring loan granted by lenders	3.25	4	1.58
Securities contribution by shareholder	3.04	3	1.55
Repayment of debt	2.43	2	1.46
Extension, conversion or deferral of existing debt	2.66	3	1.35
Debt write-off or debt-to-equity-swap	1.86	1	1.48
Turnaround context			
Development of market segment during turnaround	2.95	3	1.09
Stakeholder management during turnaround	3.29	4	1.14

Table 4: Descriptive statistics of the turnaround management variables.

N = 209.

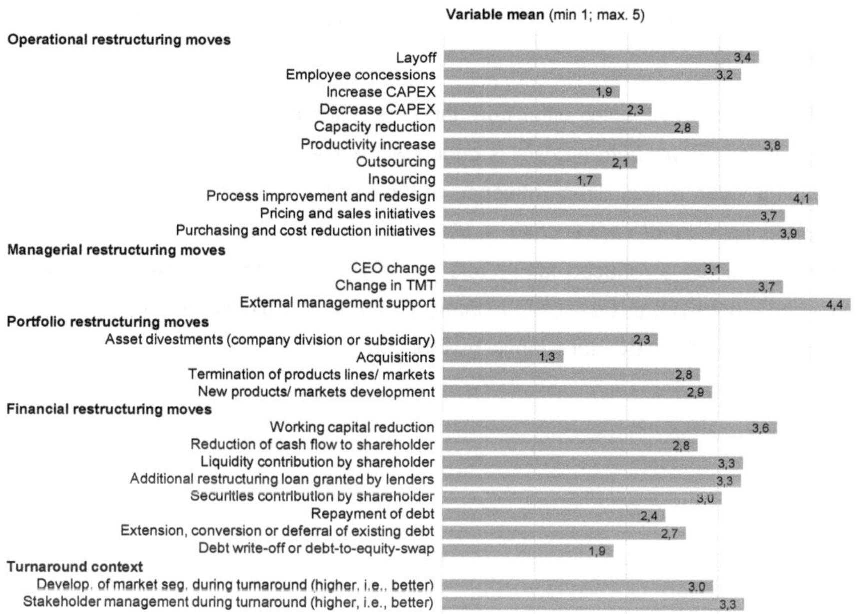

Figure 29: Mean comparison for turnaround management.

Source: Own illustration.

5.2.1.3 Internal and external context

The variable coding of the internal and external context is more diverse than that for the crisis and turnaround management variables. The context variables *'company size (turnover) before crisis,' 'share of biggest shareholder before crisis,' 'CEOs time with the company before crisis,' 'pre-crisis profitability,' 'family share in the company before crisis'* and *'owner family generation before crisis (majority of shares)'* are coded in intervals; in each case, an increasing in the respective variable is reflected by increasing coding values. The numbers of the intervals and thus the maximum values differ for each variable.

'Primary strategy before crisis' was collected as a categorical variable, which is converted into three binary variables for each of the possible strategies to allow statistical analysis. The variables *'slack resources before crisis,' 'lender security situation*

before crisis,' 'equity ratio before crisis' and *'long-term growth perspectives of market segment'* are coded with five-level Likert scales, each of the variables increasing with the code value.

The family control variables differ from the other variables. The *'role of owner family in supervisory board before crisis'* is coded with values from 2 to 5 – reflecting with increasing value a less direct influence of the family on the company. Similarly for *'owner family control before crisis – structure of TMT,'* coded from 1 to 3, higher numbers indicate a reduced family role in the top management team. The *'owner family control before crisis – CEO is family member'* is a binary variable (1 = CEO is family member; 2 = CEO not a family member).

Variable	Remarks and coding
Company size (turnover) before crisis	Values increasing with size. 1 = EUR 10m – EUR 50m 2 = EUR 50m – EUR 150m 3 = EUR 150m – EUR 500m
Share of biggest shareholder before crisis	Values increasing with family share. 2 = below 25% 3 = 25% – 49% 4 = 50% – 74% 5 = 75% and higher
CEOs time with the company before crisis	Values decreasing with longer time with the company. 1 = >15 years 2 = 5 – 15 years 3 = 1 – 4 years 4 = less than 1 year
For each of the three different possible primary strategies before crisis	Binary variable: 0 = not applicable 1 = applicable
Slack resources before crisis	Likert scale: From 1 = lean organization – no slack by 3 = normal organization – medium slack to 5 = inflated organization – high slack
Lender security situation before crisis	Likert scale: From 1 = very poor to 5 = very good
Equity ratio before crisis	Likert scale: From 1 = insufficient to 5 = very high
Pre-crisis profitability	Values increasing with higher profitability. 1 = minor <5% 2 = medium 5%-10% 3 = high >10%
Family share in the company before crisis	Values increasing with higher family share. 1 = no family share 2 = below 25% 3 = 25% – 49% 4 = 50% – 74% 5 = 75% and higher
Role of owner family in supervisory board before crisis	Values increasing with more external control in supervisory board. 2 = no supervisory board 3 = only family members in supervisory board 4 = family and non-family in supervisory board 5 = only non-family in supervisory board
Owner family control before crisis – CEO is family member	1 = yes 2 = no

Variable	Remarks and coding
Owner family control before crisis – structure of TMT	Values increasing with more external control in management. 1 = only family members 2 = family and non-family members 3 = only non-family members
Owner family generation before crisis (majority of shares)	Values increasing with generations. 2 = founder generation 3 = 2nd generation 4 = 3rd and later generation
Long-term growth perspectives of market segment	Likert scale: From 1 = contraction by 3 = stagnation to 5 = growth

Table 5: Variable coding of the context variables.

The context variables characterize the composition of the sample. They allow assessing the characteristics of the firms, which are part of this analysis.

The *'company size (turnover) before crisis'* (mean = 1.85; SD = 0.84) reflects the fact that 44% of the companies have a turnaround above EUR 10m and below EUR 50m, 27% are between EUR 50m and EUR 150m and 29% have a turnover above EUR 150m and below EUR 500m. The *'share of biggest shareholder before crisis'* (mean = 4.28; SD = 0.95) is differently distributed. While blockholders holding 75% and above account for 57% of the sample blockholders, those holding below 25% are only 6% of the sample, thus showing a strong tendency toward companies with large blockholders. The *'CEOs time with the company before crisis'* (mean = 1.87; SD = 0.79) shows a strong tendency to long-term CEOs (37% above 15 years and 42% between 5 and 15 years).

The *'primary strategy before crisis'* is very unevenly distributed. While '*quality leadership*' and '*innovation leadership*' account for 34% respectively, 23% of the sample, '*low-cost leadership*' was only selected 5% of the time. Due to its limited applicability this strategy variable is omitted in the further statistical analysis (see details in section 5.2.3). The remaining 38% of the sample had no clear primary strategy.

'Slack resources before crisis' (mean = 3.51; SD = 0.92) are assessed to be slightly above the 'normal' level for the selected companies. It seems that a reduction of slack before the turnaround management either did not take place or was inadequately executed. The average *'lender security situation before crisis'* (mean = 2.69;

SD = 1.02) is below average. The *'equity ratio before crisis'* of the company (mean = 2.42; SD = 1.09) is assessed to be even worse, thus indicating the inadequacy of the equity situation for the business model of the company. Similarly, the *'pre-crisis profitability'* (mean = 1.43; SD = 0.60) for 63% of the sample is below 5%, while only 6% reach a level above 10%.

Among the family-related context variables, only the *'family share in the company before crisis'* (mean = 4.22; SD = 1.48) can be assessed for the full sample. In 75% of the companies in the sample the family ownership is above 75%. Of the remaining companies, 15% are without a family shareholder, and 10% have a family shareholder holding between 1% and 74%. The high number of family firms in the sample is in line with the high proportion of family firms in the total economy, as discussed in section 2.4.

As conceptually defined, the remaining family-related context variables only apply for firms with family ownership (N = 178 instead of before N = 209).

The context variable *'role of owner family in supervisory board before crisis'* (mean = 2.92; SD = 1.06) shows an unequal distribution, while 46% of the firms with any family ownership have no supervisory board, 26% of the firms have a mixed supervisory board – family and externals – installed. Only family and only external supervisory boards are, with 8% respectively 6%, rather infrequently found.

The distribution of the variable *'owner family control before crisis – CEO is family member'* (mean = 1.13; SD = 0.34) is even more uneven. A vast majority of 87% of the companies with family ownership in the sample does employ a family CEO. With a similar tendency, but less uneven is the distribution of *'owner family control before crisis – structure of TMT'* (mean = 1.57; SD = 0.68). The TMT before the crisis consists, for 46% of the firms, only of family members and for 31%, of 'mixed' teams. TMTs with exclusively external members are only found in a minority of 9% of the companies.

The *'owner family generation before crisis (majority of shares)'* (mean = 2.84; SD = 0.80) is almost evenly distributed. Of all companies with family ownership, these held by first generation owners account for 35%, second-generation owners for 29% and third- and later generation owners for 21%.

The last of the contextual variables *'long-term growth perspectives of market segment'* (mean = 3.15; SD = 1.08) is again applicable for the full sample (N = 209). It shows an above stagnation and thus on average and optimistic view for the growth perspective of the relevant market segment.

Variable	Mean	Median	SD
Internal context			
The following internal context variables do apply for the complete sample (N = 209)			
Company size (turnover) before crisis	1.85	2	0.84
Share of biggest shareholder before crisis	4.28	5	0.95
CEOs time with the company before crisis	1.87	2	0.79
Primary strategy before crisis – quality leadership	0.34	0	0.47
Primary strategy before crisis – innovation leadership	0.23	0	0.42
Primary strategy before crisis – low-cost leadership	0.05	0	0.22
Slack resources before crisis	3.51	3	0.92
Lender security situation before crisis	2.69	3	1.02
Equity ratio before crisis	2.42	2	1.09
Pre-crisis profitability	1.43	1	0.60
Family share in the company before crisis	4.22	5	1.48
The following context variables do only apply for cases with family ownership before the crisis (N = 178)			
Role of owner family in supervisory board before crisis	2.92	2	1.06
Owner family control before crisis – CEO is family member	1.13	1	0.34
Owner family control before crisis – structure of TMT	1.57	1	0.68
Owner family generation before crisis (majority of shares)	2.84	3	0.80
External context			
The following external context variables do apply for the complete sample (N = 209)			
Long-term growth perspectives of market segment	3.15	3	1.08

Table 6: Descriptive statistics of the context variables.

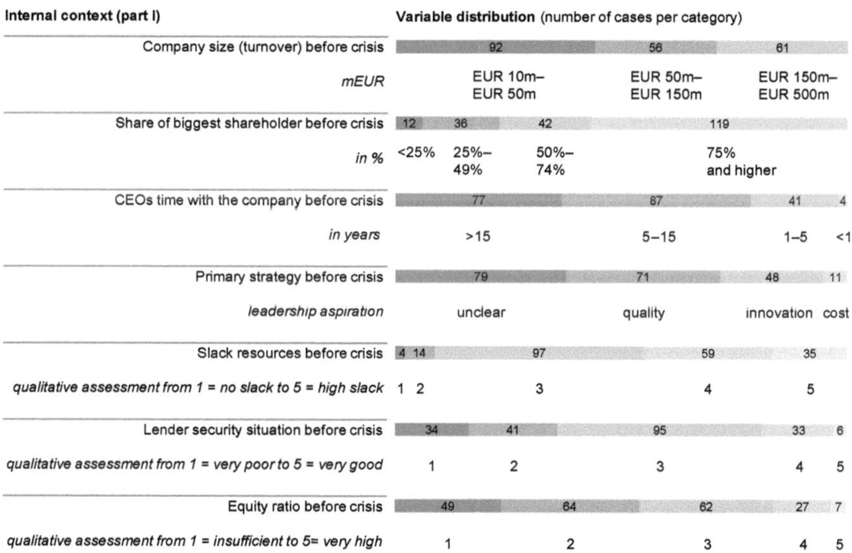

Figure 30: Distribution of context variables in sample – part I.

Source: Own illustration.

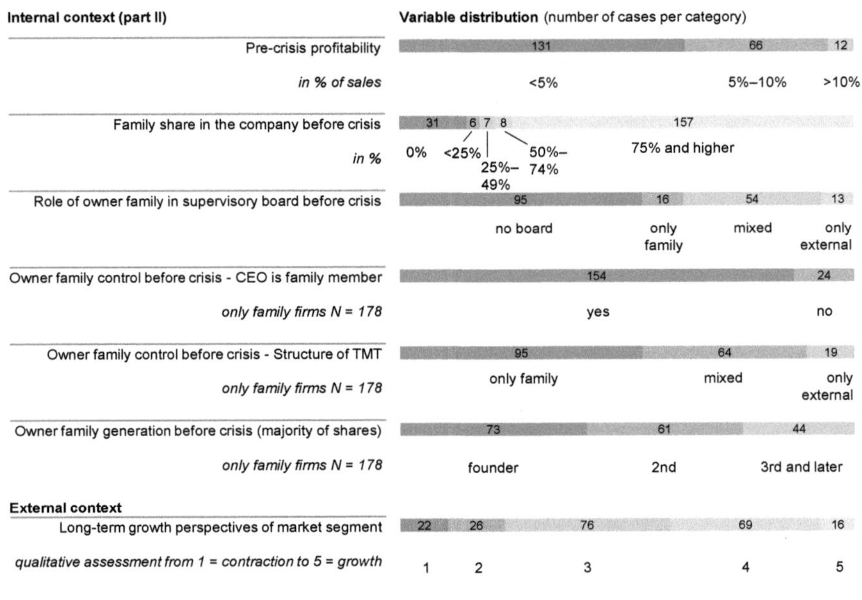

Figure 31: Distribution of context variables in sample – part II.

Source: Own illustration.

5.2.1.4 Turnaround result

The last element of the research model is the turnaround result dimension containing the fewest variables of all dimensions.

The main variable – sharing the name with the respective dimension –, *'turnaround result,'* is coded based on a five-level Likert scale. 1 indicates a failed turnaround case and 2 to 5 reflect the post-turnaround performance of the company increasing with the code value. The variable *'survival of company'* is an additional variable calculated from *'turnaround result.'* This binary variable reflects the survival of the company, takes a value of 1 for survival and 0 for the insolvency and thus per definition the failure of the company in question.

The family-specific variables *'family share in company after crisis,' 'owner family control after crisis – CEO is family member'* and *'owner family control after crisis – structure of TMT'* are coded identically to the respective context variables discussed in section 4.6.1.5.

Variable	Remarks and coding
Turnaround result	Reflecting post-turnaround performance and failed turnaround. Likert scale: From 1 = failed turnaround, i.e., insolvency to 5 = performance above pre-crisis level
Survival of company *(variable derived from turnaround result)*	Derivate of the turnaround result. 1 = survival of company (turnaround result ≥ 2) and 0 = failed turnaround (turnaround result = 1)
Family share in company after crisis	1 = no family shareholder 2 = below 25% 3 = 25%-49% 4 = 50%-74% 5 = 75% and higher
Owner family control after crisis – CEO is family member	1 = yes 2 = no
Owner family control after crisis – structure of TMT	1 = only family members 2 = family and non-family members 3 = only family members

Table 7: Variable coding of the turnaround result variables.

Different than the family-related turnaround result variables the variable *'turnaround result'* (mean = 2.88; SD = 1.66) is common for all cases in the sample. It shows a slightly below average mean with a high standard deviation. The variable *'survival of company'* (mean = 0.61; SD = 0.49) reflects the fact that 61% of the companies in this study did not file for insolvency and thus – per definition – survived the crisis.

As binary variable, it is possible to compare this number with other studies using binary definitions. The recovery rate found by Eichner (2010): 63%, by Sudarsanam and Lai (2001): 57%, by Buschmann (2006; if considering for comparability all cases with positive result after turnaround): 61% and by Jostarndt (2007; if considering all firms acquired or successfully restructured): 72% are all in a similar range, despite different selection approaches, research focus and regions.

The family-specific result variables are only applicable for the subset of the sample with family ownership. In addition, analysis is only possible for companies that did not file for insolvency, as the banks' risk managers usually transfer insolvency cases to specialized departments. Consequently, information about ownership and control in the company after insolvency are usually not available via this source and were thus not part of the questionnaire for insolvency cases (N = 113).

The *'family share in company after crisis'* (mean = 3.84; SD = 1.57) is on average significantly smaller (significance test conducted in chapter 8) than the variable *'family share in the company before crisis'* (mean = 4.22; SD = 1.88).

A similar picture emerges for the variables related to family control after the crisis: *'Owner family control after crisis – CEO is family member'* (mean = 1.44; SD = 0.50) and *'owner family control after crisis – structure of TMT'* (mean = 2.11; SD = 0.76). Both are also significantly lower than the respective variables before the crisis.

To gain a better understanding of the underlying mechanics, a detailed analysis of family control and family share development during turnaround is shown in chapter 8.

Variable	Mean	Median	SD
Company perspective			
The company perspective turnaround result variables apply for the complete sample (N = 209)			
Turnaround result	2.88	3	1.66
Survival of company	0.61	1	0.49
Owner family perspective			
The family perspective turnaround result variables only apply for the subset of companies, with both properties, surviving the crisis and having family ownership before the crisis (N = 113)			
Family share in company after crisis	3.84	5	1.57
Owner family control after crisis – CEO is family member	1.44	1	0.50
Owner family control after crisis – structure of TMT	2.11	2	0.76

Table 8: Descriptive statistics of the turnaround result variables.

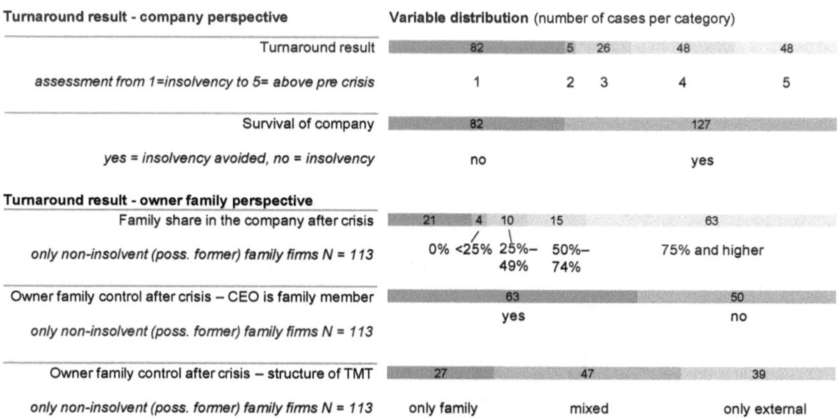

Figure 32: Distribution of the result variables in sample.

Source: Own illustration.

5.2.2 Correlations

The Pearson correlation coefficient is a measure to describe the linear relation between two variables. With respect to the conceptual model, such relations between variables are to be expected, as it is, for example, anticipated that restructuring moves depend on the crisis characteristics.

First variable	Second variable	Pearson correlation coefficient
Correlations between two crisis variables		
Ineffective/ inefficient organization	Insufficient strategy process	0.535
Insufficient strategy process	Unsuitable CEO	0.502
Ineffective financial controlling	Weak cost management	0.570
Weak cost management	Ineffective/ inefficient organization	0.548
Correlations between a crisis and a turnaround management variable		
Unsuitable CEO	CEO change	0.581
Unsuitable members of TMT	Change in TMT	0.514
Cash flow to shareholders too high	Reduction of cash flow to shareholder	0.505
Correlations between two turnaround management variables		
Layoff	Employee concessions	0.585
CEO change	Change in TMT	0.576
Correlations between a crisis and a context variable		
Initial complexity of company situation to implement turnaround	Company size (turnover) before crisis	0.518
Correlations between a turnaround management and a context variable		
Development of market segment during turnaround	Long-term growth perspectives of market segment	0.695
Correlation between two family firm-specific variables		
Owner family control before crisis – CEO is family member	Owner family control before crisis – structure of TMT	0.711
Owner family control before crisis – structure of TMT	Owner family control after crisis – structure of TMT	0.609
Family share in company after crisis	Owner family control after crisis – CEO is family member	-0.571
Family share in company after crisis	Owner family control after crisis – structure of TMT	-0.540
Owner family control after crisis – CEO is family member	Owner family control after crisis – structure of TMT	0.746

Table 9: Overview of moderate to high correlations.

Correlations between two variables with a Pearson correlation coefficient above 0.5 or below -0.5.

Since the presentation of the complete correlation matrix would require an extensive table of 71 by 71, the discussion here focuses on the analysis of all correlations with an absolute value of 0.5 and higher, thus indicating a moderate or high correlation (Field, 2013), as shown in Table 9. These relevant correlations are grouped with respect to the model dimension the pairs involve. The full correlation tables can be found in Appendix 3 – correlation tables.

Among crisis-related variables, correlations involve the three organization- and process-related crisis contribution factors and the policy-related crisis contribution factor. This can be explained with the content of these variables, as they all reflect process weaknesses. It seems that these variables indeed reflect a single underlying factor and should be consolidated into one crisis contribution factor. This option is evaluated in section 5.2.3 by performing a factor analysis.

While *'insufficient strategy process'* is also correlated to the *'unsuitable CEO,'* these two factors reflect fundamentally different content. Although an unsuitable CEO might be related to (and even causing) an 'insufficient strategy process,' a consolidation of these two factors with their very different respective content would not be in line with the model structure.

A moderate or high correlation between a crisis variable and a turnaround management variable indicates that the crisis variable is indeed influencing the chosen restructuring moves (A reverse direction of effect can be ruled out, as the crisis variables manifest in the chronological process before the turnaround management variables.). All three correlated pairs, *'unsuitable CEO'* correlating with *'CEO change,' 'unsuitable members of TMT'* correlating with *'change in TMT'* and *'cash flow to shareholders too high'* with *'reduction of cash flow to shareholder'* seem to be obvious problem-solution combinations. To further analyze the interactions between these variable pairs, they are part of the considered moderation effects, which are discussed in section 6.2.

The first of two moderately to highly correlated pairs of turnaround management variables is the combination of *'layoff'* and *'employee concessions.'* This correlation suggests that both measures are commonly combined in the course of an employee cost reduction strategy. As the differentiation between headcount reduction and cost per-head reduction is of interest for this study (both restructuring moves have different consequences for future strategic options), there is no consolidation of these two variables.

The second pair of turnaround management variables is *'CEO change'* and *'change in TMT.'* It is intuitive that changing the CEO often occurs in the context of additional top management team changes. Both of these moves have – from the restructuring-move perspective – a very different 'magnitude.' As with similar pairings, I do not consider an aggregation.

The correlation between the crisis variable *'initial complexity of company situation to implement turnaround'* and *'company size (turnover) before crisis'* can be explained by referring to the definition of the second variable. It is – among other factors – determined by the number of stakeholder and financing partners. The fact that larger firms have a more complex stakeholder structure and financing structure does make sense. A consolidation of these variables is – again due to the different informational content – not sensible.

Following the same logic, a consolidation of *'development of market segment during turnaround'* and *'long-term growth perspectives of market segment'* is not considered.

The relations between the family-specific variables are discussed and analyzed in chapter 8.

5.2.3 Model simplification

This section is dedicated to summarizing and extending the model simplifications, as already mentioned in the previous sections. The rationale for simplifying the data model is based on two key reasons: Elimination of redundant variables and reduction of model complexity.

The reduction of model complexity is achieved by the elimination of variables with little information contribution. These have been identified in the discussion of the descriptive statistics (section 5.2.1).

In a first step, the reduction of the model complexity increases the events per variable and consequently the statistical power of any statistical analysis conducted (see for more information section 6.1.2). The variables, which have been identified in the descriptive statistics section as redundant are eliminated. These are the restructuring moves *'external management support'* and *'acquisitions'* as well as the context variable *'primary strategy before crisis – low-cost leadership.'*

The second step is the elimination of redundant variables addressing the process- and policy-related CCFs (*'ineffective/ inefficient organization,' 'insufficient strategy process,' 'ineffective financial controlling'* and *'weak cost management'*), as these appear to be symptoms of one common underlying factor. The aggregation of these variables would serve two purposes:

- Further reduction of the complexity of the statistical model
- Reduction of the multicollinearity between individual variables (see detail in section 6.4.2)

To evaluate the aggregation of the four variables, a principal factor analysis is conducted with a fixed maximum of one factor. The Kaiser-Meyer-Olkin measure verified the sampling adequacy, with a KMO = 0.77. This can be interpreted as 'middling,' close to 'meritorious' according to Hutcheson and Sofroniou (1999). The reliability analysis confirms this Cronbach's $\alpha = 0.79$ (methodology adapted from Field, 2013). Consequently, the four variables are combined into one new variable for all further analyses:

Operational CCF – 'weaknesses in organization and processes' is the average of the three variables 'ineffective/ inefficient organization,' 'insufficient strategy process,' 'ineffective financial controlling' and 'weak cost management.' This CCF reflects the general state of the company's organization and processes in respect to their contribution to the crisis.

This chapter concludes the discussion of sampling process and descriptive statistics. Based on these fundamentals, the following chapters aim to analyze the collected data to achieve an improved understanding of the crisis and turnaround process.

6 Analysis of the turnaround performance

This chapter is dedicated to the core research question of this study (see section 1.2): "Which conditions enhance turnaround success?" With a broader scope than most other works (e.g., Buschmann, 2006; Eichner, 2010; Sudarsanam & Lai, 2001), I not only analyze if and how the chosen turnaround strategy impacts the '*turnaround result,*' but also integrate the effect of all aspects of turnaround management characteristics, crisis characteristics and context factors into the analysis.

This chapter has four main parts. The first part (section 6.1) discusses briefly the statistical methodology. The second part focuses on interaction effects in the model, i.e., how variables influence each other and what elements and assumptions can be and are integrated into this model (section 6.2). The third and largest part uses sequentially different statistical models and analyses to develop an understanding of the data und derive statistical results. These range from the univariate regression (section 6.3) to statistical models with different variable subsets and complexity (section 6.4 to 6.6). The fourth and last part (section 6.7) is dedicated to the discussion and interpretation of these results.

6.1 Statistical methodology

The fundamental approach of this study is to integrate the full complexity of the crisis and turnaround situation into a conceptual model as a basis for empirical data collection and statistical analysis. In doing this, variables in the model dimensions crisis, turnaround management and context are used as regressor variables (also called predictor or independent variables) for the dependent variable (also called outcome variable) *'turnaround result.'*

The complexity of the turnaround situation is reflected in the high number of regressor variables – even after the model simplification applied in section 5.2.3 – of which there are a total of 61. Adding the 13 moderating effects discussed in section 6.2, there are up to 74 variables. The data collection process provided us with a total of 209 cases. The rule of thumb calls for 10 to 15 (Field, 2013; Hair et al., 2010) events, i.e., cases, per variable; whether this rule of thumb is correct and applicable is discussed in section 6.1.2. The empirical data available in this study amounts to 3.4

events per variable if the moderating effects are not considered, and 2.9 events per variable including the moderating effects. This brings up a number of challenges and limitations, which need to be addressed by the statistical methodology:

- The statistical power of a straightforward linear regression with all variables (complete model) is limited by the number of events per variable (see section 6.1.2). There are two strategies and limitations related to this issue:
    - To overcome this limitation, I apply sequentially multiple statistical models and methods to analyze the data set, so the results will not only be based on the analysis of the complete model.

      Using this approach, it is possible to analyze the data from multiple perspectives and thus evaluate the consistency of the results, the magnitude of the calculated coefficients and their respective significance levels.
    - For the complete model itself, it has to be accepted that, as an approach inherent limitation, the detection strength (statistical power) of the analysis with all variables based on 209 cases suffices only to detect effects above a certain effect strength. This will be reflected in the comparison of the different approaches.
- A low number of events per variables can lead to overfitting issues, i.e., the resulting coefficients fit the specific data set and cannot be generalized for cases outside the data set. To avoid this issue, I validate each model using bootstrapping procedures (section 6.1.3).

6.1.1 Introduction of the statistical approaches

All statistical methods used are regression models. Regression models aim to explain the distribution of a dependent variable by one or more regressor variables (definition adapted from Fahrmeir et al., 2013). As explained, I want to use a redundant set of results from different models to cross check the respective findings. Consequently, I use sequentially different statistical models. These differ specifically in respect to complexity and variable selection. These are – in order of usage:

- *The univariate regression: As* the simplest approach, aims to explain a single dependent variable with a single regressor variable. Consequently, for each of the 61 regressor variables a univariate regression is performed. This approach is completed by the analysis of the selected 13 moderation effects (section 6.3).

- The next step is to analyze the *complete model* by using all relevant variables of the conceptual model, as well as the selected moderation effects as regressor variables (section 6.4).
- As an intermediate step, the congruence in the design of the crisis and the turnaround management models is used to analyze *partial models*, assuming that cause-effect relations exist predominantly between the similar elements of the partial models of crisis and turnaround management (section 6.5).
- In the last step, I use *simplified models* with selected variables, resulting from variable selection procedures to simplify the statistical model to a minimum number of variables (section 6.6).

The univariate regression analyzes the effect of one variable as a predictor on a second, the dependent variable. Due to the high number of cases (N = 209) and consequently the high EPV (also 209), the statistical power of this approach is able to detect even very small significant effects between the variable pairs. Due to the fact that this does not consider any of the other variables in the model, any changes of the dependent variable are attributed to the single regressor variable, ignoring the remaining variable context. This univariate analysis is a valid starting point (see e.g., Block, 2010; Eichner, 2010) to evaluate a single variable with a high statistical power while disregarding the context of this relation, i.e., the collective effect of all other variables.

The complete model – including moderation effects – is analyzed in the next step. To achieve this, five linear regression models are compiled, which include the different dimensions of the conceptual model sequentially, thus increasing the number of variables and decreasing the events per variable with each dimension added.

For the partial models, which are then analyzed, the variables of the related dimensions of the crisis and turnaround management models (e.g., operational CCFs and operational restructuring moves) are selected. In these partial models, all context variables are included as well. The model of this variable subset is based on the assumption that a turnaround strategy as the answer to the crisis has to correspond to the character of the crisis, e.g., an operational crisis requires operational measures (compare e.g., IDW, 2012).

The simplified models use variable selection procedures to select specific variable subsets. This is done with two procedures: Manual selection and automatic stepwise selection:

- *Manual selection* is based on the selection of all variables which show significant relations in either the complete or any of the four partial models, assuming that these are the variables contributing most to the explanation of the *'turnaround result.*
- *Automatic stepwise selection* is based on a common statistical procedure (Backhaus et al., 2011; Field, 2013; Hair et al., 2010). Regression variables are stepwise, i.e., sequentially selected or removed from the regression term. A variable is selected from a pool of possible variables if its contribution maximizes a specified criterion. A variable is removed again if it does not fulfill a second, possibly different criterion any more. Stepwise regression models are commonly used, but heavily criticized as the automatic variable selection tends to identify effects even for random data (Mundry & Nunn, 2009). This is why I use the stepwise regression model only in the context with all other models analyzed.

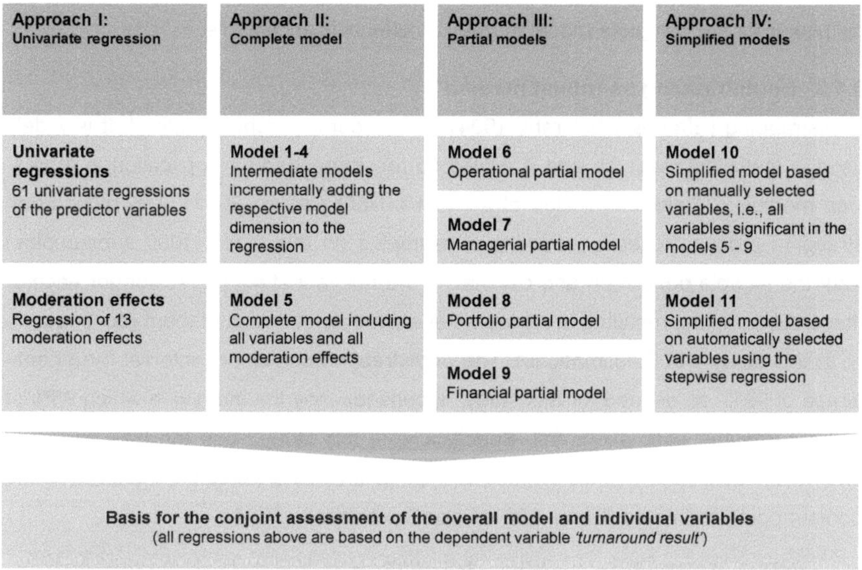

Figure 33: Overview of the statistical approaches in chapter 6.
Source: Own illustration.

6.1.2 Statistical power and sample size

The statistical power to detect effects in a regression is limited by the number of events per variable. The commonly discussed rule of thumb, asking for 10-15 events per variable, is still referred to in many statistical publications (Field, 2013; Hair et al., 2010). Fortunately, statistical analyses have shown that this rule of thumb needs to be refined. Specifically, it has been shown that the required events per variable decrease with the number of variables. It was found that to detect medium effects, i.e., $R^2 > 0.13$, the minimum sample size should be N = 104 + M, whereas N is the number of events and M is the number of regressor variables (Green, 1991; VanVoorhis & Morgan, 2007). Applying this to the maximum number of variables (complete model including moderating effects) in this study, M would be 74. Based on this formula, as N = 209 > 178 = 104 + M, it should be possible to detect effects even below the value of $R^2 = 0.13$ in the complete model.

As this study explicitly aims to generate an overview of all possible relations between the conceptual model variables and the '*turnaround result,*' a limitation of the statistical power for the complete model to medium effects is acceptable.

6.1.3 Bootstrapping as robust method

Bootstrapping (Efron & Tibshirani, 1994) is considered a robust method. It is widely used in statistical research and is a method recommended for application in regression modeling (Field, 2013; Hair et al., 2010; Núñez et al., 2011). The basic bootstrapping process relies on drawing subsamples (in this study, 1000 subsamples) from the sample population and calculating the relevant static regression for each of these subsamples, resulting in a parameter estimation for each of them (consequently, in this study, 1000 estimations). The bootstrapped confidence interval for a confidence of 95%, as defined for this study, is consequently the interval in which 95% of these parameter estimations fall. Specifically, in this study I use the bias corrected and accelerated (BCa) version of bootstrapping, which increases the accuracy of the bootstrapping estimates (Efron, 1987; Efron & Tibshirani, 1994).

A significant advantage of bootstrapping is the fact that it works even for data in which the normal distribution assumptions (e.g., concerning skewness and kurtosis) are not valid. Bootstrapping is especially helpful if overfitting issues must be addressed (Wright et al., 2011). Overfitting is, besides the limited statistical power (see section 6.1.2), the second major issue with a limited number of events per variable. It is related to the phenomenon that the statistical analysis detects significant effects and relations within data that are indeed only present in the sample. The regression parameters are then overfitted to the present sample with the consequence that the results unfortunately cannot be generalized to its parent population. Babyak (2004) illustrates the mitigating effects of bootstrapping on overfitting issues for the special case of psychosomatic research in the context of limited cases per predictor variable.

Consequently, all results in this chapter are based on bootstrapped linear regressions to improve the result quality.

6.2 Model of moderating effects

As per the assumption stated in *Proposition 5,* I assume a relation between the CCFs and the restructuring moves implemented to address them. It is uncontested in the literature that there is a relation between crisis characteristics and the chosen solution, i.e., turnaround strategy for a company. This relation is part of all turnaround phase models (e.g., Arogyaswamy et al., 1995; Faghfouri, 2013; Pearce & Robbins, 1993; Pearson & Clair, 1998; Smith & Graves, 2005; Trahms et al., 2013).

The uncontested assertion that turnaround moves are contingent upon the crisis characteristics is not an element of the statistical models in this chapter. Instead, the analysis addresses how the effect of the crisis contribution factor on the '*turnaround result*' is altered by the restructuring moves. That there is an interaction between the crisis and the turnaround management variables is the very reason why a restructuring move is implemented at all. Specifically, turnaround management is conducted to change the effect of the crisis on the '*turnaround result,*' as the crisis would otherwise lead to the company's failure.

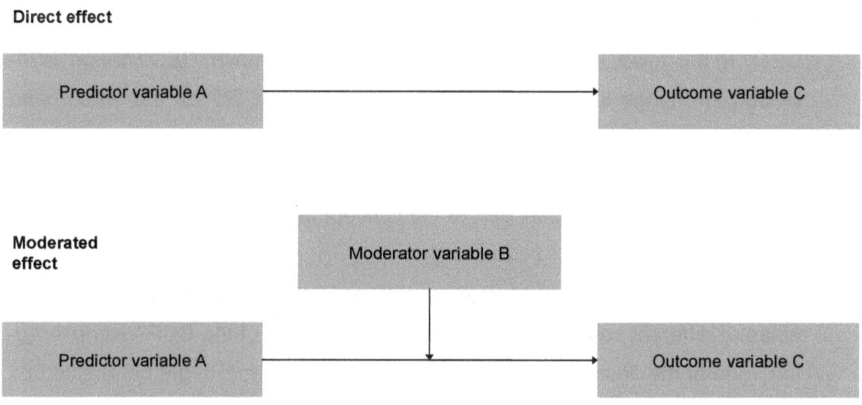

Figure 34: Moderation.

Source: Own illustration based on definition of moderation (Field, 2013; Hair et al., 2010).

Statistically, this interaction effect is defined as moderation. Moderation is defined by Hair et al. (2010):

"A moderation effect occurs when a third variable (. . .) changes the relationship between two related variables" (Hair et al., 2010; p. 770).

This describes precisely the intended effect a restructuring move should have on the relation between a CCF and the '*turnaround result,*' as a turnaround move aims to change the consequences of the crisis for the company.

For the purpose of this study, I differentiate four different levels of interaction effects; of these only the first level are addressed and analyzed in this study:

- *First level*

  Interaction effects with assumed direct cause-effect relation. These are interaction effects between variables from one specific category of restructuring moves (e.g., managerial restructuring moves) interacting with the effect of variables of the corresponding category of crisis contribution factors (e.g., managerial CCFs). One interaction – and a very obvious one – would be between the restructuring move '*CEO change*' and the effect of the CCF '*unsuitable CEO.*' In this case, it is evident that the restructuring move '*CEO change*' is intended to change the effect of the CCF *'unsuitable CEO'* on the *'turnaround result.'*

  This first group of interactions is a subcategory of the effects assumed in *Proposition 5,* introduced as part of the conceptual model in section 4.5.6.
- *Second level*

  Interaction effects between turnaround management variables and crisis variables of different categories. For example, the effect of the CCF '*overleveraging*' (one of the financial CCFs) on the '*turnaround result*' might be affected by the restructuring move '*decrease CAPEX*' (one of the operational restructuring moves).

  This second group of interactions is the second and concluding subcategory of the effects assumed in *Proposition 5,* introduced as part of the conceptual model in section 4.5.6. These interaction effects are not part of any analysis conducted in this chapter.

- *Third level*

  The context variables might influence the turnaround strategy as well as the crisis characteristics. For example, the effect of the restructuring move '*layoff*' on '*turnaround result*' might be affected by the context factor '*slack resources before the crisis.*'

  These interactions are discussed in the conceptual model as *propositions 8 and 9*. These are also not part of any analysis conducted in this chapter.

- *Fourth level*

  The context variables might influence the interaction between turnaround move and CCFs. For example, the '*long-term growth perspectives of market segment*' affects how the restructuring move '*asset divestments*' interacts with the crisis contribution factor '*overexpansion*' in its effect on '*turnaround result.*'

  This is discussed in the conceptual model as *Proposition 10*. Similar to all levels except the first, these are also not part of any analysis conducted in this chapter.

Limited by the empirical data and guided by the research questions of this study (see section 1.2), I focus on the first level of tangible interaction effects to limit the extent to which these inflate the number of variables, as well as to keep the results within a reasonable level of complexity.

This study aims to identify the role and importance of the elements of the crisis and turnaround situation on the turnaround success. An integration of all possible interactions between variables would overextend the model purpose and impede the explanatory power of the analysis, as any interaction effect would add additional variables and thus decrease the power to detect effects within the sample (see section 6.1.2).

Affected variable	Moderator
Operational CCF	*Operational restructuring move*
Incorrect investment in plant and equipment	Decrease CAPEX
Insufficient investments in plant and equipment	Increase CAPEX
Degree of company-internal value-add too high	Outsourcing
Degree of company-internal value-add too low	Insourcing
Weaknesses in organization and processes	Productivity increase
Weaknesses in organization and processes	Process improvement and redesign
Managerial CCF	*Managerial restructuring move*
Unsuitable CEO	CEO change
Unsuitable members of TMT	Change in TMT
Portfolio CCF	*Portfolio restructuring move*
Missing innovation in core products	New products/ markets development
Non-beneficial acquisitions	Asset divestments (company division or subsidiary)
Financial CCF	*Financial restructuring move*
Cash flow to shareholders too high	Reduction of cash flow to shareholder
Overleveraging	Repayment of debt
Overleveraging	Debt write-off or debt-to-equity-swap

Table 10: Selected moderation effects – considered in this study.

An overview of all moderation effects included in this analysis can be found in Table 10. The selection of these interaction effects is based on the assumption that there is an adequacy of scope between restructuring moves and the related CCFs (see, i.e., IDW, 2012).

The implementation of these statistical effects is based on a simple mathematical calculation (simplified and adapted from Field, 2013): For the variables A, B and C, where A and B are regressor variables and C is a dependent variable, the linear regression estimates the effect which each of the variables A and B have together on C, i.e., how much of the variance of C can be explained by the variance of A and B.

If a moderation effect, i.e., B is moderating the effect of A on C, is integrated into this example, the moderation effect is mathematically calculated as the product of the two variables, which is A*B or simply AB. The resulting regression, including the moderating effect, would then analyze the effects of each of the variables A, B and AB together on C, i.e., how much of the variance of C can be explained by the variance of

A, B and AB. The relevant term thus consists of all three regressor variables A, B and AB as regressor variable. Thus, adding the moderating effect increases the number of variables by one per moderation effect considered.

The integration of the moderation effects concludes the preparation of the statistical analyses that are conducted in the following sections.

6.3 Approach I: Univariate regression

This section details the results of the univariate regression. It covers sequentially the regressor variables of all model dimensions, starting with the crisis followed by turnaround management and concluding with the internal and external context.

In a further step, the regression of the moderation effects is conducted. Due to the structure of the moderation term, these are not conducted as univariate regression, but as multivariate regression involving the moderated variable as first, the moderator variables as second and the interaction effect as the third regressor variable.

The dependent variable of all regressions is '*turnaround result.*' The variable is introduced in section 4.3 and descriptively discussed in section 5.2.1.4. It has a mean of 2.88 and a standard deviation of 1.66.

The following information is provided per variable or moderation term respectively (for more information concerning these statistical figures see e.g., Backhaus et al., 2011; Fahrmeir et al., 2013; Field, 2013; Groß, 2003; Hair et al., 2010):

- *β – standardized beta (stand. beta)* is the standardized regression coefficient, resulting from the univariate parameter regression. Its value expresses how much the dependent variable changes in relation to the regressor variable. It is standardized based on the standard deviation of the two variables, i.e., $\beta = 1.00$ would imply that if the regressor variable increases by one standard deviation, the dependent variable also increases by one standard deviation. Beta can have both negative and positive values, while negative values express a negative linear relation, i.e., $\beta = -1.00$ means that if the regressor variable increases by one standard deviation, the dependent variable decreases by one standard deviation.

- *Adjusted R^2 (adj. R^2)* is the share of the variance of the dependent variable that can be predicted by the regressor variable(s).
  R^2 is calculated simply by dividing the explained variance by the total variance of the dependent variable. Thus, it is a direct measure for the effect strength of the regressor variable on the independent variable.
  'Adjusted' in this context means that this R^2 is corrected (adjusted) by using Wherry's formula. This formula reduces R^2 with an increasing number of predictors, thus accounting for the bias introduced by adding more variables (Field, 2013; Wherry, 1931). Adj. R^2 thus reflects more accurately the actual R^2 of the population the sample is drawn from.
  Adj. R^2 is also a measure for effect size. Commonly, different adj. R^2 values are labeled with the terms small, medium and large, wherein small is ±0.02, medium is ±0.13 and large is ±0.26.
- *Significance level (sign.)* of each variable – the bootstrapped (see section 6.1.3) probability *p* that the effect detected in the regression is random. For this study, all calculations are done based on a two-tailed significance, as the statistical tests allow bidirectional relations, i.e., considering negative as well as positive effects of the regressor variable on the dependent variable, whereas all significance levels $p \leq 0.05$ (5.0%) are considered significant. These sign levels are commonly marked by * for a significance level $p \leq 0.05$, ** for a significance level $p \leq 0.01$ and *** for a significance level $p \leq 0.001$.

6.3.1 Univariate regression – crisis variables

Variable name	Stand. beta	Adj. R^2	Sign.	
Operational crisis contribution factors				
Incorrect investment in plant and equipment	-0.04	0.00	0.57	
Insufficient investments in plant and equipment	-0.18	0.03	0.01	**
Degree of company-internal value-add too high	-0.06	0.00	0.37	
Degree of company-internal value-add too low	-0.06	0.00	0.46	
Weaknesses in organization and processes	-0.23	0.05	0.00	***
Managerial crisis contribution factors				
Unsuitable CEO	-0.30	0.08	0.00	***
Unsuitable members of TMT	-0.16	0.02	0.01	*
Conflict spillover from owner family to company	0.14	0.01	0.03	*
Succession problems	0.06	0.00	0.41	
Portfolio crisis contribution factors				
Incorrect market assessment	-0.18	0.03	0.01	**
Overexpansion	0.04	0.00	0.62	
Missing innovation in core products	-0.15	0.02	0.04	*
Insufficient quality and service	-0.28	0.08	0.00	***
Non-beneficial acquisitions	0.04	0.00	0.51	
Financial crisis contribution factors				
Financing structure inadequate	0.01	0.00	0.88	
Cash flow to shareholders too high	-0.03	0.00	0.65	
Overleveraging	-0.16	0.02	0.02	*
External crisis contribution factors				
Market decline	-0.08	0.00	0.22	
Increased competition	-0.16	0.02	0.02	*
Supply-side-induced crisis	-0.07	0.00	0.30	
Customer-induced crisis	-0.08	0.00	0.24	
Crisis context				
Deterioration pattern of crisis	-0.06	0.00	0.36	
Severity of crisis	0.00	0.00	1.00	
Initial complexity of company situation to implement turnaround	0.18	0.03	0.01	*

Table 11: Univariate regression of crisis variables.

Dependent variable: *'Turnaround result.'*
Significance levels at 0.05; 0.01 and 0.001 indicated by *; ** and ***.

The univariate regression of the crisis characteristics shows 11 of the 24 variables (46%) having significant statistical effects on the *'turnaround result.'* The variables with the highest adj. R^2 values are *'unsuitable CEO'* and *'insufficient quality and service'* with an adj. R^2 of 0.08. The third largest adj. R^2 is found for the combined variable (see section 5.2.3) *'weaknesses in organization and processes'* with an adj. R^2 of 0.05.

In the group of the operational CCFs, no significant effect could be found for incorrect investments and value-depth issues. Both *'insufficient investments in plant and equipment'* and *'weaknesses in organization and processes,'* have a significantly negative effect on the *'turnaround result.'*

The majority of the managerial CCFs are found to have significant effects, the only exception being the family-specific CCF *'succession problems.'* While describing a similar topic for different groups of persons, *'unsuitable CEO'* shows a much higher adj. R^2 than *'unsuitable members of TMT,'* while still being significant.

Surprisingly, *'conflict spillover from owner family to company'* shows a positive relation with the *'turnaround result,'* i.e., conflicts in the family as CCF are having a positive effect on the *'turnaround result.'* It might by hypothesized that priorities might change in a family firm when bankruptcy is imminent, i.e., family conflicts can be resolved (more easily than other CCFs) when the future of the company is in danger.

The portfolio-related CCFs, *'overexpansion'* and *'non-beneficial acquisitions'* show no significant effect on the *'turnaround result.'* On the other hand, both product-related CCFs *'missing innovation in core products'* and *'insufficient quality and service'* show a negative effect on the *'turnaround result.'* The same is the case for *'incorrect market assessment.'*

Among the financial CCFs, only *'overleveraging'* is significantly negative when related with *'turnaround result,'* although with a small effect size. No effect is found for *'inadequate financial structure'* and *'overleveraging.'*

The external CCFs only show significance with small effect sizes for *'increased competition,'* but not for the other three factors *'market decline,'* *'supply-side-induced crisis'* and *'customer-induced crisis.'*

In the crisis context, significant effects are found for the *'initial complexity of company situation to implement turnaround,'* but surprisingly with a positive relation between increasing complexity and *'turnaround result'* (adj. $R^2 = 0.03$).

Referring to section 5.2.2, the *'initial complexity of company situation to implement turnaround'* is correlated (Pearson correlation coefficient = 0.518) with *'company size (turnover) before crisis,'* which – as it is shown in section 6.3.3 – has an even stronger positive effect on *'turnaround result'* (adj. $R^2 = 0.05$). Based on this correlation, it might be assumed that the significant effect of *'initial complexity of company situation to implement turnaround'* on *'turnaround result'* can be attributed to the relation between *'company size'* and *'turnaround result,'* while the relation between *'initial complexity of company situation to implement turnaround'* to *'turnaround result'* is detected due to multicollinearity.

Interestingly, both other crisis context variables *'deterioration pattern of crisis'* and even the variable *'severity of crisis'* have no significant effect on *'turnaround result,'* despite their high relevance in literature (see section 4.6).

6.3.2 Univariate regression – turnaround management variables

Variable name	Stand. beta	Adj. R^2	Sign.
Operational restructuring moves			
Layoff	-0.17	0.02	0.01 **
Employee concessions	-0.11	0.01	0.11
Increase CAPEX	0.09	0.00	0.19
Decrease CAPEX	0.03	0.00	0.69
Capacity reduction	-0.06	0.00	0.40
Productivity increase	0.01	0.00	0.83
Outsourcing	-0.06	0.00	0.39
Insourcing	0.17	0.02	0.02 *
Process improvement and redesign	0.01	0.00	0.92
Pricing and sales initiatives	0.03	0.00	0.71
Purchasing and cost reduction initiatives	-0.08	0.00	0.26
Managerial restructuring moves			
CEO change	-0.03	0.00	0.66
Change in TMT	0.06	0.00	0.42
Portfolio restructuring moves			
Asset divestments (company division or subsidiary)	-0.06	0.00	0.42
Termination of products lines/ markets	-0.03	0.00	0.63
New products/ markets development	0.09	0.00	0.21
Financial restructuring moves			
Working capital reduction	-0.08	0.00	0.24
Reduction of cash flow to shareholder	0.08	0.00	0.24
Liquidity contribution by shareholder	0.04	0.00	0.58
Additional restructuring loan granted by lenders	-0.01	0.00	0.84
Securities contribution by shareholder	0.02	0.00	0.76
Repayment of debt	0.13	0.01	0.07
Extension. conversion or deferral of existing debt	-0.04	0.00	0.52
Debt write-off or debt-to-equity-swap	0.04	0.00	0.58
Turnaround context			
Development of market segment during turnaround	0.44	0.19	0.00 ***
Stakeholder management during turnaround	0.42	0.17	0.00 ***

Table 12: Univariate regression of turnaround management variables.

Dependent variable '*turnaround result.*'
Significance levels at 0.05; 0.01 and 0.001 indicated by *; ** and ***.

The univariate regression of the turnaround management variables shows only 4 of the 26 variables (15%) having a significant statistical effect on '*turnaround result.*'

This sheds light on the crisis and turnaround process in an interesting manner. With respect to the univariate effects, the impact of the crisis characteristics on the '*turnaround result*' is much broader (46% of the variables with significant effects), than that of the turnaround management variables (15% of the variables with significant effects).

The variables with the highest adj. R^2 are the two turnaround context variables '*development of market segment during turnaround*' and '*stakeholder management during turnaround*' with an adj. R^2 of 0.18 and 0.17, which can be assessed as medium/large positive effects. The third largest adj. R square is, with 0.02, only a small negative effect for the variable '*layoff.*'

The two variables with medium/large effects both belong to the turnaround management context and not the turnaround management content. To reiterate, the turnaround management context defines the turnaround-specific context in which the restructuring moves, the content of turnaround management, are implemented. This indicates that for the turnaround result, the turnaround context is more relevant than the actual content, the turnaround moves.

As the number of significant effects in this part of the model is limited, I focus the discussion on the two restructuring moves with significant effects on '*turnaround result*': '*Insourcing*' and '*layoff.*' Of these two, '*insourcing*' has a small positive effect, but surprisingly '*layoff*' has a small negative effect on '*turnaround result.*'

There are two ways to interpret this result for '*layoff.*'

- One way to interpret this finding, is that a focus on '*layoff*' in a turnaround does indeed trigger the negative effects discussed in the conceptual model chapter (section 4.5.1.1) and thus the negative results of such measures supersede the positive effect of the related cost savings.
- The second interpretation is that for a turnaround in which '*layoff*' is judged as a very relevant restructuring move, the turnaround strategy might be limited to retrenchment measures without being complemented by recovery measures

and the strategic repositioning often deemed to be necessary for turnaround success.

None of the other restructuring moves has a significant effect on '*turnaround result,*' explicitly none of the managerial, portfolio or financial restructuring moves.

6.3.3 Univariate regression – context variables

Variable name	Stand. beta	Adj. R^2	Sign.	
Internal context				
Company size (turnover) before crisis	0.23	0.05	0.00	***
Share of biggest shareholder before crisis	-0.01	0.00	0.90	
CEOs time with the company before crisis	-0.12	0.01	0.07	
Primary strategy before crisis – quality leadership	0.19	0.03	0.01	**
Primary strategy before crisis – innovation leadership	0.05	0.00	0.52	
Slack resources before crisis	-0.07	0.00	0.37	
Lender security situation before crisis	-0.11	0.01	0.11	
Equity ratio before crisis	0.15	0.02	0.02	*
Pre-crisis profitability	-0.07	0.00	0.33	
Family share in the company before crisis	0.16	0.02	0.02	*
External context				
Long-term growth perspectives of market segment	0.45	0.20	0.00	***

Table 13: Univariate regression of internal and external context variables.
Dependent variable '*turnaround result.*'
Significance levels at 0.05; 0.01 and 0.001 indicated by *; ** and ***.

The univariate regression of the context variables shows 5 of the 11 variables (45%) having significant statistical effect on '*turnaround result.*'

This share is comparable with the share of significant variables found for the crisis variables and is much higher than that found for the turnaround management variables.

Among these context variables, the highest adj. R^2 is found for '*long-term growth perspectives of market segment*' with an adj. R^2 of 0.20; this can be assessed as a large effect and is the variable with the highest univariate effect on '*turnaround result*' of all variables in the analysis. The second and third largest effects are found for the variables '*company size (turnover) before crisis*' and '*primary strategy before crisis – quality leadership;*' these have an adj. R^2 of 0.05 and 0.03 respectively and thus have much smaller effects on the dependent variable than *'long-term growth perspectives of market segment.'*

For five of the internal context variables – *'share of biggest shareholder before crisis,' 'CEOs time with the company before crisis,' 'primary strategy before crisis – innovation leadership,' 'slack resources before crisis,' 'lender security situation before crisis'* and *'pre-crisis profitability'* no significant effect could be found despite the fact that many of these are – as is the consensus of many authors – to be expected to affect the turnaround result (see section 4.6).

Concerning the company size, it seems that larger companies – specifically in the range of medium-sized companies in question – do indeed have a better average turnaround result.

Quality leadership strategies seem to improve the post-turnaround performance. This is in line with the findings from the crisis characteristics where product quality issues are one of the top negative factors for a company's turnaround.

A higher equity ratio, i.e., a lower level of debt on a company's balance sheet has a positive effect on the *'turnaround result.'* This is in line with the significant negative effect of the CCF *'overleveraging.'*

At the same time, an increased family share has a positive effect on the *'turnaround result.'*
While this might be explained by referring to the strengths of family firms, a second possible explanation might be the management structure of family firms and thus ultimately a principal-agent issue. As for most of these family firms, the CEO is a family member (see section 8.4), so it can also be interpreted as the manager's being more reluctant to file insolvency, as the shareholder usually has to assume a share value of zero in such a case: The average quota for debtors in insolvency cases in Germany from 2003 to 2007 was 3.6% (Kranzusc & Icks, 2009), implying that as the debtors do not receive their nominal debt value, the share value is zero.

Figure 35: Univariate regression effect strenght – result overview .
Source: Own illustration.

6.3.4 Regression of the moderation effects

The analysis of the selected moderating effects (see section 6.2) is conducted as a regression with three predictor variables: The variable that is moderated; the variable that is moderating; and the interaction effect of the two variables.

This different approach changes the structure in which the results are presented compared to the univariate regressions (see Table 14). Adj. R^2 is provided for the multivariate regression, i.e., for the complete moderation term including all three variables, not per variable. For each of the variables, the standardized beta and the significance levels are provided. To allow a further interpretation of the results, two columns showing the result of the respective univariate regressions for each of the two interacting variables are added.

Variable name	adj. R^2	Stand. beta	Sign.	Stand. beta	Sign.
	Moderation effect			Univariate results (for reference only)	
Incorrect investment in plant and equipment		-0.06	0.46	-0.04	0.57
Decrease CAPEX		0.05	0.49	0.03	0.69
'Incorrect investment in plant and equipment' × 'decrease CAPEX'		-0.02	0.83		
Adj. R^2 moderation term (referring to the multivariate moderation regression, i.e., including all three variables of the moderation – similar in all cases below)	**-0.01**				
Insufficient investments in plant and equipment		-0.25	0.00**	-0.18	0.01**
Increase CAPEX		0.19	0.01**	0.09	0.19
'Insufficient investments in plant and equipment' × 'increase CAPEX'		-0.01	0.87		
Adj. R^2 moderation term	**0.05**				
Degree of company-internal value-add too high		-0.05	0.50	-0.06	0.37
Outsourcing		-0.04	0.56	-0.06	0.39
'Degree of company-internal value-add too high' × 'outsourcing'		0.03	0.69		
Adj. R^2 moderation term	**-0.01**				
Degree of company-internal value-add too low		-0.09	0.28	-0.06	0.46
Insourcing		0.18	0.01**	0.17	0.02*
'Degree of company-internal value-add too low' × 'insourcing'		-0.02	0.79		
Adj. R^2 moderation term	**0.02**				
Weaknesses in organization and processes		-0.24	0.00***	-0.23	0.00***
Productivity increase		0.07	0.35	0.01	0.83
'Weaknesses in organization and processes' × 'productivity increase'		0.05	0.43		
Adj. R^2 moderation term	**0.05**				
Weaknesses in organization and processes		-0.26	0.00***	-0.23	0.00***
Process improvement and redesign		0.13	0.06	0.01	0.92
'Weaknesses in organization and processes' × 'process improvement and redesign'		0.08	0.11		
Adj. R^2 moderation term	**0.06**				

Variable name	adj. R^2	Stand. beta	Sign.	Stand. beta	Sign.
Unsuitable CEO		-0.33	0.00**	-0.30	0.00***
CEO change		0.18	0.02*	-0.03	0.66
'Unsuitable CEO' × 'CEO change'		0.17	0.04*		
Adj. R^2 moderation term	**0.13**				
Unsuitable members of TMT		-0.25	0.00**	-0.16	0.01*
Change in TMT		0.22	0.00**	0.06	0.42
'Unsuitable members of TMT' × 'change in TMT'		0.09	0.19		
Adj. R^2 moderation term	**0.05**				
Missing innovation in core products		-0.19	0.02*	-0.15	0.04*
New products/ markets development		0.16	0.03*	0.09	0.21
'Missing innovation in core products' × 'new products/ markets development'		-0.04	0.58		
Adj. R^2 moderation term	**0.03**				
Non-beneficial acquisitions		0.07	0.40	0.04	0.51
Asset divestments (company division or subsidiary)		-0.09	0.24	-0.06	0.42
'Non-beneficial acquisitions' × 'asset divestments (company division or subsidiary)'		0.03	0.65		
Adj. R^2 moderation term	**-0.01**				
Cash flow to shareholders too high		-0.09	0.32	-0.03	0.65
Reduction of cash flow to shareholder		0.13	0.12	0.08	0.24
'Cash flow to shareholders too high' × 'reduction of cash flow to shareholder'		-0.01	0.85		
Adj. R^2 moderation term	**0.00**				
Overleveraging		-0.23	0.00***	-0.16	0.02*
Repayment of debt		0.20	0.01**	0.13	0.07
'Overleveraging' × 'repayment of debt'		0.02	0.78		
Adj. R^2 moderation term	**0.05**				
Overleveraging		-0.18	0.01*	-0.16	0.02*
Debt write-off or debt-to-equity-swap		0.08	0.25	0.04	0.58
'Overleveraging' × 'debt write-off or debt-to-equity-swap'		0.00	0.99		
Adj. R^2 moderation term	**0.02**				

Table 14: Regression of the moderation terms.

Dependent variable *'turnaround result.'*
Significance levels at 0.05; 0.01 and 0.001 indicated by *; ** and ***.

The analysis of the moderating effects exposes three basic classes of results:

- Case 1 no interaction: The moderation effect variable itself is not significant. At the same time, there is no change in significance for either of the interacting variables. This indicates that there is indeed no moderation, and the two variables are no better at explaining the result variable together than individually.
- Case 2 compensation effect: The moderation effect itself is not significant. At the same time, there is a change in significance for one or both of the interacting variables. This indicates that there is indeed no moderation, but the two variables are better at explaining the result variable together than individually.
- Case 3 moderation effect: The moderation effect itself is significant. There is a change in significance for one or both of the interacting variables at the same time. This indicates both actual moderation and the fact that both variables are better at explaining the result variable together than individually.

Eight of the 13 interaction effects analyzed can be attributed to Case 1. The interaction effects do not show any significance, nor does the regression of the moderation term (including the two variables and the interaction effect) reveal any new information about the two analyzed variables. Nonetheless, the result is important to the extent that this means that there are no indications of the restructuring move having any effect on the consequences of the CCF (if there are any). Specifically, it can be shown that:

- There is no indication that '*decrease CAPEX'* is the right move in the case of '*incorrect investment in plant and equipment.*' Neither has any effect on the 'turnaround result.'
- There is also no indication that '*outsourcing'* is the right move if a company suffers from '*degree of company-internal value-add too high,*' while again neither variable has an effect on 'turnaround result.'
- While 'insourcing' has an overall positive effect on the *'turnaround result,'* it shows no relation with the CCF '*degree of company-internal value-add too low,'* which itself also has no effect on the '*turnaround result.*'

- *'Productivity increase'* itself not only has no effect on the *'turnaround result,'* but also does not change the significantly negative effect of 'weaknesses in organization and processes.'
- The same is the case for the restructuring move *'process improvement and redesign'* and its relation with *'weaknesses in organization and processes.'*
- Both the CCF *'non-beneficial acquisitions'* and the restructuring move *'asset divestments'* have no effect on the *'turnaround result,'* individually or together.
- The same is the case for the two variables *'cash flow to shareholders too high'* and *'reduction of cash flow to shareholder.'*
- While the CFF *'overleveraging'* significantly negatively affects the *'turnaround result,'* the same is not the case for *'debt write-off or debt-to-equity-swap.'*

Especially as there are indications of interactions in other combinations of restructuring moves and CCFs, as presented below in the context of the interactions belonging to Case 2 and Case 3, these 'non-findings' are sobering. These basically indicate that there is no statistical rationale to employ these restructuring moves as measures for the respective CCFs.

All interpretations are obviously limited by the fact that no other contextual factors are considered in these analyses. It cannot be ruled out that there are significant effects of the interaction terms in the context of more variables, thus more complex models addressing this matter are processed in sections 6.4, 6.5 and 6.6.

Four of the 13 interaction effects analyzed can be attributed to Case 2. While the interaction effect itself shows no significance, there are changes in the significance levels and betas of the two variables involved. While no indication is found for a moderation effect, the two variables together show both significant effects on the *'turnaround result,'* while before this was only the case for one of the two variables. Specifically, it could be shown that:

- While *'insufficient investments in plant and equipment'* are not moderated by *'increase CAPEX,'* the restructuring move *'increase CAPEX'* is significant in the context of CCF *'insufficient investments in plant and equipment'* (stand. beta = 0.19; sign. = 0.01), although it is insignificant in univariate regression.

The negative effect (stand. beta) of the CCF *'insufficient investments in plant and equipment'* is increased (stand. beta = -0.25 vs. -0.18).

A possible explanation could be that while an increased CAPEX does not moderate, i.e., change the negative effects of an insufficient CAPEX as CCF, this restructuring move does compensate its effects, which is only assessable if analyzing both variables concurrently. In other words, the damage is done and its effect can only (partly) be compensated.

- With an analog effect structure, but with higher significance change, a similar picture emerges for *'unsuitable members of TMT'* and *'change in TMT.'* While a significant moderation effect could not be found, the restructuring move *'change in TMT'* is significant in the context of CCF *'unsuitable members of TMT'* (stand. beta = 0.22; sign. < 0.01), while it is insignificant in the univariate regression. The negative effect (stand. beta) of the CCF *'unsuitable members of TMT'* is increased (stand. beta = -0.25 vs. -0.16). Again, a similar explanation could be given, as it appears to be a compensation instead of a moderation effect.
- The same effect could be found for the variable pair CCF *'missing innovation in core products'* and restructuring move *'new products/ markets development.'* Here, the restructuring move is now also significant (stand. beta = 0.16; sign. = 0.03) and the beta of the CCF is similarly increased (stand. beta = -0.19 vs. -0.15).
- The last pair in this group is the two variables CCF *'overleveraging'* and restructuring move *'repayment of debt,'* with a now significant restructuring move (stand. beta = 0.20; sign. < 0.01) and an increased beta of the CCF (stand beta = -0.23 vs. -0.16).

The variable combination for which moderation could be found and can thus be attributed to Case 3 is the moderation of the effect of the CCF *'unsuitable CEO'* on *'turnaround result'* by the restructuring move *'CEO change.'*

Only for this combination, the interaction effect turned out to be significant. Compared to the univariate regressions the following effects could be assessed:

- The stand. beta of the CCF is higher (-0.33 vs. -0.30).
- The restructuring move is significant (stand. beta = 0.18; sign = 0.02) compared to its being insignificant in the univariate regression.
- The interaction effect is significant (stand. beta = 0.17; sign. = 0.04) revealing that the negative effect of the CCF *'unsuitable CEO'* on *'turnaround result'* is indeed moderated by the restructuring move *'CEO change.'*

As the effects of such a moderation term are difficult to grasp based on these numbers alone, I use a scenario technique to illustrate the nature of this moderation (Table 15).

Variable name	**Value of CCF *'unsuitable CEO'***	**Value of restructuring move *'CEO change'***	**Moderated effect on *'turnaround result'***
Illustrative configurations of the CCF 'unsuitable CEO' and the restructuring move 'CEO change'			
Situation 1: CEO did not contribute to the crisis and *'CEO change'* is not a relevant part of the turnaround strategy	*1*	*1*	*+0.52*
Situation 2: *'Unsuitable CEO'* is a very important factor for the crisis and *'CEO change'* is not a relevant part of the turnaround strategy	5	1	-2.35
Situation 3: CEO did not contribute to the crisis and *'CEO change'* is very relevant part of the turnaround strategy	1	5	-0.25
Situation 4: *'Unsuitable CEO'* is a very important factor for the crisis and *'CEO change'* is very relevant part of the turnaround strategy	5	5	-0.95
Effect of different levels of the restructuring move 'CEO change' for the same level of the CCF 'unsuitable CEO'			
If the CEO did not contribute to the crisis – effect of Situation 3 minus effect of Situation 1	1	5 vs. 1	-0.77
If *'unsuitable CEO'* is a very important factor for the crisis – effect of Situation 4 minus effect of Situation 2	5	5 vs. 1	+1.40

Table 15: Illustrative CEO related moderation scenarios.

Combinations of the CCF *'unsuitable CEO'* and the restructuring move *'CEO change'* and their moderated effect on *'turnaround result.'*

The table shows clear results:

- Having an unsuitable CEO as a crisis factor is always negative for the turnaround result, as the effect on *'turnaround result'* is negative for both Situation 2 and Situation 4.
- If a CEO did contribute to the crisis, the application of the restructuring move *'CEO change'* improves the *'turnaround result.'* Comparing situation 4 with situation 2, it improves by +1.40 (while still being negative for both situations).
- If the CEO did not contribute to the crisis, the picture is less clear. For situation 1, the effect on *'turnaround result'* is positive, but for situation 3 the effect is slightly negative.
- Changing a CEO that did not contribute to the crisis has a negative effect on *'turnaround result.'* This can be assessed by comparing situation 3 with situation 1; the net effect of the change is -0.77

The results reflect common sense, but are in contrast to the majority of the research notions expressed in chapter 4. It seems that in cases of a crisis to which the CEO did not contribute, a removal of this CEO is not recommended. This rebuts the prevalent notion of *'CEO change'* as a prerequisite for turnaround, regardless of the specific context of the CEO's contribution to the crisis (see section 4.5.2 for detailed discussion of this topic). A different result emerges reviewing the other two situations in which the CEO contributes to the crisis. Here, the *'turnaround result'* is significantly increased by *'CEO change.'*

The comparison of the two combinations shows that not changing the CEO during turnaround, if he or she contributed to the crisis, endangers the turnaround more than the removal of a CEO who did not contribute to the crisis.

Concluding the moderating effects, four analyzed interaction terms show that there are no moderating effects, but rather compensating effects with restructuring moves. These reviewed pairs of CCF and restructuring moves seem to have compensating effects on the *'turnaround result.'*

For the case of *'unsuitable CEO'* and *'CEO change,'* it is shown that the restructuring move depends directly on the respective CCF. It is shown that a CEO removal in the case of his or her not contributing to the crisis has an even more negative effect on the *'turnaround result.'*

For the remaining eight analyzed interaction terms, there do not seem to be tangible relations between the paired CCF and restructuring move. All of these findings are obviously limited by the small selection of variables considered in this analysis.

6.4 Approach II: Complete model

The second approach changes the perspective from reviewing single variables and their effect on the dependent variable *'turnaround result'* to implementing multivariate models with more than one regressor variable. This is conducted in several steps, using five different models, with the last model being the model including all variables and interaction effects (as laid out in section 6.2).

6.4.1 Methodology

The complete model is set up through five steps with different subsets of variables. These are:

Model 1	Internal and external context variables
Model 2	Internal and external context variables, crisis variables
Model 3	Internal and external context variables, turnaround variables
Model 4	Internal and external context variables, crisis variables, turnaround variables
Model 5	Internal and external context variables, crisis variables, turnaround variables, interaction effects

For each of these models, model specific statistical information is provided indicating the respective model fitness and model performance:

- *Number of variables* – the number of regressor variables, which are part of the respective model. Dependent variable is *'turnaround result'* in all cases.

- *The events per variable* (EPV) are the cases per variable in the specific model – thus illustrating the statistical power of the respective model.
- For a more detailed discussion of the relation between the number of variables and the statistical power, please refer to section 6.1.2.
  To sum up: The statistical power, i.e., the ability of a regression to detect smaller effects, increases with the EPV.
- *Adjusted R^2 of the model* (adj. R^2). (Already discussed in introducing the univariate regressions – section 6.1.1). It reflects the explained share of the variance of the result variable by the model. The adjustment corrects the R^2 by the bias introduced into the model by an increasing number of model variables.
- *Significance level* of the model (sign.). The significance level is the probability for the effects found in the respective model on the dependent variable *'turnaround result'* to be coincidental.
- *Maximum variance inflation factor* (max. VIF). The maximum variance inflation factor is a measurement for multicollinearity. This issue is discussed in section 6.4.2. A maximum VIF value above 10 is a strong indication of a problem. A value above 5 indicates potential bias in the model (Hair et al., 2010).

In the presentation of the results, I deviate from the publication standard, insofar as I only show the results for a variable if these are significant in any of the models analyzed. The high number of variables would otherwise make a meaningful interpretation of the result extremely difficult and would inappropriately inflate this study without adding information.

Additionally, the standardized beta and the respective significance levels are presented for each of the presented variables (as introduced in section 6.3).

6.4.2 Multicollinearity

Collinearity is given in a regression model if two or more regressor variables are correlated (Field, 2013; Groß, 2003; Hair et al., 2010). For an ideal regression, all regression variables should be uncorrelated, but unfortunately that is usually not the case for real life data. In this data set, collinearity between the variables is to be expected; as discussed in the conceptual model (chapter 4), it is, e.g., assumed that the turnaround strategy depends on the characteristics of the crisis.

Multicollinearity in a data set has certain specific effects:

- Collinearity reduces the statistical power of a regression.
  As Hair et al. (2010) show, there is a reduction in the R^2 detected in a linear regression if multicollinearity increases. This means that for more complex models not only the EPV reduces the detection power of the regression, but so does multicollinearity (which similarly increases with more variables).
  I address this issue by comparing the results of different models and regressions. The adj. R^2 values of the different regressions play an important role in the concluding discussion.
- The regressions coefficients, the beta weights, are untrustworthy in scenarios with high multicollinearity (Field, 2013).
  If the common variance of two variables is also a predictor of the dependent variable, the betas of the two variables become unreliable, as the regression algorithm randomly distributes them between the two variables. This becomes evident if multiple models are calculated with slight changes of the variable subsets and the beta weights are very unsteady between these regressions.
  As many consecutive models are calculated with different variable subsets, the topic of high variation in the betas' weights is subject to the model assessment.

Multicollinearity can be assessed using two different approaches (Field, 2013; Hair et al., 2010):

- The analysis of the correlation matrix is the first way to identify indications for collinearity.
  The literature recommends cutoff values of 0.7 (Hair et al., 2010), 0.8 or 0.9 (Field, 2013). In this sample, the maximum correlation is at 0.695 between '*development of market segment during turnaround*' and '*long-term growth perspectives of market segment,*' and thus below the cutoff value, the next highest correlation is below 0.6.
- The second – and more precise – way to identify multicollinearity is the *variance inflation factor* (for details on its calculation please refer to Field, 2013; Hair et al., 2010).

> "The variance inflation factor (. . .) is calculated simply as the inverse of the tolerance value." The tolerance value "is defined as the amount of variability of the selected independent variable not explained by the other independent variables" (Hair et al., 2010; p. 201).
>
> The common cutoff values for the VIF are 10, as a strong indication of a problem, and 5 indicating a potential problem.

In the regressions performed for the complete model, as well as for the models analyzed in the following chapters, for one specific model the maximum VIF (max. VIF = 5.2) is slightly above the lower cutoff value of 5, indicating a potential problem. As I discuss the result of the different regression models conjointly and in their respective context, I use these different models to detect any signs of multicollinearity, such as unexplainable changes in adj. R^2 or fluctuating betas for specific variables. Using multiple different regression models to overcome multicollinearity and identify potential issues is also suggested in the literature (Backhaus et al., 2011).

For the univariate regressions as well as for the regression of the moderation effects, all VIF values are below 2, which is distinctively below any threshold indicating multicollinearity issues.

6.4.3 Results of the complete model

The result of the regressions for the five models leading up to the complete model 5, which includes all variables and the selected interaction effects, can be found in Table 16.

	Model 1	Model 2	Model 3	Model 4	Model 5
Model structure	Context	Context and crisis	Context and turn-around manage-ment	Context, crisis, turn-around manage-ment	Context, crisis, turn-around manage-ment, interaction effects
Number of variables	11	35	37	61	74
EPV	19.0	6.0	5.6	3.4	2.8
adj. R^2	0.29	0.39	0.41	0.45	0.45
Sign.	0.000	0.000	0.000	0.000	0.000
Max. VIF	1.4	2.5	2.5	4.0	5.2
Portfolio crisis contribution factors					
Insufficient quality and service	n/a	-0.16*	n/a	-0.14*	-0.16
External crisis contribution factors					
Market decline	n/a	0.21*	n/a	0.21	0.20
Financial restructuring moves					
Extension, conversion or deferral of existing debt	n/a	n/a	-0.13*	-0.12	-0.14
Turnaround context					
Stakeholder management during turna-round	n/a	n/a	0.37***	0.29***	0.29**
Internal context					
Company size (turnover) before crisis	0.16*	0.14	0.17*	0.16	0.17
Primary strategy before crisis – quality leadership	0.23**	0.12	0.14	0.06	0.07
Pre-crisis profitability	-0.14*	-0.11	-0.10	-0.06	-0.04
Family share in the company before crisis	0.12*	0.12	0.15*	0.16*	0.14
External context					
Long-term growth perspectives of mar-ket segment	0.40***	0.39***	0.28***	0.32***	0.32**

Table 16: Complete model regression.

Dependent variable '*turnaround result*,' standardized beta values shown; N = 209.
Only variables shown with significance level p≤ 0.05 in at least one model.
Significance levels at 0.05; 0.01 and 0.001 indicated by *; ** and ***.
Model 1: Context variables.
Model 2: Context variables, crisis variables.
Model 3: Context variables, turnaround management variables.
Model 4: Context variables, crisis variables, turnaround management variables.
Model 5: Context variables, crisis variables, turnaround management variables, interaction effect variables.

In each of the five consecutive steps of the model development, the respective models are highly significant. While models 2 and 3 do not build upon each other, the two models each combine the context variables with the crisis variables and the turnaround variables respectively. With the increasing number of variables, the events per variable (EPV) decrease accordingly. At the same time, the statistical power of the models, i.e., the detectable effect strength, decreases with the EPV (see section 6.1.2, not part of the information in the table).

For the complete model, the maximum variance inflation factor (VIF = 5.2) is above the warning level of 5. So when reviewing the result, caution concerning the effect of multicollinearity is appropriate, i.e., a decreased R^2 and unreliable betas (see section 6.4.2).

This effect might party explain why the adj. R^2 does not increase from Model 4 (adj. $R^2 = 0.45$) to Model 5. From this perspective, the additional consideration of interaction effects could not contribute to the model quality and its prediction properties, especially as none of the interaction effect variables emerged as a significant variable in the complete model.

These findings are reconfirmed by the significance of the changes between the models. The change from Model 2 and 3 vs. Model 1 is significant for both combinations with $p \leq 0.001$, while the change from Model 2/ 3 to Model 4 is significant with $p \leq 0.05$ only for the change from Model 2 to Model 4 and insignificant for the change from Model 3 to Model 4. The change from Model 4 to 5 is insignificant, indicating the validity of the concerns about the added value of the interaction effects.

To allow a meaningful analysis in the context of all findings, I want to defer the discussion and interpretation of individual variables until after the two next approaches have been discussed. By discussing the results conjointly, a more conclusive interpretation of the findings is reached, taking in consideration all four modeling approaches.

6.5 Approach III: Partial models

After the univariate regression as the first step and the complete models as second step, the third approach is a compromise between the two extreme points. It uses a specific slice of the model to increase statistical power by decreasing the number of variables.

6.5.1 Methodology

The third approach reflects a key notion expressed by many conceptual turnaround researchers. Early research suggested applying portfolio measures (then called strategic measures) to portfolio issues (similarly called strategic issues), while operational issues should be addressed by operational cures (Schendel et al., 1976), leading Pearce and Robbins (1993) to state that the cause of the crisis should influence the decision about turnaround strategies. An analogy to diseases is often used; expressing the conviction that the remedy has to address the illness, i.e., the scope of the measures has to be congruent with the crisis characteristics. This is similarly an integral part of the German standards for turnaround plans, the 'IDW S6' (IDW, 2012), in which the structure of the measures follows the structure of the crisis analysis. For each kind of crisis, appropriate measures have to be defined.

Following this logic, the partial models limit the scope of the variables in each of the four analyzed subsets to one dimension of the internal CCF and restructuring moves. At the same time, all other variables (i.e., context variables, crisis context variables, external CCF variables, turnaround context variables) are included as regressor variables in all four partial models. Specifically, these contain:

Model 6 operational partial model	Context variables, crisis context variables, external CCF variables, turnaround context variables, operational crisis variables, operational turnaround management variables, operational interaction effect variables
Model 7 managerial partial model	Context variables, crisis context variables, external CCF variables, turnaround context variables, managerial crisis variables, managerial turnaround management variables, managerial interaction effect variables

Model 8 portfolio partial model	Context variables, crisis context variables, external CCF variables, turnaround context variables, portfolio crisis variables, portfolio turnaround management variables, portfolio interaction effect variables
Model 9 financial partial model	Context variables, crisis context variables, external CCF variables, turnaround context variables, financial crisis variables, financial turnaround management variables, financial interaction effect variables

These partial models have a higher EPV (depending on the model from 4.5 to 6.1.) than the complete model (EPV = 2.8). This increases the statistical power of these partial models compared to the complete model, and thus allows finding statistically significant effects with lower strength than the complete model.

Considering only a subset of variables, which is the precondition to increasing the EPV, is also a limitation of these models. Nonetheless, they are considered as an additional facet to allow magnifying effects in a certain direction, thus accepting the limitations coming with it.

Moving the focus away from individual variables, the partial models also provide indications about which aspect of crisis and turnaround – i.e., operational, managerial, portfolio and financial – affects *'turnaround result'* with the highest effect strength. This allows ranking these aspects in their respective impact on the *'turnaround result.'*

6.5.2 Results of the partial models

Again, to allow a more consolidated presentation, the result table (Table 17) shows only variables that were significant in any of the four partial models.

	Model 6	Model 7	Model 8	Model 9
	Partial model (oper.)	Partial model (manag.)	Partial model (port.)	Partial model (fin.)
Number of variables	45	28	30	34
EPV	4.6	7.5	7.0	6.1
adj. R^2	0.39	0.45	0.43	0.42
Sign.	0.000	0.000	0.000	0.000
Max. VIF	2.6	2.9	2.3	2.3
Portfolio crisis contribution factors				
Insufficient quality and service	n/a	n/a	-0.19**	n/a
Financial crisis contribution factors				
Overleveraging	n/a	n/a	n/a	-0.19*
External crisis contribution factors				
Market decline	0.15*	0.10	0.12	0.18*
Turnaround context				
Development of market segment during turnaround	0.12	0.18*	0.15	0.18*
Stakeholder management during turnaround	0.31***	0.27***	0.32***	0.36***
Internal context				
Family share in the company before crisis	0.19**	0.14*	0.14*	0.13*
External context				
Long-term growth perspectives of market segment	0.33***	0.27**	0.28***	0.32***
Interaction effects				
'Unsuitable CEO' × 'CEO change'	n/a	0.17*	n/a	n/a

Table 17: Partial model regression.

Dependent variable '*turnaround result,*' standardized beta values shown; N = 209.
Only variables shown with significance level $p \leq 0.05$ in at least one model.
Significance levels at 0.05; 0.01 and 0.001 indicated by *; ** and ***.
Model 6: Context variables, crisis context variables, external CCF variables, turnaround context variables, operational crisis variables, operational turnaround management variables, operational interaction effect variables.
Model 7: Context variables, crisis context variables, external CCF variables, turnaround context variables, managerial crisis variables, managerial turnaround management variables, managerial interaction effect variables.
Model 8: Context variables, crisis context variables, external CCF variables, turnaround context variables, portfolio crisis variables, portfolio turnaround management variables, portfolio interaction effect variables.
Model 9: Context variables, crisis context variables, external CCF variables, turnaround context variables, financial crisis variables, financial turnaround management variables, financial interaction effect variables.

The regression of the partial models in all four cases shows a high significance (sign. < 0.001); at the same time, there are no indications for a high level of multicollinearity (max VIF in the range from 2.3 to 2.9).

The adj. R^2 for the four models is between 0.39 and 0.45. The managerial partial model having the highest (adj. $R^2 = 0.45$) is followed closely by the portfolio (adj. $R^2 = 0.43$) and financial (adj. $R^2 = 0.42$) partial model. The last model – in terms of adj. R^2 – is the operational model (adj. $R^2 = 0.39$).

The comprehensive discussion of the individual variables – taking into consideration the result of all four approaches – is conducted in section 6.7.

6.6 Approach IV: Simplified models

The last approach is based on the notion that it might be more appropriate to select a small subset of variables, which (together) explain the dependent variable best, instead of using many regressor variables. This eliminates many statistical hurdles, as it both drastically reduces the multicollinearity and increases the statistical power of the regression (as the EPV are much higher due to the lower number of variables). Unfortunately, there are also downsides to this approach as discussed in section 6.6.2.

6.6.1 Methodology

For the simplified models, I use two different methodologies.

Model 10 Manual variable selection
Variable subset consisting of all twelve variables, which have been significant in the complete or any of the partial models.

Model 11 Automatic variable selection
Variable subset is determined by the stepwise selection algorithm, which uses forward selection to identify the variables with the 'best' contribution to the regression term.

The manual selection approach is not a standard statistical procedure. It is based on a 'survival of the fittest' assumption, i.e., by considering the 'fitting,' i.e. significant, variables of the models calculated before. It is meant to complement the stepwise regression method – which is heavily criticized – with a variable selection procedure following a different logic. The approach to select variables for a model based on their performance in sub-models is similarly used by Eichner (2010).

"Stepwise regressions are generally frowned upon by statisticians" (Field, 2013; p. 322). By selecting automatically, they provide an easy solution to statistical problems with limited data and relatively too many variables. In my approach, I use the stepwise regression as an additional statistical lens in my analysis. To allow a proper assessment of its result (in the context of the results of the other models), a brief discussion of the specific properties and limitation of stepwise regression is necessary.

6.6.2 Stepwise regression

The general idea of evaluating multiple combinations of variables to determine a subset of variables best suited to explain the dependent variable was discussed early on by Hocking (1976). With the general availability of more computational power, these methods are widely used today and range from 'stepwise algorithm' in rating (Falkenstein et al., 2000) (with a topic very similar to the research of this study) to the much more advanced elastic net selection algorithms used in DNA analysis (Cho et al., 2010), developed by Zou and Hastie (2005). While these more advanced algorithms are well-suited to derive conclusions from datasets with an extreme number of genome variables, for my comparably simple case, the stepwise regression has been judged to be better suited than these newer algorithms. The penalty terms of the elastic net and the Lasso algorithm, in particular, make a conjoint discussion of different approaches very difficult. The stepwise regression algorithm yields results directly comparable to the other approaches used in this study and their performances and downsides are well documented in the literature.

The stepwise regression is based on a three-condition repeat loop (see e.g., Field, 2013; Hocking, 1976). These steps are:

- Step one – *adding variables*: Multiple regressions are performed, each of these based on a subset of variables, consisting of one of the variables not part of the selected subset and all variables already selected for the subset.

The variable with the highest selection criteria is added, if this is above/below a certain threshold.

For this study, the criterion is the significance level and the variable with the lowest significance level is added, as long as it is below 0.05.

- Step two – *removing variables*: If the regression of the variables, which are already in the subset, results in a value above/ below a certain value for any of these variables, this variable is removed from the model.

  In this case, the criterion for removal is again the variable's significance level: If this is above 0.10, the variable is removed.
- If no variables are added or removed, the algorithm ends.

The stepwise regression has some well-known limitations (Whittingham et al., 2006), these are:

- Selection bias – leading to overfitting and incorrect significance tests.
- Difficulty in judging quality of the final model – inflation of adj. R^2 values.
- Other models, which are equally good or better, might be overlooked.

The selection bias addresses the issue that variables are selected based on their fitness to the current regression and specifically for the sample, which is the basis for the regression. The fact that there is more than one significance test for a fixed variable set, and a significance test for many possible variable combinations, inflates the probability of misjudging the actual significance of variables. Variables are selected because of their fitness to the current sample, not because of their fitness to the general population the sample is drawn from.

Consequently, this method inflates R^2 as variables are selected that have a statistical effect on the result variable (whether this is by chance in the current sample or because the effect is actually present in the general population). Thus the R^2 values usually overestimate the actual R^2 value.

As the stepwise procedure follows a fixed path by adding one variable after another, it has been shown that the resulting subsets are usually not the best and most appropriate ones.

These limitations are part of the specific character of stepwise regression. To some extent, using a bootstrapping in the final stepwise model validates the topics of over-fitting, incorrect significance level and inflated R^2 values, but these limitations remain to be considered when interpreting the results.

Similar limitations, although on a lower level, have to be considered for the manual selection. Selection bias might be introduced into the result models through using sequential regression to select variables, as is done here.

6.6.3 Results of the simplified models

Again, as for the complete model and the partial models, the results are presented consolidated; the result table (Table 18) is limited to all variables, which are significant in any of the simplified models.

	Model 10	Model 11
	Simplified model (manual)	Simplified model (step-wise)
Number of variables	12	7
EPV	17.4	29.9
adj. R^2	0.49	0.48
Sign.	0.000	0.000
Max. VIF	2.1	2.0
Portfolio crisis contribution factors		
Insufficient quality and service	-0.19**	-0.21***
Turnaround context		
Development of market segment during turnaround	0.16*	0.18**
Stakeholder management during turnaround	0.31***	0.35***
Internal context		
Family share in the company before crisis	0.12*	0.15**
External context		
Long-term growth perspectives of market segment	0.31***	0.28***
Interaction effects		
'Unsuitable CEO' × 'CEO change'	0.17***	0.26***
'Unsuitable members of TMT' × 'change in TMT'	n/a	-0.12*

Table 18: Simplified model regression.

Dependent variable *'turnaround result,'* standardized beta values shown; N = 209.
Only variables shown with significance level p≤ 0.05 in at least one model.
Significance levels at 0.05; 0.01 and 0.001 indicated by *; ** and ***.
Model 10: Consideration of all variables significant in the complete model of any of the partial models.
Model 11: Stepwise regression with all variables. Sign. to enter variable 0.05; Sign. to remove variable 0.10.

The two simplified models show both high significance (sign. < 0.001) as well as limited multicollinearity (max. VIF in both models 2.1 and 2.0). The number of significant variables is six for Model 10 and seven for Model 11. At the same, the adj. R^2 are very similar (Model 10: Adj. $R^2 = 0.49$; Model 11: Adj. $R^2 = 0.48$) and slightly higher than for the complete model (adj. $R^2 = 0.45$) or the best partial model (managerial partial model: Adj. $R^2 = 0.45$).

The selected variables and their significance levels are consistent between the two simplified models. With the exception of the interaction effect *'unsuitable members of TMT'* × *'change in TMT,'* which is significant for the stepwise regression but not present in the manually selected model, the other six significant variables are identical for both models, despite the fact that different variable selection methods have been used.

Further variable analysis is conducted in the conjoint discussion of all four analysis approaches in the following section.

6.7 Discussion

The four different regression approaches allow applying different perspectives on the characteristics of crisis and turnaround and their effect on the '*turnaround result.*' Despite the potential risks coming from the complex model with a – in comparison – low number of cases, the results show a high level of consistency and allow identification of key factors for turnaround success, as well as highlight some factors that might affect the turnaround outcome.

The discussion is done in two steps, first a comprehensive comparison of the different models is discussed; second, the variables that have shown significant impact on the *'turnaround result'* are analyzed and discussed comprehensively.

6.7.1 Comparison of the modeling approaches

For the model comparison, seven (of the total eleven) models are considered. The first four models are steps toward the complete model and as intermediate steps are not part of this discussion.

	Model 5	Model 6	Model 7	Model 8	Model 9	Model 10	Model 11
Model structure	Complete model	Partial model (oper.)	Partial model (manag.)	Partial model (port.)	Partial model (fin.)	Simpl. model (manual)	Simpl. model (stepwise)
Number of variables	74	45	28	30	34	12	7
Number of sign. variables	2	4	5	4	6	6	7
EPV	2.8	4.6	7.5	7.0	6.1	17.4	29.9
adj. R^2	**0.45**	**0.39**	**0.45**	**0.43**	**0.42**	**0.49**	**0.48**
Sign.	0.00	0.00	0.00	0.00	0.00	0.00	0.00
Max. VIF	5.2	2.6	2.9	2.3	2.3	2.1	2.0

Table 19: Overview of the different regression approaches.

Dependent variable *'turnaround result;'* N = 209.
Number of sign. variables includes all variables with a significance level of $p \leq 0.05$.
Model 5: Context variables, crisis variables, turnaround management variables, interaction effect variables.
Model 6: Context variables, crisis context variables, external CCF variables, turnaround context variables, operational crisis variables, operational turnaround management variables, operational interaction effect variables.
Model 7: Context variables, crisis context variables, external CCF variables, turnaround context variables, managerial crisis variables, managerial turnaround management variables, managerial interaction effect variables.
Model 8: Context variables, crisis context variables, external CCF variables, turnaround context variables, portfolio crisis variables, portfolio turnaround management variables, portfolio interaction effect variables.
Model 9: Context variables, crisis context variables, external CCF variables, turnaround context variables, financial crisis variables, financial turnaround management variables, financial interaction effect variables.
Model 10: Consideration of all variables significant in the complete model of any of the partial models.
Model 11: Stepwise regression with all variables. Sign. to enter variable 0.05; Sign. to remove variable 0.10.

The comparison of the different models' explanatory power – expressed by the adj. R^2 value – shows a satisfactory level for all models, especially compared to other empirical work researching turnaround. The adj. R^2 values are all between 0.39 and 0.49 and thus able to explain 39% to 49% of the variance of the '*turnaround result*' variable. In comparison, other empirical works showed adj. $R^2 = 0.26$ (Sudarsanam & Lai, 2001), adj. $R^2 = 0.37$ (research specific for cases of financial restructuring Jostarndt, 2007) and McFadden's $R^2 = 0.48$ (Eichner, 2010), although his final model mainly (5 of 11 significant variables) relies on 'late' restructuring moves, i.e., the negative effects on turnaround probability of restructuring moves in the third and later year of the turnaround. These are, in my opinion, symptoms, not predictors of a failing turnaround – see section 2.2.2.

The lowest adj. R^2 value is found for the operational partial model. The adj. R^2 values of the remaining models are between 0.42 and 0.49 and thus within a corridor of 0.45

±10%. It seems that operational restructuring moves and operational crisis characteristics, while widely discussed in the literature (see in chapter 4, among many others, e.g., Faghfouri, 2013; Hofer, 1980; Pearce & Robbins, 1993; Robbins & Pearce, 1992; Slatter, 1984; Sudarsanam & Lai, 2001), apparently do not play a differentiating role concerning the turnaround result.

On the contrary, the managerial partial model having the best explanatory power of the partial models reflects the high relevance of the CEO role in the literature (see in chapter 4, among many others, e.g., Cater & Schwab, 2008; Clapham et al., 2005; Hofer, 1980; Trahms et al., 2013).

The comparably low R^2 value of the complete model can be explained due to the penalization term of the adjusted R^2, which reduces the R^2 for each variable added to adjust for the bias introduced by adding more variables. This specifically applies to the complete model (adj. $R^2 = 0.45$; having 74 variables), which is on a similar level to the managerial partial model (adj. $R^2 = 0.45$; having 28 variables) and thus even below both of the simplified models (Model 10: Adj. $R^2 = 0.49$; 10 variables; Model 11: Adj. $R^2 = 0.48$; 7 variables). The explanatory power gained by additional variables appears to be outweighed by the bias introduced into the model, a fact highlighted by the two simplified models with only seven, respectively twelve, variables and the highest adj. R^2.

While the complete model's adj. R^2 is on a similar level to the other models and the model itself is significant (sign. < 0.001), it shows only two variables with significant effects, thus illustrating the reduced statistical power with an increasing number of variables. As discussed before, multicollinearity (max. VIF = 5.2, which is above the warning level of 5) possibly impairs the detection of significant betas for the complete model.

While the seven models differ in conceptual and empirical design, their different approaches and content are specifically suitable to perform a cross-model variable assessment by investigating commonalities and differences between the models.

6.7.2 Comprehensive discussion of the results per variable

The research question "Which conditions enhance turnaround success?" guides the content of this chapter. Consequently, the discussion of individual variables is the most important approach to answering this question. To allow a meaningful discussion, the complementary question concerning variables widely assumed to have an effect, but which turn out not to be significant (e.g., the pre-crisis profitability – see section 4.6.1.4), is not covered. To allow a comprehensive assessment of the variables, which turn out to be significant in any of the seven models (excluding the first four models, as only intermediate steps towards the complete model), Table 20**Fehler! Verweisquelle konnte nicht gefunden werden.** shows the respective univariate results as well as the standardized betas and the significance level for each of the relevant models for each of them.

	Uni-variate	Model 5	Model 6	Model 7	Model 8	Model 9	Model 10	Model 11
		Complete model	Partial model (oper.)	Partial model (manag.)	Partial model (portfolio)	Partial model (financial)	Simpl. model (manual)	Simpl. model (stepwise)
Portfolio crisis contribution factors								
Insufficient quality and service	-0.28***	-0.16	n/a	n/a	-0.19**	n/a	-0.19**	-0.21***
Financial crisis contribution factors								
Overleveraging	-0.16*	-0.18	n/a	n/a	n/a	-0.19*	-0.08	n/a
External crisis contribution factors								
Market decline	-0.08	0.2	0.15*	0.1	0.12	0.18*	0.08	n/a
Turnaround context								
Development of market segment during turna-	0.44***	0.12	0.12	0.18*	0.15	0.18*	0.16*	0.18**
Stakeholder management during turnaround	0.42***	0.29**	0.31***	0.27***	0.32***	0.36***	0.31***	0.35***
Internal context								
Family share in the company before crisis	0.16*	0.14	0.19**	0.14*	0.14*	0.13*	0.12*	0.15**
External context								
Long-term growth perspectives of market	0.45***	0.32**	0.33***	0.27**	0.28***	0.32***	0.31***	0.28***
Interaction effects								
'Unsuitable CEO' × 'CEO change'	0.17*	0.15	n/a	0.17*	n/a	n/a	0.17***	0.26***
'Unsuitable members of TMT' × 'change in	0.09	-0.10	n/a	-0.08	n/a	n/a	n/a	-0.12*

Table 20: Variable overview for different regression approaches.

Depended variable '*turnaround result*,' standardized beta values shown; N = 209.
Only variables shown with significance level p≤ 0.05 in at least one model.
Significance levels at 0.05; 0.01 and 0.001 indicated by *; ** and ***.
For model details please refer to the respective sections 6.3, 6.4, 6.5 and 6.6.

The results are discussed on a per variable basis before concluding with a general assessment of the different model dimensions concerning their influence on the turnaround outcome (overview of concluding assessment in Table 21).

In the crisis model, three variables turn up as significant in at least one of the relevant models.

The CCF *'insufficient quality and service'* is significantly negative for the '*turnaround result'* in all models integrating this variable, excluding the complete model. For the case of the complete model, it is worth noting that all intermediate regressions in the development of the complete models show significance for this variable. While the standardized beta value is -0.28 for the univariate regression, the significant standardized beta values of the multivariate regression models for this variable range within a rather narrow corridor between -0.19 and -0.21. In the complete model – while not significant – the value is similar, with -0.16.

In the literature, the topic of product and service quality is underrepresented (see section 4.4.3.2), while this study clearly shows that it has a high relevance for turnaround success. Drawing on the contingency theory (see section 2.3.1), it seems that *'insufficient quality and service'* impairs the turnaround options of a company, thus reducing the ability to execute successful turnaround strategies. The restructuring moves in the conceptual model (chapter 4) reflect this fact, as there is no 'direct counter' for this issue.

The evidence clearly indicates that this variable is important for turnaround and has to be considered as highly likely linked to turnaround success. As the effect of '*insufficient quality and service*' is present in all models but the complete model, it seems to affect '*turnaround result*' with effect strength below the detection capability of the compete model.

'Overleveraging' is the second crisis-related variable that turns out to be significantly negative for *'turnaround result'* in at least one model. This significance is limited to the financial partial model and the univariate regression. The significance level for the other two regression models is above the 0.05 threshold. The stepwise regression

function does not select this variable. The standardized beta values fluctuate between -0.08 and -0.19, but are negative for all models.

The negative effect of *'overleveraging'* is not in line with most publications. While the effect of *'overleveraging'* is assumed to be crisis promoting, it is similarly assumed that privatized restructuring (see section 4.5.4), i.e., debt relief for the company, should ease restructuring efforts if the going concern value is above the liquidation value of the company (Gilson et al., 1990; M. C. Jensen, 1991, 2010; John, 1993). This follows the line of argument that while debt might cause a crisis, it is rational for the financing partners to give up part of the debt – and thus rectify this CCF – to preserve the value of the remaining debt of the company. This study finds neither the positive effect of the CCF *'overleveraging'* on the *'turnaround success,'* nor does it find any interaction effect between *'overleveraging'* and *'debt write-off or debt-to-equity-swap.'*

It seems – again drawing on the contingency theory (see section 2.3.1) – that overly-high debt is also a limiting factor in turnaround and has a weak, but perceivable negative impact on turnaround.

Ultimately, the assessment of this variable is based on limited evidence and thus considered as inconclusive. There seems to be a relation with turnaround success, but comparably weak in nature and thus it cannot be reliably detected with the models in this study.

The external CCF *'market decline'* shows inconsistent effects on *'turnaround result.'* Despite being part of all but one model (the stepwise regression model being the exception), the variable shows significant positive effects only for the operational and the financial partial model. Specifically for the univariate regression, there is only an insignificant negative effect. For the remaining multi-variable regression models, the insignificant beta values are consistently positive, while the variable is not selected in the stepwise regression.

Finding an insignificant negative effect for this variable in the univariate regression and a positive – for some of the models significant – effect on *'turnaround result'* indicates a complementary contribution of the variable.

A possible explanation might follow the logic of combining variables. In combination with other CCF variables, this variable allows differentiation of the cases in which there are no fundamental weaknesses to the company or changing market environment (as it would be indicated by the highly significant variables '*long-term growth perspectives of market segment*'). Having this in mind, this variable could allow identifying short-term market crunches, e.g., the sudden collapse in the automotive market 2008-2009 in Germany. It could be assumed that in these cases the CCF '*market decline*' allows discerning companies that are just experiencing a crisis due to a short-term decline from companies with fundamental issues, and thus shows a positive relation with the '*turnaround result.*' Regardless, the effect itself is comparably weak and not reliably detected in this study.

Among the turnaround management model variables, the number of variables with significant effects on '*turnaround result*' in any of the models is limited to two. None of the restructuring move variables are among these, but both of the turnaround context variables are.

The turnaround context variable '*development of market segment during turnaround*' is present in all seven models, but significantly positive in only four of them. In the three models in which the variable is not significant the respective values are not consistently close to the significance level. The beta values themselves are all in a limited range between 0.12 and 0.18, specifically the four significant values are in a narrow corridor between 0.16 and 0.18. At the same time, for the univariate regression, the beta value is much higher with a standardized beta of 0.44. This variable is correlated with '*long-term growth perspectives of market segment.*' While '*long-term growth perspectives of market segment*' is discussed later in the course of this chapter, it is clear that it consistently has a significant positive effect on the '*turnaround result*' in all models.

As in the multivariate regression, the predictor effect of the common variance of the two variables can only be attributed to either of the two variables; a lower value of the standardized beta in the multivariate models compared with the univariate regression is plausible.

The interpretation of this variable is straightforward, following the discussion in the related conceptual model chapter (section 4.5.5). The market development during turnaround sets the stage for the turnaround, either easing liquidity problems and restructuring through a positive market environment or limiting the options of the company by increased market pressure during the turnaround.

The effect is statistically consistent both in content and direction, intuitive, and thus highly likely to represent a real world relation.

The second turnaround management context variable, *'stakeholder management during turnaround,'* shows a highly significant standardized beta value through all seven models. The standardized beta values are high and within a range between 0.27 and 0.36. The univariate regression shows a value slightly above that corridor with 0.44.

"Identifying and influencing the perceptions of the critical stakeholders is essential for firm turnaround" (Trahms et al., 2013; p. 1293). This statement, similarly reflected by other authors (among others Arogyaswamy et al., 1995; Liou & Smith, 2006; Slatter, 1984; Slatter & Lovett, 1999, compare chapter 4) is reconfirmed by this study. It can be assumed that maintaining stakeholder support during turnaround is highly significant and important for any company. Much more – so it seems – than the actual content of the turnaround management.

The effect of *'stakeholder management during turnaround'* on the *'turnaround result'* is undoubted and consistently shown in all regression models.

Both internal and external context contain one variable each, which is significant in any of the seven relevant regression models.

The context variable *'family share in the company before crisis'* shows a significant effect in all but the complete models. The standardized beta values are in a corridor between 0.12 and 0.19. The significant standardized beta of the univariate regression is also in this corridor.

It seems that a higher share of family ownership increases the probability of turnaround success. There are two possible explanations for this: one drawing on the logic of the principal-agent theory (see section 2.3.2 and 2.4.3.1), the other on the SEW (see section 2.4.3.3) and RBV (see section 2.3.3 and 2.4.3.2).

The identity of CEO and ownership is the case for 87% of the companies with family ownership in the data set. Using the principal-agent theory, it can be theorized that if the owner is at the same time CEO, his shareholder role makes him strongly averse to a restructuring through insolvency, as this would usually impact the shareholder ownership and thus the family fortune (see section 6.3.3 for information of share value in insolvency). An agent, i.e., employed manager of a company, is much more inclined to restructure through insolvency, as it might be a reasonable way for the company to recover. At the same time, a late filing for insolvency might incur damage compensation and even a prison sentence for the managing director, a risk that an employed manager will try to avoid. A family manager on the other hand is incentivized to evaluate all options before filing.

Drawing on the SEW (section 2.4.3.3), this effect can be attributed to the strong desire of the family for the continuation of the company (driven by the different SEW dimensions, as conceptually defined by Berrone et al., 2012); the family is thus willing to go beyond the financially reasonable activities a rational shareholder would carry out (to promote turnaround success, i.e., personal pledges, contribution of family assets, etc.), thus providing 'familiness' to the company, helping to withstand the crisis (compare section 2.4.3.2).

The *'family share in the company before crisis'* seems to have a positive effect on '*turnaround result*,' although this effect does not seem to be strong enough to be detected by the complete model.

The effect of *'long-term growth perspectives of market segment'* is similar to the *'stakeholder management during turnaround'*: The significantly positive effect is detected through all models. The standardized beta values for the multivariate regressions are in a narrow corridor between 0.27 and 0.33. The univariate value is with 0.45 significantly higher, which can be partly attributed to the correlated variable *'development of market segment during turnaround,'* as already discussed in the assessment of this variable. The shared effect between the two variables leads to a reduction in the betas of both variables.

A growing market causes the company value to increase, but only in the going concern perspective (see section 4.5.4). In these cases, all stakeholders – especially banks, existing and new shareholders – have a high interest in ensuring the company going concern perspective. It has been shown that financial restructuring probability increases under these conditions (C. James, 1995). Specifically, these firms are able to raise additional liquidity secured against future cash flow (John, 1993), whether these are external bank financing or equity contributions. It appears that the presence of future value growth has a strong impact on the options and possibilities during turnaround, thus promoting turnaround success.

The conclusion is similar to the case of '*stakeholder management during turnaround*': '*Long-term growth perspectives of market segment*' do have an effect on '*turnaround result,*' which is undoubtedly and consistently shown by all analyzed regression models.

The interaction effects that are part of the analysis showed two variables having a significant effect on *'turnaround result'* in any of the seven relevant regression models.

The interaction effect *'unsuitable CEO'* × *'CEO change'* is the only effect that resulted as significant in the regression of the moderating effects in section 6.3.4. Among the different regression models it turned out significantly positive in all models that integrate the effect, except in the complete model. The effect is also selected by the stepwise regression algorithm. The standardized beta values are in a narrow corridor between 0.15 and 0.17 in all models but the stepwise regression (stand. beta = 0.26). There seems to be an effect from the – also in the stepwise regression selected – variable *'unsuitable members of TMT'* × *'change in TMT,'* which is correlated with '*unsuitable CEO*' × '*CEO change.*' As the second interaction effect has a negative beta
(stand. beta = -0.12) it might be speculated that this negative beta partly compensates some of the common effect with '*unsuitable CEO*' × '*CEO change,*' thus leading to inflated beta values. These inflation effects are a common downside of stepwise regression models (see 6.6.2).

As stated in the discussion of the interaction effects, there is a clear indication that for the companies analyzed in this study, the removal of a CEO is not a requirement per se, as often suggested in literature (see in chapter 4, e.g., Bibeault, 1982; Clapham et al., 2005; Grinyer & Spender, 1979; Hofer, 1980; Nystrom & Starbuck, 1984; Slatter, 1984; Slatter & Lovett, 1999), but instead the effectiveness of such a removal depends on the CEO's contribution to the crisis . Indications for this have been found (much less fine grained) in a minority of other studies, e.g., that a CEO removal in the context of industry contraction reduces the effectiveness of restructuring (Arogyaswamy et al., 1995).

The removal of a CEO has two different effects. On the positive side, it might be necessary to regain stakeholder support (Cater & Schwab, 2008; Slatter, 1984) and allow the implementation of drastic changes, impossible for CEOs with defined habits and strategies (Sudarsanam & Lai, 2001). At the same time, the downside is the loss of the CEO's know-how and transition costs for the company (Arogyaswamy et al., 1995; Cater & Schwab, 2008). It seems that these costs are outweighed by the positive effect only if the CEO was an important contributor to the crisis. Under these circumstances, the measure 'CEO change' promotes the '*turnaround result.*' It seems that the effect *'unsuitable CEO'* × *'CEO change'* has an effect on '*turnaround result,*' but below the detection capability of the complete model.

The interaction effect *'unsuitable members of TMT'* × *'change in TMT'* is significantly negative only for the stepwise regression. In all other models, as well as in the univariate regression this variable has no significant effect. Missing other models confirming the findings of the stepwise regression, I attribute this effect to the specific weaknesses of the stepwise regression as discussed in section 6.6.2.

Variable name	Assessment	Stand. beta
Portfolio crisis contribution factors		
Insufficient quality and service	Important	-0.16 – -0.21
Financial crisis contribution factors		
Overleveraging	Inconclusive	Negative, unclear strength
External crisis contribution factors		
Market decline	Inconclusive	Unclear
Turnaround context		
Development of market segment during turnaround	Limited	0.12 – 0.18
Stakeholder management during turnaround	Very important	0.27 – 0.36
Internal context		
Family share in the company before crisis	Important	0.12 – 0.19
External context		
Long-term growth perspectives of market segment	Very important	0.27 – 0.33
Interaction effects		
'Unsuitable CEO' × 'CEO change'*	Important	0.15 – 0.17
'Unsuitable members of TMT' × 'change in TMT'	Doubtful	Unclear

Table 21: Variable assessment based on multiple regression analyses.

Dependent variable *'turnaround result.'* Comprehensive cross-regression model comparison.
Assessment of the variables:
Very important – significant in all models.
Important – significant below the statistical power of complete models.
Limited – limited evidence with mixed results.
Inconclusive – limited statistical evidence with conceptual concerns.
Doubtful – little statistical evidence with strong conceptual concerns.
* beta values exclude the result of stepwise regressions, due to statistical concerns.

6.7.3 Conclusion

The comprehensive analysis of the different variables in the different regressions relates an informative picture of the relative importance of the different model dimensions: Specifically, the notion that crisis characteristics, turnaround management characteristics and context factors have an effect on turnaround, expressed in the Propositions 1, 4 and 7, could be confirmed.

It seems that the characteristics of the crisis (crisis contribution factors) have a much more prominent impact on the turnaround result than the content of the turnaround strategy (restructuring moves). While the crisis context (i.e., the crisis process: Deterioration pattern, severity and complexity) does not turn up as one of the key influencing factors for the turnaround result, the turnaround management context (i.e., market development during turnaround and stakeholder management) plays a very important role for the turnaround result. The statistically limited impact of the content of turnaround strategies might explain the mixed evidence found and criticized in turnaround research so far.

Concerning the context, many of the variables highlighted in the research (e.g., *'pre-crisis profitability'* or *'slack resources before crisis'*) do not play a key role, while the *'long-term growth perspectives of market segment,'* which heavily influence the going concern value, are one of the main factors for the turnaround result.

Researchers have maintained that family firms fail more often (Cater & Schwab, 2008; Gómez-Mejía et al., 2007; Lansberg, 1988), especially during the handover from founders to the next generation (Lansberg, 1988). This research cannot add any clarification to this topic as the probability of experiencing a crisis cannot be assessed with the present empirical data. It can be concluded though, that a family firm has a higher probability of recovering from a crisis when it materializes.

Limited by the statistical restrictions of regression functions, the complete model already stretches the sensible amount of variables to a point where only two significant effects can be detected. It can be assumed that there are many other interaction effects between the different model elements than just the relation between the CCF *'unsuitable CEO'* and the restructuring move *'CEO change.'* This interaction is the only one of the thirteen interaction effects considered to turn up with reasonably significant statistical evidence. But as the topic of top management changes plays an important role in turnaround research, it can contribute to this highly controversial subject with valid empirical evidence. This is a confirmation, as far as this proposition is reflected in this analysis, for Proposition 5 (for this specific interaction effect).

For future research, adding the most important variables uncovered by the multiple regression approach of this study seems prudent (Table 21). Research investigating specific partial cause-effect relations in crisis and turnaround, e.g., financial restructuring (Jostarndt, 2007), stakeholder relevance (Buschmann, 2006) or different turnaround moves (Eichner, 2010), should contemplate integrating, at minimum, the factors this study uncovered as important for turnaround result, to allow a possibly more meaningful attribution of effects.

7 Archetypes of crisis and archetypes of turnaround

In the discussion of the conceptual model (chapter 4), the notion of patterns in crisis and turnaround is introduced through propositions 3 and 6. The theory of gestalts (Miller, 1981), introduced in section 2.3.4, is the foundation of this notion. It is based on the assumption that there are a limited number of specific configurations of strategic variables that yield configuration-specific performances. Following Miller (1981), these configurations or 'gestalts' are labeled as archetypes in this study.

In most research contexts, this analysis is performed to identify successful strategies. The application for turnaround management is thus straightforward. It can also be extended for the case of crises, i.e., analyzing specific configurations of crisis characteristics and their respective performance.

The research of specific patterns has been employed in both crisis and turnaround research before.

This chapter consists of three major segments. First, a brief overview of the clustering and segmentation approaches conducted in other studies is given (section 7.1), followed by an introductory discussion of the statistical methodology (section 7.2). Following that, two cluster analyses are conducted sequentially and separately for the crisis characteristics (section 7.3) and the turnaround management characteristics (section 7.4). As the last step, the results of both cluster analyses are combined to identify interaction patterns and to evaluate the performance of combinations of crisis clusters and turnaround clusters (section 7.5). The chapter concludes with a brief discussion of the results (section 7.6).

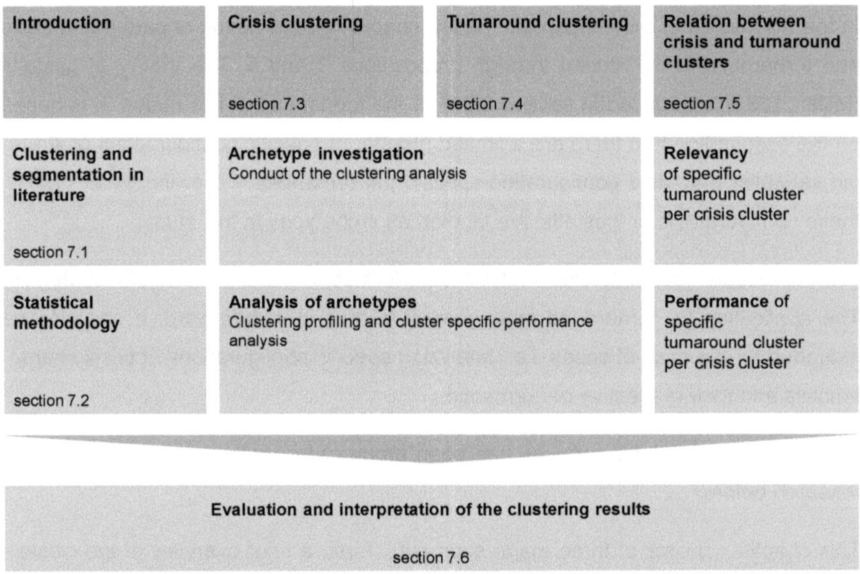

Figure 36: Overview of chapter structure (chapter 7).
Source: Own illustration.

7.1 Clustering and segmentation in crisis and turnaround research

As an initial step, this section introduces two classification approaches for crisis and one classification approach for turnaround management.

7.1.1 Classification of crisis

The first study utilizes financial data rather than cluster analysis to categorize archetypes of crises. As already mentioned in section 3.2.3, Asquith and Gertner (1994) used a scenario technique to calculate performance improvement if the cash flow improvements, e.g., specific financial variables of the company, are on the average industry level or – in case of industry-level operating performance – on the same level as the previous year. In this schematic, the largest improvement indicates the primary source of financial distress. Based on this idea, they implemented a classification scheme with three classes, which are distinct and mutually exclusive.

The classification was later extended by Eichner (2010) to four classes by adding the overexpansion category (operationalized by comparing the companies CAPEX with the average industry CAPEX).

The crises types as defined by the extended framework (Eichner, 2010) are:

- *Overleverage,* i.e., debt is too high for the company to service.
- *Overexpansion*, i.e., the firm is investing too much money in growth.
- *Operating profitability,* i.e., the company's profit is low compared to industry average.
- *Industry-level operating profitability,* i.e., while the company is in line profit-wise with the industry average, the industry itself has a profit issue.

A different approach was chosen by Hauschildt et al. (2006) – see section 2.2.3 – in the last of their three models. They used cluster analysis to segment their cases into common archetypes. Based on their 67 crisis variables characterization, they found five clusters (Hauschildt et al., 2006; p.16-17):

- *CEO with character weaknesses* ("Unternehmer mit Persönlichkeitsdefekten"): The CEO follows solely his own interests. Speculation and criminal activities are included in this archetype.
- *Companies with interpersonal interaction defects* ("Unternehmen mit Störungen der persönlichen Interaktion"): Conflicts between managers or employees are unresolved, frequent replacements in TMT, lack of supervisory board control.
- *Companies with operational defects* ("Unternehmen mit operativen Störungen"): Weaknesses in the sales channels and the sales structure. Incorrect or delayed investments in assets and R&D.
- *Companies with institutional defects* ("Unternehmen mit institutionellen Störungen"): Deficits in the organizational structure, organizational slack, weaknesses in finance and controlling.
- *Companies with unexpected sales problems* ("Unternehmen vor unerwarteten, abrupten Absatzproblemen"): Incorrect market assessment combined with sudden decline in sales.

The segmentation approaches by Eichner (2010) and Hauschildt et al. (2006) find very different clusters in their analyses. The approach by Eichner (2010) is very different in terms of the method used to structure the archetypes (i.e., based on financial figures), but it employs a perspective focused on the company which is similar to this study. The approach by Hauschildt et al. (2006) used a methodology (i.e., cluster analysis with Ward's algorithm) similar to this study, but employed a very different perspective on the crisis. The perspective is focused on the personality and the characterization of the management.

This makes the first approach the preferred reference structure when interpreting the cluster results of this study. The second segmentation is, due to its different perspective, difficult to compare with my results.

7.1.2 Classification of turnaround management

The earliest attempt to classify turnaround strategies was carried out by Hofer (1980), who established four archetypes of turnaround strategies. These were extended by Eichner (2010) to six archetypes (see section 2.2.2). As Eichner integrated and extended the Hofer scheme, the presentation here is limited to the extended version, while referencing the respective original archetypes by Hofer:

- *Radical growth strategy* (Hofer: 'Revenue growth')
  This turnaround cluster includes growth promotion strategies like new product development and acquisitions and organic growth, complemented by productivity measures.
- *Strategic reorientation* (Hofer: N/a)
  This cluster usually includes CEO removal, asset divestment, acquisitions and new product development, which are supported by equity issuance.
- *Cash flow optimization* (Hofer: 'Cost cutting')
  This archetype focuses on cash flow improvements, like working capital reduction and CAPEX reduction, usually without CEO changes and portfolio restructuring.

- *Asset retrenchment* (Hofer: 'Asset reduction')
  This gestalt consists mainly of measures like asset sales, plant closures and working capital reduction, often complemented by layoffs and reduction in CAPEX.
- *Operational reorientation* (Hofer: 'Combination strategies')
  Combines aspects of the aforementioned archetypes, specifically CEO changes and product innovation with substantial asset sales, debt repayment and productivity measures.
- *Right sizing* (Hofer: 'Combination strategies')
  This is the second combined strategy, using financial restructuring together with large asset sales.

Eichner (2010) limited his analysis to successful turnarounds. I am convinced that specific combinations of strategic moves can be similarly analyzed based on the complete sample, including both failed and successful turnarounds. This approach broadens the statistical data basis and thus the achievable significance level, but more importantly it allows achievement of the main purpose of cluster analysis, the assessment of cluster-specific performances (i.e., average *'survival of company'* and *'turnaround result'*).

7.2 Statistical methodology

The application mode of cluster analysis in strategic management research has been heavily criticized by Ketchen and Shook (1996). They pointed out as the main issues of cluster analysis the missing test statistics (unlike the significance test for linear regression) and the fact that cluster analysis even finds clusters e in data where there actually are none. Based on their critical assessment, they have suggested a guideline for the execution of cluster analysis, aiming at maximizing the value of the results by methodological consistency.

Drawing on this guideline, the cluster analysis in this study is performed as a four-step procedure:

1. Clustering variables
2. Clustering algorithm
3. Determine the number of clusters

4. Validating the clusters

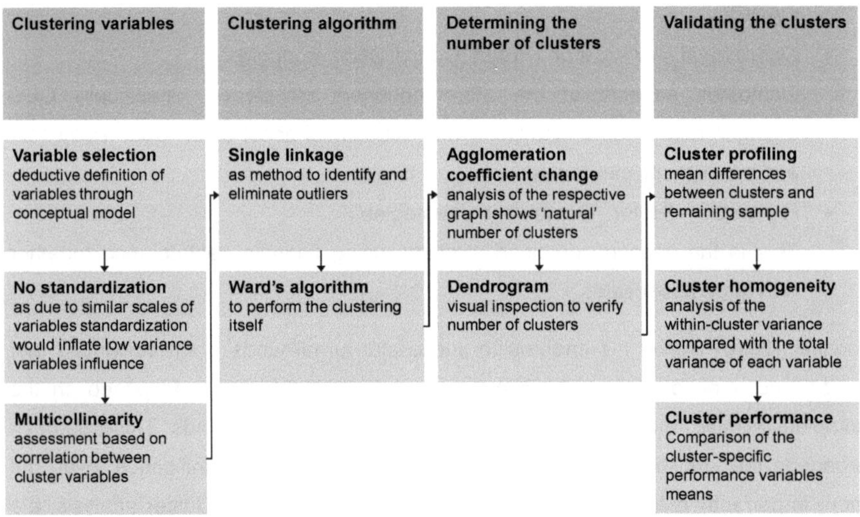

Figure 37: Conduct of cluster analysis.

Source: Adaption of procedure defined by Ketchen and Shook (1996).

7.2.1 Clustering variables

The selection of the clustering variables is the important initial step for t cluster analysis. The choice of a variable predetermines the clusters, which can be identified in the data (Gan et al., 2007). The process of selecting the clustering variable can be subdivided into three sequential steps:

- Selection of the variables.
- Standardization of variables.
- Multicollinearity of variables.

The selection of variables is based on the approach chosen by the scientific study. In the case of this study, the selection process follows a deductive approach, i.e., the structure of the conceptual model deductively defines the two variable sets chosen for both of the cluster analyses (crisis clustering and turnaround clustering). In terms of the variable selection, this is seen as the best methodological approach (Hair et al., 2010; Ketchen & Shook, 1996). It is important to note that the analyses are not restricted to the relevant variables identified by the regression analyses in chapter 6. Instead it follows the fundamental idea of the theory of gestalts, meant to be employed in complex situations with many variables (see section 2.3.4) and includes all variables of the respective conceptual model dimension in the two cluster analyses (i.e., all variables remaining after the model simplification in section 5.2.3).

The standardization of variables is commonly recommended when using variable sets with very different ranges, as otherwise variables with wider ranges dominate variables with smaller ranges (i.e., turnover in EUR would usually overshadow the headcount of a firm). In the case of my study, standardization would not suit the research purpose. As all clustering variables are specifically coded with the same range based on a five-level-Likert scale, there is no overweighing issue. At the same time, standardization would artificially increase the weight of variables with low variability in the sample and thus decrease the differentiation induced by variables with high variability. This would not improve, but would rather debase the quality of the results; thus I perform the cluster analysis using non-standardized values.

Multicollinearity is also relevant in cluster analysis, although for different reasons than for linear regression (see section 6.4.2 for the general introduction of multicollinearity and its effect in linear regression). In a cluster analysis, multicollinearity increases the weight of factors if these are reflected in more than one highly correlated variable. For that reason, I analyze the correlation coefficients within the data set to investigate whether a variable simplification is appropriate and necessary.

7.2.2 Clustering algorithm

The cluster algorithm is the second important factor determining the results of the cluster analysis. Different algorithms yield very different results as they 'grow' the clusters depending on the distance measure used. Each cluster algorithm begins with considering each data set as a single cluster (i.e., number of clusters is the number of cases). In each step of the algorithm the two clusters with the minimal distance between are merged into a new cluster. Accordingly, the structure of the result depends on the distance measure, i.e., the cluster algorithm, used to calculate the distance between any two clusters.

For the purpose of this study, I chose to use the Ward's algorithm. Ward's algorithm grows clusters based on minimizing the within-cluster variance. This means minimizing the loss of information associated with each merger (Gan et al., 2007) and thus maximizing the homogeneity within a cluster (Hair et al., 2010). It tends to yield clusters with similar size (Hair et al., 2010; Ketchen & Shook, 1996). These properties are in line with my research targets to identify disjointed and homogenous archetypes of crisis and turnaround. On the other hand, Ward's algorithm is heavily impacted by outliers. To manage that issue, single linkage clustering is used as a first step to identify and eliminate outliers, as recommended by Ketchen and Shook (1996), before performing the actual clustering process.

Ward's algorithm is the most commonly used cluster method in strategic research. 36% of the studies reviewed by Ketchen and Shook (1996) use this algorithm. At the same time, Ward's algorithm is commonly used in the research field of crisis and turnaround, both for crisis clustering (Hauschildt et al., 2006) and for turnaround strategy clustering. Specifically, the outlier analysis with a single linkage clustering followed by using Ward's algorithm as a second step has been applied previously in turnaround research (Eichner, 2010; Schmuck, 2013).

7.2.3 Number of clusters

To determine the appropriate number of clusters, two methods are used concurrently: firstly, by visually analyzing the dendrogram for a meaningful number of clusters, secondly by analyzing a graph of the agglomeration coefficient change to identify 'elbows' in the curve progression. These elbows indicate that a specific merger has aggregated two very dissimilar clusters, compared to the merger before and thus indicate that the state before this dissimilar merger is a natural number of clusters in the sample.

7.2.4 Validating the clusters

The cluster validation is done using two different measurements. For each cluster, a mean comparison (ANOVA) between the cluster and the remaining data is performed to identify the key variables, which significantly differentiate this cluster statistically from the remaining data (Hair et al., 2010). Additionally, the cluster homogeneity is analyzed by comparing the F-value, which is the in-cluster variance divided by the variance of the whole data set, for each cluster and variable. A value below one signals a higher homogeneity within the cluster than for the whole set; if all variables have F-values below one, a cluster is completely homogeneous (Backhaus et al., 2011).

Beyond the numerical validation, the most important step is the analysis of the question of whether a clustering result actually reflects distinct and relevant strategic configurations. The cluster validation is thus concluded with a per cluster evaluation of whether it actually reflects an archetype in crisis and turnaround with real world relevancy.

7.3 Cluster analysis of crisis characteristics

The first of two cluster analyses analyzes the crisis characteristics to find clusters of cases with similar variable combinations, reflecting a specific crisis archetype. As discussed in section 7.2, the choice of cluster variables is straightforward and comprises all variables belonging to the model of the crisis (see section 4.4), modified by the simplifications conducted in section 5.2.3.The analysis of these variables shows a Pearson correlation coefficient below 0.7 for all variable combinations, which is unproblematic according to Schmuck (2013), who sees problems only above an upper limit of 0.9.

To eliminate outliers, a single linkage clustering is conducted. This usually results in a snakelike cluster structure, which links all cases sequentially to one large cluster chain (Hair et al., 2010). In this process, the agglomeration coefficient steeply increases for the last few cases added, thus indicating outlying data points. This is the basis for the selection of outliers. Based on the agglomeration schedule, as well as the visual inspection of the related dendrogram, four cases are ultimately eliminated from the sample as outliers.

The cluster analysis based on Ward's algorithm shows the agglomeration coefficient change shown in Figure 38. The agglomeration coefficient development indicates two possible solutions: A three-cluster segmentation and a six-cluster segmentation of the cases. This is reconfirmed by the visual inspection of the dendrogram (not depicted). The detailed analysis of both solutions, especially the analysis of a valid representation of each cluster in a real word crisis configuration, shows much higher relevance of the segmentation in three clusters.

Change of agglomeration coefficient depending on the number of clusters

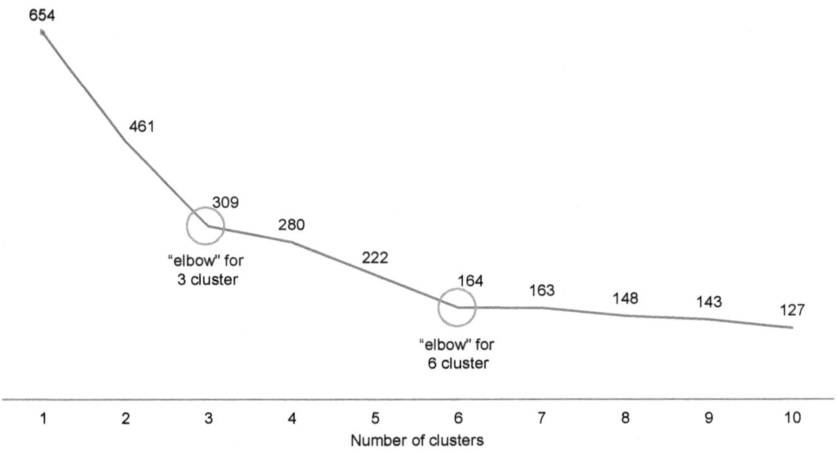

Figure 38: Change of agglomeration coefficient depending on the number of crisis clusters.
Source: Own illustration.

By comparing the cluster-specific means of all variables with the non-cluster means and assessing the significance of the difference, the profiles of each cluster emerging from the sample can be assessed. Following the presentation by Eichner (2010), the significance is complemented by the presentation of the t-statistic as additional information on the direction of the difference.

Variable name	**Total sample N = 205**	Cluster 1: ***Operational crisis*** **N = 47**		Cluster 2: ***Financial crisis*** **N = 105**		Cluster 3: ***Market crisis*** **N = 53**	
	Mean	Mean	T-stat.	Mean	T-stat.	Mean	T-stat.
Operational crisis contribution factors							
Incorrect investment in plant and equipment	2.9	3.7	4.38***	2.8	-1.66	2.5	-2.9**
Insufficient investments in plant and equipment	2	2.4	1.96	1.6	-5.10***	2.4	1.84
Degree of company-internal value-add too high	2.3	2.7	1.3	1.9	-4.83***	2.9	2.67**
Degree of company-internal value-add too low	1.6	1.7	0.41	1.5	-1.22	1.7	0.61
Weaknesses in organization and processes	3.9	4.4	5.39***	3.7	-3.91***	3.9	-1.28
Managerial crisis contribution factors							
Unsuitable CEO	3.7	4.4	6.38***	3.4	-3.8***	3.6	-1.75
Unsuitable members of TMT	3.4	3.8	2.72**	3.2	-2.88**	3.5	-0.02
Conflict spillover from owner family to company	2	3.4	8.76***	1.8	-3.58***	1.3	-7.7***
Succession problems	2.2	3.6	9.28***	1.9	-3.93****	1.5	-7.22***
Portfolio crisis contribution factors							
Incorrect market assessment	3.5	3.9	2.39*	3.1	-4.79***	3.9	2.39*
Overexpansion	2.8	2.8	0.98	3.2	4.57***	1.9	-5.45***
Missing innovation in core products	2.1	2.4	0.45	1.5	-8.42***	3.1	5.6***
Insufficient quality and service	2.4	2.6	0.73	2.2	-2.23*	2.7	1.18
Non-beneficial acquisitions	2.2	3	4.04***	2.1	-1.2	1.7	-3.8***

Variable name	Total sample N = 205	Cluster 1: *Operational crisis* N = 47		Cluster 2: *Financial crisis* N = 105		Cluster 3: *Market crisis* N = 53	
	Mean	Mean	T-stat.	Mean	T-stat.	Mean	T-stat.
Financial crisis contribution factors							
Financing structure inadequate	3	3.2	2.29*	3.3	2.84**	2.2	-4.96***
Cash flow to shareholders too high	2.2	3.2	5.64***	1.9	-3.72***	1.9	-3.15**
Overleveraging	3.6	4.1	3.22**	3.6	-0.57	3.3	-2.53*
External crisis contribution factors							
Market decline	2.9	3.4	1.89	2.2	-7.83***	3.8	4.97***
Increased competition	3.1	3.6	1.79	2.5	-9.01***	4.1	7.24***
Supply-side-induced crisis	2.4	2.7	1.88	2	-4.18***	2.7	1.81
Customer-induced crisis	3.5	3.7	1.14	3.2	-3.48***	3.9	2.19*
Crisis context							
Deterioration pattern of crisis	2.9	3.6	3.43***	2.4	-5.61***	3.3	1.28
Severity of crisis	4.1	4.1	0.42	4.1	0.66	4	-1.02
Initial complexity of company situation to implement turna-	3.6	3.9	2.63*	3.7	1.26	3.1	-4.02***

Table 22: Crisis cluster profiles.

Mean comparison; N = 205.
Significance levels at 0.05; 0.01 and 0.001 indicated by *; ** and ***.

Based on the analysis of the cluster properties, the three crisis clusters can be attributed to three distinct archetypes of crisis. The character of these clusters is defined by the distinct variables that differ significantly from the remaining data sample:

- Cluster 1: *Operational crisis*
- Cluster 2: *Financial crisis*
- Cluster 3: *Market crisis*

Operational crisis – the first cluster is characterized by two key elements:

firstly, an unsuitable CEO and management team, and secondly, weaknesses in processes and organization, which are found combined with incorrect investments.

The operational and managerial issues go along with the frequent occurrences of succession problems and conflict spillover from the owner family.

The deterioration pattern matches these characteristics of company facing operational and managerial issues and is significantly longer than for the average case in the remaining data sample, i.e., with a tendency towards long-term decline instead of shock-based crisis due to sudden events.

The operational issues often occur concurrently with other CCFs, e.g., overexpansion, incorrect investments and high cash flow to shareholders.

This depicts a company with operational issues and an inadequate management that is unable to properly execute its management duties, leading to a long-term decline process.

Financial crisis – the second cluster is less clearly identified. Specifically, it shows significantly lower values for the variables defining Cluster 1: *Operational crisis* and Cluster 3: *Market crisis*. It can be concluded that the absence of these crisis symptoms is one of the characterizing properties of Cluster 2. On the other hand, it shows a significantly higher value for variables, indicating issues with the financial structure and overexpansion, thus indicating that neither market nor operations is a key contribution factor for the crisis of the company; instead, the crisis is rooted in too much growth combined with an inadequate financial structure.

The mean of the context variable *'deterioration pattern of crisis'* of this cluster matches this picture, with a significant tendency towards quicker crisis development caused by sudden events. This depicts a fundamentally healthy company with an inadequate financial structure, making it vulnerable to sudden crisis developments.

The third cluster – *market crisis* – is characterized by increased competition complemented by market decline and customer issues, with a significantly higher contribution from *'missing innovation in core products'* and *'incorrect market assessment.'*

Cluster 3 depicts the typical market crisis scenario precipitated mainly by external market-related issues, pressuring the company with declining markets and increasing competition into a crisis. Incorrect market assessment and missing innovation indicate at the same time that the company has failed to adjust its strategy to the changing market environment.

After characterizing the clusters based on their variable profiles, the next step is to evaluate the specific mean of the performance variable *'turnaround result'* and *'survival of company'* (which are not part of the clustering variables) for each cluster.

The mean value of *'turnaround result'* as a performance measure of the average company per cluster shows a differentiated picture, depending on the cluster affiliation (Table 23). Cluster 1: *Operational crisis* does not differ significantly from the remaining sample – neither in terms of performance nor in terms of survival rate. While the *financial crisis* cluster shows a significantly better performance after turnaround, the survival rate is not significantly different from the remaining data set. Cluster 3: *'Market crisis,'* on the other hand, is significantly worse in both respects – *'turnaround result'* and survival rate. It seems that a *market crisis* provokes the highest risk to a company and its survival.

Cluster	*Turnaround result*		*Survival of company*	
	Mean	T-stat.	Mean	T-stat.
Cluster 1: *Operational crisis*	2.9	0.45	68%	1.63
Cluster 2: *Financial crisis*	3.2	2.49*	67%	1.63
Cluster 3: *Market crisis*	2.3	-2.58*	43%	-2.99**
Total sample	2.9		61%	

Table 23: Performance per crisis cluster.

Mean of 'turnaround result' and mean of '*survival of company*' per crisis cluster; N = 205.
Significance levels at 0.05 and 0.01 indicated by * and **.

Crisis cluster	Cluster 1: **Operational crisis cluster** N = 47	Cluster 2: **Financial crisis cluster** N = 105	Cluster 3: **Market crisis cluster** N = 53
Key defining variables	**Unsuitable CEO and TMT;** Weaknesses in organization and processes	**Inadequate financing structure**	**Increased competition; Market decline**
Complementing cluster characterization	Issues with owning family both from conflicts and succession more frequent Long-term decline	Overexpansion issues Absence of any operational, management and market issues No issues with product quality or innovation Sudden crisis development	Internal value-add too high Missing innovation in products
Cluster performance	**Average** result 2.9 **Average** survival rate 68%	**Better** result 3.2 **Average** survival rate 67%	**Worse** result 2.3 **Worse** survival rate 43%

Figure 39: Crisis cluster characterization.

Source: Own illustration.

The homogeneity of the clusters can be assessed by the F-values of each cluster (Table 24). None of the clusters is completely homogenous, as the maximum F-value is in all cases above 1. It is apparent that while the *operational crisis* cluster and the *market crisis* cluster show a much lower within-cluster variance than the complete sample with a mean F-value of 0.79 and 0.82, the *financial crisis* cluster shows, with 0.95, an only slightly lower within-cluster variance.

Most other authors do not offer validity measures like the F-value for the emerging clusters; an exception is Eichner (2010). In his six-cluster solution for turnaround strategies, he has reported mean F-values between 0.43 and 1.04, thus showing a value range similar to the solutions in this study.

Crisis cluster	Mean F-value	Median F-value	Max. F-value
Cluster 1: *Operational crisis*	0.79	0.80	1.22
Cluster 2: *Financial crisis*	0.95	0.98	1.22
Cluster 3: *Market crisis*	0.82	0.86	1.22

Table 24: F-values of crisis clusters.
N=205.

For further discussion of the results, please refer to section 7.6.

7.4 Cluster analysis of turnaround management characteristics

The second cluster analysis investigates turnaround strategies for archetypical combinations of turnaround management characteristics. Again, the choice of the variables is deduced from the model of the turnaround management (see section 4.5), modified by the respective simplifications (see section 5.2.3).

The maximum correlations coefficient between any two turnaround management variables is uncritically below 0.6 (Pearson correlation coefficient).

The single-linkage clustering shows no outliers in the data set for the turnaround management; thus, no cases are eliminated from the sample.

The agglomeration coefficient development in relation to the number of clusters (based on Ward's algorithm) can be assessed in Figure 40.

The agglomeration coefficient change suggests a two-cluster segmentation. This is reconfirmed by the visual inspection of the dendrogram.

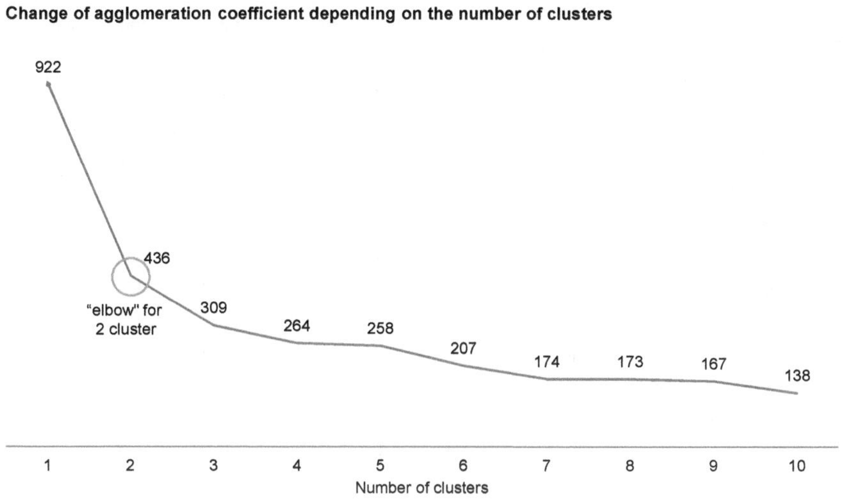

Figure 40: Change of agglomeration coefficient depending on the number of turnaround clusters.
Source: Own illustration.

The profiles of the two clusters found show significantly different means for many turnaround management variables, again, the mean comparison shown together with the respective t-statistic to assess direction and significance levels per variables (Table 25).

Variable name	Total sample N = 209	CEO change/ retrenchment focus N = 131		No CEO change/ no retrenchment focus N = 78	
	Mean	Mean	T-stat.	Mean	T-stat.
Operational restructuring moves					
Layoff	3.4	3.7	4.72***	2.9	-4.72***
Employee concessions	3.2	3.4	2.88**	2.9	-2.88**
Increase CAPEX	1.9	2.0	1.17	1.8	-1.17
Decrease CAPEX	2.3	2.7	6.38***	1.6	-6.38***
Capacity reduction	2.8	3.2	5.12***	2.1	-5.12***
Productivity increase	3.8	3.9	1.73	3.6	-1.73
Outsourcing	2.1	2.3	3.40***	1.7	-3.40***
Insourcing	1.7	1.8	1.63	1.6	-1.63
Process improvement and redesign	4.1	4.4	6.20***	3.5	-6.20***
Pricing and sales initiatives	3.7	3.7	-0.66	3.8	0.66
Purchasing and cost reduction initiatives	3.9	4.1	3.67***	3.6	-3.67***
Managerial restructuring moves					
CEO change	3.1	4.0	14.56***	1.6	-14.56***
Change in TMT	3.7	4.4	10.58***	2.6	-10.58***
Portfolio restructuring moves					
Asset divestments (company division or subsidiary)	2.3	2.7	4.56***	1.8	-4.56***
Termination of products lines/ markets	2.8	3.2	5.22***	2.2	-5.22***
New products/ markets development	2.9	3.0	1.50	2.7	-1.50
Financial restructuring moves					
Working capital reduction	3.6	3.8	2.78**	3.4	-2.78**
Reduction of cash flow to shareholder	2.8	2.9	1.86	2.5	-1.86
Liquidity contribution by shareholder	3.3	3.6	4.36***	2.7	-4.36***
Additional restructuring loan by lenders	3.3	3.3	-0.02	3.3	0.02
Securities contribution by shareholder	3.0	3.2	2.44*	2.7	-2.44*
Repayment of debt	2.4	2.7	3.70***	2.0	-3.70***
Extension, conversion or deferral of existing debt	2.7	2.7	0.63	2.6	-0.63
Debt write-off or debt-to-equity-swap	1.9	2.1	3.75***	1.4	-3.75***
Turnaround context					
Develop. of market segment during turnaround	3.0	3.0	0.69	2.9	-0.69
Stakeholder management during turnaround	3.3	3.3	0.22	3.3	-0.22

Table 25: Turnaround cluster profiles.

Mean comparison; N = 209.
Significance levels at 0.05; 0.01 and 0.001 indicated by *; ** and ***.

The analysis of the two turnaround clusters shows a distinct and significant characterization of the two clusters based on significantly different means.

The two emerging clusters are

- Cluster 1: *'CEO change/ retrenchment focus'*
- Cluster 2: *'No CEO change/ no retrenchment focus'*

As for the comparison of two clusters, the differences between the two are obviously mirrored respectively by the other cluster. The clusters are thus discussed conjointly.

Changing the CEO and the management team is the most defining element in this cluster differentiation. Key indications for this are the extremely high t-statistic values (*'CEO change'* – t-stat.: ±14.56; $p < 0.001$/ *'change in TMT'* – t-stat.: ±10.58; $p < 0.001$).

The second defining element is the clear differentiation in terms of retrenchment-oriented operational restructuring moves. *'Decrease CAPEX,' 'capacity reduction,' 'outsourcing,' 'layoff, 'process improvement and redesign'* and *'purchasing and cost reduction initiatives'* all show significantly higher values for Cluster 1 ($3.4 \leq$ t-stat. ≤ 6.2; $p < 0.001$). These effects are obviously mirrored for Cluster 2 with inverse direction.

Completing the picture, the portfolio retrenchment moves *'asset divestment'* and *'termination of product lines/markets'* are also significantly higher in Cluster 1 ($4.56 \leq$ t-stat. ≤ 5.22; $p < 0.001$). It seems that the liquidity needed to implement these retrenchment moves (Cluster 1) is achieved by a higher level of shareholder contributions (t-stat.: 4.36; $p < 0.001$), while the reduced debt capacity (due to the retrenchment actions) for the cases in Cluster 1 is reflected by '*repayment of debt*' and '*debt write-off or debt-to-equity-swap*' ($3.70 \leq$ t-stat. ≤ 3.75; $p < 0.001$). All these observations are true with inverse direction for Cluster 2.

It seems that the two turnaround clusters are mainly differentiated by the respective retrenchment orientation, with specific emphasis on the CEO change. The main recovery-oriented moves do not significantly differ between the two clusters; nor does the '*severity of crisis*' (not shown in table; not a cluster variable).

Despite the significant difference between the two clusters, the mean performance after turnaround (not part of the cluster variables) shows no significant differences (Table 26). This again reconfirms the findings of chapter 6, that the restructuring move variables alone contain little information about the *'turnaround result.'*

Cluster	Turnaround result		Survival of company	
	Mean	T-stat.	Mean	T-stat.
Cluster 1: *CEO change/ retrenchment focus*	2.9	0.57	63%	0.98
Cluster 2: *No CEO change/ no retrenchment focus*	2.8	-0.57	56%	-0.98
Total sample	2.9		61%	

Table 26: Performance per turnaround cluster.

Mean of *'turnaround result'* and '*survival of company'* per turnaround cluster; N = 209.
No significance levels $p \leq 0.05$ observed.

Turnaround cluster	Cluster 1: **CEO change/ retrenchment focus** N = 131	Cluster 2: **No CEO change/ no retrenchment focus** N = 78
Key defining variables	**Change of CEO**	**No change of CEO**
Complementing cluster characterization	Intensive changes in TMT CAPEX and capacity reduction Higher relevance of layoffs and employee concessions Very high relevance of process improvements and redesign Divestment of assets and termination of products Liquidity from shareholder	Nearly no CAPEX reduction and much less capacity reduction Lower intensity of layoffs and employee concessions Low intensity of asset divestments Hardly any debt-to-equity-swap
Cluster performance	**Average** result 2.9 **Average** survival rate 63%	**Average** result 2.8 **Average** survival rate 56%

Figure 41: Turnaround cluster characterization.

Source: Own illustration.

The homogeneity assessment of the two turnaround clusters is shown in Table 27. With a lower number of clusters the diversity of these clusters increases, as more clusters allow a better segmentation of data. Thus it is not unexpected for the two clusters that both are not completely homogenous and the mean F-value is, with 0.90 and 0.96 for Cluster 1 and Cluster 2 respectively, higher than for the crisis clusters.

In investigating the key differentiating variables of '*CEO change*' and '*change in TMT*' it is clear that in this respect the two clusters are quite homogenous ('*CEO change*': F-value = 0.58; '*Change in TMT*': F-value = 0.35).

Cluster			**F-value**
	Mean	Median	Max
Cluster 1: CEO change/ retrenchment focus	0.90	0.95	1.21
Cluster 2: No CEO change/ no retrenchment focus	0.96	1.00	1.50

Table 27: F-values of turnaround clusters.
N=209.

Please refer to section 7.6 for further discussion of the results.

7.5 Relations between crisis and turnaround clusters

When examining the two sequential cluster analyses, an obvious question arises: "Is there a relation between the crisis and the turnaround clusters?" This question can be analyzed two-fold:

- Is there a common path from crisis cluster to turnaround cluster, i.e., do cases belonging to a specific crisis cluster also commonly belong to one of the two turnaround clusters?
- Is there a difference in terms of resulting performance after turnaround and the survival rate for cases within the same crisis cluster, depending on the turnaround cluster these belong to?

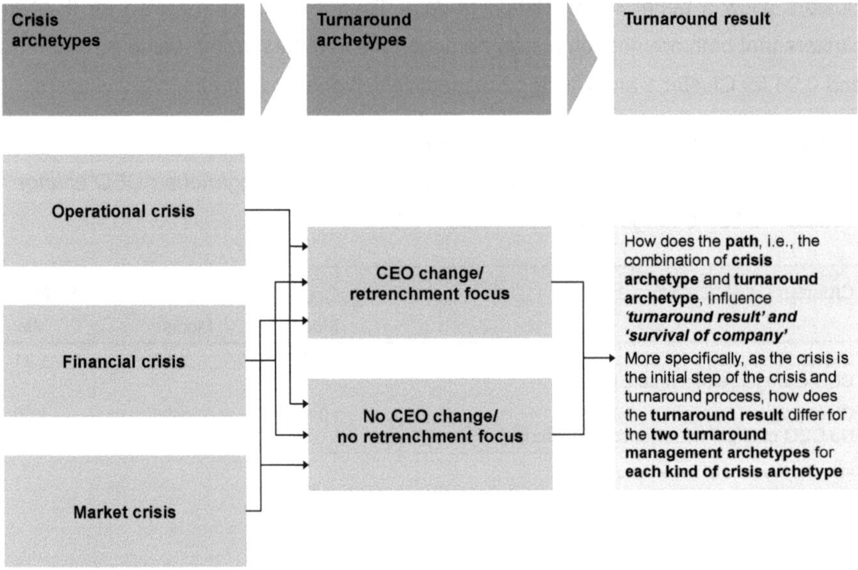

Figure 42: Structure of the combination of crisis and turnaround archetypes.
Source: Own illustration.

The analysis to answer the first question is shown in Table 28. For obvious reasons, this analysis is restricted to all cases clustered in both analyses; These are 205 cases for crisis clustering due to outlier elimination and all cases for turnaround clustering, thus a total of 205 cases. The analysis shows that nearly 90% of the cases belonging to the *operational crisis* cluster also belong to the *'CEO change/retrenchment focus'* cluster, while for the two other crisis clusters the distribution is less one-sided, but with a slight tendency towards the turnaround cluster *'CEO change/retrenchment focus.'*

Meta cluster analysis turnaround cluster per crisis cluster	Cluster 1: *CEO change/ retrenchment focus*		Cluster 2: *No CEO change/ no retrenchment focus*	
	Number. of cases	Share of cases	Number of cases	Share of cases
Cluster 1: *Operational crisis*	42	89%	5	11%
Cluster 2: *Financial crisis*	57	54%	48	46%
Cluster 3: *Market crisis*	29	55%	24	45%

Table 28: Case distribution on turnaround clusters per crisis cluster
(N = 205)

To answer the second question, the means of the two variables *'turnaround result'* and *'survival of company'* are compared for both turnaround clusters within each crisis cluster. The analysis shows that within the crisis cluster *operational crisis*, the cases attributed to the turnaround Cluster 1: *'CEO change/ retrenchment'* show a significantly higher performance and survival rate after turnaround than those attributed to the second turnaround cluster. For both other crisis clusters, the difference between the two turnaround clusters is not significant.

Meta cluster analysis *'Turnaround result'* and *'survival of company'* depending on turnaround cluster per crisis cluster	**Crisis cluster total**	***CEO change/ retrenchment focus***	***No CEO change/ no retrenchment focus***
	Mean	Mean	Mean
Turnaround result			
Cluster 1: *Operational crisis*	2.9	3.0*	1.4*
Cluster 2: *Financial crisis*	3.2	3.1	3.3
Cluster 3: *Market crisis*	2.3	2.4	2.2
Survival of company			
Cluster 1: *Operational crisis*	68%	74%*	20%*
Cluster 2: *Financial crisis*	67%	67%	67%
Cluster 3: *Market crisis*	43%	41%	46%

Table 29: Performance of turnaround cluster per crisis cluster.
Mean comparison within crisis cluster depending on turnaround cluster attribution; N = 205.
Significance level at 0.05 indicated by *.

7.6 Discussion

The cluster analysis showed distinct strategic configurations for both crisis and turnaround, thus far confirming Propositions 3 and 6.

The profiling of the clusters for the crisis variables led to the clusters *operational crisis*, *financial crisis* and *market crisis.* These results can be matched with the structure developed by Asquith and Gertner (1994) and extended by Eichner (2010):

- *Operational crisis* can be compared to his category 'operating profitability'
- *Financial crisis* can be seen as a combination of both 'overleverage' and 'overexpansion'
- *Market crisis* is similarly reflected by 'industry level operating profitability decline'

The comparison with the structure chosen by Hauschildt et al. (2006) does not seem feasible. The categories he chose are too different in terms of content due to his extensive focus on persons and interaction of CEO and management team.

The two turnaround clusters reflecting the discussion of retrenchment and recovery have been recurrent in turnaround management research since the publication of Pearce and Robbins (1993). It seems that the intensity of retrenchment, combined with the decision to change the CEO, is the main differentiation item for turnaround strategy.

Matching these two with the clusters of turnaround strategies found by Eichner (2010) is possible although the two-cluster structure is necessarily a significant simplification compared to his six-cluster result.

- *'CEO change, retrenchment focus'* might be seen as a combination of the clusters 'strategic reorientation,' 'asset retrenchment,' 'operational reorientation' and 'right sizing'
- *'No CEO change/ no retrenchment focus'* can similarly be seen as reflected by the clusters 'radical growth strategy' and 'cash flow optimization.'

The implication of the crisis cluster attribution for *'turnaround result'* and *'survival of company'* reconfirm the findings in chapter 6 that market development plays a crucial role for the turnaround chances of the company, which is the first key finding of this cluster analysis beyond the existence of the cluster themselves.

The significantly lower survival rate of 43% in the *market crisis* cluster, compared to the average survival rate of 61%, gives way to the assumption that an externally induced market crisis is far more dangerous for the survival of a company than financial or operational issues.

The CCF *'increased competition,'* being the variable with the highest significance in terms of cluster differentiation, in conjunction with *'market decline'* (similar combinations are also conceptually anticipated; see section 4.4.5) together lead not only to reduced turnovers and thus a decline in the economics of scale, but also at the same time, price and margin decline.

This impedes the current as well as the expected future cash flow, which reduces the resources of the company at present and the going concern value of a company. The reduced going concern value is thus closer to the liquidation value of the firm, and thus decreases the value loss for debt and shareholders in the case of the failure of the company, all reducing the willingness to provide further support.

The second key finding is related to the combination of *operational crisis* and the two turnaround clusters. It seems in the case of an *operational crisis*, the choice of the *'CEO change/ retrenchment focus'* strategy significantly promotes the survival of the company. This reconfirms similar findings in chapter 6 in relation to the moderation effect *'unsuitable CEO'* × *'CEO change.'*

It is reconfirmed that if there is an unsuitable CEO – significant for any case belonging the *operational crisis* cluster – changing the CEO is virtually a precondition for the survival of the company. This is very well illustrated by the survival rate, which is 74%, for this crisis cluster if the case is attributed to the turnaround cluster *'CEO change/ retrenchment focus,'* but only 20% otherwise.

The third finding is related to non-significance. The analysis of the turnaround clusters themselves similarly reconfirms the findings in chapter 6. The content of turnaround management, in this chapter clustered in two distinct strategies, in chapter 6 analyzed as linear regressions, is not significantly related to the success of a turnaround. In terms of information content, the crisis characteristics are superior to the turnaround strategies and an assessment of the turnaround management is only possible in the context of all relevant variables of the crisis and turnaround process.

8 Impact of turnaround on family ownership and control

The family-owned company, as a system of family and company, has been receiving increasing attention in research (Gomez-Mejia et al., 2011). The specific configuration of the founding family and their descendants as company owners influence both family and firm. This has been discussed in respect to the specific impact of the common identity of management and shareholder (see section 5.2.1.3), utilizing the principal agency theory (e.g., Anderson & Reeb, 2003), or by asserting these differences based on the resource-based view, thereby attributing family-specific resources to the family firm, labeled 'familiness' (Habbershon & Williams, 1999), which add positive and negative resources to the companies. An important theoretical addition has been the concept of socioemotional wealth (SEW) (Gómez-Mejía et al., 2007), which has introduced the notion that family firms pursue additional, non-financial goals. All these basis theories are introduced briefly in section 2.4.3.

The specific properties of family firms influence the occurrence and result of crisis. It has been shown, for example, that family firms are vulnerable during transgenerational handover (Lansberg, 1988) and fail more often (Gómez-Mejía et al., 2007; Lansberg, 1988). Concerning the turnaround process, it has been shown that while many strategies are very similar for family firms, there are differences (Bruton et al., 2003; Cater & Schwab, 2008; Faghfouri, 2013; Gómez-Mejía et al., 2007; Rüsen, 2008; Trahms et al., 2013).

While this research stream is extremely valuable to better understand the crisis and turnaround process in family firms, I want to move the focus away from the actual process of crisis and turnaround, instead investigating how the role of the family, in respect to the company, changes during turnaround. To my knowledge, up until now there has been no published empirical research reviewing the influence of the crisis and turnaround process on the role of the family in the family firm.

This is surprising, as retaining family ownership and family influence in a family firm is an important motivation for shareholding families, according to the SEW theory (see section 2.4.3.3) of Gómez-Mejía et al. (2007). As introduced in section 2.4.3.3

Berrone et al. (2012) have differentiated the SEW into five elemental constructs, abbreviated FIBER:

1. *Family control and influence* refer to the family's need to influence decisions and the course of the company.
2. *Identification of family members with the firm* refers to the family members' perception of the company as part of their identity.
3. *Binding social ties* refer to the wish that the company be perceived positively by society, stakeholders and community beyond what could be explained by expected financial returns.
4. *Emotional attachment of family members* refers to the fact that a family firm is perceived not as a financial vehicle, but as an entity to which there is an emotional connection.
5. *Renewal of family bonds through dynastic succession* refers to the wish to hand over the family business to future generations.

These SEW motivations can be directly linked to the family ownership, as all FIBER elements require family ownership as a prerequisite. Similarly, there is also a link between the first FIBER element and the role of the family in the firm's management. Consequently, it is assumed that retaining family control and ownership is important for the shareholding family.

The fact that the family role might change during turnaround has been conceptually pointed out before (Rüsen, 2008). It is intuitively a valid scenario that a family firm might be successfully restructured, while reducing the family role. The underlying factors and mechanisms for the change of the family role during crisis and turnaround are investigated for successful turnarounds in this chapter.

This chapter employs the statistical methods, already introduced in chapters 6 and 7, to analyze if and what elements of the crisis and turnaround process influence a change in the role of the family. As the respective empirical data is available only for firms that did not fail in the crisis (see section 4.7 – banks' risk managers hand over responsibility for insolvency cases to different departments, thus there is no information available about the company's future after insolvency) all analyses in this chapter are limited to companies that did not file for insolvency.

In these analyses, all firms with any family ownership before the crisis are considered. These are not restricted by implementing a lower threshold, as is commonly done in the literature (see section 2.4.1); instead, the context variable *'family share in the company before crisis'* is part of the analyses as an input variable. Should the share be relevant for the family role change, this variable would turn out to be significant in these analyses.

This chapter is structured in seven parts:

- In section 8.1, the key definitions are introduced
- In section 8.2, the exploratory propositions are discussed and introduced.
- In section 8.3, the statistical methodology is highlighted.
- In section 8.4, the descriptive results in respect to the role of the family in the company are presented.
- In section 8.5 and 8.6, the statistical analysis is conducted
  In section 8.5 by using univariate regression models and in section 8.6 by the application of the cluster analysis results presented in chapter 7 and analyzing its effects on the family role change.
- Section 8.7 concludes this chapter with the results discussion.

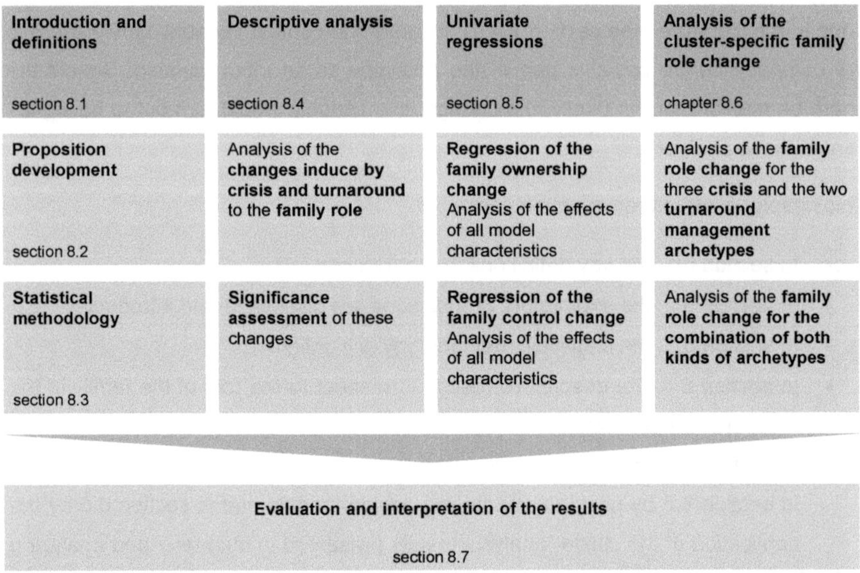

Figure 43: Overview of chapter structure (chapter 8).
Source: Own illustration.

8.1 Definitions

While the dependent variable for all analyzes in chapters 6 and 7 is *'turnaround result,'* i.e., the result of the turnaround from the company's perspective, this chapter is dedicated to analyzing the family role as dependent variable (the exact operationalization of the family role is introduced in section 8.3).

The family role refers to the relation between family and firm, specifically the ownership and managerial influence on the company. The family role is operationalized based on the variables already introduced in the conceptual model chapter 4. These variables belong to two model dimensions; the variables defining the family role before the crisis are discussed in the context model in section 4.6.1.5, while the variables defining the family role after the turnaround are discussed in the turnaround result model in section 4.7.

The family role *before* the crisis is defined by the internal context variables:

- The family ownership by two variables
    - The context variable *'family share in the company before crisis.'*
    - The context variable *'owner family generation before crisis (majority of shares).'*
- The family control by three variables:
    - The context variable *'role of owner family in supervisory board before crisis.'*
    - The context variable *'owner family control before crisis – CEO is family member.'*
    - The context variable *'owner family control before crisis – structure of TMT.'*

The family role *after* the crisis is defined by the following turnaround result variables:

- The family ownership by the turnaround result variable *'family share in company after crisis'*
- The family control by two variables:
    - The turnaround result variable *'owner family control after crisis – CEO is family member'*
    - The turnaround result variable *'owner family control after crisis – structure of TMT'*

To measure the change of family ownership and control, the comparison of the three family-related turnaround result variables with the corresponding internal context variables is used to operationalize the role of the family. Consequently, this role is based on two dimensions, ownership and control.

Family ownership is defined as follows:

Family ownership is defined by the variable 'family share in the company,' i.e., the share of the founding families and their descendants in the company. The change in family ownership is reflected by the difference of this variable before and after the crisis.

Family control is defined as follows:

Family control is the level of managerial influence of the family on the firm, i.e., the operational management functions of family members in the company.

This is differentiated into two aspects:

- *'Owner family control – structure of TMT,' i.e., the role of the founding families and their descendants in the TMT.*
- *'Owner family control – CEO is family member,' i.e., if the CEO belongs to the founding family and its descendants.*

The change of family control is similarly segregated in the two dimensions and reflected by the difference between the two variables before and after the crisis.

Both dimensions are jointly referred to as family role, which is defined as follows:

The family role in the company is defined by family ownership and family control. Family role change is the difference between the situation before the crisis and after the turnaround.

The remaining variables defining the family role have been assessed for the time before the crisis only. These are treated as context factors, as a dynamic change in these variables due to crisis and turnaround is not expected. These are *'owner family generation before crisis (majority of shares)'* and *'role of owner family in supervisory board before crisis.'*

8.2 Proposition development

Due to the exploratory nature of this work, the propositions (Figure 44) are broadly structured, similar to those laid out in chapter 4. There are three propositions for this chapter, the first relating to the general direction of family role change, the second related to the fact that the family role change is assumed to be influenced by crisis and turnaround management characteristics and the third with similar content, but based on the clusters identified in chapter 7, i.e., the assumption of cluster-specific family role change.

The general direction of family role change is assumed to decline, i.e., it is assumed that the role of the family is diminished during crisis and successful turnaround. The argumentation needs to be conducted separately for the two dimensions, family ownership and family control.

Regarding the family ownership, the proposition is based on the general shift of power between shareholder and debt holder in distressed firms. In a crisis situation, the future of a company is threatened (Arogyaswamy et al., 1995; Hauschildt et al., 2006). This threatens, per se, the going concern perspective. The value of the company is thus reduced, as it is based on the future cash flow expectations. These are discounted due to both the impaired profit situation during the crisis and the threat of the company failure in turnaround. At the same time, the obligations towards external stakeholders (e.g., banks) remain at a contractually fixed value. This reduces the value of the equity (share value), changes the role of the debt holders and increases their influence (Asquith & Gertner, 1994). For family firms, this can lead to a scenario in which a family that is unwilling or unable to contribute new funds either has to sell shares to an investor, who has better options to turn the company around (e.g., through contribution of new funds), or to invite a new investor (e.g., through equity increase) who contributes liquidity and thus diminishes the family shareholding (Rüsen, 2008). This constellation is the basis for the assumption of a reduction in family shareholding during turnaround.

The family control change follows a similar structure as *'CEO change'* is a frequent (see chapter 6) and defining (see chapter 7) element of the turnaround strategy. Two different arguments support the assumption of reduced family control after crisis:

- First and simplest, the reduction of family share – as discussed – might bring in new shareholder(s), who put in place a new CEO and TMT.
- Secondly, as shown in chapter 6, if the CEO specifically contributed to a crisis, and respectively, if the company faces an *operational crisis* (chapter 7), the restructuring move *'CEO change'* strongly supports turnaround success. Because the pool of willing and able family-member management candidates is limited (Dyer, 1989; Sharma & Irving, 2005), another family member might not be available to replace the family-member manager; thus the employment of

non-family managers might be the only alternative, leading to a reduction of family control in the company.

Thus it is assumed that in time of crisis and turnaround, the family role will diminish in both respects, resulting in the following proposition:

Proposition 8.1: For a company emerging from turnaround (i.e., not filing for insolvency), the family role, both in terms of ownership and management control, will on average be reduced, compared to the situation before the crisis.

As already discussed above, there are specific characteristics of crisis, turnaround management and context that could influence the change of the family role during turnaround. While this general notion is rather intuitive, I want to substantiate it with four examples from the three model dimensions.

- Among the crisis characteristics, it could be argued that the relevance of the CCF *'missing innovation in core products'* signals that the company's management lacks the necessary competencies surrounding the technologies required in the respective market. This could make it necessary to employ a new non-family manager, who brings in required know-how to overcome these weaknesses, thus reducing family control.
- Among the turnaround management characteristics, the implementation of the restructuring move '*CEO change*' makes a loss of family control more likely, as already discussed for Proposition 8.1.
- The financial restructuring move '*debt write-off or debt-to-equity-swap*' has a direct impact on family ownership if implemented as debt-to-equity-swap. This transaction converts debt into equity for the debt holders and thus directly reduces the percentage of family shareholding.
- The context factor *'leverage'* can be seen similarly. As the influence of debt holder increases during turnaround (Asquith & Gertner, 1994), it could be argued that a higher leverage promotes this shift of influence and also makes the sale of shares by the family and thus the loss of family ownership more likely.

An exhaustive discussion of all possible relations between single variables of the conceptual model and the different variables defining the family role change would not suit the purpose of this research approach. Especially the lack of current conceptual and empirical literature would make such a hypothesis compilation highly speculative.

Thus, these examples should serve only as illustrations for the proposition, fundamentally following the logic of the propositions already analyzed in chapter 6 and 7. It is assumed that the specific setup of the crisis and turnaround process influences the change in family ownership and family control.

Proposition 8.2: Some or all of the crisis and turnaround management variables discussed and developed in the conceptual model significantly influence the direction and extent of the family role change during turnaround. These effects might differ for family control and family ownership.

With similar content, the next proposition reflects the arguments made as the basis for Proposition 8.2. Instead of individual variables, it addresses the cluster perspective. Chapter 7 showed that there are specific archetypes of crisis and turnaround influencing the turnaround result. It is assumed that there is a similar relation between the family role change and the cluster affiliation of the sample cases.

Proposition 8.3: The cluster means for the family role change differ for the crisis and turnaround clusters, as well as within a crisis cluster for the two turnarounds clusters. These effects might differ for family control and family ownership.

The statistical methodology to test these propositions is briefly presented in the following part of this chapter.

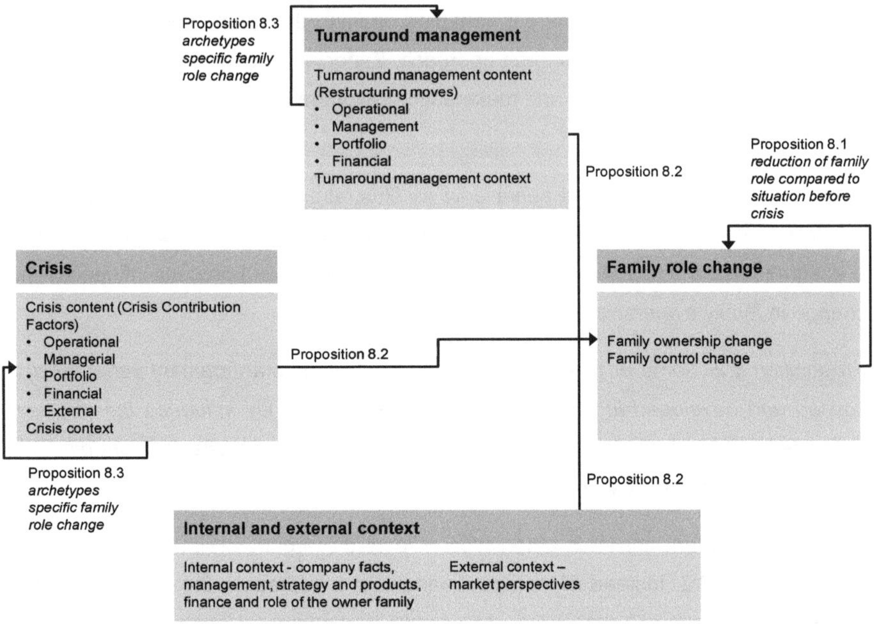

Figure 44: Family role change propositions.
Source: Own illustration.

8.3 Statistical methodology

The statistical methodology employed in this chapter was introduced in chapters 6 and 7. As an extensive reiteration would be redundant, the respective introduction is referenced instead.

To conduct the family role change analysis, a set of four new variables is required. The family role change is based on the comparison of the family role before and after the crisis. Thus, these role change variables are calculated based on the respective variables already introduced in the conceptual model:

- The situation before the crisis is based on the family-firm-specific internal context variables (section 4.6.1.5)
- The situation after the crisis is based on the owner-family-specific turnaround result variables (section 4.7)

Variable	Remarks and coding
Company lost	As the sample is limited to companies with any family ownership before the crisis, this variable reflects loss of all family shares in the company. 1: No family ownership after the crisis 0: Family ownership after the crisis
Loss of family share	Higher variable value reflects higher loss of family shares. *'Family share in company before crisis'* minus *'Family share in company after crisis'* From -3 = highest gain of shares by family by 0 = no family share change to 4 = highest loss of shares by family
Loss of family control – CEO	1 = family CEO – before crisis: Yes, after crisis: No 0 = no change in family CEO situation 1 = family CEO – before crisis: No, after crisis: Yes
Loss of family control – role of family in TMT	Higher variable value reflects higher loss of family influence in top management team. *'Owner family control before crisis – structure of TMT'* minus *'Owner family control after crisis – structure of TMT'* From -2 = highest gain of family control in TMT by 0 = no change of family control in TMT to 2 = highest loss of family control in TMT

Table 30: Variable coding of the family role change variables.

The four family role change variables reflect changes in family ownership, differentiated in one variable for the total loss of ownership and a second variable for a gradual change in ownership share, as well as family control changes, both for CEO and TMT. Details can be assessed in Table 30.

In the first step, the descriptive analysis is conducted (section 8.4). The four family role change variables are descriptively analyzed and assessed. The mean and standard deviation, but also the correlation between the variables is calculated. To evaluate the validity of Proposition 8.1, a one-sample t-test is conducted for each of the variables to evaluate the significance of the variables' deviation from 0, as 0 would imply the family role remains unchanged by crisis and turnaround.

In the pursuit of Proposition 8.3, a univariate regression is conducted, analyzing the effect of crisis, turnaround management and context variables on both family control and family ownership changes. The univariate regression employs the same methodology used for the regression of the dependent variable *'turnaround result'* in section 6.3. For both the family role aspects, family control and family ownership, a separate univariate regression is conducted (section 8.5).

The last analytical step is the comparison of cluster-specific means for family ownership and family control change in two steps for both crisis and turnaround cluster, separately and combined (section 8.6). It is important to note that the cluster attribution of the individual cases is based on the cluster analysis in chapter 7. The methodology is a straightforward adaption of the methods introduced in section 7.2.

8.4 Descriptive analysis of family role changes

The first step of the descriptive analysis addresses the family control change. It is worth noting that in the vast majority (88%) of the family firms the family has a share of 75% and higher. So if there is a founding family shareholding, it is in most cases the most influential or even the sole shareholder.

This situation changes during crisis and turnaround for a significant share of all family firms. While an increase of share can be found for only fewer than 1% of family firms, for more than one third (35.4%) the family share is reduced after crisis. In nearly one fifth (18.6%) of the family firms, the company has ceased to be a family firm, as the family ownership is zero after the crisis.

At this point I want to assess this information in the general context of this study. As discussed in this chapter's introduction, all numbers in this chapter refer to companies that did not file for insolvency. If one wants to evaluate the consequences for the family shareholding of crisis and turnaround, the cases that did file for insolvency would have to be included. In my view, it has to be assumed that for insolvency cases the relation between family and company is usually terminated as well.

This assumption is based on indirect evidence only, as there is unfortunately no direct empirical data available. The indirect evidence is based on the following line of argument:

The average quota for debtors in insolvency cases in Germany in the time from 2003 to 2007 reached a value of 3.6% (Kranzusc & Icks, 2009). An insolvency case, wherein debtors do not receive their nominal value, will (in Germany) usually devalue the share price to zero, i.e., the administrator will sell the company assets to the highest bidder, using the revenues to pay the quota to the debtors without the shareholders receiving any cash flow or assets. Based on this evidence, it can be assumed that for nearly all family firms filing for insolvency the firm/ family relation is terminated.

A total number of 65 (36.5%) of the 178 firms with family shareholding did file for insolvency. Of the 21 former family firms not filing for insolvency, none retained a family shareholding after the crisis (Table 31). Based on the assumption that the family/ firm relation ends with insolvency, for 86 (48.3%) of the 178 firms with family shareholding before the crisis the family lost their ownership stake in the former family firm during the crisis and insolvency process.

Variable	Before crisis		After crisis	
	Cases	Percentage	Cases	Percentage
Family share				
No family share			21	18.6%
Below 25%	1	0.9 %	4	3.5%
25% – 49%	6	5.3%	10	8.8%
50% – 74%	7	6.2%	15	13.3%
75% and higher	99	87.6%	63	55.8%
Loss of family share				
< 0 (gain of gamily share)			1	0.9%
0 (same family share)			72	63.7%
> 0 (loss of family share)			40	35.4%
Loss of company				
No more family ownership			21	18.6%
Family ownership			92	81.4%

Table 31: Family shareholding before and after crisis.
Any company with family share before crisis; companies not filing for insolvency; N = 113.

The family control signifies a prominent role of the family members in the firm's management before the crisis. Among the family firms 85.0% had a family member as CEO before the crisis. Nearly half of the companies (48.7%) had only family members in the top management team. Only slightly more than one in ten companies had no family members in the top management team (11.5%).

The family role in management is also drastically changed by crisis and turnaround for many family firms. The share of family firms with family-member CEOs is reduced from 85.0% before, to 55.8% after crisis. For 36.5% of the 96 companies that had a family CEO before the crisis, the CEO after the crisis is not a family member. Only for two firms (1.8% of the sample) the new CEO after the crisis is a family member, while the CEO before the crisis has not belonged to the family. Similarly, in 43.4% of the companies the role of the family in the TMT is reduced.

Variable	Before crisis		After crisis	
	Cases	Percentage	Cases	Percentage
Family control – CEO is family member				
Yes	96	85.0%	63	55.8%
No	17	15.0%	50	44.2%
Family control – structure of TMT				
Only family members	55	48.7%	27	23.9%
Family and non-family members	45	39.8%	47	41.6%
Only non-family members	13	11.5%	39	34.5%
Loss of family control – CEO				
before crisis: No, after crisis: Yes			2	1.8%
No change			76	67.3%
before crisis: Yes, after crisis: No			35	31.0%
Loss of family control – role of family in TMT				
< 0 more family in top management team			2	1.8%
= 0 no change of family role in top management team			62	54.9%
> 0 less family in top management team			49	43.4%

Table 32: Family control before and after crisis.

Any company with family share before crisis; companies not filing for insolvency; N = 113.

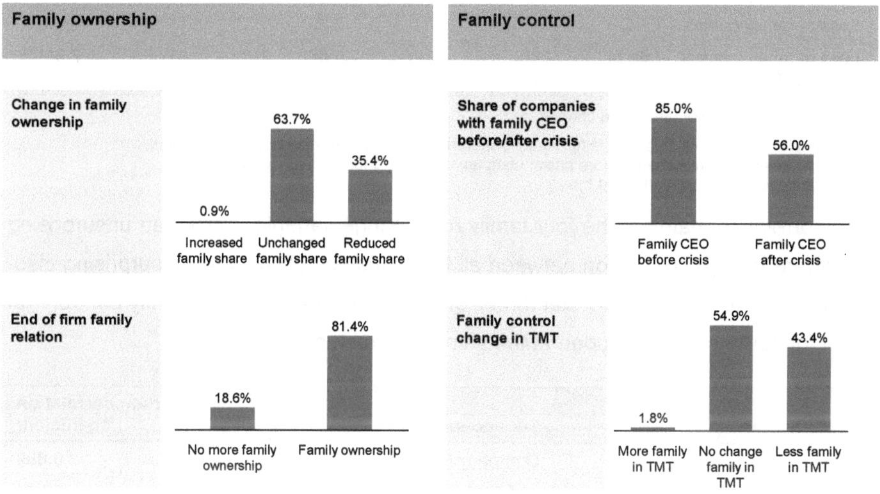

Figure 45: Changes in family role.

Source: Own illustration.

To test the significance of these family role changes, a bootstrapped one-sample t-test is conducted. It evaluates the probability that an observed distribution of a variable originates from a distribution with a mean of zero (Table 33). For the four family role change variables, the probability that the variable mean is zero, i.e., there is no diminishing of the family role, is below 0.001. This indicates that the loss of family role during crisis and turnaround is highly significant in respect to all four variables and thus consistent for family ownership and family control. This confirms Proposition 8.1.

Variable	Mean	T-stat.
Company lost	0.19	5.06***
Loss of family share	0.97	6.68***
Loss of family control – CEO	0.29	6.28***
Loss of family control – role of family in TMT	0.48	7.91***

Table 33: Significance of family role change.

One sample t-test vs. null hypothesis for family ownership loss and family control loss variables.
All companies with family share before crisis; companies not filing for insolvency; N = 113.
Significance level at 0.001 indicated ***.

The correlation matrix of the four family role change variables shows an unsurprising moderate to high correlation between all four variables (Table 34), unsurprising insofar as it has to be assumed that family ownership loss and loss of family control – at least for some cases – happen at the same time (see section 8.2).

First variable	Second variable	Pearson correlation coefficient
Loss of family share	Company lost	0.889
Loss of family share	Loss of family control – CEO	0.626
Loss of family share	Loss of family control – role of family in TMT	0.525
Loss of family control – CEO	Loss of family control – role of family in TMT	0.625

Table 34: Correlation between family role change variables.

Pearson correlation coefficient for family ownership loss and family control loss variables.
Any company with family share before crisis; companies not filing for insolvency; N = 113.

The analysis in the following sections is restricted to two of the four family role change variables to ease the presentation and interpretation of the results. For each of the two aspects, family ownership and family control, one variable is selected.

As a measure for family shareholding, the variable '*loss of family share*' is used, as the variable '*company lost*' only reflects one specific case of this variable.

The analysis of family control is conducted based on the variable '*loss of family control – role of family in TMT*' as empirically it does change more often during the crisis (45.2% of the cases vs. 31.0% of the cases for the variable '*loss of family control – CEO* '). At the same time, '*loss of family control – CEO*' is nearly always combined with '*loss of family control – role of family in TMT,*' while this is not the case vice versa (88.6% of all CEO changes go in concert with a change in the TMT, while only

63.3% of the changes in the TMT also happen at the same time as a CEO change). Furthermore, compared to *'loss of family control – CEO'* it is less correlated with the *'loss of family share'* variable (0.525 vs. 0.626), which might imply that it contains more independent information.

8.5 Univariate analysis of the family role change

The univariate analysis investigates the effect of a single predictor variable on a single dependent variable. As the research in the field of family role changes in crisis and turnaround is very limited, this rather simple approach is a valid initial step in investigating possible relationships between variables (see section 6.1). Due to the fact that the sample size is limited (N = 113), multivariate approaches would face severe limitations of statistical power (see section 6.1.2) and are thus not to be conducted; for similar reasons, interaction effects (see section 6.2) are not part of the analysis.

Due to the already-mentioned lack of research related to family role change in turnaround, the scope of this chapter differs from that of chapters 6 and 7. The next two sections describe the empirically observed effects and effect directions. These are later discussed together with possible hypotheses (see section 8.7) but with much broader strokes and less detail. The univariate analyses in this section as well as the cluster analyses in section 8.5 are not intended to yield a concluding research result, but instead are meant to be a valid starting point for future conceptual and empirical studies, demonstrating that there are significant effects between crisis, turnaround management and context and the family role change, effects that require additional conceptual and empirical research attention.

As for the result presentation, the figures presented are very similar to the information shown in section 6.3. To allow a more comprehensive assessment of the results of respective univariate regression, the presentation is limited to the variables with significant effects ($p \leq 0.05$) similar to the model presentation in section 6.4 to 6.6.

8.5.1 Analysis of family ownership change

The results of the first univariate regression with the dependent variable *'loss of family share in company'* are shown in Table 35. To allow an easier assessment, the presentation is limited to the variables with significant effect. Positive beta values indicate a promotion effect and negative values indicate a reduction effect on *'loss of family share in company.'* The respective subsample for this regression includes all cases of the total sample that did not file for insolvency and had any family shareholding before the crisis (N = 113).

Variable name	Stand. beta	Adj. R^2	Sign.
Positive standardized beta values indicate a promotion of family share loss; negative values an opposite effect on family share loss.			
Managerial crisis contribution factors			
Unsuitable CEO	0.37	0.13	0.00***
Succession problems	0.19	0.03	0.04*
Operational restructuring moves			
Insourcing	-0.22	0.04	0.01**
Managerial restructuring moves			
CEO change	0.34	0.11	0.00**
Change in TMT	0.19	0.03	0.01**
Internal context			
Family share in the company before crisis	0.13	0.01	0.05*

Table 35: Univariate regression of family ownership change.

Dependent variable *'loss of family share in company;'* only significant variables $p \leq 0.05$; N = 113.
Significance levels at 0.05; 0.01 and 0.001 indicated by *; ** and ***.

The results show six predictors with significant effect on *'loss of family share in company.'* These are

- Two variables of the managerial crisis contribution factors.
- Two variables of the managerial restructuring moves.
- One variable of the operational restructuring moves, *'insourcing.'*
- One context variable, *'family share in the company before crisis.'*

The two significant managerial crisis characteristics variables, *'unsuitable CEO'* (adj. $R^2 = 0.13$; $p < 0.001$) and *'succession problems'* (adj. $R^2 = 0.03$; $p < 0.05$), both promote the reduction of family ownership, while *'unsuitable CEO'* shows a much stronger effect.

Similarly negative is the effect of the corresponding managerial restructuring move *'CEO change'* (adj. $R^2 = 0.11$; $p < 0.001$). While the CCF *'unsuitable members of TMT'* does not have a significant effect, the corresponding restructuring move *'change in TMT'* (adj. $R^2 = 0.03$; $p < 0.01$) also significantly positively affects *'loss of family share in company.'*

The only restructuring move with significant adverse effects, i.e., reducing the probability of *'loss of family share in company'* is *'insourcing'* (adj. $R^2 = 0.04$; $p < 0.01$).

The context variable *'family share in the company before crisis'* (adj. $R^2 = 0.01$; $p < 0.05$) shows that a higher family share in the company increases the risk of ownership reduction.

Management-related variables account for four of the six variables with significant effect on *'loss of family share in company.'* Among those are the two variables with the strongest effects. It seems that although management crisis contribution factors and management restructuring moves at first glance are not directly related, they have a strong impact on family shareholding.

While these findings already confirm Proposition 8.2 for the family ownership change, a further discussion of the results is conducted in the context of all findings in the concluding section 8.7 of this chapter.

8.5.2 Analysis of family control change

The results of the second univariate regression with the dependent variable *'loss of family control – role of family in TMT'* are shown in Table 36, again limited to the variables with significant effect.

As this analysis is only meaningful for companies that had family members in the TMT before the crisis, the subsample for this analysis is further restricted to all cases that had any family members in the TMT before the crisis. Specifically, this means that the cases selected are all those that did not file for insolvency, had any family shareholding before the crisis and family members in the TMT before the crisis (N = 100).

Variable name	Stand. beta	Adj. R^2	Sign.
Positive standardized beta values indicate a promotion of family control loss; negative values an opposite effect on family control loss.			
Operational crisis contribution factors			
Degree of company-internal value-add too high	0.28	0.07	0.01*
Weaknesses in organization and processes	0.28	0.07	0.00**
Managerial crisis contribution factors			
Unsuitable CEO	0.46	0.20	0.00***
Unsuitable members of TMT	0.24	0.05	0.02*
Conflict spillover from owner family to company	0.25	0.05	0.00**
Succession problems	0.27	0.06	0.01**
Portfolio crisis contribution factors			
Missing innovation in core products	0.34	0.11	0.00***
Insufficient quality and service	0.29	0.08	0.01**
Financial crisis contribution factors			
Financing structure inadequate	-0.21	0.04	0.02*
External crisis contribution factors			
Market decline	0.28	0.07	0.00**
Operational restructuring moves			
Productivity increase	0.23	0.04	0.02*
Layoff	0.24	0.05	0.01**
Employee concessions	0.32	0.09	0.00***
Process improvement and redesign	0.23	0.04	0.00**
Purchasing and cost reduction initiatives	0.26	0.06	0.00**
Managerial restructuring moves			
CEO change	0.53	0.27	0.00***
Change in TMT	0.31	0.08	0.00***
Portfolio restructuring moves			
Termination of products lines/ markets	0.26	0.06	0.01*
Turnaround context			
Development of market segment during turnaround	-0.30	0.08	0.00**
Internal context			
Slack resources before crisis	0.28	0.07	0.01**
External context			
Long-term growth perspectives of market segment	-0.37	0.12	0.00**

Table 36: Univariate regression of family control change.

Dependent variable '*loss of family control – role of family in TMT*;' only significant variables $p \leq 0.05$; N = 100. Significance levels at 0.05; 0.01 and 0.001 indicated by *; ** and ***.

It is immediately apparent that the effects influencing *'loss of family control – role of family in TMT'* are much more complex than the effects on *'loss of family share in company.'* A total number of 21 variables with significant effects, compared to only six variables with significant effects on *'loss of family share in company,'* clearly illustrate that.

Among the variables that are part of the model of the crisis, all categories of crisis characteristics are present.

- From the operational CCFs, process-related issues, specifically '*degree of company-internal value-add too high*' and '*weaknesses in organization and processes*' both promoted the loss of family control in the TMT.
- All four managerial CCFs promote '*loss of family control – role of family in TMT.*' As the dependent variable addresses the TMT composition, it is interesting that the CCF *'unsuitable CEO'* (adj. $R^2 = 0.20$; $p<0.001$) has the strongest effect of all crisis variables, stronger than that of the CCF *'unsuitable members of TMT'* (adj. $R^2 = 0.05$; $p<0.05$).
- Both product-related portfolio CCFs (*'missing innovation in core products'* and '*insufficient quality and service'*) are significantly negative for the family control in the TMT.
- An inverse effect can be found for the financial CCF '*financing structure inadequate*' (adj. $R^2 = 0.04$; $p< 0.05$), i.e., a higher crisis contribution of the financial structure reduced the probability of a family control loss in the TMT.
- The external CCF '*market decline*' promotes control loss in the TMT.

Among the nine significant turnaround variables, the operational restructuring moves are the focal point with five significant variables, followed by two managerial restructuring moves and one of each for portfolio restructuring moves and turnaround context.

- The operational restructuring moves with significant effects are related to two topics, human resource and processes/policies. Among the human resources topic, both '*layoff*' and '*employee concessions*' promote family control loss in the TMT. The same is the case for '*process improvement and redesign,*' '*pur-*

chasing and cost reduction initiatives' and '*productivity increase.*' Of these, '*employee concessions*' shows the strongest effect (adj. $R^2 = 0.09$; $p < 0.001$).

- Both of the managerial restructuring moves are significant. While '*change in TMT*' (adj. $R^2 = 0.08$; $p < 0.001$) significantly promotes the family control loss in the TMT, its effective strength is less than the significant effect of the '*CEO change*' (adj. $R^2 = 0.27$; $p < 0.001$).
- Among the portfolio restructuring moves, *'termination of product lines/ markets'* promotes a control loss of the family in the management team.
- Reducing the probability of family control loss in the TMT is the turnaround context variable *'development of market segment during turnaround'* (adj. $R^2 = 0.08$; $p<0.01$). It seems a growing market stabilizes the family control in the TMT during turnaround.

Among the context variables, only two show a significant effect on *'loss of family control – role of family in TMT':*

- In line with the findings for the turnaround context variable, the *'Long-term growth perspectives of market segment'* has a similarly negative effect on the *'loss of family control – role of family in TMT*. The effect for the long-term market growth is even stronger than for the development of the market during turnaround (adj. $R^2 = 0.12$; $p < 0.01$).
- The only internal context variable with significant effect is *'slack resources before crisis,'* which does promote family control loss in the TMT with increasing slack resources.

Due to this diverse field of significant variables, a concluding assessment is challenging. The following is an attempt to group these effects into four main aspects that seem to influence the family control change:

- The first group I want to label as managerial/operational aspects. For grouping these I draw upon the cluster analysis where managerial and operational CCFs are found together in the '*operational crisis'* as the analysis in chapter 7 shows.

  Indeed, all the variables belonging to managerial CCFs and restructuring moves significantly promote control loss. The operational CCFs and restructuring moves are focused on process and human resource topics. A similar pattern is found for the cluster-specific analysis in section 8.6, where the family control loss is also higher for the *operational crisis* cluster.

It seems that managerial weaknesses and the operational weaknesses that go along with them (see cluster analysis chapter 7), as well as the related restructuring moves, promote family control loss.

- The second group of issues leading to loss of family control consists of strategic product problems related to innovation and quality as well as the restructuring move *'termination of products lines/markets.'* It seems that strategic issues and the related restructuring moves similarly promote family control loss.
- The third group is related to the market perspective, the CCF '*market decline*' and the two context variables related to market growth. These show that if the market is impeding the company's success, a reduction of family control becomes more likely, whereas if the market perspective is positive, the probability of family control loss is decreased.

  It seems market growth supports and market decline reduces family control.
- The fourth group is related to the financial CCFs and the financial restructuring. Among these, the exception is the CCF '*financing structure inadequate,*' which has a positive effect on the family control, reducing the probability of family control loss. None of the other financial CCFs' restructuring moves or context factors seems to have any influence on the family control.

  It appears that financial issues have little, and in some cases even a positive, impact on the family control.

In conclusion, it might be stated that although these groups appear to make sense of the effects found, the effect structure for family control change is much more complex than that found for family ownership change.

Similar to section 8.5.1, the presence of significant effects confirms Proposition 8.2 for the family control change. A further evaluation of the results is conducted in the final section of this chapter, in section 8.7.

8.6 Crisis and turnaround archetypes and the family role change

The aim of cluster analysis in strategic management research is to analyze archetypical strategic configurations with respect to cluster-specific performance variables (which are not part of the clustering algorithm) (Ketchen & Shook, 1996). Similar to the use of this approach in chapter 7 to assess the cluster-specific '*turnaround result,*' it is employed in this chapter to analyze the impact of these strategic configurations on the variables '*loss of family share*' and '*loss of family control – role of family in TMT,*' i.e., the cluster specific family role change. The family role change is a performance indicator from the perspective of the owner families, as these are assumed to be interested not only in a successful turnaround, but also in continued family ownership and control (see introduction of this chapter).

To analyze the cluster performance, the cluster-specific means of the two variables '*loss of family share*' and '*loss of family control – role of family in TMT*' are compared. The basis for this is the cluster analysis conducted in chapter 7. The clusters that emerge there, as well as the case specific cluster attributions identified there, are reused in this chapter.

To reiterate, the subsamples used in this section are restricted to cases that did not file for insolvency and had family shareholding before the crisis. Additionally, the outliers eliminated in chapter 7 are also excluded from the subsample, as a cluster attribution for these outliers is not available, resulting in a total of 111 cases.

The analysis is done in three steps, first for the crisis clusters (8.6.1), then for the turnaround clusters (8.6.2), followed by the analysis of the combined effect of both cluster attributions on the family role change (8.6.3).

8.6.1 Crisis-cluster-specific family role change

In the first step, the crisis clusters are analyzed. The crisis cluster-specific means for the variables '*loss of family share*' and '*loss of family control – role of family in TMT*' are calculated. These are complemented by the t-statistics indicating whether the mean differences between the clusters are significant. The results are presented in Table 37.

Cluster	Loss of family share.		Loss of family control – role of family in TMT		
	Mean	T-stat.	Mean	T-stat.	
Cluster 1: *Operational crisis* N = 31	0.8	-0.60	0.8	2.39	*
Cluster 2: *Financial crisis* N = 61	1.0	0.46	0.3	-2.75	**
Cluster 3: *Market crisis* N = 19	0.9	0.15	0.5	-0.09	
Total sample	0.9		0.5		

Table 37: Family role change per crisis cluster.

'Loss of family share' and *'loss of family control – role of family in TMT'* per crisis cluster; N = 111.
Significance levels at 0.05 and 0.01 indicated by * and **.

While the *'loss of family share'* shows no significant means differences between the three clusters, the mean of *'loss of family control – role of family in TMT'* is significantly lower for Cluster 2: *Financial crisis* and a significantly higher for the Cluster 3: *Operational crisis.*

Cluster 2: *Financial crisis* is characterized by overexpansion and inadequate financial structure and the absence of operational and market-related issues. Cluster 3: *Operational crisis* is characterized by a much higher relevance of managerial and operational CCFs (see cluster profiles in chapter 7, Table 22).

It seems that the difference might originate in the respective presence and absence of operational and managerial issues. The crisis cluster profiles show that specifically these factors are significantly higher for the *operational crisis* cluster, while being significantly lower for the *financial crisis* cluster. At the same time, for the *market crisis* cluster these factors do not significantly deviate from the remaining sample.

This pattern regarding operational and managerial CCFs matches the effects on *'loss of family control – role of family in TMT'* found in the univariate regression for the family control change (see section 8.4.2).

8.6.2 Turnaround-cluster-specific family role change

In the second step, the turnaround clusters and the cluster-specific means for *'loss of family share'* and *'loss of family control – role of family in TMT'* are analyzed.

Again the calculated means as well as the t-statistics are shown in Table 38.

Cluster	Loss of family share		Loss of family control – role of family in TMT	
	Mean	T-stat.	Mean	T-stat.
Cluster 1: *CEO change/ re-trenchment focus* N = 72	1.1	2.21*	0.7	4.54***
Cluster 2: *No CEO change/ no retrenchment focus* N = 39	0.5	-2.21*	0.2	-4.54***
Total sample	0.9		0.5	

Table 38: Family role change per turnaround cluster

'Loss of family share' and *'loss of family control – role of family in TMT'* per turnaround cluster; N = 111
Significance levels at 0.05 and 0.001 indicated by * and ***.

While the turnaround cluster attribution does not show significant differences in regard to the *'turnaround result,'* as analyzed in chapter 7, this is not the case for the family role change. The family role change appears heavily influenced by the cluster attribution of the chosen turnaround strategy. The mean values for the turnaround cluster '*CEO change, retrenchment focus'* show significantly higher means for '*loss of family share'* and '*loss of family control – role of family in TMT.'* Viewed purely from the owner family perspective, choosing a turnaround strategy from the cluster '*no CEO change/ no retrenchment focus*' is advantageous.

The cluster profiles for the two turnaround clusters (chapter 7, Table 25) show the restructuring move '*CEO change'* as the main differentiating variable between the two clusters. The restructuring move '*CEO change'* promoting a reduction of the family role ('*loss of family share'* and '*loss of family control – role of family in TMT*') would be in line with the findings of the two univariate regressions performed in section 8.5.1 and 8.5.2. For both, the restructuring move '*CEO change*' turns out to be a significant variable with high R^2 values.

8.6.3 Combined effects of crisis and turnaround clusters

Similar to the analysis in section 7.5, the combined effects of both crisis and turnaround clusters are analyzed. To reiterate, this is based on the fact that all cases go through the following two steps:

- A crisis belonging to one of the three crisis clusters, i.e., *operational*, *financial* or *market crisis*.

- Turnaround management belonging to one of the two turnaround clusters, i.e., '*CEO change/ retrenchment focus*' or '*no CEO change/ no retrenchment focus.*'

The crisis cluster attribution is chronologically prior to the turnaround cluster attribution. Thus the analysis investigates the turnaround clusters per crisis cluster. This structure is illustrated in chapter 7 in Figure 42.

The turnaround cluster attribution within a specific crisis cluster is referred to as sub-cluster. I.e. the sub-cluster '*CEO change/ retrenchment focus*' within the crisis cluster *market crisis* contains all cases experiencing a *market crisis* and a turnaround strategy attributed to the turnaround cluster *'CEO change/ retrenchment focus.'*

In a first step, the distribution of the cases on turnaround sub-clusters per crisis cluster in shown in Table 39.

Meta cluster analysis turnaround sub-cluster per crisis cluster	Cluster 1: ***CEO change/ retrenchment focus***		Cluster 2: ***No CEO change/ no retrenchment focus***	
	Number of cases	Share of cases within crisis cluster	Number of cases	Share of cases within crisis cluster
Cluster 1: *Operational crisis*	30	97%	1	3%
Cluster 2: *Financial crisis*	33	54%	28	46%
Cluster 3: *Market crisis*	9	47%	10	53%

Table 39: Case distribution on turnaround clusters per crisis cluster.

Number of cases in turnaround clusters per crisis cluster.
Firms with any family share before turnaround, surviving turnaround; N = 111.

It is apparent, that the distribution is very similar to the distribution of the complete sample as found in chapter 7, shown there in Table 28. For the cases belonging to the *operational crisis* cluster most belong to a turnaround strategy attributed to Cluster 1: '*CEO change/ retrenchment focus.*' For the other two clusters the cases are almost equally divided between the two turnaround clusters.

In the next step, the family role change variable means for the combinations of the two clusters are calculated, i.e., the mean for all cases belonging to both a specific crisis cluster and a specific turnaround cluster. For the turnaround management sub-cluster within a specific crisis cluster, a t-test is performed to analyze the significance of the mean difference between the two turnaround sub-clusters within a crisis cluster. These results are shown in Table 40.

Meta cluster analysis *'Loss of family share'* and *'loss of family control – role of family in TMT'* depending on turnaround sub-cluster per crisis cluster	**Crisis cluster total**	Cluster 1: ***CEO change/ retrenchment focus***	Cluster 2: ***No CEO change/ no retrenchment focus***
	mean	mean	mean
Loss of family share (higher value indicated higher average loss of family ownership)			
Cluster 1: *Operational crisis*	0.8	0.7*	2.0*
Cluster 2: *Financial crisis*	1.0	1.4*	0.5*
Cluster 3: *Market crisis*	0.9	1.4	0.5
Loss of family control – role of family in TMT (higher value indicated higher average loss of family control)			
Cluster 1: *Operational crisis*	0.8	0.8	1.0
Cluster 2: *Financial crisis*	0.3	0.5*	0.1*
Cluster 3: *Market crisis*	0.5	0.9*	0.2*

Table 40: Performance of turnaround clusters per crisis cluster.

Mean comparison within crisis cluster depending on turnaround cluster attribution.
Firms with any family share before turnaround, surviving turnaround; N = 111.
Significance levels at 0.05 indicated by *.

The results are discussed sequentially, first for the *'loss of family share,'* then for *'loss of family control – role of family in TMT.'*

- For the cases belonging to the archetype *operational crisis,* choosing a turnaround strategy belonging to *'CEO change/ retrenchment focus'* is better for family ownership, as it shows a lower mean for *'loss of family share.'* This is surprising: While generally this turnaround cluster is disadvantageous for family ownership, it seems that for the special case of an *operational crisis* the inverse is true.
- For the financial crisis cluster, choosing a turnaround strategy of the cluster '*no CEO change/ no retrenchment focus*' is significantly better for the family ownership, as it shows a lower mean *'loss of family share.'*
- For the *market crisis*, there is no significant difference in the family ownership change for the two turnaround sub-clusters.

Analyzing the '*loss of family control – role of family in TMT*' the picture is slightly more consistent.

- For the archetype *operational crisis*, the two turnaround clusters show no significant difference in regard to the turnaround sub cluster-specific mean of '*loss of family control – role of family in TMT.*'
- For the two clusters *financial* and *market crisis,* the mean differences between the two turnaround sub-clusters have the same direction. For both kinds of crisis the turnaround strategy '*no CEO change/ no retrenchment focus*' is better for family control, as the mean of '*loss of family control – role of family in TMT*' is lower for this turnaround sub-cluster.

Combining both dimensions of the family role change perspective, a clear pattern emerges:

- For the cluster *operational crisis*, the turnaround strategy '*CEO change/ retrenchment focus*' yields better results for the family than the turnaround strategy '*no CEO change/ no retrenchment focus.*' The mean for the variable *'loss of family share'* is significantly lower and the mean of *'loss of family control – role of family in TMT'* is insignificantly lower.
- For the other two clusters, the turnaround strategy '*no CEO change/ no retrenchment focus'* is better for the family. For both clusters, the means of the variables *'loss of family share'* and *'loss of family control – role of family in TMT*' are lower – in three of the four comparisons significantly – for the cluster *'no CEO change/ no retrenchment focus'* than for the cluster *'CEO change/ retrenchment focus.*'

This can be cross-referenced with the analysis performed in chapter 7 for the variable '*turnaround result.'* There, the analysis of turnaround sub-clusters per crisis cluster shows the turnaround strategy '*CEO change/ retrenchment focus'* to be more beneficial only for the *operational crisis.* For the other two crisis clusters there is no significant difference between the turnaround sub-clusters.

This indicates that the preferred turnaround strategy archetype from owner family perspective is not in conflict with the findings in respect to the *'turnaround result.'* It could be concluded with the simple formula:

- *Operational crisis → 'CEO change/ retrenchment focus'*
- Other crisis archetypes → *'no CEO change/ no retrenchment focus'*

Obviously, this is a very simplistic perspective on the turnaround, purely based on the cluster analysis, but illustrates the findings of this section.

The cluster-specific mean differences for the family role change variables found in this section confirm Proposition 8.3.

8.7 Discussion

As discussed in the introduction of this chapter, there is almost no conceptual and empirical research related to the mechanisms leading to loss of family ownership and loss of family control during crisis and turnaround. Therefore, the results of the analyses conducted in this chapter are exploratory in nature rather than confirmatory. Consequently, I attempt to grasp the diverse results by structuring them into four key items and complement them with a hypothesis referring to possible explanations and rationales. This is not meant to be an exhaustive analysis of all effects found, but a rough overview of the key relations between crisis and turnaround management characteristics and the family role change. These key items are:

- Suitability and removal of the CEO.
- Employee concessions and layoff.
- Product-related portfolio issues.
- Market development.

Suitability and removal of the CEO

The person of the CEO (CCF *'unsuitable CEO'*) and the removal of the CEO (restructuring move *'change CEO'*) seem to be key factors for the family role change. Both the CCF and the restructuring move strongly promote the loss of family ownership as well as the loss of family control.

The fact that family control is reduced if there is an unsuitable CEO and he/she is removed can be straightforwardly explained: Changing a CEO is obviously a high risk for the family, in that the successor is a non-family member resulting in a reduction in family control.

More interesting is the relation between the CEO and family ownership, as there is no similarly obvious direct effect structure. The univariate regression found that the effect of an '*unsuitable CEO*' (adj. $R^2 = 0.13$) on '*loss of family share*' is even stronger than the effect of the *'CEO change'* (adj. $R^2 = 0.11$) on the same variable; this indicates that indeed the loss of family ownership has its origins in the unsuitable person of the CEO, not in the related measure of changing the CEO. Two possible explanations could explain these findings:

- In the case of an unsuitable shareholding CEO, a removal might not be possible. As the introduction of new shareholders reduces the shareholding CEO's influence, other stakeholders might push for new shareholders and thus a reduction in family ownership.
- Another possible explanation is that an unsuitable CEO is also an unsuitable shareholder, thus promoting share loss.

Although having less effect and thus possibly only a derived finding for the CCF '*unsuitable CEO,*' there are two explanations for the effect of the restructuring move '*change CEO*' on the family ownership change:

- The first hypothesis is based on the assumption that the replacement of a CEO leads to a non-family CEO being installed (indicated by the fact that the share of family CEOs drops during crisis – see section 8.4). Based on the principal-agent theory, it might be assumed that this newly installed agent in the company (the new non-family CEO) has different interests than the shareholders and behaves differently from a family member CEO. Specifically, he has no interest in maintaining the shareholder structure, while the contrary is usually the case for family CEOs (according to the SEW theory). Thus he might be more likely to promote measures that bring in new shareholders (e.g., by increasing equity) and thus increase the probability of share loss.

- The CEO removal jointly with a family ownership reduction might also be due to an inverse cause-effect relation, as a new shareholder replaces the CEO with his own (non-family) candidate.

Employee concessions and layoff

A second finding concerns the restructuring moves '*employee concessions*' and '*layoff.*' These employee-based restructuring moves appear to promote the loss of family control (adj. R^2 = 0.09 and 0.05 respectively). It might be hypothesized that the family has to pay a price for their employees' contribution to the turnaround success. My hypothesis is that employees demand as a price for their contribution the constitution of a more diverse, less family-focused composition of the TMT and thus less family control.

Product-related portfolio issues

Product-related portfolio issues are also related to family control loss (CCFs '*missing innovation in core products*' and '*insufficient quality and service*' with adj. R^2 = 0.11 and 0.08 respectively). These effects might indicate that specifically, if the product portfolio shows weaknesses, the company is forced to add non-family TMT members to bring in external resources and know how to improve the product portfolio.

Market development

The market development (turnaround context *'development of market segment during turnaround'* and external context factor *'Long-term growth perspectives of market segment'*) are both negatively related to *'loss of family control'* (adj. R^2 = 0.08 and 0.12 respectively). There is no significant relation between any of these variables and the family ownership change.

It is assumed that a market growth perspective increases the negotiation power of the shareholders (higher going concern value means higher share value) in relation with the debt holders. This would imply a positive effect of market growth on family ownership. As this is not the case, a different explanation is required.

It could be speculated that market growth promotes turnaround success (as found in chapter 6) and thus decreases the pressure on the company to replace its managers, which in consequence would consolidate family control.

The cause-effect relations discussed above and the hypotheses for these effects are highly speculative in nature. One fact remains certain with the empirical evidence found: In crisis and turnaround, the role of the family, both in terms of ownership and in terms of family control, is reduced. Crisis and turnaround are extremely critical for a family and defining for the relation between family and company in the future.

Especially because it could be shown that there are strong effects between the characteristics of crisis and turnaround and the results of turnaround for the family, I want to argue that additional research – especially conceptually – is required to understand how crisis and turnaround affect the future of a family in their family firm.

9 Conclusions

As each of the three result chapters closes with a concluding assessment of the respective findings, this chapter reiterates the content of these statements while aggregating them into a bigger picture.

This chapter consists of four parts. In the first section, 9.1, the key findings are summarized and aggregated, allowing a concluding assessment of the results at a glance. The next two sections address the implications and recommendations for both the managers and stakeholders (section 9.2) as well as for future turnaround research (section 9.3). This chapter closes with limitations of this study's approach and its relevance for the results (see section 9.4).

9.1 Summary of key findings

To navigate through the summary of this study's findings, I want to refer back to the research questions discussed in the introduction of this study addressing the current state and specifically the weaknesses of turnaround research:

1. What are the conceptually relevant factors influencing the turnaround success?
2. Which conditions enhance turnaround success?
3. Are there common patterns in and out of crisis?
   What is their respective performance?
4. How is the relation between family and family firm affected by crisis and turnaround?

This study provides answers for each of these four questions. Unfortunately, as expected, these answers are by far neither conclusive nor exhaustive. Nonetheless, the answers add significantly to the relevant research. At the same time, many additional questions, both conceptual and empirical, can be derived from the findings in this study. On the following pages, I want to sum up the findings for each of the four questions.

What are the conceptually relevant factors influencing the turnaround success?

The identification of relevant variables is conducted in chapters 3 and 4. The model design decisions concerning both content and structure of the model are derived and discussed in chapter 3. The model dimensions are defined as 'crisis characteristics,' 'turnaround management characteristics,' 'context factors' and 'turnaround result characteristics.' One key decision that is an innovation compared to other research approaches, is the description of crisis content using crisis contribution factors (CCFs), allowing an assessment based on symptoms, departing from the traditional usage of the misleading term 'crisis causes.' Based on these decisions, the conceptual model is developed in chapter 4. The foundation for the model development is a set of four robust model decision criteria: '*Limitation to a homogenous research sample,' consideration of all relevant dimensions of the turnaround situation,' 'congruence in complexity in these dimensions'* and *'the principle of visibility and relevancy'* (see section 4.1).

In a bottom-up approach, the variables are selected according to these criteria, meaning that initially all variables discussed in the literature are considered relevant. This variable pool is then grouped and structured. In a review cycle, each variable is challenged for its explanatory contribution together with a group of restructuring experts (see Appendix 1 – list of restructuring specialists). This process concludes in a final conceptual model. The structure of the model confirms the assumption of high complexity in turnaround. It yields 27 variables for the crisis characteristics, 28 variables for the turnaround management characteristics, 16 variables (or 14, if the categorical '*primary strategy before crisis'* variables is considered as one) for the context, and 4 variables for the turnaround result.

Based on this conceptual model, a study-specific sample collection process was conducted with banks' risk management experts. Asking risk managers of banks for their contribution was possible due to the specific regulations in the German banking system; these risk managers have two unique properties: They are required and eligible to collect detailed information about the distressed company, and they have extensive experience with turnaround, as their sole function is to supervise the business with distressed companies. In this sample collection process, 209 valid cases of mid-sized companies in distress entering a turnaround were recorded from 22 different banks. Among the contributing banks are large listed institutions including Deutsche Bank, Commerzbank, the DZ Bank and Postbank, along with smaller institutes. The contributing banks derive from all three pillars of the German banking system (see section 5.1.3) and represent over 50% of the aggregated balance sheet sum of all German banks.

Which conditions enhance turnaround success?

Chapter 6 researches the relation between all relevant variables and the *'turnaround result'* as outcome variable, i.e., the performance of the company after turnaround, with the lowest value representing failed turnaround. The statistical analysis is conducted based on a sequential approach, using four approaches and eleven different multivariate regression models to confirm the consistency of results through the multiple approaches.

The first approach uses univariate regression of all model variables as predictors and *'turnaround result'* as outcome variable (section 6.3). This approach has the highest statistical power (see section 6.1.2) and is thus able to detect even small significant effects. It shows significance for 11 crisis variables, four turnaround management variables and five context variables. These numbers result in an immediate first insight, showing that in terms of numbers the crisis variables are more relevant than turnaround management variables, reconfirming the assumption that if these variables were not considered, the result might depend on the (possibly not random) distribution of these factors in the sample.

The univariate regression yields some counterintuitive results, as the CCF *'conflict spillover from owner family to company'* shows a significantly positive and the restructuring move *'layoff'* a significantly negative effect on the *'turnaround result.'* The first might be explained by the notion that family conflicts are easier to resolve in the face of crisis than actual company issues. The second might be seen as a sign that layoffs as a key element of the turnaround strategy are not an ideal measure for the sustainable recovery of a firm.

As part of the first approach, selected moderation effects are analyzed (section 6.3.4). Of the 13 interaction effects, four combined variables are shown to explain the effects better; a moderation effect itself is not present, thus indicating compensation, not a moderation effect.

Only one moderation effect is reconfirmed as significant. The restructuring move *'change CEO'* is found to moderate the effect of the CCF *'unsuitable CEO'* on the *'turnaround result,'* i.e., the restructuring move changes the effect strength and direction of the CCF on the dependent variable. This evidence indicates that changing a CEO only affects the turnaround result positively if the CEO contributes to the crisis. The common notion of a mandatory CEO change does not seem to be generally valid (see section 4.5.2).

While the detection strength of the univariate regression is very high, it does not consider how multiple variables simultaneously affect the *'turnaround result.'* Consequently, this is analyzed using eleven multivariate regression models with different model structures and different variable subsets; these include complete, partial and simplified models. The results show that the models are all significant, and able to explain 42% to 49% of the variance of the *'turnaround result'* variable.

The assessments of the variables that are ultimately significant in one or more of the regressions appear in the table below. The variables in this table are based on the multivariate analyses of the conceptual model, representing the main influencing factors for the turnaround result.

Variable name	Assessment	Stand. beta
Portfolio crisis contribution factors		
Insufficient quality and service	Important	-0.16 – -0.21
Financial crisis contribution factors		
Overleveraging	Inconclusive	Negative, unclear strength
External crisis contribution factors		
Market decline	Inconclusive	Unclear
Turnaround context		
Development of market segment during turnaround	Limited	0.12 – 0.18
Stakeholder management during turnaround	Very important	0.27 – 0.36
Internal context		
Family share in the company before crisis	Important	0.12 – 0.19
External context		
Long-term growth perspectives of market segment	Very important	0.27 – 0.33
Interaction effects		
'Unsuitable CEO' × 'CEO change'*	Important	0.15 – 0.17
'Unsuitable members of TMT' × 'change in TMT'	Doubtful	Unclear

Table 41: Variable assessment based on multiple regression analyses.

Dependent variable *'turnaround result.'* Comprehensive cross-regression model comparison.
Assessment of the variables:
Very important – significant in all models.
Important – significant below the statistical power of complete models.
Limited – limited evidence with mixed results.
Inconclusive – limited statistical evidence with conceptual concerns.
Doubtful – little statistical evidence with strong conceptual concerns.
* beta values exclude the result of stepwise regressions due to statistical concerns.

This nine-variable table is the result of a cross-regression model comparison of all analyzed variables and includes all variables that turned out significant in a least one relevant model. Stakeholder management and the long-term perspective of the market segment appear to be the most important factors for a successful turnaround.

Are there common patterns in and out of crisis?
What is their respective performance?

To answer this research question, the focus of the analysis in chapter 7 moves away from assessing individual variables to clustering the data in the search for common archetypes. The cluster analysis is conducted sequentially for both crisis and turnaround management characteristics. For both dimensions, distinct patterns are detected; three crisis clusters and two turnaround clusters emerge. The clusters show distinct differences in regard to the cluster variables. For the crisis, these are labeled as *operational*, *financial* and *market crisis*. For the turnaround management, the two clusters '*CEO change/ retrenchment focus*' and *'no CEO change/no retrenchment focus'* are identified.

The cluster-specific means for the performance variable '*turnaround result*' yield two key findings.

The mean *'turnaround result'* for the *market crisis* cluster is significantly worse, while the mean for the *financial crisis* cluster is better than the respective remaining sample.

The mean of *'survival of company'* is significantly lower for the *market crisis* with 43% compared to 67% for the *operational* and 68% for the *financial crisis*.

The turnaround clusters do not yield any significant differences in terms of *'turnaround result'* and '*survival of company*.'

The combination of both clusters shows significant differences only for the *operational crisis* cluster. For these kinds of crises, the strategies attributed to the turnaround cluster '*CEO change/ retrenchment focus*' are on average far better, with a mean survival rate of 74%, than strategies attributed to the turnaround cluster '*no CEO change/ no retrenchment focus*,' where the mean survival rate is only 20%.

> *How is the relation between family and family firm affected by crisis and turnaround?*

The relation between family and firm is addressed in chapter 8. The focus is the under-researched topic of the family role change during turnaround. The role of the family is analyzed in two aspects: Family ownership and family control. Due to data availability, this is restricted to successful turnarounds of family firms.

The analysis is conducted in three consecutive steps: The descriptive assessment of the data, followed by a univariate regression and finally the mean family role change assessment for the crisis and turnaround clusters.

The descriptive analysis shows a significant reduction of the family role in both respects, control and ownership, during turnaround. For 35% of the firms, the ownership share is reduced during turnaround; for 19% of the firms, the family has no share in the firm after turnaround. Similarly, the share of companies with family CEOs is reduced from 85% to 55% with a parallel loss of influence in the TMT.

The univariate regression shows six variables with significant effect on the loss of family ownership. The majority of the significant factors are related to the company's management, specifically the crisis contribution of the CEO, succession problems, as well as CEO change and TMT changes, all promoting ownership reduction.

The univariate regression of the family loss of control shows a much more complex result with 21 variables having a significant effect on the family loss of control. A rough aggregation shows four main trends:

- Operational and managerial CCFs and restructuring moves promote family control loss.
- Product-related strategic issues and restructuring moves promote family control loss.
- Market growth perspectives reduce the control loss of the family.
- Financial crisis items and measures do not influence the control loss.

The analysis of the crisis and turnaround clusters for their respective mean family role change concludes with a differentiated picture:

While the crisis clusters have no significant effect on the family ownership change, they affect the loss of family control. It is found that the control loss is significantly higher for the *operational crisis*, while it is significantly lower for the *financial crisis*. These findings are in line with the univariate regression results.

In comparison, the turnaround strategy has a stronger significant effect on the family role. Strategies belonging to the cluster '*CEO change/retrenchment focus*' promote on average a diminishing of the family role in both aspects, while the *'no CEO change/no retrenchment focus'* turnaround archetype shows less family control and family ownership loss.

The cross cluster comparison complements these results, as it shows that from a family role change perspective, for an *'operational crisis'* the *'CEO change/retrenchment focus'* is better, while for the other two kinds of crises the *'no CEO change/no retrenchment focus'* is superior.

This study's results show clearly that an integrated approach using an adequately complex model for crisis and turnaround produces more differentiated and meaningful results. The effects of the crisis and the context on the turnaround probability are extensive, strong and significant and an analysis neglecting these can only yield inferior insights.

There are effects of the crisis and turnaround on the firm family relation. While these effects have been shown to be strongly significant, their conceptual foundation can only be the subject of speculation as there is currently no conceptual research available to explain these effects theoretically.

9.2 Implications for managers, shareholders and stakeholders

The practical implications of this work can be differentiated for three affected parties involved in crisis and turnaround:

- *Managers and shareholders* are interested in how to act, i.e., how to avoid or solve a crisis.
- *Family shareholders* have interests similar to other shareholders, but are additionally interested in preserving the family ownership and control in the firm.
- *Stakeholders, especially banks,* are interested in how to assess a crisis, i.e., how to conduct a prognosis of whether a specific company is likely to recover from a given crisis

9.2.1 Managers and shareholders

The implications for managers and owners lie in two aspects: Before a crisis and during turnaround management.

Managers and shareholders – before a crisis

The univariate analysis of the crisis variables on the *'turnaround result'* may offer some guidance, specifically the 11 significant variables and their respective strength of effect. These can be used to assess the dangers of these variables in a crisis scenario. The crisis characteristics that significantly negatively influence the turnaround result can be seen as more dangerous crisis properties and should thus be avoided.

Based on the multivariate models, there is one CCF *'insufficient quality and service'* that is assessed as particularly important, as it significantly reduces the turnaround chances. It appears advisable to implement a specific risk management measure to mitigate this factor.

Of even higher relevance, but with different characteristics, is the market situation. This is indicated by both the very important and significant context variable *'Long-term growth perspectives of market segment'* and the significantly lower mean of *'survival of company'* for the cluster *market crisis*.

While the market situation cannot be changed by managers, it seems to be prudent to intensify crisis avoidance and preparation activities in long-term shrinking market environments, as a crisis is then more lethal and recovering from a crisis much more difficult.

Related to the cluster analysis, a last finding directly affects the person of the CEO and the implications of a crisis for him. There is strong evidence that a crisis belonging to the *operational crisis* cluster makes a '*CEO change/retrenchment focus*' turnaround strategy much more likely, making it highly attractive for a CEO to avoid such crises, as otherwise his removal becomes very likely.

Managers and shareholders – during turnaround management

Similarly, the univariate regression of the turnaround management characteristics offers limited guidance for managers and shareholders during turnaround management. More guidance can be gained from the analysis of the moderation effects, as it shows a clear relation between crisis characteristic and restructuring move for five combinations.

Based on the findings of the multivariate analysis, a clear message for managers and shareholders is implied: Move the focus away from the content of turnaround management and focus specifically on stakeholder management, which is a consistently very important variable for turnaround success.

From the shareholders' perspective, it is important to understand the role of the CEO in the crisis development. If he is perceived as a contributing factor, a removal is advisable. This harsh fact is reconfirmed by different approaches, including cluster analysis, moderation effect analysis and multivariate analyses.

9.2.2 Family shareholders

For family shareholders there is good news from the univariate and multivariate analysis: The chances are better for a family firm to recover from a crisis. As such, it might be advisable to utilize the possibilities and strengths of the unique situation of a family firm to the maximum degree, as these seem to make an actual difference.

When it comes to preserving the family firm ownership, the CEO topic is found to be most relevant. Having a suitable CEO, a smooth succession process and – if possible – not changing the CEO in crisis seems to support retaining family ownership.

Family control is, by contrast, much more complex. The effects described in the last section of chapter 8 are lengthy and are not repeated here. They may offer some guidance how to retain family control during turnaround.

In comparison, a clearer result can be derived from the cluster analysis. It results in a decision tree: For family firms in an operational crisis, a '*CEO change/retrenchment focus*' strategy is advisable, while in all other kinds of crises the strategies belonging to the cluster '*no CEO change/no retrenchment focus*' are better for the family role in the company after turnaround.

This is emphasized by the fact that except for the *operational crisis* cluster, there are no significant differences between the two turnaround clusters in regard to '*survival of company*' and '*turnaround result.*' From the family perspective, the decision for the cluster '*no CEO change/no retrenchment focus*' is thus (for all crises not belonging to the *operational crisis* cluster) not in conflict with the '*turnaround result*' perspective.'

9.2.3 Stakeholders, especially banks

For stakeholders in general, the results of this study can offer some guidance in assessing the likelihood of success for a specific turnaround. Based on the cross-cluster analysis together with the significant moderation effect of *'unsuitable CEO'* and *'CEO change,'* stakeholders should use their influence on the company to demand the removal of the CEO, if the CEO's is perceived to have contributed to the crisis. At the same time, if the stakeholder management is perceived as lacking, this is a warning indicator that failure of the company is more likely.

Similarly, as there is always interaction between stakeholders and the company, the results of this study can also be used as a basis for critical discussion with the company about crisis and measures taken.

Specifically for banks working with companies in distress, it seems feasible to implement a rating system based on the content of the restructuring opinion, both in terms of crisis diagnosis, turnaround strategy and context factors. This could complement traditional rating approaches and would allow the bank to make decisions during the restructuring process, e.g., debt conversion, new debt or debt waiver, based on a rating system as a firm factual basis. As the regression models are able to explain a significant part of the *'turnaround result'* variance, such a rating system would be able to contribute significantly to the banks' risk management procedures.

9.3 Implications for future research

My perspective on the implications for future research is briefly mentioned in the concluding sections of chapters 6 to 8. I repeat and aggregate these in this section.

The issues with turnaround research – specifically the lack of integration – appear to be valid. The study shows that factors from the neglected areas of crisis characteristics and context factors, but also non-content related aspects of turnaround management, such as the stakeholder management, have a significant impact on the turnaround result, resulting in the first two recommendations:

- A minimum number of crisis and context factors, specifically those that have turned out to have a significant effect on *'turnaround result,'* should be considered in a study of turnaround if only to make sure that by integrating them as control variables the result is not distorted by a non-random distribution of these variables. At a minimum, it seems prudent to refer to Table 41, discussing variables that turned out significant for all relevant regression analysis.

- The second recommendation is related to the complexity of the crisis. The results show that an overgeneralization, for instance, of all operational restructuring moves as one operational restructuring move, leads to limited information content. Concerning a study's design, both consideration of the criteria of congruency in complexity and a minimum level of detail is recommended, as the effects might consistently be diluted.

Similarly, a focus adjustment away from a pure assessment of turnaround strategies to a more holistic approach is indicated by this study. The research on the effects of crisis characteristics and context factors on turnaround – specifically conceptual research – is scarce. The same can be stated for the context and process elements of both crisis and turnaround.

The topic of moderation effects between the different variables has only been analyzed in this study very superficially. The interactions between crisis characteristics, context factors and the turnaround strategy are extremely complex. The compensation effects for some factors and the moderation for one factor ('*CEO change*' moderating the effect of '*unsuitable CEO*') have shown (see section 6.2) that there are effect structures that could be an interesting topic for future research. Unfortunately, even for these few selective interaction effects, their effect strengths are mostly below the statistical power of the multivariate analyses conducted in this study. It is my view that, a significant part of the unexplained variance can be attributed to these interactions.

The use of scale variables instead of binary variables is shown to be effective. Especially in the cluster performance assessment, where both variables are used in parallel, differences in content can be seen (see chapter 7). Consequently, a simultaneous usage of binary and scale variable might be the best approach.

While the medical analogies only carry so far, in my opinion there is a great deal to be learned for turnaround management research from medical studies and how they are conducted. This involves both the clear structure and consideration of context variables to assess a treatment, as well as the use of more complex statistical methods (briefly mentioned in section 6.6.2) applied in medical and genetic research. Perceiving a company crisis as an illness and turnaround management as a treatment are deemed to be a valid plausibility check for a study setup.

For the field of family firm research, specifically concerning the effect of crisis and turnaround on the role of the family in a firm, there are differentiated findings in this study. The results show firstly that crisis and turnaround are a critical time (i.e., a time when many families lose ownership and control) for a family and their firm, and secondly, that there are significant effects between the characteristics of crisis and turnaround on family ownership and control. In my view, this field definitely deserves conceptual and empirical research attention to understand these effects.

9.4 Limitations

This section discusses the key limitations of this study with regard to the research approach chosen.

While the researcher aspires to include all relevant factors for the crisis and turnaround process in the conceptual model, the possibility cannot be excluded that either important items may be missing or the congruency of model complexity is not fully satisfied. A case-study-based analysis of factors and interaction for several turnaround cases could help to identify further relevant factors and help to achieve a consistent level of complexity. In general, a more standardized model of turnaround could benefit both the quality of research and the comparability of results.

The second limitation is common to nearly all empirical studies and addresses the issue of whether the analyzed sample is representative of the population it is drawn from. Specifically, the sampling process gave little control over the selection of the cases in the sample (see chapter 5). The absence of selection bias can thus not be guaranteed. A different approach would be to sample all cases of one bank for a specific year or time period. However, a limited time period and limited participating banks would then introduce a new bias. A randomized selection – according to a standardized procedure – involving both a reasonably long period of time and a large number of banks would be best. Such was unfortunately not possible for this study, as convincing the banks to participate was already a challenge.

It is important to note that this study does specifically address a homogenous research sample as specified in section 4.2. An extension of the finding on companies not within the sample characteristics, both in terms of bank financing, industry segment or country, but also in terms of company size, is speculative in nature and cannot be directly derived from the findings in this study.

The approach was also limited due to the way the data was collected. Missing information and personal judgment may cloud the assessment of the participating bank risk managers. Although the researcher assumes that these individuals are ideal independent witnesses – as laid out in section 3.1.3 – this is a specific weakness of this expert-opinion-based approach. On the other hand, research based on financial data has been shown to be similarly diluted by window dressing effects (see section 3.2.2).

The sample size is one of the most obvious limitations. A larger sample would make detection of more and weaker effects possible. At the same time, it would allow inclusion of additional interaction effects, which are assumed to be present within the data. I hope that the findings of this study make additional research based on the privileged information of German banks' risk managers possible to address these items and to better understand the process of crisis and turnaround.

Appendix 1 – list of restructuring specialists

Alban Baiker – Director, working at AlixPartners (www.alixpartners.com), an international consulting company with focus on turnaround and restructuring.

Holmer Glietz – Founder and partner of AuxilPartner (www.auxil-partner.com), a consulting company specialized on turnaround and restructuring.

Felix Schwabedal – Independent interim manager and restructuring specialist.

More than 10 risk managers of German banks provided input, but requested anonymity.

Appendix 2 – questionnaire

Wittener Institut für Familienunternehmen der Universität Witten/Herdecke

Wissenschaftliche Studie –

Krise, Turnaround und Sanierungserfolg im Mittelstand

Analyse von Einflussfaktoren und Zusammenhängen mit besonderem Fokus auf Unterschiede zwischen Familien- und Nicht-Familienunternehmen

Thomas Wittig
Dipl. Wirt.-Ing.

Prof. Dr. Andreas Hack

Prof. Dr. Arist von Schlippe

Hintergrund

- Ziel dieser Studie ist ein **verbessertes Verständnis von Krise und Turnaround in mittelständischen Unternehmen**. Dazu sollen typische Krisenarten, Turnaround-Strategien und **Erfolgsfaktoren** der Sanierung identifiziert werden. Besonderer Fokus wird dabei auf **Unterschiede und Gemeinsamkeiten von Familienunternehmen** und Nicht-Familienunternehmen gelegt.
- Die internationale Forschung zu Sanierung und Turnaround konzentriert sich auf börsennotierte Großunternehmen. Ein zentraler Pfeiler der deutschen Wirtschaft, der Mittelstand, unterscheidet sich jedoch grundlegend von diesen Großunternehmen.
- Als ein auf die Betreuung von Problemkrediten spezialisierter Mitarbeiter eines Kreditinstitutes haben Sie **im Rahmen Ihrer täglichen professionellen Arbeit Erfahrungen mit Unternehmen in der Krise** und kennen positive und negative Beispiele für Sanierungen. Diese Kenntnisse wollen wir im Rahmen dieser Studie mit diesem Fragebogen **anonymisiert erfassen und systematisch wissenschaftlich analysieren.**

Unser Dankeschön für Ihre Teilnahme:

- **Exklusiver Ergebnisbericht** dieser Studie (anonym und aggregiert) für Sie.
- Für **jeden vollständigen Fragebogen** werden wir jeweils **10 EUR spenden**. Begünstigt werden zu gleiche Teilen die deutsche Kindernothilfe und das Kinderhospiz Regenbogenland. Wenn Sie den Fragebogen für **mehrere Fälle** bearbeiten, so erfolgt die Spende für **jeden ausgefüllten Fragebogen.**
(Sie finden unter https://www.betterplace.org/de/fundraising-events/studie_krise_mittelstand das offizielle Spendenbarometer dieser Studie, Spenden bis zum Maximalbetrag von 3.000 EUR)

Hinweise zum Fragebogen:

- Für das vollständige Ausfüllen des Fragebogens werden für den ersten Fall ca. **20-25 Minuten** benötigt. Wir freuen uns, wenn Sie den Fragebogen für mehrere Praxisfälle ausfüllen – die Erfassung **weiterer Fälle** dauert nach unserer Erfahrung **deutlich kürzer**.
- Der Fragebogen dient rein **wissenschaftlichen Zwecken**.
- Alle Ihre Angaben unterliegen den **deutschen Datenschutzrichtlinien** und werden ausschließlich in **anonymisierter** Form ausgewertet. Rückschlüsse auf die betrachteten Unternehmen sind nicht möglich!
- Um wissenschaftlich verwertbare Ergebnisse zu erzielen, ist es sehr wichtig, dass Sie den Fragebogen **vollständig ausfüllen**.

1. Erläuterungen zur Fallorientierung des Fragbogens

Um eine systematische, vergleichende Analyse zu ermöglichen, wurden die im Rahmen dieser Studie betrachteten Unternehmen eingeschränkt. Bitte beachten Sie hierzu die folgenden Kriterien:

- **Produzierendes** Unternehmen (keine reinen Handels- oder Dienstleistungsunternehmen)
- Hauptsitz des Unternehmens in **Deutschland**
- Umsatz zwischen **10 und 500 Mio. EUR** – „Mittelstand"
- Krisensituation des Unternehmens ist **„beendet"** – entweder durch **Insolvenz** oder durch eine (mehr oder weniger) **erfolgreiche Sanierung**
- Unternehmen hatte im Rahmen der Krise einen **Liquiditätsengpass** oder zusätzlichen Finanzierungsbedarf
- Der Krisenfall war **nach dem Jahr 2000**

Wir freuen uns, wenn Sie im Rahmen der Studie **einen Fall** erfassen, idealer Weise füllen Sie jedoch – wenn möglich – diesen Fragebogen für **mehrere unterschiedliche Fälle** (Problemkreditnehmer) aus Ihrer persönlichen Erfahrung aus.

Wenn Sie mehr als einen Fall betrachten, möchten wir Sie bitten möglichst **mindestens ein positives und ein negatives Beispiel** einer Sanierung zu betrachten (nur der Vergleich erlaubt die **Identifikation von Erfolgsfaktoren**).

HINWEIS: Für **jeden erfassten Fall** erfolgt eine Spende von **10 EUR** (bis zum Limit von 3.000 EUR).

Führen Sie sich nun bitte im Folgenden jeweils **einen Fall** vor Augen und beantworten Sie alle Fragen für diesen Fall. Sind Ihnen die Fakten nicht genau bekannt, so **schätzen Sie bitte die Werte**, die Genauigkeit ist weniger wichtig als die **vollständige Beantwortung** des Fragebogens, da dies Voraussetzung für die wissenschaftliche Verarbeitung ist.

2. Mittelstand – Familienunternehmen oder Nicht-Familienunternehmen

Für diese Studie werden Familienunternehmen und Nicht-Familienunternehmen unterschieden. Hierbei wird im ersten Fall die Rolle der Familie durch weitere Fragen differenzierter betrachtet. Zur Abgrenzung von privat erworbenen Unternehmen bedeutet Familie im Sinne dieser Studie die **Familie(n) des/der Gründer des Unternehmens**.

Eigentumsanteil der *Gründerfamilie(n)* und ihrer Nachkommen am Unternehmens vor der Krise
(Durch die Gründerfamilie(n) gehaltene Anteile, ggf. bei mehreren Familien (Nachkommen der/ des Gründers) insgesamt. Nicht zutreffend bei durch Privatpersonen nach Gründung übernommener Unternehmen)

Kein Familienanteil	*unter 25%*	*25%–49%*	*50%–74%*	*75% und höher*
O	O	O	O	O

Wenn Sie hier mit „kein Familienanteil" geantwortet haben, so überspringen Sie bitte die übrigen Fragen auf dieser Seite und setzen den Fragebogen auf der folgenden Seite fort.

Aufsichtsrat(AR) / Beirat (BR) und die *Rolle* der Familie in diesem Gremium vor der Krise

unbekannt	*Kein AR/ BR*	*Nur Familien im AR/ BR*	*Auch Externe im AR/ BR*	*Nur Externe im AR/ BR*
O	O	O	O	O

(Bitte nur beantworten, wenn die Gründerfamilie Anteile am Unternehmen hält)

Operativer Einfluss der Familie vor der Krise – Vorstandsvorsitzender, Sprecher der Geschäftsführung oder Alleingeschäftsführer ist *Familienmitglied*
(Bitte nur beantworten, wenn die Gründerfamilie Anteile am Unternehmen hält)

Ja	*Nein*
O	O

Operativer Einfluss der Familie vor der Krise – *Zusammensetzung* von Geschäftsführung/ Vorstand
(Bitte nur beantworten, wenn die Gründerfamilie Anteile am Unternehmen hält)

Nur Familienmitglieder (ggf. auch Alleingeschäftsführer)	*Externe und Familienmitglieder*	*Nur Externe*
O	O	O

Generation der Familie, in der die *meisten* Anteile gehalten wurden (vor der Krise)
(Bitte nur beantworten, wenn die Gründerfamilie Anteile am Unternehmen hält)

Unbekannt	*Gründergeneration*	*2. Generation*	*3. oder spätere Generation*
O	O	O	O

3. Beschreibung der Einflussfaktoren auf die Entstehung und Entwicklung der Krise

Beschreiben Sie die Einflussfaktoren, welche die Krise bei dem betrachteten Fall **verursacht und verstärkt** haben. Beurteilen Sie die jeweilige **Relevanz** für die Schieflage des Unternehmens nach Ihrer heutigen Auffassung.

Diese Faktoren **beeinflussen** sich teilweise gegenseitig (z.B. können fehlende Investitionen zu schlechterer Produktqualität führen) – bitte wählen Sie in solchen Fällen alle relevanten Optionen.

Operationelle Kriseneinflussfaktoren	***keine Relevanz für die Krise***				***hohe Relevanz für die Krise***
***Falsche Investitionen** des Unternehmens in operatives Anlagevermögen* (Nicht notwendige, nicht sinnvolle, zu komplexe oder nicht ausgereifte Investitionen in Maschinen, Gebäude, Infrastruktur, Grundstücke.)	○	○	○	○	○
***Fehlende Investitionen** in operatives Anlagevermögen* (Fehlende Investitionen führen zu veralteter Produktion/ Gebäude/ Infrastruktur. Anlagen und Prozesse sind nicht Stand der Technik, dadurch z.B. häufige Instandhaltung, häufige Ausfälle, hoher Ausschuss oder schlechte Qualität.)	○	○	○	○	○
*Zu **hohe Wertschöpfungstiefe*** (Unternehmen macht „zu viel selbst". Leistungen werden nicht eingekauft, dadurch hohe Investitionen außerhalb der Kernkompetenzen. Fehlende Spezialisierung. Eingekaufte Leistungen wären günstiger und/oder besser.)	○	○	○	○	○
*Zu **geringe Wertschöpfungstiefe*** (Schlüsselprozesse in der Produktion oder in der Entwicklung werden nicht selbst erbracht. Dadurch Abhängigkeit, keine Kontrolle, zu schlechte Qualität oder zu hohe Preise.)	○	○	○	○	○
***Schwächen im Finanzbereich** oder im Controlling* (Fehlende oder schwach ausgeprägte kaufmännische Unternehmenssteuerung. Unzuverlässige oder fehlende Unternehmenskennzahlen. Fehlendes oder schlechtes Berichtswesen.)	○	○	○	○	○
*Fehlendes/ schwaches **Kostenmanagement*** (Verschwendung in den Prozessen. Zu wenig Kostenkontrolle und -steuerung. Hohe Sachkosten.)	○	○	○	○	○
*Schwächen in der **Organisation*** (Schlechte Vorbereitung und Umsetzung von Entscheidungen. Zu viele Hierarchieebenen. Unklare Zuständigkeiten. Schwächen in Schlüsselprozessen wie z.B. Marketing oder Vertrieb.)	○	○	○	○	○
*Schwächen im **Strategieprozess/-vermittlung*** (Keine strukturierte Strategieentwicklung. Fehlende Einbindung oder fehlende Kommunikation der Strategie mit den betroffenen Mitarbeitern.)	○	○	○	○	○

Einflussfaktoren auf die Krise aus dem Management	***keine Relevanz für die Krise***				***hohe Relevanz für die Krise***
Ungeeigneter ***Vorstandsvorsitzender/ Sprecher der Geschäftsführung/ Alleingeschäftsführer*** *(fachlich und/oder persönlich)* **Bitte bei gleichrangigen Geschäftsführern/ Vorständen auch beantworten, wenn es nur auf eine der Personen zutrifft.** (Fehlende Fähigkeiten oder ungeeignete Persönlichkeit. Krise nicht erkannt/ realisiert. Persönliche oder fachliche Fehler. Zu viel oder fehlende Konfliktfreudigkeit)	O	O	O	O	O
Ungeeignete ***Mitglieder des Management-Teams*** *(fachlich und/ oder persönlich)* (Alle in Managementfunktionen an der Steuerung des Unternehmens beteiligten Mitarbeiter. Fehlende Fähigkeiten oder ungeeignete Persönlichkeiten. Konflikte im Team oder mit Mitarbeitern.)	O	O	O	O	O

Wenn Sie im *Abschnitt 2. Mittelstand – Familienunternehmen oder Nicht-Familienunternehmen* mit „kein Familienanteil" geantwortet haben, so können Sie die folgenden Fragen zum Familieneinfluss überspringen und setzen den Fragebogen auf der Folgeseite fort.

Auswirkung des Familieneinflusses auf die Krise *Wenn die Gründerfamilie keine Anteile am Unternehmen hält, so überspringen Sie diese Fragen bitte.*	***keine Relevanz für die Krise***				***hohe Relevanz für die Krise***
Negative Auswirkungen von ***Konflikten*** *in der/den Eigentümerfamilie/-n* (Konflikte aus dem familiären Umfeld wirken sich auf das Unternehmen negativ aus.)	O	O	O	O	O
Probleme bei der ***Unternehmensnachfolge*** (Konflikte oder Probleme bei der Unternehmensübergabe auf Folgegenerationen. Ungeeignete Nachfolger. Verlust des Netzwerks/ Wissens des Vorgängers. Zu viele Veränderungen durch Nachfolger. Unternehmen auf Vorgänger zugeschnitten.)	O	O	O	O	O

Portfoliobedingte Einflussfaktoren auf die Krise	***keine Relevanz für die Krise***				***hohe Relevanz für die Krise***
***Fehlende** innovative* Produkte (Fehlende Innovationen in Schlüsselprodukten. Rückfall hinter Wettbewerb hinsichtlich der Produkteigenschaften.)	O	O	O	O	O
*Schwächen bei **Produktqualität** und -service* (Reklamationen und Ausfall der Produkte. Schlechter Kundenservice bzw. schlechte Logistik, Lieferperformance oder andere Schwächen bei produktbegleitenden Leistungen.)	O	O	O	O	O
*Fehleinschätzung der **Marktentwicklung*** (Fehleinschätzung bzgl. Marktwachstum und -bedarf. Fehleinschätzung bzgl. zukünftiger Produkte und Produkteigenschaften.)	O	O	O	O	O
*Zu schnelles oder schlecht beherrschtes **Wachstum*** (Finanzierungsprobleme durch Wachstum. Komplexität wird nicht beherrscht. Probleme bei der Diversifizierung auf andere Märkte oder Marktsegmente. Verluste auf neuen Märkten oder neuen Marktsegmenten.)	O	O	O	O	O
*Fehler bei **Unternehmensakquisitionen** und Beteiligungen* (Zukäufe von Unternehmen oder Unternehmensteilen, die sich negativ auswirken. Akquisitionen zu groß, zu komplex oder in der Krise.)	O	O	O	O	O

Finanzielle Kriseneinflussfaktoren	***keine Relevanz für die Krise***				***hohe Relevanz für die Krise***
*Unpassende **Finanzierung*** (Finanzierung zu komplex oder zu teuer. Finanzierung nicht fristenkongruent. Nutzung nicht geeigneter oder nicht beherrschter finanzieller Instrumente. Spekulation statt Finanzierung.)	O	O	O	O	O
*Liquiditätsabfluss an **Gesellschafter*** (Zu hohe Dividenden oder zu hoher anderer Liquiditätsabfluss an Gesellschafter. Gilt auch für den Gesellschaftern nahestehende dritte Unternehmen z.B. Holding, Vermieter)	O	O	O	O	O
*Verbindlichkeiten zu **hoch*** („Overleverage". Zu hohe Belastung mit Fremdkapital. Fremdkapital und Tilgungen bzw. Zinsen aufgrund der Fremdkapitalbelastung nicht tragbar – dadurch Kapitaldienstfähigkeit gefährdet.)	O	O	O	O	O

Externe Kriseneinflussfaktoren	***keine Relevanz für die Krise***				***hohe Relevanz für die Krise***
***Schrumpfung** des/ der Kernmärkte des Unternehmens* (Einkauf der Kunden auf anderen Märkten, z.B. in Niedriglohnländern. Zyklischer Abschwung. Substitution der Produkte durch neue Produkte, z.B. Digitalkamera vs. Analogkamera.)	O	O	O	O	O
*Zunahme der **Wettbewerbsintensität*** (Eintritt neuer Marktteilnehmer. Steigende Aktivitäten oder Effizienz andere Wettbewerber)	O	O	O	O	O
***Lieferantenseitige** Einflussfaktoren* (Preissteigerungen für Vorprodukte und Rohmaterialien. Verfügbarkeitsprobleme bei eingekauften Produkten. Ausfall von Schlüssellieferanten. Veränderung von Zahlungszielen.)	O	O	O	O	O
***Kundenseitige** Einflussfaktoren* (Erzwungene Preissenkungen. Mengenreduzierungen/ Reduzierung der Lieferanteile des Unternehmens. Verlust von Schlüsselkunden. Forderungsausfälle.)	O	O	O	O	O

Sonstige wichtige Einflussfaktoren auf die Krise

4. Beschreibung der Sanierungsstrategie des Unternehmens

Beschreiben Sie die gewählten Strategien und Maßnahmen zur (angestrebten) Bewältigung der Krise beim betrachteten Fall. Beurteilen Sie deren Relevanz für die (geplante) **nachhaltige Sanierung** des Unternehmens.

Tun Sie dies bitte unabhängig davon, ob diese abschließend erfolgreich war. Ist die **Sanierung fehlgeschlagen** (im Sinne dieser Studie bedeutet dies Insolvenzanmeldung), so geben Sie bitte die entsprechende **Relevanz für die ursprünglich angestrebte und geplante Sanierung** an.

Operative Restrukturierung – Investitionen und Produktion	***keine Relevanz für die Sanierung***				***sehr wichtig für die Sanierung***
***Mehr** Investitionen* (Zusätzliche Investitionen. Steigerung der Ausgaben für Investitionen in neue Maschinen oder Infrastruktur. Ggf. in Kombination mit Innovation oder Insourcing.)	O	O	O	O	O
***Weniger** Investitionen* (Kürzungen des Investitionsvolumens. Reduzierung von Investitionen in Maschinen oder Infrastruktur. Ggf. in Kombination mit Outsourcing oder Kapazitätsreduktion.)	O	O	O	O	O
Kapazitätsreduzierung (Schließung oder Teilschließung von Werken. Reduzierung von Anlagennutzungszeiten, z.B. Schichten.)	O	O	O	O	O
Outsourcing (Outsourcing von Produktionsschritten und Leistungen mit oder ohne Verkauf des zugehörigen Anlagevermögens.)	O	O	O	O	O
Insourcing (Insourcing von Produktionsschritten und Leistungen. Aufbau von Kapazitäten für neue Produktionsschritte bzw. andere Produktionsverfahren. Ggf. aus Kosten- oder Qualitätsgründen.)	O	O	O	O	O
Produktivitätssteigerung (Implementierung von Maßnahmen zur Produktivitätserhöhung. Steigerung der Anlagen- bzw. Personalproduktivität, auch durch Ausschussreduzierung und Automatisierung. Einführung von Lean Production oder anderen Methoden.)	O	O	O	O	O

Operative Restrukturierung – Personal, Prozesse und Abläufe	*keine Relevanz für die Sanierung*				*sehr wichtig für die Sanierung*
Personalabbau (Kündigung von Mitarbeitern. Übertragung von Mitarbeitern an eine Transfergesellschaft oder Angebot von Aufhebungsverträgen.)	O	O	O	O	O
Mitarbeiterbeiträge/*-verzichte* (Finanzielle Zugeständnisse bei der Bezahlung des Personals. Verzicht auf Urlaubs- bzw. Weihnachtsgeld. Gehaltsreduzierung. Aussetzung von tariflichen oder anderen Erhöhungen.)	O	O	O	O	O
Organisationsveränderung *und -optimierung* (Veränderung der Organisation – z.B. Aufbauorganisation – und Zuständigkeiten. Optimierung der Prozesse durch Veränderungen von Abläufen und Schnittstellen.)	O	O	O	O	O
Umsatzausweitung *und/oder Preiserhöhung* (Initiativen des Vertriebs und Marketings zur Erhöhung von Preisen oder zur Ausweitung des Umsatzes.)	O	O	O	O	O
Kostensenkungsmaßnahmen (Einkaufsoptimierung und Sachkostensenkung.)	O	O	O	O	O

Veränderungen im Management	*keine Relevanz für die Sanierung*				*sehr wichtig für die Sanierung*
Austausch *des Vorstandsvorsitzenden, Alleingeschäftsführers oder des Sprechers der Geschäftsführung* Bitte bei gleichrangigen Geschäftsführern/ Vorständen auch positiv beantworten, wenn es nur auf eine der Personen zutrifft.	O	O	O	O	O
Veränderungen *im Management-Team* (Veränderungen bei den in Managementfunktionen an der Steuerung des Unternehmens beteiligten Mitarbeiter.)	O	O	O	O	O
Externe *Unterstützung und Beratung des Managements* (Einsatz externer Berater bzw. eines externen Geschäftsführers oder Vorstands für Restrukturierung – CRO.)	O	O	O	O	O

Strategische (Portfolio) Restrukturierung	***keine Relevanz für die Sanierung***				***sehr wichtig für die Sanierung***
***Einstellung** von Produkten oder Rückzug von Märkten* (Einstellung von Produkten oder Produktlinien. Rückzug von bestimmten Märkten oder Marktsegmenten.)	O	O	O	O	O
*Neue **Produkte** oder Eintritt in neue Märkte* (Produktinnovationen oder neue Produktlinien. Eintritt in neue Märkte.)	O	O	O	O	O
***Verkauf** von Unternehmensteilen* (Verkauf von Beteiligungen, Werken, Standorten bzw. Teilen von Standorten.)	O	O	O	O	O
***Kauf** von Unternehmensbeteiligungen* (Beteiligung an oder kompletter Erwerb von Unternehmen im Rahmen der nachhaltigen Sanierung. Gründung von Joint Ventures.)	O	O	O	O	O

Finanzielle Restrukturierung	***keine Relevanz für die Sanierung***				***sehr wichtig für die Sanierung***
*Reduzierung des **Working Capitals*** (Erhöhung der Lieferantenverbindlichkeiten. Reduzierung von Kundenverbindlichkeiten bzw. Lagerbeständen.)	O	O	O	O	O
*Reduzierung von **Dividenden** und Zahlungen an Gesellschafter* (Gilt ebenso für den Gesellschaftern nahestehende Unternehmen – z.B. vermietende Gesellschaften.)	O	O	O	O	O
*Zusätzliche **Sicherheiten** durch Gesellschafter* (Einbringung von zusätzlichen Sicherheiten. Persönliche Bürgschaft. Bürgschaft Dritter durch den/ die Gesellschafter veranlasst. Rangrücktritt oder Verzicht auf Gesellschafterdarlehen.)	O	O	O	O	O
***Liquiditätsbeitrag** der Gesellschafter* (Der/ Die Gesellschafter bringt/-en mittels Gesellschafterdarlehen oder Kapitalerhöhungen liquide Mittel ein.)	O	O	O	O	O
*Zusätzliches **Fremdkapital*** (Bankkredite, Kreditlinien, Mezzanine, Anleihen oder Finanzmarktinstrumente.)	O	O	O	O	O

Finanzielle **Restrukturierung** (Fortsetzung)	***keine Relevanz für die Sanierung***				***sehr wichtig für die Sanierung***
Konditionenänderungen *bei existierenden Verbindlichkeiten* (Veränderung von Kosten (Zinsen), Fristen oder Modalitäten bei existierenden Finanzierungen.)	O	O	O	O	O
Tilgung *von Fremdkapital* (Rückzahlung von externen Verbindlichkeiten, Anleihen oder Krediten, z.B. nach dem Verkauf von Beteiligungen.)	O	O	O	O	O
Hair-Cut *oder Debt-to-Equity Swap* (Teil-/Verzicht auf Verbindlichkeiten durch Finanzierer. Umwandlung von Verbindlichkeiten in Eigenkapital.)	O	O	O	O	O

Sonstige wichtige Sanierungsmaßnahmen

5. Eigenschaften des Unternehmens, der Krise, der Sanierung

Neben den Eigenschaften der Krise und den gewählten Sanierungsstrategien/-maßnahmen beeinflussen auch andere Faktoren die Entstehung und Entwicklung der Krise in der Sanierung.

Bitte beantworten Sie die Fragen zu den **anderen Einflussfaktoren** für den gewählten Fall. Im Besonderen für diesen Abschnitt gilt: **Falls Ihnen die Information nicht vorliegen, schätzen Sie die Angaben bitte.**

Daten & Fakten

Wie hoch war der *Umsatz* des Unternehmens vor der Krise?	***10–50 Mio. EUR***	***50–150 Mio. EUR***	***150–500 Mio. EUR***
	O	O	O

Wie hoch war der *Anteil des größten Gesellschafters* des Unternehmens vor der Krise?	***unbekannt***	***bis 24%***	***25%–49%***	***50%–74%***	***75% und höher***
	O	O	O	O	O

Management

Wie *lange* war der Vorstandsvorsitzende, Alleingeschäftsführer oder Sprecher der Geschäftsführung vor der Krise für das Unternehmen (in dieser Funktion) tätig? *(Bei mehreren gleichgestellten Geschäftsführern oder Vorständen der jeweils längste Zeitraum.)*	***>15 Jahre***	***5–15 Jahre***	***1–4 Jahre***	***weniger als 1 Jahr***
	O	O	O	O

Unternehmensstrategie und -produkte

Beschreiben Sie grob die *primäre* Strategie des Unternehmens vor der Krise	***Keine/ Unklar***	***Qualitäts-führer***	***Innovations-führer***	***Kosten-führer***
	O	O	O	O

Wie beurteilen Sie die *Ausstattung* des Unternehmens mit Personal und Ressourcen vor der Krise?	***schlanke und ressourcenarme Organisation (lean)***		***normale Organisation***		***überschüssige Ressourcen – schlagkräftig, aber auch Wasserkopf/ „aufgeblasen"***
	O	O	O	O	O

Finanzen und Finanzierung des Unternehmens

Wie war vor der Krise die Sicherheitensituation der Kreditgeber *insgesamt* betrachtet?

sehr schlecht				*sehr gut*
O	O	O	O	O

Wie beurteilen Sie die Eigenkapitalquote des Unternehmens vor der Krise *in Relation* zum jeweiligen Geschäftsmodell?

zu gering				*sehr hoch*
O	O	O	O	O

Wie beurteilen Sie die *Profitabilität* des Unternehmens vor der Krise (Umsatzrendite)?
(Umsatzrendite hier EBIT dividiert durch Umsatz.)

gering <5%	*mittel 5%-10%*	*hoch >10%*
O	O	O

Beurteilung der Krise

Wie war die *Dynamik* des Krisenverlaufs bis zur aktiven Begleitung der Sanierung durch Sie/ Ihr Haus?
(Ist die Krise schlagartig durch ein oder mehrere Ereignisse eingetreten oder handelt es sich um einen längerfristigen sukzessiven Abwärtstrend.)

schlagartig durch Ereignis(se)				*längerfristiger Abwärtstrend*
O	O	O	O	O

Wie *kritisch* war die Situation für das Unternehmen zu Beginn der aktiven Begleitung der Sanierung durch Sie/ Ihr Haus?

weniger ernstes Krisenstadium				*sehr ernste Krise*
O	O	O	O	O

Marktbeurteilung

Wie beurteilen Sie die *langfristigen* Wachstumsaussichten des Marktsegments, in dem das Unternehmen vorwiegend aktiv ist?

Schrumpfung		*Stagnation*		*Wachstum*
O	O	O	O	O

Wie entwickelte sich dieses Marktsegment *während der Sanierung*?

Schrumpfung		*Stagnation*		*Wachstum*
O	O	O	O	O

Beurteilung des Turnaroundprozesses

	schlecht				*sehr gut*
Wie war Information und Einbindung *wichtiger* Interessengruppen während der Sanierung? *(Information und Einbindung von Banken, Kunden, Lieferanten und Mitarbeitern.)*	O	O	O	O	O

	einfach				*sehr komplex*
Wie komplex war die *Ausgangssituation* zu Beginn der aktiven Begleitung der Sanierung? *(Anzahl der beteiligten Banken. Komplexität der Finanzierungen. Rolle von Gewerkschaften, wesentlicher Kunden oder Lieferanten)*	O	O	O	O	O

Sonstige wichtige Eigenschaften des in der Krise befindlichen Unternehmens

6. Resultat der Sanierung

Die **Unternehmenskrise** kann für das Unternehmen im Sinne dieser Studie **enden mit**

- **„Insolvenz"** (als im Sinne dieser Studie negativstem Resultat)
- „Unternehmensperformance unter Vorkrisenniveau"
- **„Unternehmensperformance über Vorkrisenniveau"** (als im Sinne dieser Studie besten Resultat)

Bei Familienunternehmen kann sich im Rahmen der Sanierung die **Rolle der Familie** verändern.

Ergebnis der Sanierung *für das Unternehmen*	***Insolvenz***				***Performance über Vorkrisenniveau***
	O	O	O	O	O

Wenn Sie hier mit „Insolvenz" geantwortet haben oder die Gründerfamilie keine Anteile am Unternehmen hält, so können Sie die übrigen Fragen dieses Abschnittes überspringen und auf die Folgeseite wechseln.

Anteil des Unternehmens im Besitz der Gründerfamilie(n) und ihrer Nachkommen *nach der Krise* *(Bitte nur für den Fall beantworten, dass keine Insolvenz angemeldete worden ist.)*	***Kein Familien-anteil***	***unter 25%***	***25%–49%***	***50%–74%***	***75% und höher***
	O	O	O	O	O

Operativer Einfluss der Familie *nach der Krise* – Vorstandsvorsitzender, Sprecher der Geschäftsführung oder Alleingeschäftsführer ist Familienmitglied	***Ja***	***Nein***
	O	O

(Bitte nur für den Fall beantworten, dass keine Insolvenz angemeldete worden is.t)

Operativer Einfluss der Familie *nach der Krise* – Zusammensetzung von Geschäftsführung/ Vorstand *(Bitte nur für den Fall beantworten, dass keine Insolvenz angemeldete worden ist.)*	***Nur Familienmitglieder (ggf. auch Alleingeschäftsführer)***	***Externe und Familienmitglieder***	***Nur Externe***
	O	O	O

Appendix 3 – correlation tables

The tables on the following pages show the Pearson correlation coefficients for all variable pairs before the model simplification in section 5.2.3 (as referred to in section 5.2.2).

Crisis characteristics part I **Pearson correlation coefficient** N = 209 ****. Correlation is significant at the 0.01 level (2-tailed).** ***. Correlation is significant at the 0.05 level (2-tailed).**	Incorrect investment in plant and equipment	Insufficient investments in plant and equipment	Degree of company-internal value-add too high	Degree of company-internal value-add too low	Ineffective/ inefficient organization	Insufficient strategy process	Ineffective financial controlling	Weak cost management	Unsuitable CEO
Operational crisis contribution factors									
Incorrect investment in plant and equipment	1	0.051	0.141*	0.108	0.200**	0.01	0.126	0.09	0.347**
Insufficient investments in plant and equipment	0.051	1	0.230**	0.220**	0.165*	0.318**	0.109	0.181**	0.250**
Degree of company-internal value-add too high	0.141*	0.230**	1	0.042	0.140*	0.280**	0.054	0.185**	0.156*
Degree of company-internal value-add too low	0.108	0.220**	0.042	1	0.204**	0.211**	0.106	0.203**	0.105
Ineffective/ inefficient organization	0.200**	0.165*	0.140*	0.204**	1	0.373**	0.488**	0.570**	0.474**
Insufficient strategy process	0.01	0.318**	0.280**	0.211**	0.373**	1	0.535**	0.457**	0.446**
Ineffective financial controlling	0.126	0.109	0.054	0.106	0.488**	0.535**	1	0.548**	0.502**
Weak cost management	0.09	0.181**	0.185**	0.203**	0.570**	0.457**	0.548**	1	0.484**
Managerial crisis contribution factors									
Unsuitable CEO	0.347**	0.250**	0.156*	0.105	0.474**	0.446**	0.502**	0.484**	1
Unsuitable members of TMT	0.132	0.290**	0.249**	0.112	0.439**	0.437**	0.463**	0.425**	0.423**
Conflict spillover from owner family to company	0.231**	0.129	0.11	0.03	0.205**	0.241**	0.238**	0.227**	0.359**
Succession problems	0.189**	0.032	-0.063	0.066	0.245**	0.182**	0.196**	0.152*	0.337**
Portfolio crisis contribution factors									
Incorrect market assessment	0.141*	0.088	0.191**	0.026	0.044	0.184**	0.029	0.006	0.031
Overexpansion	0.338**	-0.125	0.071	0.067	0.128	0.142*	0.198**	0.063	0.258**
Missing innovation in core products	0.04	0.300**	0.295**	0.118	0.021	0.298**	0.143*	0.137*	0.153*
Insufficient quality and service	-0.006	0.150*	-0.012	0.087	-0.027	0.075	0.158*	0.131	0.08
Non-beneficial acquisitions	0.093	-0.026	0.038	0	0.031	0.186**	0.139*	0.01	0.097
Financial crisis contribution factors									
Financing structure inadequate	0.084	-0.096	-0.159*	0.026	0.109	0.045	0.091	0.003	-0.018
Cash flow to shareholders too high	0.055	0.033	-0.016	0.153*	0.189**	0.213**	0.217**	0.194**	0.198**
Overleveraging	0.170*	0.058	-0.013	0.074	0.045	0.09	0.004	0.084	0.138*
External crisis contribution factors									
Market decline	0.119	0.162*	0.229**	0.052	-0.157*	0.143*	-0.033	-0.053	0.012
Increased competition	0.044	0.205**	0.257**	0.084	-0.014	0.139*	0.008	0.019	0.061
Supply side induced crisis	0.104	0.146*	0.144*	0.171*	0.099	0.087	0.039	0.108	-0.001
Customer induced crisis	0.022	0.082	0.071	0.131	-0.092	0.042	-0.121	-0.044	-0.002
Crisis context									
Deterioration pattern of crisis	0.067	0.135	0.175*	0.079	0.071	0.197**	0.140*	0.122	0.155*
Severity of crisis	0.097	0.072	-0.078	-0.015	0.144*	0.022	0.012	0.104	0.111
Initial complexity of company situation to implement turnaround	0.201**	-0.118	0.029	-0.034	0.027	-0.013	-0.013	-0.02	0.03

Crisis characteristics part II **Pearson correlation coefficient** **N = 209** ****. Correlation is significant at the 0.01 level (2-tailed).** ***. Correlation is significant at the 0.05 level (2-tailed).**	Unsuitable members of TMT	Conflict spillover from owner family to company	Succession problems	Incorrect market assessment	Overexpansion	Missing innovation in core products	Insufficient quality and service	Non-beneficial acquisitions	Financing structure inadequate
Operational crisis contribution factors									
Incorrect investment in plant and equipment	0.132	0.231**	0.189**	0.141*	0.338**	0.04	-0.006	0.093	0.084
Insufficient investments in plant and equipment	0.290**	0.129	0.032	0.088	-0.125	0.300**	0.150*	-0.026	-0.096
Degree of company-internal value-add too high	0.249**	0.11	-0.063	0.191**	0.071	0.295**	-0.012	0.038	-0.159*
Degree of company-internal value-add too low	0.112	0.03	0.066	0.026	0.067	0.118	0.087	0	0.026
Ineffective/ inefficient organization	0.439**	0.205**	0.245**	0.044	0.128	0.021	-0.027	0.031	0.109
Insufficient strategy process	0.437**	0.241**	0.182**	0.184**	0.142*	0.298**	0.075	0.186**	0.045
Ineffective financial controlling	0.463**	0.238**	0.196**	0.029	0.198**	0.143*	0.158*	0.139*	0.091
Weak cost management	0.425**	0.227**	0.152*	0.006	0.063	0.137*	0.131	0.01	0.003
Managerial crisis contribution factors									
Unsuitable CEO	0.423**	0.359**	0.337**	0.031	0.258**	0.153*	0.08	0.097	-0.018
Unsuitable members of TMT	1	0.250**	0.137*	0.053	0.114	0.199**	0.088	0.163*	-0.022
Conflict spillover from owner family to company	0.250**	1	0.431**	-0.012	0.082	0.096	-0.063	0.123	-0.05
Succession problems	0.137*	0.431**	1	-0.064	0.067	0.033	-0.044	0.171*	-0.015
Portfolio crisis contribution factors									
Incorrect market assessment	0.053	-0.012	-0.064	1	0.160*	0.259**	0.123	0.159*	0.055
Overexpansion	0.114	0.082	0.067	0.160*	1	-0.153*	-0.129	0.317**	0.259**
Missing innovation in core products	0.199**	0.096	0.033	0.259**	-0.153*	1	0.238**	0.072	-0.192**
Insufficient quality and service	0.088	-0.063	-0.044	0.123	-0.129	0.238**	1	0.04	-0.056
Non-beneficial acquisitions	0.163*	0.123	0.171*	0.159*	0.317**	0.072	0.04	1	0.086
Financial crisis contribution factors									
Financing structure inadequate	-0.022	-0.05	-0.015	0.055	0.259**	-0.192**	-0.056	0.086	1
Cash flow to shareholders too high	0.06	0.316**	0.185**	0.011	-0.027	0.032	-0.001	0.063	0.072
Overleveraging	0.042	-0.014	-0.03	0.232**	0.198**	-0.104	-0.009	0.157*	0.465**
External crisis contribution factors									
Market decline	0.083	-0.06	-0.053	0.458**	-0.115	0.298**	0.003	-0.02	0.05
Increased competition	0.141*	0.029	0.035	0.283**	-0.091	0.354**	0.064	-0.053	-0.001
Supply side induced crisis	0.145*	0.087	-0.04	0.084	-0.116	0.103	0.053	-0.006	-0.141*
Customer induced crisis	-0.019	0.009	0.004	0.266**	-0.108	0.094	-0.131	-0.141*	0.005
Crisis context									
Deterioration pattern of crisis	0.142*	0.061	0.197**	0.003	-0.142*	0.228**	-0.02	0.165*	-0.228**
Severity of crisis	0.083	0.036	0.039	-0.048	0.014	-0.066	-0.06	-0.047	0.144*
Initial complexity of company situation to implement turnaround	0.091	0.058	0.011	0.074	0.236**	-0.104	0.026	0.314**	0.262**

Crisis characteristics part III **Pearson correlation coefficient** **N = 209** ****. Correlation is significant at the 0.01 level (2-tailed).** ***. Correlation is significant at the 0.05 level (2-tailed).**	Cash flow to share-holders too high	Overlev eraging	Market decline	In-creased compe-tition	Supply side induced crisis	Cus-tomer induced crisis	Deterio-ration pattern of crisis	Severity of crisis	Initial com-plexity of compa-ny situation
Operational crisis contribution factors									
Incorrect investment in plant and equipment	0.055	0.170*	0.119	0.044	0.104	0.022	0.067	0.097	0.201**
Insufficient investments in plant and equipment	0.033	0.058	0.162*	0.205**	0.146*	0.082	0.135	0.072	-0.118
Degree of company-internal value-add too high	-0.016	-0.013	0.229**	0.257**	0.144*	0.071	0.175*	-0.078	0.029
Degree of company-internal value-add too low	0.153*	0.074	0.052	0.084	0.171*	0.131	0.079	-0.015	-0.034
Ineffective/ inefficient organization	0.189**	0.045	-0.157*	-0.014	0.099	-0.092	0.071	0.144*	0.027
Insufficient strategy process	0.213**	0.09	0.143*	0.139*	0.087	0.042	0.197**	0.022	-0.013
Ineffective financial controlling	0.217**	0.004	-0.033	0.008	0.039	-0.121	0.140*	0.012	-0.013
Weak cost management	0.194**	0.084	-0.053	0.019	0.108	-0.044	0.122	0.104	-0.02
Managerial crisis contribution factors									
Unsuitable CEO	0.198**	0.138*	0.012	0.061	-0.001	-0.002	0.155*	0.111	0.03
Unsuitable members of TMT	0.06	0.042	0.083	0.141*	0.145*	-0.019	0.142*	0.083	0.091
Conflict spillover from owner family to company	0.316**	-0.014	-0.06	0.029	0.087	0.009	0.061	0.036	0.058
Succession problems	0.185**	-0.03	-0.053	0.035	-0.04	0.004	0.197**	0.039	0.011
Portfolio crisis contribution factors									
Incorrect market assessment	0.011	0.232**	0.458**	0.283**	0.084	0.266**	0.003	-0.048	0.074
Overexpansion	-0.027	0.198**	-0.115	-0.091	-0.116	-0.108	-0.142*	0.014	0.236**
Missing innovation in core products	0.032	-0.104	0.298**	0.354**	0.103	0.094	0.228**	-0.066	-0.104
Insufficient quality and service	-0.001	-0.009	0.003	0.064	0.053	-0.131	-0.02	-0.06	0.026
Non-beneficial acquisitions	0.063	0.157*	-0.02	-0.053	-0.006	-0.141*	0.165*	-0.047	0.314**
Financial crisis contribution factors									
Financing structure inadequate	0.072	0.465**	0.05	-0.001	-0.141*	0.005	-0.228**	0.144*	0.262**
Cash flow to shareholders too high	1	0.152*	-0.018	0.026	0.08	-0.081	0.064	0.116	-0.128
Overleveraging	0.152*	1	0.245**	0.117	0.150*	0.089	-0.038	0.189**	0.218**
External crisis contribution factors									
Market decline	-0.018	0.245**	1	0.487**	0.085	0.286**	0.121	-0.113	0.085
Increased competition	0.026	0.117	0.487**	1	0.277**	0.284**	0.193**	-0.148*	-0.013
Supply side induced crisis	0.08	0.150*	0.085	0.277**	1	0.193**	0.054	0.035	0.003
Customer induced crisis	-0.081	0.089	0.286**	0.284**	0.193**	1	0.038	-0.094	-0.045
Crisis context									
Deterioration pattern of crisis	0.064	-0.038	0.121	0.193**	0.054	0.038	1	-0.242**	-0.163*
Severity of crisis	0.116	0.189**	-0.113	-0.148*	0.035	-0.094	-0.242**	1	0.147*
Initial complexity of company situation to im-plement turnaround	-0.128	0.218**	0.085	-0.013	0.003	-0.045	-0.163*	0.147*	1

Crisis characteristics part IV **Pearson correlation coefficient** **N = 209** ****. Correlation is significant at the 0.01 level (2-tailed).** ***. Correlation is significant at the 0.05 level (2-tailed).**	Layoff	Employee concessions	Increase CAPEX	Decrease CAPEX	Capacity reduction	Productivity increase	Outsourcing	Insourcing	Process improvement and redesign
Operational crisis contribution factors									
Incorrect investment in plant and equipment	0.069	0.140*	-0.076	0.371**	0.185**	0.021	0.041	0.03	0.088
Insufficient investments in plant and equipment	0.175*	0.173*	0.385**	-0.008	0.04	0.211**	0.194**	0.039	0.084
Degree of company-internal value-add too high	0.296**	0.172*	0.1	0.232**	0.219**	0.262**	0.394**	0.162*	0.248**
Degree of company-internal value-add too low	-0.027	0.039	0.171*	0.04	-0.048	0.072	0.044	0.160*	0.054
Ineffective/ inefficient organization	0.09	0.087	0.032	0.026	0.102	0.06	0.048	-0.135	0.192**
Insufficient strategy process	0.161*	0.091	0.149*	0.12	0.196**	0.183**	0.205**	0.077	0.364**
Ineffective financial controlling	0.108	0.106	-0.007	0.065	0.148*	0.091	0.125	0.002	0.382**
Weak cost management	0.163*	0.122	0.028	0.095	0.116	0.233**	0.106	-0.053	0.250**
Managerial crisis contribution factors									
Unsuitable CEO	0.182**	0.138*	-0.023	0.132	0.137*	0.109	0.071	-0.196**	0.225**
Unsuitable members of TMT	0.301**	0.206**	0.045	0.199**	0.349**	0.166*	0.214**	-0.036	0.376**
Conflict spillover from owner family to company	0.058	0.052	0.124	0.175*	0.091	0.063	0.119	0.001	0.220**
Succession problems	0.096	0.139*	-0.017	0.199**	0.133	-0.093	0.075	-0.101	0.112
Portfolio crisis contribution factors									
Incorrect market assessment	0.275**	0.170*	0.081	0.104	0.217**	0.029	0.053	0.125	0.103
Overexpansion	-0.047	-0.073	0.016	0.199**	0.118	0.013	-0.06	0.034	0.147*
Missing innovation in core products	0.242**	0.210**	0.174*	0.061	0.183**	0.099	0.149*	0.161*	0.148*
Insufficient quality and service	0.106	0.116	0.097	-0.084	-0.073	0.168*	-0.006	0.043	0.073
Non-beneficial acquisitions	0.097	0.025	-0.013	0.115	0.182**	0.012	0.05	0.056	0.167*
Financial crisis contribution factors									
Financing structure inadequate	-0.116	-0.054	-0.025	0.164*	0.002	-0.018	-0.09	0.051	0.015
Cash flow to shareholders too high	-0.042	-0.052	0.037	0.106	-0.072	-0.111	-0.015	0.043	0.1
Overleveraging	0.101	0.023	0.011	0.269**	0.068	0.037	-0.019	-0.007	-0.009
External crisis contribution factors									
Market decline	0.342**	0.257**	0.107	0.193**	0.285**	0.114	0.179**	0.179**	0.046
Increased competition	0.399**	0.185**	0.077	0.094	0.203**	0.028	0.186**	-0.034	0.181**
Supply side induced crisis	0.123	0.042	0.09	0.002	0.032	-0.024	0.158*	0.128	0.172*
Customer induced crisis	0.183**	0.205**	0.087	0.02	0.143*	0.075	0.045	0.036	-0.084
Crisis context									
Deterioration pattern of crisis	0.065	-0.036	0.011	0.106	0.054	0.062	0.047	0.008	0.199**
Severity of crisis	0.016	0.092	0.014	0.033	-0.106	0.046	-0.022	-0.036	0.044
Initial complexity of company situation to implement turnaround	0.094	0.123	0.014	0.186**	0.209**	0.125	0.125	0.034	0.099

Crisis characteristics part V Pearson correlation coefficient N = 209 **. Correlation is significant at the 0.01 level (2-tailed). *. Correlation is significant at the 0.05 level (2-tailed).	Pricing and sales initia-tives	Pur-chasing and cost reduc-tion initia-tives	CEO change	Change in TMT	External man-age-ment support	Asset divest-ments	Acquisi-tions	Termi-nation of prod-ucts lines/ markets	New prod-ucts/ markets devel-opment
Operational crisis contribution factors									
Incorrect investment in plant and equipment	0.114	0.051	0.140*	0.149*	-0.009	0.230**	-0.082	0.035	-0.059
Insufficient investments in plant and equipment	0.086	0.203**	0.209**	0.115	0.124	0.01	0.054	0.072	0.204**
Degree of company-internal value-add too high	0.019	0.238**	0.141*	0.111	0.195**	0.074	0.034	0.285**	0.199**
Degree of company-internal value-add too low	0.115	0.078	0.081	0.171*	0.170*	0.094	0.12	-0.001	0.08
Ineffective/ inefficient organization	0.087	0.034	0.250**	0.309**	0.214**	0.147*	0.006	0.046	0.015
Insufficient strategy process	0.200**	0.319**	0.337**	0.335**	0.187**	0.146*	0.04	0.329**	0.158*
Ineffective financial controlling	0.112	0.128	0.327**	0.352**	0.205**	0.154*	0.044	0.104	-0.054
Weak cost management	0.177*	0.227**	0.361**	0.278**	0.244**	0.07	0.03	0.093	-0.078
Managerial crisis contribution factors									
Unsuitable CEO	0.112	0.154*	0.581**	0.351**	0.240**	0.270**	-0.106	0.162*	-0.140*
Unsuitable members of TMT	0.032	0.300**	0.412**	0.514**	0.243**	0.234**	0.057	0.187**	0.067
Conflict spillover from owner family to company	0.09	0.104	0.458**	0.354**	0.111	0.255**	0.101	0.212**	0
Succession problems	-0.019	-0.071	0.356**	0.258**	0.125	0.251**	0.069	0.103	-0.012
Portfolio crisis contribution factors									
Incorrect market assessment	0.128	0.111	-0.033	0.075	-0.078	0.034	0.101	0.224**	0.222**
Overexpansion	-0.017	0.031	0.108	0.229**	0.023	0.194**	0.058	0.185**	-0.034
Missing innovation in core products	0.106	0.099	0.139*	0.082	0.134	0.042	0.021	0.241**	0.329**
Insufficient quality and service	-0.003	0.083	0.085	0.015	0.072	0.041	-0.024	0.014	-0.038
Non-beneficial acquisitions	-0.084	0.056	0.114	0.220**	0.026	0.364**	0.146*	0.306**	-0.09
Financial crisis contribution factors									
Financing structure inadequate	0.025	-0.048	-0.12	0.089	0.005	0.094	-0.038	-0.022	-0.07
Cash flow to shareholders too high	0.076	-0.039	0.211**	0.086	0.064	0.098	0.127	0.049	-0.044
Overleveraging	0.061	0.161*	0.087	0.160*	-0.023	0.219**	0.082	-0.106	-0.094
External crisis contribution factors									
Market decline	0.132	0.206**	0.135	0.01	-0.017	-0.036	0.007	0.164*	0.291**
Increased competition	-0.02	0.230**	0.076	0.011	0.086	-0.01	-0.005	0.179**	0.246**
Supply side induced crisis	0.106	0.274**	0.094	0.113	0.047	0.017	0.104	0.036	0.062
Customer induced crisis	0.196**	0.232**	0.006	0.055	0.169*	-0.069	-0.008	0.001	0.07
Crisis context									
Deterioration pattern of crisis	0.042	0.1	0.174*	0.091	0.05	0.081	0.012	0.096	0.049
Severity of crisis	0.077	0.04	0.159*	0.138*	0.055	0.014	-0.047	-0.125	-0.075
Initial complexity of company situation to implement turnaround	-0.064	0.145*	0.159*	0.227**	-0.001	0.295**	0.007	0.170*	0.056

Crisis characteristics part VI **Pearson correlation coefficient** **N = 209** ****. Correlation is significant at the 0.01 level (2-tailed).** ***. Correlation is significant at the 0.05 level (2-tailed).**	Working capital reduction	Reduction of cash flow to shareholder	Liquidity contribution by shareholder	Additional restructuring loan granted by lenders	Securities contribution by shareholder	Repayment of debt	Extension, conversion or deferral of existing debt	Debt write-off or debt-to-equity-swap	Development of market segm. during turnaround
Operational crisis contribution factors									
Incorrect investment in plant and equipment	0.016	0.026	0.005	0.054	0.118	0.253**	0.219**	0.180**	0.029
Insufficient investments in plant and equipment	0.167*	-0.096	0.047	-0.012	0.062	-0.027	0.032	-0.064	-0.016
Degree of company-internal value-add too high	0.211**	0.033	0.104	0.013	0.193**	0.1	0.055	0.017	-0.174*
Degree of company-internal value-add too low	0.164*	0.003	0.06	0.069	0.198**	0.01	0.11	-0.002	0.06
Ineffective/ inefficient organization	0.047	0.122	0.174*	0	0.200**	0.047	-0.005	0.059	0.023
Insufficient strategy process	0.165*	0.073	0.185**	-0.06	0.173*	0.099	0.019	-0.01	-0.091
Ineffective financial controlling	0.071	0.117	0.087	0.09	0.139*	0.095	-0.009	0.042	-0.039
Weak cost management	0.082	0.023	0.140*	0.054	0.166*	0.013	-0.124	-0.006	-0.051
Managerial crisis contribution factors									
Unsuitable CEO	0.114	0.04	0.137*	0.05	0.156*	0.178*	-0.032	0.13	-0.098
Unsuitable members of TMT	0.205**	0.026	0.144*	0.004	0.109	0.228**	-0.031	0.178**	0.107
Conflict spillover from owner family to company	0.051	0.240**	0.12	0.067	0.117	0.227**	-0.002	0.022	0.055
Succession problems	-0.035	0.199**	0.096	-0.096	0.094	0.140*	0.054	0.104	0.018
Portfolio crisis contribution factors									
Incorrect market assessment	0.099	0.018	0.174*	-0.132	0.064	0.073	0.123	0.049	-0.254**
Overexpansion	-0.025	-0.082	0.047	0.109	0.067	0.301**	0.155*	0.195**	0.112
Missing innovation in core products	0.129	-0.025	0.052	-0.082	0.066	-0.05	-0.045	-0.06	-0.229**
Insufficient quality and service	0.106	-0.059	-0.014	0.105	-0.047	-0.055	-0.002	0.01	-0.147*
Non-beneficial acquisitions	0.105	-0.013	0.028	0.028	0.075	0.305**	0.103	0.274**	-0.058
Financial crisis contribution factors									
Financing structure inadequate	-0.014	0.002	0.098	0.133	0.105	0.273**	0.233**	0.107	0.108
Cash flow to shareholders too high	0.063	0.505**	0.044	0.092	0.236**	0.072	0.028	-0.095	0.008
Overleveraging	0.155*	-0.03	0.052	0.098	0.146*	0.350**	0.336**	0.239**	-0.033
External crisis contribution factors									
Market decline	0.209**	0.009	0.103	-0.045	0.05	0.052	0.176*	-0.003	-0.303**
Increased competition	0.170*	0.016	0.105	-0.078	0.039	0.126	0.139*	0.071	-0.286**
Supply side induced crisis	0.138*	0.035	0.172*	-0.039	0.183**	0.108	0.08	0.143*	-0.068
Customer induced crisis	0.109	-0.019	0.04	-0.005	0.007	0.051	0.099	0.054	-0.229**
Crisis context									
Deterioration pattern of crisis	0.038	0.007	0.007	-0.114	0.044	-0.024	-0.068	0.003	-0.104
Severity of crisis	0.140*	0.111	0.03	0.188**	0.007	0.056	0.058	0.133	0.156*
Initial complexity of company situation to implement turnaround	0.123	-0.065	0.154*	0.137*	0.052	0.291**	0.218**	0.314**	0.126

Crisis characteristics part VII **Pearson correlation coefficient** **N = 209** ****. Correlation is significant at the 0.01 level (2-tailed).** ***. Correlation is significant at the 0.05 level (2-tailed).**	Stake-holder man-age-ment during turna-round	Com-pany size (turno-ver) before crisis	Share of biggest share-holder before crisis	CEOs time with the compa-ny before crisis	Primary strategy before crisis - Quality leader-ship	Primary strat. before crisis - Innova-tion leader-ship	Primary strat. before crisis - Low-cost leader-ship	Slack re-sources before crisis	Lender security situation before crisis
Operational crisis contribution factors									
Incorrect investment in plant and equipment	-0.115	0.085	-0.093	-0.055	0.06	-0.031	-0.026	0.200**	-0.054
Insufficient investments in plant and equipment	-0.242**	-0.034	0.04	0.093	-0.041	-0.083	-0.027	0.195**	0.009
Degree of company-internal value-add too high	-0.048	-0.017	-0.074	-0.12	0.150*	-0.062	-0.087	0.249**	-0.095
Degree of company-internal value-add too low	-0.099	-0.028	0.031	0.027	0.014	-0.051	-0.015	0.092	0.11
Ineffective/ inefficient organization	-0.261**	0.008	0.09	-0.134	-0.187**	0.058	-0.014	0.190**	-0.029
Insufficient strategy process	-0.168*	-0.008	-0.037	-0.069	-0.011	-0.111	-0.031	0.225**	-0.077
Ineffective financial controlling	-0.13	-0.021	0.118	-0.053	-0.096	-0.054	0.054	0.269**	-0.032
Weak cost management	-0.153*	-0.094	0.083	0.042	-0.028	-0.046	-0.08	0.378**	0.08
Managerial crisis contribution factors									
Unsuitable CEO	-0.244**	-0.06	0.103	-0.001	-0.064	-0.097	0.022	0.299**	0.045
Unsuitable members of TMT	-0.106	0.202**	-0.057	-0.057	0.024	-0.107	-0.075	0.331**	0.014
Conflict spillover from owner family to company	0.052	0.116	-0.178**	-0.049	0.1	-0.063	-0.071	0.152*	-0.146*
Succession problems	-0.012	-0.001	0.132	-0.197**	0.073	-0.111	-0.005	0.164*	0.012
Portfolio crisis contribution factors									
Incorrect market assessment	-0.036	0.155*	-0.016	-0.066	-0.02	-0.009	-0.067	0.044	-0.108
Overexpansion	-0.093	0.237**	0.033	-0.071	-0.026	0.116	0.084	-0.014	-0.045
Missing innovation in core products	-0.063	-0.039	-0.091	-0.058	0.112	-0.228**	-0.01	0.167*	0.008
Insufficient quality and service	-0.012	-0.024	-0.071	0.03	-0.101	-0.146*	0.092	0.099	-0.029
Non-beneficial acquisitions	0.026	0.308**	-0.124	0.046	-0.071	0.022	0.099	0.152*	-0.074
Financial crisis contribution factors									
Financing structure inadequate	-0.058	0.123	-0.008	0.04	-0.018	0.112	0.023	-0.021	0.032
Cash flow to shareholders too high	-0.176*	-0.203**	0.069	-0.173*	0.054	-0.074	-0.027	0.066	-0.028
Overleveraging	-0.09	0.088	-0.011	0.058	0.042	0.008	0.05	0.043	0.004
External crisis contribution factors									
Market decline	0.035	0.089	-0.027	0.056	0.223**	-0.157*	-0.119	0.156*	0.004
Increased competition	-0.044	0.1	-0.059	-0.119	0.107	-0.136*	-0.012	0.125	-0.036
Supply side induced crisis	-0.032	0.027	-0.007	-0.111	-0.032	0.002	0.056	0.063	-0.092
Customer induced crisis	-0.023	0.044	-0.052	0.04	0.075	-0.079	0.082	0.035	0.031
Crisis context									
Deterioration pattern of crisis	-0.098	-0.175*	0.045	-0.003	-0.075	-0.08	-0.02	0.197**	0.149*
Severity of crisis	0.045	-0.022	-0.024	0.014	-0.036	0.028	-0.064	0.07	0.084
Initial complexity of company situation to implement turnaround	0.254**	0.518**	-0.155*	0.11	0.062	0.033	0.012	0.178**	-0.139*

Crisis characteristics part VIII **Pearson correlation coefficient** N = 209 ****. Correlation is significant at the 0.01 level (2-tailed).** ***. Correlation is significant at the 0.05 level (2-tailed).**	Equity ratio before crisis	Pre-crisis profitability	Family share in the company before crisis	Long-term growth perspect. of mark. Segm.	Turnaround result
Operational crisis contribution factors					
Incorrect investment in plant and equipment	-0.055	0.031	0.058	0.044	-0.041
Insufficient investments in plant and equipment	0.017	-0.073	-0.016	0.016	-0.185**
Degree of company-internal value-add too high	0.067	-0.069	0.07	-0.094	-0.06
Degree of company-internal value-add too low	-0.005	-0.02	0.007	0.082	-0.059
Ineffective/ inefficient organization	0.053	0.038	0.186**	-0.007	-0.205**
Insufficient strategy process	-0.005	-0.053	0.065	-0.139*	-0.187**
Ineffective financial controlling	0.041	0.128	0.072	-0.06	-0.143*
Weak cost management	-0.03	0.031	0.095	-0.064	-0.203**
Managerial crisis contribution factors					
Unsuitable CEO	0	0.068	0.088	-0.12	-0.299**
Unsuitable members of TMT	0.064	0.043	0.08	-0.084	-0.160*
Conflict spillover from owner family to company	0.003	0.044	0.305**	0.114	0.137*
Succession problems	0.027	-0.045	0.352**	0.01	0.056
Portfolio crisis contribution factors					
Incorrect market assessment	-0.104	0.078	0.026	-0.296**	-0.180**
Overexpansion	-0.066	0.066	0.201**	0.045	0.036
Missing innovation in core products	0.012	-0.032	-0.014	-0.305**	-0.150*
Insufficient quality and service	0.055	-0.016	-0.144*	-0.098	-0.282**
Non-beneficial acquisitions	-0.022	-0.041	0.07	-0.035	0.043
Financial crisis contribution factors					
Financing structure inadequate	-0.216**	0.007	-0.013	0.112	0.01
Cash flow to shareholders too high	-0.153*	0.009	0.067	-0.025	-0.031
Overleveraging	-0.399**	-0.033	-0.054	-0.012	-0.163*
External crisis contribution factors					
Market decline	-0.064	0.122	-0.156*	-0.337**	-0.083
Increased competition	0.082	0.035	-0.028	-0.255**	-0.162*
Supply side induced crisis	-0.094	0.043	-0.042	-0.018	-0.068
Customer induced crisis	-0.069	-0.074	0.102	-0.183**	-0.083
Crisis context					
Deterioration pattern of crisis	0.005	-0.203**	0.036	-0.128	-0.064
Severity of crisis	-0.142*	-0.091	-0.140*	0.115	0
Initial complexity of company situation to implement turnaround	0.056	-0.015	-0.087	0.163*	0.183**

Crisis characteristics part IX **Pearson correlation coefficient** **family-firm-specific context variables N = 178** ****. Correlation is significant at the 0.01 level (2-tailed).** ***. Correlation is significant at the 0.05 level (2-tailed).**	Role of owner family in sup. board before crisis	Owner family control before crisis - CEO is family member	Owner family control bef. crisis - struc-ture of TMT	Owner family genera-tion before crisis
Operational crisis contribution factors				
Incorrect investment in plant and equipment	-0.162*	-0.133	-0.083	-0.058
Insufficient investments in plant and equipment	-0.047	0.043	0.069	0.055
Degree of company-internal value-add too high	0.122	0.039	-0.008	0.029
Degree of company-internal value-add too low	-0.102	-0.142	-0.103	-0.036
Ineffective/ inefficient organization	-0.159*	-0.079	-0.074	0.009
Insufficient strategy process	-0.063	-0.024	-0.044	0.044
Ineffective financial controlling	-0.066	-0.091	-0.089	0.021
Weak cost management	-0.099	-0.034	-0.072	0.053
Managerial crisis contribution factors				
Unsuitable CEO	-0.148*	-0.195**	-0.164*	-0.02
Unsuitable members of TMT	0.082	-0.005	0.034	0.086
Conflict spillover from owner family to company	0.079	-0.02	0.071	0.142
Succession problems	-0.091	-0.102	-0.092	-0.008
Portfolio crisis contribution factors				
Incorrect market assessment	-0.049	0.005	0.031	0.05
Overexpansion	0.079	-0.129	-0.038	-0.252**
Missing innovation in core products	-0.007	0.095	0.063	0.131
Insufficient quality and service	-0.038	-0.014	0.031	0.078
Non-beneficial acquisitions	-0.015	0.014	0.179*	0.143
Financial crisis contribution factors				
Financing structure inadequate	-0.036	-0.066	0.007	-0.190*
Cash flow to shareholders too high	-0.143	-0.044	-0.054	-0.034
Overleveraging	-0.053	-0.150*	-0.079	-0.107
External crisis contribution factors				
Market decline	-0.019	0.049	-0.006	0.031
Increased competition	0.068	0.052	0.015	0.075
Supply side induced crisis	-0.033	-0.045	0.017	0.041
Customer induced crisis	0.009	-0.052	-0.013	0.055
Crisis context				
Deterioration pattern of crisis	-0.044	0.011	-0.042	-0.006
Severity of crisis	-0.200**	-0.108	-0.168*	-0.025
Initial complexity of company situation to im-plement turnaround	0.133	0.133	0.259**	0.036

Crisis characteristics part X **Pearson correlation coefficient** **family-firm-specific result variables – non insolvent cases only N = 113** ****. Correlation is significant at the 0.01 level (2-tailed).** ***. Correlation is significant at the 0.05 level (2-tailed).**	Family share in compa-ny after crisis	Owner family control after crisis - CEO is family member	Owner family control after crisis - struc-ture of TMT
Operational crisis contribution factors			
Incorrect investment in plant and equipment	-0.095	0.042	-0.047
Insufficient investments in plant and equipment	-0.043	0.123	0.151
Degree of company-internal value-add too high	0.03	0.161	0.165
Degree of company-internal value-add too low	0.007	-0.039	0.059
Ineffective/ inefficient organization	-0.12	0.250**	0.093
Insufficient strategy process	-0.026	0.116	0.195*
Ineffective financial controlling	-0.142	0.157	0.133
Weak cost management	-0.113	0.297**	0.194*
Managerial crisis contribution factors			
Unsuitable CEO	-0.356**	0.328**	0.267**
Unsuitable members of TMT	-0.117	0.141	0.186*
Conflict spillover from owner family to company	-0.135	0.18	0.214*
Succession problems	-0.168	0.166	0.126
Portfolio crisis contribution factors			
Incorrect market assessment	0.095	-0.097	0.023
Overexpansion	-0.128	0.066	-0.009
Missing innovation in core products	-0.181	0.234*	0.287**
Insufficient quality and service	-0.089	0.112	0.203*
Non-beneficial acquisitions	0.033	-0.009	0.066
Financial crisis contribution factors			
Financing structure inadequate	0.047	-0.095	-0.084
Cash flow to shareholders too high	0.016	0.043	0.017
Overleveraging	0.017	-0.159	-0.063
External crisis contribution factors			
Market decline	-0.006	-0.006	0.145
Increased competition	-0.097	0.038	0.131
Supply side induced crisis	-0.021	-0.098	0.062
Customer induced crisis	0.1	-0.156	-0.049
Crisis context			
Deterioration pattern of crisis	0.135	-0.088	-0.075
Severity of crisis	-0.063	-0.054	-0.088
Initial complexity of company situation to im-plement turnaround	-0.127	0.227*	0.262**

Turnaround management characteristics part I **Pearson correlation coefficient** **N = 209** ****. Correlation is significant at the 0.01 level (2-tailed).** ***. Correlation is significant at the 0.05 level (2-tailed).**	Incorrect investment in plant and equipment	Insufficient investments in plant and equipment	Degree of company-internal value-add too high	Degree of company-internal value-add too low	Ineffective/ inefficient organization	Insufficient strategy process	Ineffective financial controlling	Weak cost management	Unsuitable CEO
Operational restructuring moves									
Layoff	0.069	0.175*	0.296**	-0.027	0.09	0.161*	0.108	0.163*	0.182**
Employee concessions	0.140*	0.173*	0.172*	0.039	0.087	0.091	0.106	0.122	0.138*
Increase CAPEX	-0.076	0.385**	0.1	0.171*	0.032	0.149*	-0.007	0.028	-0.023
Decrease CAPEX	0.371**	-0.008	0.232**	0.04	0.026	0.12	0.065	0.095	0.132
Capacity reduction	0.185**	0.04	0.219**	-0.048	0.102	0.196**	0.148*	0.116	0.137*
Productivity increase	0.021	0.211**	0.262**	0.072	0.06	0.183**	0.091	0.233**	0.109
Outsourcing	0.041	0.194**	0.394**	0.044	0.048	0.205**	0.125	0.106	0.071
Insourcing	0.03	0.039	0.162*	0.160*	-0.135	0.077	0.002	-0.053	-0.196**
Process improvement and redesign	0.088	0.084	0.248**	0.054	0.192**	0.364**	0.382**	0.250**	0.225**
Pricing and sales initiatives	0.114	0.086	0.019	0.115	0.087	0.200**	0.112	0.177*	0.112
Purchasing and cost reduction initiatives	0.051	0.203**	0.238**	0.078	0.034	0.319**	0.128	0.227**	0.154*
Managerial restructuring moves									
CEO change	0.140*	0.209**	0.141*	0.081	0.250**	0.337**	0.327**	0.361**	0.581**
Change in TMT	0.149*	0.115	0.111	0.171*	0.309**	0.335**	0.352**	0.278**	0.351**
External management support	-0.009	0.124	0.195**	0.170*	0.214**	0.187**	0.205**	0.244**	0.240**
Portfolio restructuring moves									
Asset divestments (company division or subsidiary)	0.230**	0.01	0.074	0.094	0.147*	0.146*	0.154*	0.07	0.270**
Acquisitions	-0.082	0.054	0.034	0.12	0.006	0.04	0.044	0.03	-0.106
Termination of products lines/ markets	0.035	0.072	0.285**	-0.001	0.046	0.329**	0.104	0.093	0.162*
New products/ markets development	-0.059	0.204**	0.199**	0.08	0.015	0.158*	-0.054	-0.078	-0.140*
Financial restructuring moves									
Working capital reduction	0.016	0.167*	0.211**	0.164*	0.047	0.165*	0.071	0.082	0.114
Reduction of cash flow to shareholder	0.026	-0.096	0.033	0.003	0.122	0.073	0.117	0.023	0.04
Liquidity contribution by shareholder	0.005	0.047	0.104	0.06	0.174*	0.185**	0.087	0.140*	0.137*
Additional restructuring loan granted by lenders	0.054	-0.012	0.013	0.069	0	-0.06	0.09	0.054	0.05
Securities contribution by shareholder	0.118	0.062	0.193**	0.198**	0.200**	0.173*	0.139*	0.166*	0.156*
Repayment of debt	0.253**	-0.027	0.1	0.01	0.047	0.099	0.095	0.013	0.178*
Extension, conversion or deferral of existing debt	0.219**	0.032	0.055	0.11	-0.005	0.019	-0.009	-0.124	-0.032
Debt write-off or debt-to-equity-swap	0.180**	-0.064	0.017	-0.002	0.059	-0.01	0.042	-0.006	0.13
Turnaround context									
Development of market segment during turnaround	0.029	-0.016	-0.174*	0.06	0.023	-0.091	-0.039	-0.051	-0.098
Stakeholder management during turnaround	-0.115	-0.242**	-0.048	-0.099	-0.261**	-0.168*	-0.13	-0.153*	-0.244**

Turnaround management part II **Pearson correlation coefficient** **N = 209** ****. Correlation is significant at the 0.01 level (2-tailed).** ***. Correlation is significant at the 0.05 level (2-tailed).**	Unsuitable members of TMT	Conflict spillover from owner family to company	Succession problems	Incorrect market assessment	Overexpansion	Missing innovation in core products	Insufficient quality and service	Non-beneficial acquisitions	Financing structure inadequate
Operational restructuring moves									
Layoff	0.301**	0.058	0.096	0.275**	-0.047	0.242**	0.106	0.097	-0.116
Employee concessions	0.206**	0.052	0.139*	0.170*	-0.073	0.210**	0.116	0.025	-0.054
Increase CAPEX	0.045	0.124	-0.017	0.081	0.016	0.174*	0.097	-0.013	-0.025
Decrease CAPEX	0.199**	0.175*	0.199**	0.104	0.199**	0.061	-0.084	0.115	0.164*
Capacity reduction	0.349**	0.091	0.133	0.217**	0.118	0.183**	-0.073	0.182**	0.002
Productivity increase	0.166*	0.063	-0.093	0.029	0.013	0.099	0.168*	0.012	-0.018
Outsourcing	0.214**	0.119	0.075	0.053	-0.06	0.149*	-0.006	0.05	-0.09
Insourcing	-0.036	0.001	-0.101	0.125	0.034	0.161*	0.043	0.056	0.051
Process improvement and redesign	0.376**	0.220**	0.112	0.103	0.147*	0.148*	0.073	0.167*	0.015
Pricing and sales initiatives	0.032	0.09	-0.019	0.128	-0.017	0.106	-0.003	-0.084	0.025
Purchasing and cost reduction initiatives	0.300**	0.104	-0.071	0.111	0.031	0.099	0.083	0.056	-0.048
Managerial restructuring moves									
CEO change	0.412**	0.458**	0.356**	-0.033	0.108	0.139*	0.085	0.114	-0.12
Change in TMT	0.514**	0.354**	0.258**	0.075	0.229**	0.082	0.015	0.220**	0.089
External management support	0.243**	0.111	0.125	-0.078	0.023	0.134	0.072	0.026	0.005
Portfolio restructuring moves									
Asset divestments (company division or subsidiary)	0.234**	0.255**	0.251**	0.034	0.194**	0.042	0.041	0.364**	0.094
Acquisitions	0.057	0.101	0.069	0.101	0.058	0.021	-0.024	0.146*	-0.038
Termination of products lines/ markets	0.187**	0.212**	0.103	0.224**	0.185**	0.241**	0.014	0.306**	-0.022
New products/ markets development	0.067	0	-0.012	0.222**	-0.034	0.329**	-0.038	-0.09	-0.07
Financial restructuring moves									
Working capital reduction	0.205**	0.051	-0.035	0.099	-0.025	0.129	0.106	0.105	-0.014
Reduction of cash flow to shareholder	0.026	0.240**	0.199**	0.018	-0.082	-0.025	-0.059	-0.013	0.002
Liquidity contribution by shareholder	0.144*	0.12	0.096	0.174*	0.047	0.052	-0.014	0.028	0.098
Additional restructuring loan granted by lenders	0.004	0.067	-0.096	-0.132	0.109	-0.082	0.105	0.028	0.133
Securities contribution by shareholder	0.109	0.117	0.094	0.064	0.067	0.066	-0.047	0.075	0.105
Repayment of debt	0.228**	0.227**	0.140*	0.073	0.301**	-0.05	-0.055	0.305**	0.273**
Extension, conversion or deferral of existing debt	-0.031	-0.002	0.054	0.123	0.155*	-0.045	-0.002	0.103	0.233**
Debt write-off or debt-to-equity-swap	0.178**	0.022	0.104	0.049	0.195**	-0.06	0.01	0.274**	0.107
Turnaround context									
Development of market segment during turnaround	-0.107	0.055	0.018	-0.254**	0.112	-0.229**	-0.147*	-0.058	0.108
Stakeholder management during turnaround	-0.106	0.052	-0.012	-0.036	-0.093	-0.063	-0.012	0.026	-0.058

Turnaround management part III **Pearson correlation coefficient** N = 209 ****. Correlation is significant at the 0.01 level (2-tailed).** ***. Correlation is significant at the 0.05 level (2-tailed).**	Cash flow to share-holders too high	Overlev eraging	Market decline	In-creased compe-tition	Supply side induced crisis	Cus-tomer induced crisis	Deterio-ration pattern of crisis	Severity of crisis	Initial com-plexity of compa-ny situation
Operational restructuring moves									
Layoff	-0.042	0.101	0.342**	0.399**	0.123	0.183**	0.065	0.016	0.094
Employee concessions	-0.052	0.023	0.257**	0.185**	0.042	0.205**	-0.036	0.092	0.123
Increase CAPEX	0.037	0.011	0.107	0.077	0.09	0.087	0.011	0.014	0.014
Decrease CAPEX	0.106	0.269**	0.193**	0.094	0.002	0.02	0.106	0.033	0.186**
Capacity reduction	-0.072	0.068	0.285**	0.203**	0.032	0.143*	0.054	-0.106	0.209**
Productivity increase	-0.111	0.037	0.114	0.028	-0.024	0.075	0.062	0.046	0.125
Outsourcing	-0.015	-0.019	0.179**	0.186**	0.158*	0.045	0.047	-0.022	0.125
Insourcing	0.043	-0.007	0.179**	-0.034	0.128	0.036	0.008	-0.036	0.034
Process improvement and redesign	0.1	-0.009	0.046	0.181**	0.172*	-0.084	0.199**	0.044	0.099
Pricing and sales initiatives	0.076	0.061	0.132	-0.02	0.106	0.196**	0.042	0.077	-0.064
Purchasing and cost reduction initiatives	-0.039	0.161*	0.206**	0.230**	0.274**	0.232**	0.1	0.04	0.145*
Managerial restructuring moves									
CEO change	0.211**	0.087	0.135	0.076	0.094	0.006	0.174*	0.159*	0.159*
Change in TMT	0.086	0.160*	0.01	0.011	0.113	0.055	0.091	0.138*	0.227**
External management support	0.064	-0.023	-0.017	0.086	0.047	0.169*	0.05	0.055	-0.001
Portfolio restructuring moves									
Asset divestments (company division or subsidiary)	0.098	0.219**	-0.036	-0.01	0.017	-0.069	0.081	0.014	0.295**
Acquisitions	0.127	0.082	0.007	-0.005	0.104	-0.008	0.012	-0.047	0.007
Termination of products lines/ markets	0.049	-0.106	0.164*	0.179**	0.036	0.001	0.096	-0.125	0.170*
New products/ markets development	-0.044	-0.094	0.291**	0.246**	0.062	0.07	0.049	-0.075	0.056
Financial restructuring moves									
Working capital reduction	0.063	0.155*	0.209**	0.170*	0.138*	0.109	0.038	0.140*	0.123
Reduction of cash flow to shareholder	0.505**	-0.03	0.009	0.016	0.035	-0.019	0.007	0.111	-0.065
Liquidity contribution by shareholder	0.044	0.052	0.103	0.105	0.172*	0.04	0.007	0.03	0.154*
Additional restructuring loan granted by lenders	0.092	0.098	-0.045	-0.078	-0.039	-0.005	-0.114	0.188**	0.137*
Securities contribution by shareholder	0.236**	0.146*	0.05	0.039	0.183**	0.007	0.044	0.007	0.052
Repayment of debt	0.072	0.350**	0.052	0.126	0.108	0.051	-0.024	0.056	0.291**
Extension, conversion or deferral of existing debt	0.028	0.336**	0.176*	0.139*	0.08	0.099	-0.068	0.058	0.218**
Debt write-off or debt-to-equity-swap	-0.095	0.239**	-0.003	0.071	0.143*	0.054	0.003	0.133	0.314**
Turnaround context									
Development of market segment during turnaround	0.008	-0.033	-0.303**	-0.286**	-0.068	-0.229**	-0.104	0.156*	0.126
Stakeholder management during turnaround	-0.176*	-0.09	0.035	-0.044	-0.032	-0.023	-0.098	0.045	0.254**

Turnaround management part IV Pearson correlation coefficient N = 209 **. Correlation is significant at the 0.01 level (2-tailed). *. Correlation is significant at the 0.05 level (2-tailed).	Layoff	Employee concessions	Increase CAPEX	Decrease CAPEX	Capacity reduction	Productivity increase	Outsourcing	Insourcing	Process improvement and redesign
Operational restructuring moves									
Layoff	1	0.585**	0.03	0.242**	0.457**	0.273**	0.331**	-0.067	0.222**
Employee concessions	0.585**	1	0.08	0.182**	0.298**	0.240**	0.241**	0.041	0.132
Increase CAPEX	0.03	0.08	1	-0.183**	-0.160*	0.225**	0.092	0.215**	0.029
Decrease CAPEX	0.242**	0.182**	-0.183**	1	0.414**	-0.038	0.216**	0.095	0.117
Capacity reduction	0.457**	0.298**	-0.160*	0.414**	1	0.165*	0.316**	-0.053	0.193**
Productivity increase	0.273**	0.240**	0.225**	-0.038	0.165*	1	0.171*	0.177*	0.280**
Outsourcing	0.331**	0.241**	0.092	0.216**	0.316**	0.171*	1	0.183**	0.244**
Insourcing	-0.067	0.041	0.215**	0.095	-0.053	0.177*	0.183**	1	0.111
Process improvement and redesign	0.222**	0.132	0.029	0.117	0.193**	0.280**	0.244**	0.111	1
Pricing and sales initiatives	-0.079	0.088	0.122	-0.005	-0.057	0.241**	-0.074	0.066	0.054
Purchasing and cost reduction initiatives	0.428**	0.264**	0.056	0.112	0.213**	0.499**	0.215**	0.046	0.386**
Managerial restructuring moves									
CEO change	0.222**	0.152*	0.109	0.201**	0.178**	0.159*	0.117	-0.073	0.355**
Change in TMT	0.162*	0.132	0.068	0.273**	0.207**	0.179**	0.135	0.018	0.411**
External management support	0.228**	0.325**	-0.029	0.058	0.163*	0.180**	0.133	0.025	0.252**
Portfolio restructuring moves									
Asset divestments (company division or subsidiary)	0.131	0.112	-0.069	0.248**	0.307**	-0.079	0.231**	-0.034	0.142*
Acquisitions	0.009	0.059	0.121	0.109	0.077	-0.01	0.035	0.088	0.002
Termination of products lines/ markets	0.253**	0.124	0.024	0.185**	0.358**	0.106	0.296**	0.156*	0.292**
New products/ markets development	0.035	0.106	0.303**	-0.05	-0.021	0.086	0.148*	0.186**	0.133
Financial restructuring moves									
Working capital reduction	0.295**	0.240**	0.062	-0.007	0.113	0.154*	0.179**	0.125	0.175*
Reduction of cash flow to shareholder	0.005	0.047	-0.055	0.095	-0.002	-0.089	0.037	0.122	0.121
Liquidity contribution by shareholder	0.099	0.072	0.200**	-0.022	0.103	0.098	0.145*	0.160*	0.165*
Additional restructuring loan granted by lenders	0.02	0.138*	0.091	0.002	-0.08	0.123	0.017	0.058	-0.005
Securities contribution by shareholder	0.075	0.028	0.242**	0.029	0.021	0.037	0.073	0.013	0.170*
Repayment of debt	0.143*	0.09	0.071	0.291**	0.197**	0.008	0.112	-0.011	0.113
Extension, conversion or deferral of existing debt	-0.05	0.056	0.075	0.143*	0.062	-0.008	0.026	0.159*	-0.049
Debt write-off or debt-to-equity-swap	0.057	0.135	0.027	0.174*	0.240**	0.082	0.047	-0.041	0.087
Turnaround context									
Development of market segment during turnaround	-0.245**	-0.153*	0.132	-0.021	-0.173*	0.039	-0.148*	0.149*	-0.063
Stakeholder management during turnaround	0.039	0.149*	-0.036	0.066	0.12	0.198**	-0.001	0.074	0.036

Turnaround management part V **Pearson correlation coefficient** **N = 209** ****. Correlation is significant at the 0.01 level (2-tailed).** ***. Correlation is significant at the 0.05 level (2-tailed).**	Pricing and sales initia-tives	Pur-chasing and cost reduc-tion initia-tives	CEO change	Change in TMT	External man-age-ment support	Asset divest-ments	Acquisi-tions	Termi-nation of prod-ucts lines/ markets	New prod-ucts/ markets devel-opment
Operational restructuring moves									
Layoff	-0.079	0.428**	0.222**	0.162*	0.228**	0.131	0.009	0.253**	0.035
Employee concessions	0.088	0.264**	0.152*	0.132	0.325**	0.112	0.059	0.124	0.106
Increase CAPEX	0.122	0.056	0.109	0.068	-0.029	-0.069	0.121	0.024	0.303**
Decrease CAPEX	-0.005	0.112	0.201**	0.273**	0.058	0.248**	0.109	0.185**	-0.05
Capacity reduction	-0.057	0.213**	0.178**	0.207**	0.163*	0.307**	0.077	0.358**	-0.021
Productivity increase	0.241**	0.499**	0.159*	0.179**	0.180**	-0.079	-0.01	0.106	0.086
Outsourcing	-0.074	0.215**	0.117	0.135	0.133	0.231**	0.035	0.296**	0.148*
Insourcing	0.066	0.046	-0.073	0.018	0.025	-0.034	0.088	0.156*	0.186**
Process improvement and redesign	0.054	0.386**	0.355**	0.411**	0.252**	0.142*	0.002	0.292**	0.133
Pricing and sales initiatives	1	0.129	0.028	0.06	0.098	-0.178**	0.160*	-0.08	0.142*
Purchasing and cost reduction initiatives	0.129	1	0.246**	0.304**	0.230**	0.029	-0.026	0.215**	0.062
Managerial restructuring moves									
CEO change	0.028	0.246**	1	0.576**	0.220**	0.249**	0.012	0.244**	0.048
Change in TMT	0.06	0.304**	0.576**	1	0.271**	0.205**	0.035	0.129	0.115
External management support	0.098	0.230**	0.220**	0.271**	1	0.178**	-0.01	0.039	-0.015
Portfolio restructuring moves									
Asset divestments (company division or subsidiary)	-0.178**	0.029	0.249**	0.205**	0.178**	1	0.044	0.315**	-0.104
Acquisitions	0.160*	-0.026	0.012	0.035	-0.01	0.044	1	0.045	0.135
Termination of products lines/ markets	-0.08	0.215**	0.244**	0.129	0.039	0.315**	0.045	1	0.191**
New products/ markets development	0.142*	0.062	0.048	0.115	-0.015	-0.104	0.135	0.191**	1
Financial restructuring moves									
Working capital reduction	0.097	0.177*	0.134	0.1	0.316**	0.027	-0.014	0.063	-0.031
Reduction of cash flow to shareholder	0.037	-0.084	0.033	0.067	0.037	0.028	0.001	0.048	-0.021
Liquidity contribution by shareholder	0.134	0.097	0.170*	0.161*	0.085	0.042	0.067	0.119	0.184**
Additional restructuring loan granted by lenders	0.097	0.125	0.012	0.024	0.259**	0.11	0.023	-0.12	-0.163*
Securities contribution by shareholder	0.149*	0.06	0.047	0.076	0.156*	0.160*	-0.036	0.062	0.037
Repayment of debt	-0.017	0.124	0.119	0.250**	0.045	0.422**	0.058	0.128	-0.019
Extension, conversion or deferral of existing debt	0.075	0.102	0.05	0.109	0.042	0.159*	0.093	-0.005	0.046
Debt write-off or debt-to-equity-swap	0.06	0.129	0.207**	0.160*	0.11	0.242**	0.107	0.134	-0.103
Turnaround context									
Development of market segment during turnaround	0.034	-0.13	-0.054	0.045	-0.037	-0.015	0.084	-0.107	0.02
Stakeholder management during turnaround	0.044	0.104	0.01	0.066	0.019	-0.066	-0.01	0.042	-0.015

Turnaround management part VI **Pearson correlation coefficient** **N = 209** ****. Correlation is significant at the 0.01 level (2-tailed).** ***. Correlation is significant at the 0.05 level (2-tailed).**	Working capital reduction	Reduction of cash flow to shareholder	Liquidity contribution by shareholder	Additional restructuring loan granted by lenders	Securities contribution by shareholder	Repayment of debt	Extension, conversion or deferral of existing debt	Debt write-off or debt-to-equity-swap	Development of market segm. during turnaround
Operational restructuring moves									
Layoff	0.295**	0.005	0.099	0.02	0.075	0.143*	-0.05	0.057	-0.245**
Employee concessions	0.240**	0.047	0.072	0.138*	0.028	0.09	0.056	0.135	-0.153*
Increase CAPEX	0.062	-0.055	0.200**	0.091	0.242**	0.071	0.075	0.027	0.132
Decrease CAPEX	-0.007	0.095	-0.022	0.002	0.029	0.291**	0.143*	0.174*	-0.021
Capacity reduction	0.113	-0.002	0.103	-0.08	0.021	0.197**	0.062	0.240**	-0.173*
Productivity increase	0.154*	-0.089	0.098	0.123	0.037	0.008	-0.008	0.082	0.039
Outsourcing	0.179**	0.037	0.145*	0.017	0.073	0.112	0.026	0.047	-0.148*
Insourcing	0.125	0.122	0.160*	0.058	0.013	-0.011	0.159*	-0.041	0.149*
Process improvement and redesign	0.175*	0.121	0.165*	-0.005	0.170*	0.113	-0.049	0.087	-0.063
Pricing and sales initiatives	0.097	0.037	0.134	0.097	0.149*	-0.017	0.075	0.06	0.034
Purchasing and cost reduction initiatives	0.177*	-0.084	0.097	0.125	0.06	0.124	0.102	0.129	-0.13
Managerial restructuring moves									
CEO change	0.134	0.033	0.170*	0.012	0.047	0.119	0.05	0.207**	-0.054
Change in TMT	0.1	0.067	0.161*	0.024	0.076	0.250**	0.109	0.160*	0.045
External management support	0.316**	0.037	0.085	0.259**	0.156*	0.045	0.042	0.11	-0.037
Portfolio restructuring moves									
Asset divestments (company division or subsidiary)	0.027	0.028	0.042	0.11	0.160*	0.422**	0.159*	0.242**	-0.015
Acquisitions	-0.014	0.001	0.067	0.023	-0.036	0.058	0.093	0.107	0.084
Termination of products lines/ markets	0.063	0.048	0.119	-0.12	0.062	0.128	-0.005	0.134	-0.107
New products/ markets development	-0.031	-0.021	0.184**	-0.163*	0.037	-0.019	0.046	-0.103	0.02
Financial restructuring moves									
Working capital reduction	1	0.088	0.109	0.105	0.11	0.109	0.078	0.182**	-0.01
Reduction of cash flow to shareholder	0.088	1	0.104	-0.017	0.227**	-0.005	0.102	-0.041	0.051
Liquidity contribution by shareholder	0.109	0.104	1	-0.084	0.300**	0.093	0.034	0.066	-0.003
Additional restructuring loan granted by lenders	0.105	-0.017	-0.084	1	0.219**	0.101	0.205**	0.098	0.063
Securities contribution by shareholder	0.11	0.227**	0.300**	0.219**	1	0.213**	0.103	-0.054	-0.013
Repayment of debt	0.109	-0.005	0.093	0.101	0.213**	1	0.127	0.410**	0.08
Extension, conversion or deferral of existing debt	0.078	0.102	0.034	0.205**	0.103	0.127	1	0.181**	0.018
Debt write-off or debt-to-equity-swap	0.182**	-0.041	0.066	0.098	-0.054	0.410**	0.181**	1	0.026
Turnaround context									
Development of market segment during turnaround	-0.01	0.051	-0.003	0.063	-0.013	0.08	0.018	0.026	1
Stakeholder management during turnaround	0.099	0.047	0.009	0.049	-0.034	-0.012	0.053	0.138*	0.077

Turnaround management part VII **Pearson correlation coefficient** **N = 209** ****. Correlation is significant at the 0.01 level (2-tailed).** ***. Correlation is significant at the 0.05 level (2-tailed).**	Stake-holder man-age-ment during turna-round	Com-pany size (turno-ver) before crisis	Share of biggest share-holder before crisis	CEOs time with the compa-ny before crisis	Primary strategy before crisis - Quality leader-ship	Primary strat. before crisis - Innova-tion leader-ship	Primary strat. before crisis - Low-cost leader-ship	Slack re-sources before crisis	Lender security situation before crisis
Operational restructuring moves									
Layoff	0.039	0.184**	-0.157*	0.01	0.099	-0.140*	-0.046	0.267**	-0.028
Employee concessions	0.149*	0.113	-0.161*	0.118	0.103	-0.054	-0.140*	0.235**	-0.018
Increase CAPEX	-0.036	0.07	-0.061	0.034	0.024	-0.03	-0.038	-0.041	-0.009
Decrease CAPEX	0.066	0.136*	-0.036	-0.053	0.191**	0.029	-0.078	0.101	0.003
Capacity reduction	0.12	0.241**	-0.078	-0.111	0.018	-0.049	-0.037	0.182**	0.003
Productivity increase	0.198**	0.079	-0.127	0.088	0.088	-0.147*	-0.078	0.262**	0.069
Outsourcing	-0.001	0.127	-0.036	0.032	0.197**	-0.087	-0.052	0.175*	-0.087
Insourcing	0.074	0.012	-0.148*	0.041	0.175*	-0.147*	-0.06	0.006	-0.150*
Process improvement and redesign	0.036	0.091	-0.031	-0.078	0.039	-0.062	-0.144*	0.345**	-0.049
Pricing and sales initiatives	0.044	-0.201**	0.136*	0.018	0.01	0.006	0.002	0.04	0.031
Purchasing and cost reduction initiatives	0.104	0.151*	-0.091	0.025	0.108	-0.155*	-0.09	0.224**	-0.025
Managerial restructuring moves									
CEO change	0.01	0.122	0.027	0.054	0.047	-0.043	-0.028	0.383**	0.034
Change in TMT	0.066	0.222**	-0.012	0.016	0.04	0.012	-0.105	0.188**	0.054
External management support	0.019	-0.021	-0.028	-0.091	0.075	-0.139*	-0.043	0.189**	-0.004
Portfolio restructuring moves									
Asset divestments (company division or subsidiary)	-0.066	0.208**	-0.102	-0.153*	0.01	-0.075	0.043	0.046	-0.074
Acquisitions	-0.01	0.018	0.034	-0.059	-0.037	0.108	-0.061	-0.014	0.005
Termination of products lines/ markets	0.042	0.218**	-0.166*	0.002	0.047	-0.089	0.002	0.202**	-0.085
New products/ markets development	-0.015	0.057	-0.004	-0.039	0.042	0.067	-0.097	-0.101	-0.083
Financial restructuring moves									
Working capital reduction	0.099	0.061	-0.101	0.011	0.014	-0.101	-0.04	0.279**	-0.021
Reduction of cash flow to shareholder	0.047	-0.108	-0.048	-0.199**	0.170*	-0.096	-0.096	-0.052	-0.116
Liquidity contribution by shareholder	0.009	-0.034	0.179**	0.085	-0.021	-0.029	-0.067	0.1	-0.142*
Additional restructuring loan granted by lenders	0.049	0.036	-0.1	0.004	0.019	-0.095	-0.011	-0.064	-0.068
Securities contribution by shareholder	-0.034	-0.109	0.09	-0.073	0.078	-0.074	-0.131	0.079	-0.138*
Repayment of debt	-0.012	0.240**	-0.127	-0.004	0.045	0.05	0.004	0.054	-0.148*
Extension, conversion or deferral of existing debt	0.053	0.203**	-0.066	-0.066	0.153*	-0.054	-0.003	-0.043	-0.018
Debt write-off or debt-to-equity-swap	0.138*	0.219**	-0.089	-0.041	-0.035	0.09	0.095	0.149*	0.032
Turnaround context									
Development of market segment during turnaround	0.077	0.107	-0.024	-0.019	0.05	0.066	0.01	-0.178**	-0.087
Stakeholder management during turnaround	1	0.220**	-0.117	0.012	0.180**	-0.02	-0.098	0.031	-0.051

Turnaround management part VIII **Pearson correlation coefficient** **N = 209** ****. Correlation is significant at the 0.01 level (2-tailed).** ***. Correlation is significant at the 0.05 level (2-tailed).**	Equity ratio before crisis	Pre-crisis profitability	Family share in the company before crisis	Long-term growth perspect. of mark. Segm.	Turnaround result
Operational restructuring moves					
Layoff	0.014	0.058	0.068	-0.203**	-0.171*
Employee concessions	0.018	0.012	0.048	-0.166*	-0.108
Increase CAPEX	0.158*	-0.072	0.057	0.190**	0.086
Decrease CAPEX	-0.129	-0.016	0.126	-0.067	0.027
Capacity reduction	0.072	0.042	0.126	-0.186**	-0.056
Productivity increase	0.099	-0.068	-0.041	0.07	0.014
Outsourcing	0.117	0.076	0.015	-0.031	-0.058
Insourcing	0.063	-0.104	0.008	0.157*	0.167*
Process improvement and redesign	0.152*	0.052	0.051	-0.085	0.008
Pricing and sales initiatives	-0.1	0.011	0.093	-0.084	0.027
Purchasing and cost reduction initiatives	-0.014	0.008	-0.029	-0.061	-0.082
Managerial restructuring moves					
CEO change	0.093	0.064	-0.084	0.001	-0.033
Change in TMT	0.128	0.065	0.067	0.04	0.06
External management support	0.074	-0.093	0.196**	-0.198**	-0.108
Portfolio restructuring moves					
Asset divestments (company division or subsidiary)	-0.009	-0.135	0.177*	-0.038	-0.055
Acquisitions	0.008	-0.084	0.084	0.038	0.081
Termination of products lines/ markets	0.06	-0.002	0.048	-0.117	-0.033
New products/ markets development	0.143*	-0.04	-0.023	0	0.09
Financial restructuring moves					
Working capital reduction	-0.05	0.017	0.021	-0.06	-0.079
Reduction of cash flow to shareholder	-0.014	0.135	0.143*	0.012	0.08
Liquidity contribution by shareholder	0.104	-0.037	0.032	0.051	0.039
Additional restructuring loan granted by lenders	-0.183**	-0.116	0.063	0.065	-0.014
Securities contribution by shareholder	-0.108	-0.092	0.175*	0.002	0.021
Repayment of debt	-0.109	-0.136*	0.159*	0.072	0.125
Extension, conversion or deferral of existing debt	-0.061	-0.012	-0.063	0.061	-0.044
Debt write-off or debt-to-equity-swap	-0.056	-0.052	-0.028	0.022	0.038
Turnaround context					
Development of market segment during turnaround	0.086	-0.049	0.108	0.695**	0.435**
Stakeholder management during turnaround	0.156*	0.019	-0.12	0.113	0.415**

Turnaround management part IX **Pearson correlation coefficient** **family-firm-specific context variables - N = 178** ****. Correlation is significant at the 0.01 level (2-tailed).** ***. Correlation is significant at the 0.05 level (2-tailed).**	Role of owner family in sup. board before crisis	Owner family control before crisis - CEO is family member	Owner family control bef. crisis - structure of TMT	Owner family generation before crisis
Operational restructuring moves				
Layoff	0.099	0.069	0.094	0.230**
Employee concessions	-0.007	0.104	0.142	0.244**
Increase CAPEX	-0.008	-0.011	-0.02	-0.009
Decrease CAPEX	0.076	-0.017	0.064	-0.11
Capacity reduction	0.147	0.055	0.037	0.054
Productivity increase	0.067	0.062	0.031	0.084
Outsourcing	0.088	0.109	0.083	0.058
Insourcing	0.108	0.099	0.131	0.058
Process improvement and redesign	0.012	-0.097	-0.133	0.108
Pricing and sales initiatives	-0.124	-0.034	-0.161*	-0.047
Purchasing and cost reduction initiatives	0.114	0.044	0.101	0.034
Managerial restructuring moves				
CEO change	0.045	-0.078	0.009	-0.051
Change in TMT	0.1	-0.102	0.064	-0.02
External management support	0.018	0.029	0.007	0.079
Portfolio restructuring moves				
Asset divestments (company division or subsidiary)	0.059	-0.137	0.016	0.018
Acquisitions	0.025	-0.063	-0.037	-0.107
Termination of products lines/ markets	0.168*	-0.05	0.039	0.094
New products/ markets development	0.08	-0.019	-0.019	-0.059
Financial restructuring moves				
Working capital reduction	-0.107	-0.055	-0.026	0.218**
Reduction of cash flow to shareholder	-0.137	-0.042	-0.097	0.079
Liquidity contribution by shareholder	-0.036	0.075	0.012	0.041
Additional restructuring loan granted by lenders	0.05	-0.059	-0.064	-0.013
Securities contribution by shareholder	-0.059	-0.132	-0.097	0.014
Repayment of debt	0.115	-0.081	0.008	-0.016
Extension, conversion or deferral of existing debt	0.057	-0.134	0.003	-0.163*
Debt write-off or debt-to-equity-swap	0.180*	-0.035	-0.005	-0.064
Turnaround context				
Development of market segment during turnaround	0.019	0.004	0.001	0.037
Stakeholder management during turnaround	0.06	0.106	0.174*	0.121

Turnaround management part X **Pearson correlation coefficient** **family-firm-specific result variables – non insolvent cases only N = 113** ****. Correlation is significant at the 0.01 level (2-tailed).** ***. Correlation is significant at the 0.05 level (2-tailed).**	Family share in company after crisis	Owner family control after crisis - CEO is family member	Owner family control after crisis - structure of TMT
Operational restructuring moves			
Layoff	-0.118	0.158	0.294**
Employee concessions	-0.197*	0.228*	0.374**
Increase CAPEX	-0.049	0.108	0.025
Decrease CAPEX	-0.069	0.09	0.17
Capacity reduction	-0.135	0.179	0.216*
Productivity increase	-0.066	0.220*	0.193*
Outsourcing	0.042	0.081	0.093
Insourcing	0.148	0.061	0.106
Process improvement and redesign	0.015	0.046	0.043
Pricing and sales initiatives	0.09	-0.091	-0.017
Purchasing and cost reduction initiatives	-0.095	0.059	0.247**
Managerial restructuring moves			
CEO change	-0.347**	0.377**	0.357**
Change in TMT	-0.164	0.187*	0.217*
External management support	-0.055	0.163	0.185*
Portfolio restructuring moves			
Asset divestments (company division or subsidiary)	-0.173	0.124	0.214*
Acquisitions	0.082	-0.114	-0.073
Termination of products lines/ markets	-0.102	0.139	0.244**
New products/ markets development	0.048	-0.087	-0.107
Financial restructuring moves			
Working capital reduction	0.056	0.011	0.085
Reduction of cash flow to shareholder	0.104	-0.001	-0.079
Liquidity contribution by shareholder	0.081	0.089	0.098
Additional restructuring loan granted by lenders	-0.183	0.06	0.03
Securities contribution by shareholder	-0.138	0.125	0.083
Repayment of debt	-0.054	-0.099	0.055
Extension, conversion or deferral of existing debt	0.007	-0.031	-0.024
Debt write-off or debt-to-equity-swap	-0.199*	-0.04	0.067
Turnaround context			
Development of market segment during turnaround	0.131	-0.032	-0.188*
Stakeholder management during turnaround	-0.019	0.148	0.181

Context and turnaround result part I **Pearson correlation coefficient** **N = 209** ****. Correlation is significant at the 0.01 level (2-tailed).** ***. Correlation is significant at the 0.05 level (2-tailed).**	Incorrect investment in plant and equipment	Insufficient investments in plant and equipment	Degree of company-internal value-add too high	Degree of company-internal value-add too low	Ineffective/ inefficient organization	Insufficient strategy process	Ineffective financial controlling	Weak cost management	Unsuitable CEO
Internal context									
Company size (turnover) before crisis	0.085	-0.034	-0.017	-0.028	0.008	-0.008	-0.021	-0.094	-0.06
Share of biggest shareholder before crisis	-0.093	0.04	-0.074	0.031	0.09	-0.037	0.118	0.083	0.103
CEOs time with the company before crisis	-0.055	0.093	-0.12	0.027	-0.134	-0.069	-0.053	0.042	-0.001
Primary strategy before crisis - Quality leadership	0.06	-0.041	0.150*	0.014	-0.187**	-0.011	-0.096	-0.028	-0.064
Primary strategy before crisis - Innovation leadership	-0.031	-0.083	-0.062	-0.051	0.058	-0.111	-0.054	-0.046	-0.097
Primary strategy before crisis - Low-cost leadership	-0.026	-0.027	-0.087	-0.015	-0.014	-0.031	0.054	-0.08	0.022
Slack resources before crisis	0.200**	0.195**	0.249**	0.092	0.190**	0.225**	0.269**	0.378**	0.299**
Lender security situation before crisis	-0.054	0.009	-0.095	0.11	-0.029	-0.077	-0.032	0.08	0.045
Equity ratio before crisis	-0.055	0.017	0.067	-0.005	0.053	-0.005	0.041	-0.03	0
Pre-crisis profitability	0.031	-0.073	-0.069	-0.02	0.038	-0.053	0.128	0.031	0.068
Family share in the company before crisis	0.058	-0.016	0.07	0.007	0.186**	0.065	0.072	0.095	0.088
External context									
Long-term growth perspectives of market segment	0.044	0.016	-0.094	0.082	-0.007	-0.139*	-0.06	-0.064	-0.12
Turnaround result									
Turnaround result	-0.041	-0.185**	-0.06	-0.059	-0.205**	-0.187**	-0.143*	-0.203**	-0.299**

Context and turnaround result part II **Pearson correlation coefficient** N = 209 ****. Correlation is significant at the 0.01 level (2-tailed).** ***. Correlation is significant at the 0.05 level (2-tailed).**	Unsuitable members of TMT	Conflict spillover from owner family to company	Succession problems	Incorrect market assessment	Overexpansion	Missing innovation in core products	Insufficient quality and service	Nonbeneficial acquisitions	Financing structure inadequate
Internal context									
Company size (turnover) before crisis	0.202**	0.116	-0.001	0.155*	0.237**	-0.039	-0.024	0.308**	0.123
Share of biggest shareholder before crisis	-0.057	-0.178**	0.132	-0.016	0.033	-0.091	-0.071	-0.124	-0.008
CEOs time with the company before crisis	-0.057	-0.049	-0.197**	-0.066	-0.071	-0.058	0.03	0.046	0.04
Primary strategy before crisis - Quality leadership	0.024	0.1	0.073	-0.02	-0.026	0.112	-0.101	-0.071	-0.018
Primary strategy before crisis - Innovation leadership	-0.107	-0.063	-0.111	-0.009	0.116	-0.228**	-0.146*	0.022	0.112
Primary strategy before crisis - Low-cost leadership	-0.075	-0.071	-0.005	-0.067	0.084	-0.01	0.092	0.099	0.023
Slack resources before crisis	0.331**	0.152*	0.164*	0.044	-0.014	0.167*	0.099	0.152*	-0.021
Lender security situation before crisis	0.014	-0.146*	0.012	-0.108	-0.045	0.008	-0.029	-0.074	0.032
Equity ratio before crisis	0.064	0.003	0.027	-0.104	-0.066	0.012	0.055	-0.022	-0.216**
Pre-crisis profitability	0.043	0.044	-0.045	0.078	0.066	-0.032	-0.016	-0.041	0.007
Family share in the company before crisis	0.08	0.305**	0.352**	0.026	0.201**	-0.014	-0.144*	0.07	-0.013
External context									
Long-term growth perspectives of market segment	-0.084	0.114	0.01	-0.296**	0.045	-0.305**	-0.098	-0.035	0.112
Turnaround result									
Turnaround result	-0.160*	0.137*	0.056	-0.180**	0.036	-0.150*	-0.282**	0.043	0.01

Context and turnaround result part III **Pearson correlation coefficient** **N = 209** ****. Correlation is significant at the 0.01 level (2-tailed).** ***. Correlation is significant at the 0.05 level (2-tailed).**	Cash flow to share-holders too high	Overlev eraging	Market decline	In-creased compe-tition	Supply side induced crisis	Cus-tomer induced crisis	Deterio-ration pattern of crisis	Severity of crisis	Initial com-plexity of compa-ny situation
Internal context									
Company size (turnover) before crisis	-0.203**	0.088	0.089	0.1	0.027	0.044	-0.175*	-0.022	0.518**
Share of biggest shareholder before crisis	0.069	-0.011	-0.027	-0.059	-0.007	-0.052	0.045	-0.024	-0.155*
CEOs time with the company before crisis	-0.173*	0.058	0.056	-0.119	-0.111	0.04	-0.003	0.014	0.11
Primary strategy before crisis - Quality leader-ship	0.054	0.042	0.223**	0.107	-0.032	0.075	-0.075	-0.036	0.062
Primary strategy before crisis - Innovation leadership	-0.074	0.008	-0.157*	-0.136*	0.002	-0.079	-0.08	0.028	0.033
Primary strategy before crisis - Low-cost lead-ership	-0.027	0.05	-0.119	-0.012	0.056	0.082	-0.02	-0.064	0.012
Slack resources before crisis	0.066	0.043	0.156*	0.125	0.063	0.035	0.197**	0.07	0.178**
Lender security situation before crisis	-0.028	0.004	0.004	-0.036	-0.092	0.031	0.149*	0.084	-0.139*
Equity ratio before crisis	-0.153*	-0.399**	-0.064	0.082	-0.094	-0.069	0.005	-0.142*	0.056
Pre-crisis profitability	0.009	-0.033	0.122	0.035	0.043	-0.074	-0.203**	-0.091	-0.015
Family share in the company before crisis	0.067	-0.054	-0.156*	-0.028	-0.042	0.102	0.036	-0.140*	-0.087
External context									
Long-term growth perspectives of market segment	-0.025	-0.012	-0.337**	-0.255**	-0.018	-0.183**	-0.128	0.115	0.163*
Turnaround result									
Turnaround result	-0.031	-0.163*	-0.083	-0.162*	-0.068	-0.083	-0.064	0	0.183**

Context and turnaround result part IV **Pearson correlation coefficient** **N = 209** ****. Correlation is significant at the 0.01 level (2-tailed).** ***. Correlation is significant at the 0.05 level (2-tailed).**	Layoff	Em-ployee conces-sions	In-crease CAPEX	De-crease CAPEX	Capaci-ty reduc-tion	Produc-tivity in-crease	Out-sourc-ing	Insourc-ing	Process im-prove-ment and rede-sign
Internal context									
Company size (turnover) before crisis	0.184**	0.113	0.07	0.136*	0.241**	0.079	0.127	0.012	0.091
Share of biggest shareholder before crisis	-0.157*	-0.161*	-0.061	-0.036	-0.078	-0.127	-0.036	-0.148*	-0.031
CEOs time with the company before crisis	0.01	0.118	0.034	-0.053	-0.111	0.088	0.032	0.041	-0.078
Primary strategy before crisis - Quality leader-ship	0.099	0.103	0.024	0.191**	0.018	0.088	0.197**	0.175*	0.039
Primary strategy before crisis - Innovation leadership	-0.140*	-0.054	-0.03	0.029	-0.049	-0.147*	-0.087	-0.147*	-0.062
Primary strategy before crisis - Low-cost lead-ership	-0.046	-0.140*	-0.038	-0.078	-0.037	-0.078	-0.052	-0.06	-0.144*
Slack resources before crisis	0.267**	0.235**	-0.041	0.101	0.182**	0.262**	0.175*	0.006	0.345**
Lender security situation before crisis	-0.028	-0.018	-0.009	0.003	0.003	0.069	-0.087	-0.150*	-0.049
Equity ratio before crisis	0.014	0.018	0.158*	-0.129	0.072	0.099	0.117	0.063	0.152*
Pre-crisis profitability	0.058	0.012	-0.072	-0.016	0.042	-0.068	0.076	-0.104	0.052
Family share in the company before crisis	0.068	0.048	0.057	0.126	0.126	-0.041	0.015	0.008	0.051
External context									
Long-term growth perspectives of market segment	-0.203**	-0.166*	0.190**	-0.067	-0.186**	0.07	-0.031	0.157*	-0.085
Turnaround result									
Turnaround result	-0.171*	-0.108	0.086	0.027	-0.056	0.014	-0.058	0.167*	0.008

Context and turnaround result part V **Pearson correlation coefficient** **N = 209** ****. Correlation is significant at the 0.01 level (2-tailed).** ***. Correlation is significant at the 0.05 level (2-tailed).**	Pricing and sales initiatives	Purchasing and cost reduction initiatives	CEO change	Change in TMT	External management support	Asset divestments	Acquisitions	Termination of products lines/ markets	New products/ markets development
Internal context									
Company size (turnover) before crisis	-0.201**	0.151*	0.122	0.222**	-0.021	0.208**	0.018	0.218**	0.057
Share of biggest shareholder before crisis	0.136*	-0.091	0.027	-0.012	-0.028	-0.102	0.034	-0.166*	-0.004
CEOs time with the company before crisis	0.018	0.025	0.054	0.016	-0.091	-0.153*	-0.059	0.002	-0.039
Primary strategy before crisis - Quality leadership	0.01	0.108	0.047	0.04	0.075	0.01	-0.037	0.047	0.042
Primary strategy before crisis - Innovation leadership	0.006	-0.155*	-0.043	0.012	-0.139*	-0.075	0.108	-0.089	0.067
Primary strategy before crisis - Low-cost leadership	0.002	-0.09	-0.028	-0.105	-0.043	0.043	-0.061	0.002	-0.097
Slack resources before crisis	0.04	0.224**	0.383**	0.188**	0.189**	0.046	-0.014	0.202**	-0.101
Lender security situation before crisis	0.031	-0.025	0.034	0.054	-0.004	-0.074	0.005	-0.085	-0.083
Equity ratio before crisis	-0.1	-0.014	0.093	0.128	0.074	-0.009	0.008	0.06	0.143*
Pre-crisis profitability	0.011	0.008	0.064	0.065	-0.093	-0.135	-0.084	-0.002	-0.04
Family share in the company before crisis	0.093	-0.029	-0.084	0.067	0.196**	0.177*	0.084	0.048	-0.023
External context									
Long-term growth perspectives of market segment	-0.084	-0.061	0.001	0.04	-0.198**	-0.038	0.038	-0.117	0
Turnaround result									
Turnaround result	0.027	-0.082	-0.033	0.06	-0.108	-0.055	0.081	-0.033	0.09

Context and turnaround result part VI **Pearson correlation coefficient** **N = 209** ****. Correlation is significant at the 0.01 level (2-tailed).** ***. Correlation is significant at the 0.05 level (2-tailed).**	Working capital reduction	Reduction of cash flow to shareholder	Liquidity contribution by shareholder	Additional restructuring loan granted by lenders	Securities contribution by shareholder	Repayment of debt	Extension, conversion or deferral of existing debt	Debt write-off or debt-to-equity-swap	Development of market segm. during turnaround
Internal context									
Company size (turnover) before crisis	0.061	-0.108	-0.034	0.036	-0.109	0.240**	0.203**	0.219**	0.107
Share of biggest shareholder before crisis	-0.101	-0.048	0.179**	-0.1	0.09	-0.127	-0.066	-0.089	-0.024
CEOs time with the company before crisis	0.011	-0.199**	0.085	0.004	-0.073	-0.004	-0.066	-0.041	-0.019
Primary strategy before crisis - Quality leadership	0.014	0.170*	-0.021	0.019	0.078	0.045	0.153*	-0.035	0.05
Primary strategy before crisis - Innovation leadership	-0.101	-0.096	-0.029	-0.095	-0.074	0.05	-0.054	0.09	0.066
Primary strategy before crisis - Low-cost leadership	-0.04	-0.096	-0.067	-0.011	-0.131	0.004	-0.003	0.095	0.01
Slack resources before crisis	0.279**	-0.052	0.1	-0.064	0.079	0.054	-0.043	0.149*	-0.178**
Lender security situation before crisis	-0.021	-0.116	-0.142*	-0.068	-0.138*	-0.148*	-0.018	0.032	-0.087
Equity ratio before crisis	-0.05	-0.014	0.104	-0.183**	-0.108	-0.109	-0.061	-0.056	0.086
Pre-crisis profitability	0.017	0.135	-0.037	-0.116	-0.092	-0.136*	-0.012	-0.052	-0.049
Family share in the company before crisis	0.021	0.143*	0.032	0.063	0.175*	0.159*	-0.063	-0.028	0.108
External context									
Long-term growth perspectives of market segment	-0.06	0.012	0.051	0.065	0.002	0.072	0.061	0.022	0.695**
Turnaround result									
Turnaround result	-0.079	0.08	0.039	-0.014	0.021	0.125	-0.044	0.038	0.435**

Context and turnaround result part VII **Pearson correlation coefficient** **N = 209** ****. Correlation is significant at the 0.01 level (2-tailed).** ***. Correlation is significant at the 0.05 level (2-tailed).**	Stake-holder man-age-ment during turna-round	Com-pany size (turno-ver) before crisis	Share of biggest share-holder before crisis	CEOs time with the compa-ny before crisis	Primary strategy before crisis - Quality leader-ship	Primary strat. before crisis - Innova-tion leader-ship	Primary strat. before crisis - Low-cost leader-ship	Slack re-sources before crisis	Lender security situation before crisis
Internal context									
Company size (turnover) before crisis	0.220**	1	-0.248**	-0.015	0.09	0.069	0.067	0.08	-0.126
Share of biggest shareholder before crisis	-0.117	-0.248**	1	-0.180**	-0.118	0.054	0.066	-0.012	0.165*
CEOs time with the company before crisis	0.012	-0.015	-0.180**	1	0.019	0.049	-0.096	0.188**	0.098
Primary strategy before crisis - Quality leader-ship	0.180**	0.09	-0.118	0.019	1	-0.392**	-0.169*	0.129	0.067
Primary strategy before crisis - Innovation leadership	-0.02	0.069	0.054	0.049	-0.392**	1	-0.129	-0.119	-0.06
Primary strategy before crisis - Low-cost lead-ership	-0.098	0.067	0.066	-0.096	-0.169*	-0.129	1	-0.156*	0.05
Slack resources before crisis	0.031	0.08	-0.012	0.188**	0.129	-0.119	-0.156*	1	0.03
Lender security situation before crisis	-0.051	-0.126	0.165*	0.098	0.067	-0.06	0.05	0.03	1
Equity ratio before crisis	0.156*	0.089	0.005	-0.096	0.113	0.019	-0.052	0.053	0.065
Pre-crisis profitability	0.019	0.051	0.073	0.061	0.260**	0.006	0.009	-0.044	0.02
Family share in the company before crisis	-0.12	0.003	0.152*	-0.360**	0.005	-0.041	0.024	-0.121	-0.1
External context									
Long-term growth perspectives of market segment	0.113	0.13	-0.032	0.091	0.042	0.083	0.027	-0.102	-0.147*
Turnaround result									
Turnaround result	0.415**	0.235**	-0.009	-0.119	0.187**	0.046	-0.048	-0.067	-0.111

Context and turnaround result part VIII **Pearson correlation coefficient** **N = 209** ****. Correlation is significant at the 0.01 level (2-tailed).** ***. Correlation is significant at the 0.05 level (2-tailed).**	Equity ratio before crisis	Pre-crisis profitability	Family share in the company before crisis	Long-term growth perspect. of mark. Segm.	Turnaround result
Internal context					
Company size (turnover) before crisis	0.089	0.051	0.003	0.13	0.235**
Share of biggest shareholder before crisis	0.005	0.073	0.152*	-0.032	-0.009
CEOs time with the company before crisis	-0.096	0.061	-0.360**	0.091	-0.119
Primary strategy before crisis - Quality leadership	0.113	0.260**	0.005	0.042	0.187**
Primary strategy before crisis - Innovation leadership	0.019	0.006	-0.041	0.083	0.046
Primary strategy before crisis - Low-cost leadership	-0.052	0.009	0.024	0.027	-0.048
Slack resources before crisis	0.053	-0.044	-0.121	-0.102	-0.067
Lender security situation before crisis	0.065	0.02	-0.1	-0.147*	-0.111
Equity ratio before crisis	1	0.207**	0.015	0.119	0.151*
Pre-crisis profitability	0.207**	1	-0.034	-0.032	-0.069
Family share in the company before crisis	0.015	-0.034	1	-0.017	0.159*
External context					
Long-term growth perspectives of market segment	0.119	-0.032	-0.017	1	0.454**
Turnaround result					
Turnaround result	0.151*	-0.069	0.159*	0.454**	1

Context and turnaround result part IX **Pearson correlation coefficient** **family-firm-specific context variables - N = 178** ****. Correlation is significant at the 0.01 level (2-tailed).** ***. Correlation is significant at the 0.05 level (2-tailed).**	Role of owner family in sup. board before crisis	Owner family control before crisis - CEO is family member	Owner family control bef. crisis - structure of TMT	Owner family generation before crisis
Internal context				
Company size (turnover) before crisis	0.355**	0.142	0.414**	0.144
Share of biggest shareholder before crisis	-0.177*	-0.280**	-0.266**	-0.274**
CEOs time with the company before crisis	-0.049	0.295**	0.240**	0.258**
Primary strategy before crisis - Quality leadership	0.079	0.101	0.099	0.042
Primary strategy before crisis - Innovation leadership	0.132	-0.015	-0.018	-0.195**
Primary strategy before crisis - Low-cost leadership	-0.096	-0.025	0.046	-0.011
Slack resources before crisis	0.022	0.073	0.059	0.139
Lender security situation before crisis	-0.072	-0.155*	-0.195**	-0.146
Equity ratio before crisis	0.111	0.058	0.089	0.036
Pre-crisis profitability	-0.07	0.004	0.044	-0.025
Family share in the company before crisis	-0.113	-0.307**	-0.309**	0.099
External context				
Long-term growth perspectives of market segment	0.119	0.014	0.077	0.045
Turnaround result				
Turnaround result	0.180*	0.096	0.133	0.096

Context and turnaround result part X **Pearson correlation coefficient** **family-firm-specific result variables – non insolvent cases only - N = 113** ****. Correlation is significant at the 0.01 level (2-tailed).** ***. Correlation is significant at the 0.05 level (2-tailed).**	Family share in company after crisis	Owner family control after crisis - CEO is family member	Owner family control after crisis - structure of TMT
Internal context			
Company size (turnover) before crisis	-0.106	0.223*	0.260**
Share of biggest shareholder before crisis	0.017	-0.181	-0.168
CEOs time with the company before crisis	-0.071	0.127	0.168
Primary strategy before crisis - Quality leadership	0.071	0.04	0.101
Primary strategy before crisis - Innovation leadership	-0.007	-0.033	-0.099
Primary strategy before crisis - Low-cost leadership	0.132	-0.192*	-0.087
Slack resources before crisis	-0.076	0.189*	0.228*
Lender security situation before crisis	-0.019	-0.102	-0.118
Equity ratio before crisis	0.032	0.156	0.076
Pre-crisis profitability	-0.003	0.013	0.011
Family share in the company before crisis	0.237*	-0.167	-0.201*
External context			
Long-term growth perspectives of market segment	0.118	-0.029	-0.154
Turnaround result			
Turnaround result	0.141	-0.018	-0.029

References

Ahlers, O. (2014). *Family Firms and Private Equity: A Collection of Essays on Value Creation, Negotiation, and Soft Factors*. Wiesbaden: Springer Gabler.

Altman, E. I. (1968). Financial ratios, discriminant analysis and the prediction of corporate bankruptcy. *Journal of Finance, 23*(4), 589-609.

Altman, E. I., & Hotchkiss, E. (2006). *Corporate financial distress and bankruptcy: Predict and avoid bankruptcy, analyze and invest in distressed debt* (3rd ed.): John Wiley & Sons.

Anand, J., & Singh, H. (1997). Asset redeployment, acquisitions and corporate strategy in declining industries. *Strategic Management Journal, 18*(Summer Special Issue), 99-118.

Anderson, R. C., & Reeb, D. M. (2003). Founding-Family Ownership and Firm Performance: Evidence from the S&P 500. *Journal of Finance, 58*(3), 1301-1328.

Arogyaswamy, K., Barker, I. I. I. V. L., & Yasai-Ardekani, M. (1995). Firm turnarounds: An intergrative two-stage model. *Journal of Management Studies, 32*(4), 493-525.

Ashta, A., & Tolle, L. (2005). Criteria for selecting restructuring strategies for distressed or declining enterprises. *CEREN, 6*, 1-20.

Asquith, P., & Gertner, R. (1994). Anatomy of financial distress: An examination of junk-bond issuers. *Quarterly Journal of Economics, 109*(3), 625-658.

Astrachan, J. H., Klein, S. B., & Smyrnios, K. X. (2002). The F-PEC Scale of Family Influence: A Proposal for Solving the Family Business Definition Problem. *Family Business Review, 15*(1), 45-58.

Astrachan, J. H., & Kolenko, T. A. (1994). A neglected factor explaining family business success: Human resource practices. *Family business review, 7*(3), 251-262.

Audia, P. G., & Greve, H. R. (2006). Less likely to fail: Low performance, firm size, and factory expansion in the shipbuilding industry. *Management Science, 52*(1), 83-94.

Babyak, M. A. (2004). What you see may not be what you get: a brief, nontechnical introduction to overfitting in regression-type models. *Psychosomatic medicine, 66*(3), 411-421.

Backhaus, K., Erichson, B., Plinke, W., & Weiber, R. (2011). *Multivariate Analysemethoden: Eine anwendungsorientierte Einführung*: Springer.

BaFin. (2012). Mindestanforderungen an das Risikomanagement - MaRisk: Bundesanstalt für Finanzdienstleistungsaufsicht (BaFin).

Bankenverband, B. D. B. (2000). Daten, Fakten, Arguemente - Private Banken–Partner des Mittelstandes. Berlin: Bundesverband Deutscher Banken.

Barker, V. L., & Duhaime, I. M. (1997). Strategic change in the turnaround process: theory and empirical evidence. *Strategic Management Journal, 18*(1), 13-38.

Barker, V. L., & Mone, M. A. (1994). Retrenchment: Cause of turnaround or consequence of decline? *Strategic Management Journal, 15*(5), 395-405.

Barker, V. L., & Patterson, P. W. (1996). Top management team tenure and top manager causal attributions at declining firms attempting turnarounds. *Group & Organization Management, 21*(3), 304-336.

Barker, V. L., Patterson, P. W., & Mueller, G. C. (2001). Organizational causes and strategic consequences of the extent of top management team replacement during turnaround attempts. *Journal of Management Studies, 38*(2), 235-270.

Barney, J. (1991). Firm Resources and Sustained Competitive Advantage. *Journal of Management, 17*(1), 99-120.

Barr, P. S., Stimpert, J. L., & Huff, A. S. (1992). Cognitive change, strategic action, and organizational renewal. *Strategic Management Journal, 13*(Strategy Process: Managing), 15-36.

Bergauer, A. (2001). *Erfolgreiches Krisenmanagement in der Unternehmung - Eine empirische Analyse*. Berlin: Erich Schmidt.

Berrone, P., Cruz, C., & Gomez-Mejia, L. R. (2012). Socioemotional Wealth in Family Firms: Theoretical Dimensions, Assessment Approaches, and Agenda for Future Research. *Family Business Review, 25*(3), 258-279.

Bethel, J. E., & Liebeskind, J. (1993). The effects of ownership structure on corporate restructuring. *Strategic Management Journal, 14*(Corporate Restructuring), 15-31.

Bethge, I. (2014). Zahlen, Daten, Fakten der Kreditwirtschaft: Bundesverband deutscher Banken e.V.

Bibeault, D. B. (1982). *Corporate Turnaround: How managers turn losers into winners*. Ohio: McGraw-Hill.

Bjuggren, P.-O., & Sund, L.-G. (2001). Strategic decision making in intergenerational successions of small-and medium-size family-owned businesses. *Family Business Review, 14*(1), 11-23.

Block, J. (2010). Family Management, Family Ownership, and Downsizing: Evidence From S&P 500 Firms. *Family Business Review, 23*(2), 109-130.

Böckenförde, B. (1996). *Unternehmenssanierung*. Stuttgart: Schäffer-Poeschel Verlag.

Bolton, M. K. (1993). Organizational innovation and substandard performance: when is necessity the mother of innovation? *Organization science, 4*(1), 57-75.

Bonnier, K.-A., & Bruner, R. F. (1989). An analysis of stock price reaction to management change in distressed firms. *Journal of Accounting and Economics, 11*(1), 95-106.

Bowman, E. H., & Singh, H. (1993). Corporate restructuring: Reconfiguring the firm. *Strategic Management Journal, 14*(Special issue), 5-14.

Bowman, E. H., Singh, H., Useem, M., & Bhadury, R. (1999). When Does Restructuring Improve Economic Performance? *California Management Review, 41*(2), 33-54.

Bozeman, B., & Slusher, E. A. (1979). Scarcity and Environmental Stress in Public organizations A Conjectural Essay. *Administration & Society, 11*(3), 335-355.

Bradley, S. W., Aldrich, H., Shepherd, D. A., & Wiklund, J. (2011). Resources, environmental change, and survival: Asymmetric paths of young independent and subsidiary organizations. *Strategic Management Journal, 32*(5), 486-509.

Brown, D. T., James, C. M., & Mooradian, R. M. (1994). Asset sales by financially distressed firms. *Journal of Corporate finance, 1*(2), 233-257.

Bruton, G. D., Ahlstrom, D., & Wan, J. C. (2003). Turnaround in East Asian firms: Evidence from ethnic overseas Chinese communities. *Strategic Management Journal, 24*(6), 519-540.

Buchalik, R. (2004). Restrukturierungs-/Sanierungsmöglichkeiten aus der Sicht der finanzierenden Bank. In A. K. Buth & M. Hermanns (Eds.), *Restrukturierung, Sanierung und Insolvenz* (2nd ed., pp. 30-65). München: Verlag C. H. Beck.

Buschmann, H. (2006). *Erfolgreiches Turnaround-Management - Empirische Untersuchung mit Schwerpunkt auf dem Einfluss der Stakeholder*. Wiesbaden: Deutscher Universitäts-Verlag.

Buth, A. K., & Hermanns, M. (2004). Finanzwirtschaftliche Aspekte bei Fortführung von Krisenunternehmen. In A. K. Buth & M. Hermanns (Eds.), *Restrukturierung, Sanierung und Insolvenz* (2nd ed., pp. 257 – 278). München: C. H. Beck.

Cameron, K. S., Kim, M. U., & Whetten, D. A. (1987). Organizational Effects of Decline and Turbulence. *Administrative Science Quarterly, 32*(2), 222-240.

Cameron, K. S., Sutton, R. I., & Whetten, D. A. (1988). Issues in organizational decline. In K. S. Cameron, R. I. Sutton & D. A. Whetten (Eds.), *Readings in Organizational Decline: Frameworks, Research and Prescriptions* (pp. 3-19). Cambridge: Ballinger Publishing.

Campbell, S. V. (1996). Predicting bankruptcy reorganization for closely held firms. *Accounting Horizons, 10*(3), 12-25.

Carmeli, A., & Schaubroeck, J. (2006). Top management team behavioral integration, decision quality, and organizational decline. *The Leadership Quarterly, 17*(5), 441-453.

Castrogiovanni, G. J., & Bruton, G. D. (2000). Business turnaround processes following acquisitions: Reconsidering the role of retrenchment. *Journal of Business Research, 48*(1), 25-34.

Cater, J., & Schwab, A. (2008). Turnaround Strategies in Established Small Family Firms. *Family Business Review, 21*(1), 31-50.

Cho, S., Kim, K., Kim, Y. J., Lee, J.-K., Cho, Y. S., Lee, J.-Y., et al. (2010). Joint Identification of Multiple Genetic Variants via Elastic-Net Variable Selection in a Genome-Wide Association Analysis. *Annals of Human Genetics, 74*(5), 416-428.

Chowdhury, S. D., & Lang, J. R. (1993). Crisis, Decline, and Turnaround: A Test of Competing Hypotheses for Short-Term Performance Improvement in Small Firms. *Journal of Small Business Management, 31*(4), 8-17.

Chowdhury, S. D., & Lang, J. R. (1996). Turnaround in small firms: An assessment of efficiency strategies. *Journal of Business Research, 36*(2), 169-178.

Chrisman, J. J., Chua, J. H., & Sharma, P. (2005). Trends and Directions in the Development of a Strategic Management Theory of the Family Firm. *Entrepreneurship: Theory & Practice, 29*(5), 555-575.

Chrisman, J. J., Kellermanns, F. W., Chan, K. C., & Liano, K. (2010). Intellectual Foundations of Current Research in Family Business: An Identification and Review of 25 Influential Articles. *Family Business Review, 23*(1), 9-26.

Chua, J. H., Chrisman, J. J., & Bergiel, E. B. (2009). An agency theoretic analysis of the professionalized family firm. *Entrepreneurship Theory and Practice, 33*(2), 355-372.

Chua, J. H., Chrisman, J. J., & Sharma, P. (1999). Defining the Family Business by Behavior. *Entrepreneurship: Theory & Practice, 23*(4), 19-39.

Clapham, S. E., Schwenk, C. R., & Caldwell, C. (2005). CEO perceptions and corporate turnaround. *Journal of Change Management, 5*(4), 407-428.

Coughlan, A. T., & Schmidt, R. M. (1985). Executive compensation, management turnover, and firm performance: An empirical investigation. *Journal of Accounting and Economics, 7*(1), 43-66.

D'Aunno, T., & Sutton, R. I. (1992). The responses of drug abuse treatment organizations to financial adversity: A partial test of the threat-rigidity thesis. *Journal of Management, 18*(1), 117-131.

Daily, C. M., & Dalton, D. R. (1994). Bankruptcy and corporate governance: The impact of board composition and structure. *Academy of Management journal, 37*(6), 1603-1617.

Daily, C. M., & Dalton, D. R. (1995). CEO and director turnover in failing firms: An illusion of change? *Strategic Management Journal, 16*(5), 393-400.

Davis, P. S., & Harveston, P. D. (2001). The phenomenon of substantive conflict in the family firm: a cross-generational study. *Journal of Small Business Management, 39*(1), 14-30.

de Vries, M. F. K. (1994). The dynamics of family controlled firms: The good and the bad news. *Organizational dynamics, 21*(3), 59-71.

DeAngelo, H., & DeAngelo, L. (1990). Dividend policy and financial distress: An empirical investigation of troubled NYSE firms. *The Journal of Finance, 45*(5), 1415-1431.

Denis, D. J., & Kruse, T. A. (2000). Managerial discipline and corporate restructuring following performance declines. *Journal of Financial Economics, 55*(3), 391-424.

DeWitt, R.-L. (1993). The structural consequences of downsizing. *Organization Science, 4*(1), 30-40.

DeWitt, R.-L. (1998). Firm, industry, and strategy influences on choice of downsizing approach. *Strategic Management Journal, 19*(1), 59-79.

Donaldson, G. (1994). *Corporate Restructuring: Managing the change process from within*. Boston: Harvard Business School Press.

Dowell, G., & Swaminathan, A. (2006). Entry timing, exploration, and firm survival in the early US bicycle industry. *Strategic Management Journal, 27*(12), 1159-1182.

Dyer, W. G. (1986). *Cultural change in family firms: anticipating and managing family business transitions*. San Francisco: Jossey-Bass Inc.

Dyer, W. G. (1989). Integrating professional management into a family owned business. *Family Business Review, 2*(3), 221-235.

Efron, B. (1987). Better bootstrap confidence intervals. *Journal of the American statistical Association, 82*(397), 171-185.

Efron, B., & Tibshirani, R. J. (1994). *An introduction to the bootstrap*. New York: Chapman & Hall.

Eichner, T. (2010). *Restructuring and Turnaround of Distressed Manufacturing Firms: An International Empirical Study*. Frankfurt am Main: Lang, Peter.

Eisenhardt, K. M. (1989). Agency theory: An assessment and review. *Academy of management review, 14*(1), 57-74.

European Commission. (2003). Definition of Micro, Small and Medium-sized Enterprises, OJEU L 124. In E. Commission (Ed.), *46* (Vol. L 124, pp. 6). Official Journal of the European Union: European Union.

Faghfouri, P. (2013). *The Role of Governance Structure in the Context of Crisis Management: An Empirical Analysis on a German Sample of Non-family and Family Businesses.* Wiesbaden: Springer.

Faghfouri, P., Kraiczy, N. D., Hack, A., & Kellermanns, F. W. (2015). Ready for a crisis? How supervisory boards affect the formalized crisis procedures of small and medium-sized family firms in Germany. *Review of Managerial Science, 9*(2), 317-338.

Fahrmeir, L., Kneib, T., Lang, S., & Marx, B. (2013). *Regression: models, methods and applications*: Springer Science & Business Media.

Falkenstein, E. G., Boral, A., & Carty, L. V. (2000). RiskCalc for private companies: Moody's default model. *As published in Global Credit Research, May*.

Field, A. (2013). *Discovering statistics using IBM SPSS statistics*. London: Sage.

Filatotchev, I., & Toms, S. (2003). Corporate Governance, Strategy and Survival in a Declining Industry: A Study of UK Cotton Textile Companies. *Journal of Management Studies, 40*(4), 895-920.

Filatotchev, I., & Toms, S. (2006). Corporate Governance and Financial Constraints on Strategic Turnarounds. *Journal of Management Studies, 43*(3), 407-433.

Finkin, E. F. (1985). Company Turnaround. *Journal of Business Strategy, 5*(4), 14-24.

Francis, J. D., & Desai, A. B. (2005). Situational and organizational determinants of turnaround. *Management Decision, 43*(9), 1203-1224.

Franks, J. R., & Sanzhar, S. V. (2006). *Evidence on debt overhang from distressed equity issues.* Paper presented at the EFA 2005 Moscow Meetings Paper.

Freeman, J., & Hannan, M. T. (1989). Setting the record straight on organizational ecology. *American Journal of Sociology, 95*(2), 425-439.

Freeman, S. J., & Cameron, K. S. (1993). Organizational downsizing: A convergence and reorientation framework. *Organization Science, 4*(1), 10-29.

Furrer, O., Pandian, J. R., & Thomas, H. (2007). Corporate strategy and shareholder value during decline and turnaround. *Management Decision, 45*(3), 372-392.

Gan, G., Ma, C., & Wu, J. (2007). *Data Clustering: Theory, Algorithms, and Applications*. Philadelphia: SIAM.

Gertner, R., & Scharfstein, D. (1991). A theory of workouts and the effects of reorganization law*. *The Journal of Finance, 46*(4), 1189-1222.

Gilson, S. C. (1989). Management turnover and financial distress. *Journal of financial Economics, 25*(2), 241-262.

Gilson, S. C. (1990). Bankruptcy, boards, banks, and blockholders: Evidence on changes in corporate ownership and control when firms default. *Journal of Financial Economics, 27*(2), 355-387.

Gilson, S. C., John, K., & Lang, L. H. (1990). Troubled debt restructurings: An empirical study of private reorganization of firms in default. *Journal of financial economics, 27*(2), 315-353.

Gomez-Mejia, L. R., Cruz, C., Berrone, P., & De Castro, J. (2011). The bind that ties: Socioemotional wealth preservation in family firms. *The academy of management annals, 5*(1), 653-707.

Gómez-Mejía, L. R., Haynes, K. T., Núñez-Nickel, M., Jacobson, K. J. L., & Moyano-Fuentes, J. (2007). Socioemotional Wealth and Business Risks in Family-controlled Firms: Evidence from Spanish Olive Oil Mills. *Administrative Science Quarterly, 52*(1), 106-137.

Górriz, C. G., & Fumás, V. S. (1996). Ownership structure and firm performance: Some empirical evidence from Spain. *Managerial and Decision Economics, 17*(6), 575-586.

Grape, C. (2006). *Sanierungsstrategien - Empirisch-qualitative Untersuchung zur Bewältigung schwerer Unternehmenskrisen*. Wiesbaden: Deutscher Universitäts-Verlag.

Green, S. B. (1991). How many subjects does it take to do a regression analysis. *Multivariate behavioral research, 26*(3), 499-510.

Grinblatt, M., & Titman, S. (1989). Mutual fund performance: An analysis of quarterly portfolio holdings. *The Journal of Business, 62*(3), 393-416.

Grinyer, P. H., Mayes, D. G., & McKiernan, P. (1988). *Sharpbenders: The secrets of unleashing corporate potential*. Oxford: Basil Blackwell.

Grinyer, P. H., & McKiernan, P. (1990). Generating major change in stagnating companies. *Strategic Management Journal, 11*(Corporate Entrepreneurship), 131-146.

Grinyer, P. H., & Spender, J.-C. (1979). Recipes, crises, and adaptation in mature businesses. *International Studies of Management & Organization, 9*(3), 113-133.

Groß, J. (2003). *Linear regression* (Vol. 175): Springer Science & Business Media.

Günterberg, B. (2012). *Unternehmensgrößenstatistik: Unternehmen, Umsatz und sozialversicherungspflichtig Beschäftigte 2004 bis 2009 in Deutschland, Ergebnisse des Unternehmensregisters (URS 95)*: Daten und Fakten, Institut für Mittelstandsforschung (IfM) Bonn.

Habbershon, T. G., & Williams, M. L. (1999). A resource-based framework for assessing the strategic advantages of family firms. *Family Business Review, 12*(1), 1-25.

Hair, J. F., Black, W. C., Babin, B. J., & Anderson, R. E. (2010). *Multivariate data analysis* (7 ed.): Pearson.

Hambrick, D. C., & D'Aveni, R. A. (1988). Large corporate failures as downward spirals. *Administrative Science Quarterly, 33*(1), 1-23.

Hambrick, D. C., & Schecter, S. M. (1983). Turnaround strategies for mature industrial-product business units. *Academy of Management Journal, 26*(2), 231-248.

Handler, W. C. (1994). Succession in family business: A review of the research. *Family business review, 7*(2), 133-157.

Hannan, M. T., & Freeman, J. (1984). Structure inertia and organizational change. *American Sociological Review, 49*(2), 149-164.

Harrigan, K. R. (1980). Strategy formulation in declining industries. *Academy of Management Review, 5*(4), 599-604.

Harrigan, K. R., & Porter, M. E. (1983). End-game strategies. *Harvard Business Review, 61*(4).

Harris, D., Martinez, J. I., & Ward, J. L. (1994). Is Strategy Different for the Family-Owned Business? *Family Business Review, 7*(2), 159-174.

Hauschildt, J. (2000). Unternehmenskrisen - Herausforderungen an die Bilanzanalyse. In J. L. Hauschildt, Jens (Ed.), *Krisendiagnose durch Bilanzanalyse*. Köln: Dr. Otto Schmidt.

Hauschildt, J., Grape, C., & Schindler, M. (2006). Typologien von Unternehmenskrisen im Wandel. *Die Betriebswirtschaft, 66*(1), 7-24.

Healy, P. M., & Palepu, K. G. (1988). Earnings information conveyed by dividend initiations and omissions. *Journal of financial Economics, 21*, 149-175.

Heany, D. F. (1985). Business in profit trouble. *Journal of Business Strategy, 5*(4), 4-12.

Hedberg, B., & Jönsson, S. (1977). Strategy formulation as a discontinuous process. *International Studies of Management & Organization, 7*(2), 88-109.

Hedberg, B. L., Bystrom, P. C., & Starbuck, W. H. (1976). Camping on seesaws: Prescriptions for a self-designing organization. *Administrative Science Quarterly, 21*, 41-65.

Hirschmann, S. (2015). Top 100 der deutschen Kreditwirtschaft. *Die Bank, 08*(2015).

Hocking, R. R. (1976). A Biometrics invited paper. The analysis and selection of variables in linear regression. *Biometrics*, 1-49.

Hofer, C. W. (1980). Turnaround strategies. *The Journal of Business Strategy, 1*(1), 19-31.

Hoffman, R. C. (1989). Strategies for corporate turnarounds: What do we know about them. *Journal of General Management, 14*(3), 46-66.

Hoskisson, R. E., Johnson, R. A., & Moesel, D. D. (1994). Corporate divestiture intensity in restructuring firms: Effects of governance, strategy, and performance. *Academy of Management Journal, 37*(5), 1207-1251.

Hutcheson, G. D., & Sofroniou, N. (1999). *The multivariate social scientist: Introductory statistics using generalized linear models*. London: Sage.

IDW. (2012). IDW S6 Standard: Anforderungen an die Erstellung von Sanierungskonzepten. Düsseldorf: IDW Verlag.

Indro, D. C., Leach, R. T., & Lee, W. Y. (1999). Sources of gains to shareholders from bankruptcy resolution. *Journal of Banking & Finance, 23*(1), 21-47.

James, C. (1995). When do banks take equity in debt restructurings? *Review of Financial Studies, 8*(4), 1209-1234.

James, H. S. (1999). Owner as Manager, Extended Horizons and the Family Firm. *International Journal of the Economics of Business, 6*(1), 41-55.

Jensen, G. R., & Johnson, J. M. (1995). The dynamics of corporate dividend reductions. *Financial Management, 24*(4), 31-51.

Jensen, M. C. (1991). Corporate control and the politics of finance. *Journal of applied corporate finance, 4*(2), 13-34.

Jensen, M. C. (2010). Active investors, LBOs, and the privatization of bankruptcy. *Journal of Applied Corporate Finance, 22*(1), 77-85.

Jensen, M. C., & Meckling, W. H. (1976). Theory of the firm: Managerial behavior, agency costs and ownership structure. *Journal of financial economics, 3*(4), 305-360.

Jensen, R. (2003). Tradition is double-edged sword in family business. *Journal of Corporate Renewal, 16*(6), 8-10.

Jenter, D., & Kanaan, F. (2015). CEO turnover and relative performance evaluation. *The Journal of Finance, 70*(5), 2155–2184.

John, K. (1993). Managing Financial Distress and Valuing Distressed Securities: A Survey and a Research Agenda. *Financial Management, 22*(3), 60-78.

John, K., Lang, L. H. P., & Netter, J. (1992). The Voluntary Restructuring of Large Firms in Response to Performance Decline. *Journal of Finance, 47*(3), 891-917.

Johnson, R. A. (1996). Antecedents and Outcomes of Corporate Refocusing. *Journal of Management, 22*(3), 439-483.

Johnson, R. A., Hoskisson, R. E., & Hitt, M. A. (1993). Board of director involvement in restructuring: The effects of board versus managerial controls and characteristics. *Strategic Management Journal, 14*, 33-50.

Jostarndt, P. (2007). *Financial Distress, Corporate Restructuring and Firm Survival - An Empirical Analysis of German Panel Data* (Vol. 116). Wiesbaden: Deutscher Universitäts-Verlag.

Kahl, M. (2002). Economic distress, financial distress, and dynamic liquidation. *Journal of Finance, 57*(1), 135-168.

Kang, J.-K., & Shivdasani, A. (1997). Corporate restructuring during performance declines in Japan. *Journal of Financial Economics, 46*(1), 29-65.

Ketchen, D. J., & Palmer, T. B. (1999). Strategic responses to poor organizational performance: A test of competing perspectives. *Journal of Management, 25*(5), 683-706.

Ketchen, D. J., & Shook, C. L. (1996). The Application of Cluster Analysis in Strategic Management Research: An Analysis and Critique. *Strategic Management Journal, 17*(6), 441-458.

Khanna, N., & Poulsen, A. B. (1995). Managers of financially distressed firms: Villains or scapegoats? *The Journal of Finance, 50*(3), 919-940.

Klein, S. B. (2000). Family businesses in Germany: Significance and structure. *Family Business Review, 13*(3), 157-181.

Koetter, M. (2013). Market structure and competition in German banking (pp. 166). Report commissioned by the Council of Economic Experts and the Monopolies Commission: German Council of Economic Experts.

Kraaijenbrink, J., Spender, J.-C., & Groen, A. J. (2010). The resource-based view: a review and assessment of its critiques. *Journal of management, 36*(1), 349-372.

Kranzusc, P., & Icks, A. (2009). Die Quoten der Insolvenzgläubiger in Regel- und Insolvenzplanverfahren - Ergebnisse von Insolvenzverfahren nach der Insolvenzrechtsreform. Bonn: Institut für Mittelstandsforschung.

Kraus, A., & Litzenberger, R. H. (1973). A State-Preference Model of Optimal Financial Leverage. *Journal of Finance, 28*(4), 911-922.

Krueger, D. A., & Willard, G. E. (1991). *Tunrarounds: A process, not an event.* Paper presented at the Academy of Management Proceedings.

Krystek, U. (1980). Organisatorische Möglichkeiten des Krisen-Managements. *Zeitschrift für Organisation, 49*(2), 63-71.

Lai, J., & Sudarsanam, S. (1997). Corporate restructuring in response to performance decline: Impact of ownership, governance and lenders. *European Finance Review, 1*(2), 197-233.

Lang, L. H., Poulsen, A., & Stulz, R. M. (1995). Asset sales, firm performance, and the agency costs of managerial discretion. *Journal of Financial Economics, 37*(1), 3-37.

Langer, C., Eschenburg, K., & Eschbach, R. (2012). *Rating und Finanzierung im Mittelstand: Leitfaden für erfolgreiche Bankgespräche*: Springer-Verlag.

Lansberg, I. (1988). The Succession Conspiracy. *Family Business Review, 1*(2), 119-143.

Lasfer, M. A., Sudarsanam, P. S., & Taffler, R. J. (1996). Financial distress, asset sales, and lender monitoring. *Financial Management, 25*(3), 57-66.

Latham, S. F., & Braun, M. (2009). Managerial risk, innovation, and organizational decline. *Journal of Management, 35*(2), 258-281.

Le Breton-Miller, I., & Miller, D. (2006). Why Do Some Family Businesses Out-Compete? Governance, Long-Term Orientations, and Sustainable Capability. *Entrepreneurship: Theory & Practice, 30*(6), 731-746.

Lie, E. (2005). Operating performance following dividend decreases and omissions. *Journal of Corporate Finance, 12*(1), 27-53.

Liou, D.-K., & Smith, M. (2006). Financial distress and corporate turnaround: a review of the literature and agenda for research. *SSRN Electronic Journal.*

Longenecker, J. G., & Schoen, J. E. (1978). Management succession in the family business. *Journal of small business management, 16*(3), 1-6.

Lovallo, D., & Kahneman, D. (2003). Delusions of Success. *Harvard Business Review, 81*(7), 56-63.

Love, G. E., & Nohria, N. (2005). Reducing slack: the performance consequences of downsizing by large industrial firms, 1977–93. *Strategic Management Journal, 26*(12), 1087-1108.

MacKenzie, J. E. (2002). Downsizing family businesses: Family dynamics increase challenges. *Journal of Corporate Renewal, 15*(5), 18-21.

Markides, C. C. (1995). Diversification, Restructuring and Economic Performance. *Strategic Management Journal, 16*(2), 101-118.

Martínez, J. I., Stöhr, B. S., & Quiroga, B. F. (2007). Family ownership and firm performance: Evidence from public companies in Chile. *Family Business Review, 20*(2), 83-94.

Meyer, M. W., & Zucker, L. G. (1989). *Permanently failing organizations*. Newbury Park: Sage Publications.

Miller, D. (1981). Toward a new contingency approach: The search for organizational gestalts. *Journal of management studies, 18*(1), 1-26.

Miller, D., Steier, L., & Le Breton-Miller, I. (2003). Lost in time: intergenerational succession, change, and failure in family business. *Journal of Business venturing, 18*(4), 513-531.

Morgan, G. (1997). *Images of organization*: Sage Publications Ltd.

Morrow, J., Sirmon, D. G., Hitt, M. A., & Holcomb, T. R. (2007). Creating value in the face of declining performance: Firm strategies and organizational recovery. *Strategic Management Journal, 28*(3), 271-283.

Moulton, W. N., Thomas, H., & Pruett, M. (1996). Business Failure Path ways: Environmental Stress and Organizational Response. *Journal of Management, 22*(4), 571-595.

Mundry, R., & Nunn, Charles L. (2009). Stepwise Model Fitting and Statistical Inference: Turning Noise into Signal Pollution. *The American Naturalist, 173*(1), 119-123.

Musteen, M., Liang, X., & Barker, V. L. (2011). Personality, perceptions and retrenchment decisions of managers in response to decline: Evidence from a decision-making study. *The Leadership Quarterly, 22*(5), 926-941.

Myers, S. C. (1977). Determinants of corporate borrowing. *Journal of financial economics, 5*(2), 147-175.

Ndofor, H. A., Vanevenhoven, J., & Barker, V. L. (2013). Software firm turnarounds in the 1990s: An analysis of reversing decline in a growing, dynamic industry. *Strategic Management Journal, 34*, 1123-1133.

Nixon, R. D., Hitt, M. A., Lee, H. U., & Jeong, E. (2004). Market reactions to announcements of corporate downsizing actions and implementation strategies. *Strategic Management Journal, 25*(11), 1121-1129.

Nothardt, F. (2001). *Corporate turnaround and corporate stakeholders: an empirical examination of the determinants of corporate turnaround in Germany with a focus on financial stakeholder theory*. St. Gallen: Disseration, Universität St. Gallen (HSG).

Núñez, E., Steyerberg, E. W., & Núñez, J. (2011). Regression modeling strategies. *Revista Española de Cardiología (English Edition), 64*(6), 501-507.

Nystrom, P. C., & Starbuck, W. H. (1984). To avoid organizational crises, unlearn. *Organizational dynamics, 12*(4), 53-65.

O'Neill, H. M. (1986). Turnaround and recovery: What strategy do you need? *Long Range Planning, 19*(1), 80-88.

Ofek, E. (1993). Capital structure and firm response to poor performance: An empirical analysis. *Journal of financial economics, 34*(1), 3-30.

Pajunen, K. (2006). Stakeholder influences in organizational survival. *Journal of Management Studies, 43*(6), 1261-1288.

Pandit, N. R. (2000). Some recommendations for improved research on corporate turnaround. *Management, 3*(2), 31-56.

Park, N. K., & Mezias, J. M. (2005). Before and after the technology sector crash: The effect of environmental munifience on stock market response to alliances to E-Commerce Firms. *Strategic Management Journal, 26*(11), 987-1007.

Pearce, J. A. (2007). The Value of Corporate Financial Measures in Monitoring Downturn and Managing Turnaround: An Exploratory Study. *Journal of Managerial Issues, 19*(2), 253-270.

Pearce, J. A., & Robbins, D. K. (1993). Toward Improved Theory and Research on Business Turnaround. *Journal of Management, 19*(3), 613-636.

Pearce, J. A., & Robbins, D. K. (1994). Research notes and communications: Retrenchment remains the foundation of business turnaround. *Strategic Management Journal, 15*(5), 407-417.

Pearson, C. M., & Clair, J. A. (1998). Reframing crisis management. *Academy of management review, 23*(1), 59-76.

Pettigrew, A. M. (1988). *The management of strategic change*. Oxford: Basil Blackwell.

Pijanowski, T. (2014). *Lending Behavior toward Family Firms*. Witten/ Herdecke, Germany: Springer.

Porter, M. E. (1985). *Competitive Advantage: Creating and Sustaining Superior Performance* (Export 2004 ed.). New York: Free Press.

Robbins, D. K., & Pearce, J. A. (1992). Turnaround: Retrenchment and recovery. *Strategic Management Journal, 13*(4), 287-309.

Rosenbauer, C. C. (1994). *Strategische Erfolgsfaktoren des Familienunternehmens im Rahmen seines Lebenszyklus: Ein eignerorientiertes Konzept zur Steigerung der Lebens-und Entwicklungsfähigkeit des Familienunternehmens*. Hallstadt: Rosch-Buch.

Rosenblatt, Z., & Mannheim, B. (1996). Organizational response to decline in the Israeli electronics industry. *Organization Studies, 17*(6), 953-984.

Rosenblatt, Z., Rogers, K. S., & Nord, W. R. (1993). Toward a political framework for flexible management of decline. *Organization Science, 4*(1), 76-91.

Routledge, J., & Gadenne, D. (2004). An exploratory study of the company reorganisation decision in voluntary administration. *Pacific Accounting Review, 16*(1), 31-56.

Rüsen, T. A. (2008). *Krisen und Krisenmanagement in Familienunternehmen: Schwachstellen erkennen, Lösungen erarbeiten, Existenzbedrohung meistern*: Springer DE.

Schendel, D. E. (1993). Introduction to the summer 1993 special issue on 'corporate restructuring'. *Strategic Management Journal, 14*(S1), 1-3.

Schendel, D. E., & Patton, G. R. (1976). Corporate stagnation and turnaround. *Journal of Economics and Business, 28*(3), 236-241.

Schendel, D. E., Patton, G. R., & Riggs, J. (1976). Corporate Turnaround Strategies: Study of Profit Decline and Recovery. *Journal of General Management, 3*(3), 3-11.

Schmuck, M. (2013). *Financial Distress and Corporate Turnaround: An Empirical Analysis of the Automotive Supplier Industry*. Wiesbaden: Springer Gabler.

Schuler, R. S., & Jackson, S. E. (1987). Linking competitive strategies with human resource management practices. *The Academy of Management Executive, 1*(3), 207-219.

Schulze, W. S., Lubatkin, M. H., Dino, R. N., & Buchholtz, A. K. (2001). Agency Relationships in Family Firms: Theory and Evidence. *Organization Science, 12*(2), 99-116.

Sharma, P., Chrisman, J. J., & Chua, J. H. (2003). Predictors of satisfaction with the succession process in family firms. *Journal of Business Venturing, 18*(5), 667-687.

Sharma, P., Chrisman, J. J., Pablo, A. L., & Chua, J. H. (2001). Determinants of initial satisfaction with the succession process in family firms: A conceptual model. *Entrepreneurship Theory and Practice, 25*(3), 1-19.

Sharma, P., & Irving, P. G. (2005). Four bases of family business successor commitment: Antecedents and consequences. *Entrepreneurship Theory and Practice, 29*(1), 13-33.

Shleifer, A., & Vishny, R. W. (1986). Large shareholders and corporate control. *The Journal of Political Economy, 47*, 461-488.

Shleifer, A., & Vishny, R. W. (1992). Liquidation values and debt capacity: A market equilibrium approach. *The Journal of Finance, 47*(4), 1343-1366.

Short, J. C., Ketchen, D. J., Palmer, T. B., & Hult, G. T. M. (2007). Firm, strategic group, and industry influences on performance. *Strategic Management Journal, 28*(2), 147-167.

Siebels, J.-F., & zu Knyphausen-Aufseß, D. (2012). A Review of Theory in Family Business Research: The Implications for Corporate Governance. *International Journal of Management Reviews, 14*(3), 280-304.

Sirmon, D. G., & Hitt, M. A. (2003). Managing resources: Linking unique resources, management, and wealth creation in family firms. *Entrepreneurship theory and practice, 27*(4), 339-358.

Slatter, S. (1984). *Corporate Recovery: Successful Turnaround Strategies and their Implementation*. Harmondsworth: Penguin Books Ltd.

Slatter, S., & Lovett, D. (1999). *Corporate turnaround: Managing Companies in Distress*. London: Penguin Books.

Smith, M., & Graves, C. (2005). Corporate turnaround and financial distress. *Managerial Auditing Journal, 20*(3), 304-320.

Starbuck, W. H., Greve, A., & Hedberg, B. L. T. (1985). Responding to crises. In S. J. Andriole (Ed.), *Corporate Crisis Management* (pp. 155-188). Princetown: Petrocelli Books.

Staw, B. M., Sandelands, L. E., & Dutton, J. E. (1981). Threat rigidity effects in organizational behavior: A multilevel analysis. *Administrative science quarterly, 26*(4), 501-524.

Stopford, J. M., & Baden-Fuller, C. (1990). Corporate rejuvenation. *Journal of Management Studies, 27*(4), 399-415.

Sudarsanam, S., & Lai, J. (2001). Corporate Financial Distress and Turnaround Strategies: An Empirical Analysis. *British Journal of Management, 12*(3), 183-199.

Sutton, J. (1997). Gibrat's legacy. *Journal of economic literature, 35*(1), 40-59.

Suzuki, N. (1985). *The Cross-National Comparison of Turnaround Strategies: The U.S. and Japan.* Paper presented at the Academy of Management Proceedings.

Tagiuri, R., & Davis, J. A. (1992). On the Goals of Successful Family Companies. *Family Business Review, 5*(1), 43-62.

Thietart, R. A. (1988). Success strategies for businesses that perform poorly. *Interfaces, 18*(3), 32-45.

Thornhill, S., & Amit, R. (2003). Learning About Failure: Bankruptcy, Firm Age, and the Resource-Based View. *Organization Science, 14*(5), 497-509.

Trahms, C. A., Ndofor, H. A., & Sirmon, D. G. (2013). Organizational Decline and Turnaround: A Review and Agenda for Future Research. *Journal of Management, 39*(5), 1277-1307.

Tsai, W. H., Hung, J. H., Kuo, Y. C., & Kuo, L. (2006). CEO tenure in Taiwanese family and nonfamily firms: An agency theory perspective. *Family Business Review, 19*(1), 11-28.

van Witteloostuijn, A. (1998). Bridging behavioral and economic theories of decline: Organizational inertia, strategic competition, and chronic failure. *Management Science, 44*(4), 501-521.

VanVoorhis, C. R. W., & Morgan, B. L. (2007). Understanding power and rules of thumb for determining sample sizes. *Tutorials in Quantitative Methods for Psychology, 3*(2), 43-50.

Varaiya, N., Kerin, R. A., & Weeks, D. (1987). The relationship between growth, profitability, and firm value. *Strategic Management Journal, 8*(5), 487-497.

Wan, W. P., & Yiu, D. W. (2009). From crisis to opportunity: Environmental jolt, corporate acquisitions, and firm performance. *Strategic Management Journal, 30*(7), 791-801.

Ward, J. L. (1997). Growing the Family Business: Special Challenges and Best Practices. *Family Business Review, 10*(4), 323-337.

Warner, J. B., Watts, R. L., & Wruck, K. H. (1988). Stock prices and top management changes. *Journal of financial Economics, 20*, 461-492.

Weisbach, M. S. (1988). Outside directors and CEO turnover. *Journal of financial Economics, 20*, 431-460.

Weitzel, W., & Jonsson, E. (1989). Decline in organizations: A literature integration and extension. *Administrative Science Quarterly, 34*(1), 91-109.

Wernerfelt, B. (1984). A resource-based view of the firm. *Strategic management journal, 5*(2), 171-180.

Wherry, R. J. (1931). A New Formula for Predicting the Shrinkage of the Coefficient of Multiple Correlation. 440-457.

Whetten, D. A. (1987). Organizational growth and decline processes. *Annual review of sociology, 13*, 335-358.

Whitaker, R. B. (1999). The early stages of financial distress. *Journal of Economics and Finance, 23*(2), 123-132.

Whitney, J. O. (1999). *Taking charge: Management guide to troubled companies and turnarounds*. Washington: Beard Books.

Whittingham, M. J., Stephens, P. A., Bradbury, R. B., & Freckleton, R. P. (2006). Why do we still use stepwise modelling in ecology and behaviour? *Journal of Animal Ecology, 75*(5), 1182-1189.

Winn, J. (1993). Performance measures for corporate decline and turnaround. *Journal of General Management, 19*(2), 48-63.

Withers, M. C., Corley, K. G., & Hillman, A. J. (2012). Stay or leave: Director identities and voluntary exit from the board during organizational crisis. *Organization Science, 23*(3), 835-850.

Witte, E. (1981). Die Unternehmenskrise–Anfang vom Ende oder Neubeginn. In R. Bratschitsch & W. Schnellinger (Eds.), *Unternehmenskrisen–Ursachen, Früherkennung, Bewältigung, Stuttgart* (pp. 7-24). Stuttgart: C.E. Poeschel Verlag.

Woodward, J. (1965). *Industrial organization: Theory and practice* (2nd edition ed.). London: Oxford University Press.

Wright, D., London, K., & Field, A. P. (2011). Using Bootstrap Estimation and the Plug-in Principle for Clinical Psychology Data. *Journal of Experimental Psychopathology, 2*(2), 252-270.

Zahra, S. A. (2005). Entrepreneurial risk taking in family firms. *Family Business Review, 18*(1), 23-40.

Zammuto, R. F., & Cameron, K. S. (1982). Environmental Decline and Organizational Response. *Academy of management proceedings, 1982*(1), 250-254.

Zellweger, T. (2007). Time Horizon, Costs of Equity Capital, and Generic Investment Strategies of Firms. *Family Business Review, 20*(1), 1-15.

Zimmerman, F. M. (1989). Managing a successful turnaround. *Long Range Planning, 22*(3), 105-124.

Zou, H., & Hastie, T. (2005). Regularization and variable selection via the elastic net. *Journal of the Royal Statistical Society: Series B (Statistical Methodology), 67*(2), 301-320.

MIX
Papier aus verantwortungsvollen Quellen
Paper from responsible sources
FSC® C105338
FSC
www.fsc.org

If you have any concerns about our products,
you can contact us on
ProductSafety@springernature.com

In case Publisher is established outside the EU,
the EU authorized representative is:
Springer Nature Customer Service Center GmbH
Europaplatz 3, 69115 Heidelberg, Germany

Printed by Libri Plureos GmbH
in Hamburg, Germany